The Essence of Islam

About the Author

Born on December 1, 1939 at Utraon close to Allahabad, Professor Saiyed Jafar Reza is an internationally known scholar, thinker and litterateur. His father late Saiyed Khairat Hasan was a freedom fighter, scholar and writer. Reza has not only continued the family tradition of scholarship but also broadened and enriched it. He did his Ph.D. in both Urdu and Hindi at the University of Allahabad and thus brought the two literary traditions of India closer to each other. University of Kashmir, Srinagar honoured him with D. Litt. degree for his outstanding contributions to Urdu Literature.

Reza started his academic career at the University of Allahabad in 1965. After a short stay at the University of Kashmir (1980-83) as a reader, he returned to the University of Allahabad where he served as a Prem Chand Chair Professor until his retirement in 2000.

Reza has more than three dozen books to his credit. His literary work is path breaking and his verse is personal discovery and vision of life. His books on Islam give insights into the liberal and spiritual dimensions of the message of Prophet Muḥammad. He looks at all religions from spiritual perspectives and hence his views on Islam are different from that of a professional clergy, who has a rigid mindset and not prepared to listen to any other point of view. His writings are among those writings, which are read again and again, read in bits and pondered over.

Reza is an academic of great repute, an educational administrator of wide experience and above all a true human being full of love and compassion.

The Essence of Islam

SAIYED JAFAR REZA
M.A., Ph.D., D.Phil., D.Litt.

Concept Publishing Company Pvt. Ltd.
New Delhi-110059

ISBN-13: 978-81-8069-832-3

First Published 2012

Published and Printed by

Concept
Since 1974

Concept Publishing Company Pvt. Ltd.
A/15-16, Commercial Block, Mohan Garden
New Delhi-110059 (India)
T: 25351460, 25351794, *F*: 091-11-25357109
E: publishing@conceptpub.com, W: www.conceptpub.com
Editorial Office: H-13, Bali Nagar, New Delhi-110 015, India.

Reza, Saiyed Jafar, 1939-
The essence of Islam / Saiyed Jafar Reza.
p. cm.
Includes bibliographical references (p.) and index.
ISBN 9788180698323

1. Islam—Essence, genius, nature. 2. Islam—Apologetic works. I. Title.

DDC 297 23

Dedicated to the living pious
memory of my late parents :
Kulthūm Sābi'ā
Saiyed Khairāt Ḥasan

"And if God had desired, He would have made you (*all*) a single community but that He might try you in what He hath given (*to each of*) you. Therefore compete ye excelling one another in goodness."

(*Qur'an : 5 /48*)

Preface

Islam, like any other religion, is being challenged by modern civilization process of the impetuous globalizing economy and society. Its role, scope and relevance are being redefined and addressed afresh. The meaning and necessity of a global religion cutting across all organized faiths is in the offing. While one group proposes to replace the word *religion* with any other word, which can stand for mutual human relationship, common human virtues and spiritual basis of human refinement.

In the foreground of this emerging need of reconsidering the issue of religion, ample light may be culled from the epoch making life-ideology of Islam, which can be discussed with a matured and re-interpretative approach. There are those who consider the label religion for Islam as too narrow. Since Islam stands for human brotherhood, mutual respect, common human values and spiritual basis of life and living; it is far more than rituals. Of course, those who like to narrow down Islam to a few day-to-day practices and rituals are still more in number. In this book I would like to draw the attention of the reader to the epoch making life-ideology of Islam, which, if seen by people in proper perspectives, can lead the world to eternal peace and harmony. While doing so I have no intention to suggest that other faiths are less ennobling, peace engendering and humane. For me all religions are great; they all have been inspired by God Almighty and laid down and propagated by some messenger of God. I also believe that all religions are universal and if their followers do not deviate from the path charted for them, this world would be a far better place to live. Islam too is a great religion and a true follower of Islam would never falter and would ever try to reach higher levels of human consciousness to know his Maker. But there are many misgivings about Islam as they are about other religions of the world. It is partly because people tend to image Islam from how its adherents practice it; and partly because it has been identified with *Jihād* and terrorism. This book is intended to present Islam in a holistic and true perspectives so that it is better understood and less misunderstood.

We can change the stereotypical image of religion with rational and scientific approach. An impassioned examination is necessary to transform ourselves into a true knowledge society imbued with spirituality. The revolutionary advances in science and technology have changed the mindset of the people. In modern days, scientific speculation and discovery has opened new dimensions in monopolizaion of nature. It has changed our outlook and behaviour pattern, with respect to both nature and our fellow human beings. Globalization has reduced our planet into a village at least in physical terms. Things, which were unknown yesterday, are widely known today. At the same time, the negative consequences are not few. Nature has become a resource for exploitation and humans as the means of production of goods and services.

We have more knowledge but less wisdom to use that knowledge in the interest of all. The mind, which is considered to be the sixth sense, is now full of baser attributes like greed, attachment to material objects and egoism. Life is being spent in the blind race of material gains. Enormous time and effort are spent in trying to realize imaginary objects, which have no intrinsic value in life. The other dimension of life, that is the inner self, or soul could result in eternal peace, satisfaction, bliss with both material and spiritual benefits, necessary for life to exist and culture to prosper. A new socio-intellectual set-up is emerging so far; a new one in many respects. The difference between the humans and the beasts is narrowing fast. Eternal human values, and moral standards are dancing in divergent directions or have taken back seat. Religious faith can overcome selfishness, give a sense of purpose and transform attitudes. It resists dogma, emphasizes human well-being and safeguard freedom in order to remain a force for good. It is the time for various religions to play their creative roles and this could take place only if various faiths work in tandem and send out a message of harmony all-over the world.

Islam is the religion of tolerance, harmony and peaceful coexistence. One of its basic articles of faith is the belief in God, His Messengers and His Books are, confined to any particular faith but all Messengers from Adam down the history bringing into fold all the Divine figures and scriptures of all the times and religions of this Universe. Among the other guiding principles of Islam are equality, and harmonious social and family relationships and issues related with inheritance, etc. In the backdrop of the contemporary state of things, it has become imperative to introduce the real and true spirit of Islam in the world. This will not only dispel the darkness of mistrust and suspicion about Islam, but also give a new and true image of Islam, as a religion of peace will also be awakened to study it afresh in the light of the modern global imperatives, with a view to afresh exploration of science-religion debate, as well as discussion of the impact of recent terrorism.

Islam today is at the crossroads; its image in the contemporary world is not positive. Muslims rightfully struggle for self-determination, justice and democracy in their own lands are being devastated, by the onslaughts of the monarchical and dictatorial rulers. The protest of the people ends in socio-political turmoil and senseless use of violence. It is the time to revive and protect the democratic traditions, including the rule of law, that have survived even in the face of repression and conquests; and the fundamental rights guaranteed to us and liberties that were realized after years of struggle and our resolve to adhere to these values and liberties will be tested in the crucible of extremism.

It is not for the first time that the Nimrod's pyre of terrorism has been lit for Islam. It was done even in the past, and every time it was extinguished, a garden of peace was born, and this time too it will be put out and peace would be restored. The sad part of it is that a handful of misled, indiscrete and reckless hands of so-called Muslims too have joined those who have inflamed this Nimrod-pyre to set Islam on fire. These fanatics call other religions, and faiths as unholy. To kill people and plunder their hearths and homes, to attack other nations and to subjugate them in the name of Islam is un-Islamic to the core. Actually, it is another face of fascism, which plays its part sometimes in the form of an imperial terror indulging in capturing other nations and shedding blood, killing people and plunder their hearths and homes. Sometimes, it comes in the form of a reformer seeking to dislodge other cultures to establish dominance of his own way of life, and sometimes in the form of a *thinker* and *theorist* to captivate the masses by conditioning their thoughts.

Extremism in a religion has borne the worst consequences when the fascism in the form of terrorism has found its ways into human instinct and manifests itself in different fashions. History is witness to the blind fury of the people of one religion let loose the brutal tyranny on the people of other religion. Sometimes, one sect of the same religion makes devastating onslaughts on other sects. The followers of Islam are no exception to it. The injustice and oppression heaped on people of other faiths by the Muslim invaders, kings and emperors, makes real and sensible Muslims lower their heads in shame and repentance. The tyranny the conquering Muslim armies, supported by pseudo Muslim scholars and jurists inflicted on the innocent people. Even in the name of Islamic reformation, extremism and terrorism has been allowed to openly play its part is unimaginable. Even today terrorism as a means to punish the 'enemies of Islam' and spread Islam, is being glorified. Not a long ago, the monuments of some Muslim saints were demolished, graves were levelled, people were looted and tortured, all in the name of Islamic reforms.

To counter not only the powerful Muslim nations, there has been vicious attempt to hold the whole world in bondage in a way are the top rung of international power pedestal, putting them at the destinies of the billions around the world, are responsible for contemporary global *Jihād,* which has resulted in the creation and steady enlargement of an alternative pan-Islamic front to fight for sharing power polity with the petro-rich Muslim kingdoms, and oil-rich Shaykhs, who live without any regard to everybody, even Muslims of their own countries, especially have no regard for the right of women. But the trouble is that this front uses un-Islamic means and methods to achieve its aims and objectives, noble as they may in theory. They do not spare even Muslim children and women. It has virtually bulldozed the global peace. It is determined to take a revenge for the various imaginary or real atrocities committed on Islam; and do away with all those who toe their line.

Exteremist outfits are being organized and fully armed with the most modern weapons; and used to incite trouble all-over the world, the Muslim countries included. Focus is on the oil-rich countries of West Asia and North Africa 'to save and spread Islam'. What they are doing is un-Islamic; history will laugh at what they are indulging in. The author believes that these terrorists constitute the lunatic fringes, of the Muslim society which in due course of time would disappear from the scene.

All through the history, it was the power struggle among the Muslim rulers, which enslaved Muslim masses politically, economically but mentally. Many of them have become politically free but the mental enslavement has persisted to this day. This mental slavery prevents people from grasping the true meaning of Islam. Today Islam is the most misunderstood and misrepresented religion of the world. If Islam is treated as one of the several God-inspired religions of the world, not the only one, the question of fighting other religionists does not arise. Let all follow their faith and become good human beings. In a society of good human beings all will prosper.

The tendency of discrimination against Islam will end only by removing the tendency of isolation and mistrust. Contrary to the popular belief that the *Jihādis* are against the non-Muslims alone, they have heaped untold miseries on the followers of other sects of Islam as well. Their mosques and shrines are being demolished, their peaceful religious congregations and processions have been bombed. And thousands of people have been killed in mosques while they were praying. These fanatics call themselves *Jihādis* in the service of God. In their own estimation they are the soldiers of Islam and are engaged in the noblest service of Islam.

These are the people who blew up and bombed important places in various countries, killing and wounding millions of innocent people and destroying cultural heritages that reminded man of what their ancestors were able to create and recreate. Several thousand year old histories of human races and their artistic achievements brought to light by archaeological excavation teams have been destroyed in few days by these fanatics in the name of Islam. These handful Muslim but un-Islamic extremists have earned shame and disgrace for Islam and Muslims all-over the world. It is not wrong in calling them the worst enemies of Islam. 'Adjudge yourselves', says the Holy Qur'an.

> "Let there be no compulsion in religion." (*Qur'an : 2/256*)
>
> "To you be your religion, and to me mine." (*Qur'an : 6/109*)
>
> "Whosoever killeth a human being for other than man slaughter or corruption in the earth, it shall be as if he had killed all mankind." (*Qur'an : 5/32*)

The religiousness of these misguided men and women is based largely on sentiments rooted in false premises, paradigm and ignorance, which can create contradictions and confusion and lead to very dangerous consequences. No true Muslim can ever be a terrorist; nor would a true follower of any faith could become a terrorist. It deserves to be cursed and condemned by all those who believe in God. It is because of these unholy people that the Muslims settled in Europe and America and other countries for many generations, and who have played significant roles in shaping their national and cultural life, are being looked down with suspicion.

Muslims as other religionists regard their respective religions as the fountain of cultural and social life. Emphasis is laid on reaching truth following the path of spirituality, which unites all religions into a single religion of human brotherhood. Islam is the latest among the major religions of the world; it called for puritan lifestyle. No religion of the world spread so rapidly as Islam but it never chose to remain isolated as an island. It became a part of the local culture and society, and adopted local norms and practices. True, it was different in thoughts and rituals, but in the choice of God and the forms of worship every individual enjoyed his right to go his own ways. And so there could be no conflict of the old natives of that country with Muslims in matter related to God and the way of worship. The conflicts, if any, were borne out of factors other than religion.

Despite the Qur'anic guiding principles and the general adherence to them by the Muslims, a number of orientalists have tried to find fault with Islam and the holy Prophet Muḥammad for all that some misguided and ignorant Muslims have done. They drew wrong inferences and arrived at wrong conclusions. Since the public opinion about Islam in the intellectual circles, is shaped by the books and articles written by these scholars, Islam got a very distorted image in the minds of other religionists. For instance, Swiss historian Jacob Bark Hardt severely condemned Islam and propagated that no reformist movement could ever originate in Islam because it has no concern with enlightenment.

But, there were scholars, like Lutheran Bishop, Nar Andre and contemporary expert of Islamic studies, Anne-Marie Schimmel, in whose considered opinion the attempts of anti-Islamic European orientalists, is nothing short of 'religious colonialism.' Some Islamic organizations, in recent times, have done a good job of recovering the Muslim readers from the sway of pseudo academics, by exposing their designs and removing the doubts created by them. But they have so far proved to be drops in the ocean.

The blame for the prevailing anti-Islamic environment goes to the Muslim scholars more than to the western orientalists. Instead of treading on the footsteps of the holy Prophet, in thought, words and deeds, they followed the Muslim rulers and dictators making them the standard bearers of Islam. While the rulers were interested in serving their own interests, the clergy in their hands sanctified their actions as Islamic. Islam thus got the colour of politics and it became difficult to disengage the two. Under the pressure of Muslim polity, the real Islam suffered and became a tool in the hands of the rulers. When they invaded other countries, and killed thousands of innocent people, they did so in the name of Islam.

The reader will now appreciate that the main factor at the root of the general hostile attitude towards Islam among the followers of other faiths, is lack of knowledge and right understanding of Islam. The treasure of books on Islam in English and other European languages is large enough to fill many racks in libraries, but it would not be easy to lay hand on those, which truly represent Islam in its original form. There are several sects in Islam and each one calls itself to be the original and true. Most of the authors look at Islam from the perspectives of their own respective religions or faiths. They advance arguments to contradict each other. The missionaries of other religions too have published books on Islam in English and other European languages. Obviously their mission is not to introduce Islam as it really is but to trace the flaws and cracks in Islam and thus defend their own and establish their superiority over Islam.

Want of true knowledge of spiritual, and practical aspects of Islam has given rise to confusions. It has even alienated the followers of other religions. Islam sans knowledge is ignorance. It is futile to expect any good and auspicious thing from ignorance. Knowledge takes us forward to attain spirituality, which is the core of all religions. If spirituality is propagated, the religious divisions within Islam and among various religions would disappear. Islam has to be interpreted in the spirit of what the holy Prophet had said, and not by modifying verses containing words like *Kāfir* and *Jihād*, as suggested by some.

Muslims believe in Qur'an as the book revealed by God. None can have the power of amending or changing it. This power was not available to even the holy Prophet of Islam, Muḥammad. Hence no amendment would be acceptable to Muslims. Instead of changing Qur'an, they should try to look at the real meaning of, say, *Kāfir*. *Kāfir* is one who is infidel; he may be a Muslim too. So it is not against any religion or religious practice. If Islam allows other religions to live in harmony with it, it does allow infidels in other religions to co-exist with Islamists. Similarly, *Jihād*, is interpreted wrongly. The sense in which the impeder depicts *Jihād*, is not *Jihād,* which means struggling against injustice, but it is *Qattāl,* the slaughtering, which is permitted only in very exceptional circumstances. It has to be used against any unjust and inhuman system not necessarily a Hindu, Christian or Jewish system, it may be used against Muslims as well and has been used against Muslim despotic system. In the present context several Muslim countries have been fighting each other.

This book elaborates many of the issues raised above. The point of departutue is the holy Qur'an, which is the code of religious belief of entire Muslim world. I have couched my arguments in Qur'anic verses. No Muslim, of whatever sect, can refute Qur'an, he will have to submit to it, for even a little defiance to Qur'an will turn him out of the pale of Islam, and as for the non-Muslims, they too would regard Qur'an as the most credible reference and authentic source for the understanding of

Islam. Qur'an is a Divinely revealed scripture, as are other religious books, fully protected from any type of tampering. Memorized by numerous men and women, there is no possibility of change neither of words nor even dots. It is obligatory on all Muslims to accept all its contents. Denying any part of this suffices to be thrown out of Islamic fold. So its references are acceptable to all. The holy Qur'an has been translated into each and every important language of the world. In English too, several scholars of eminence have translated and some of them have also given notes or commentaries on it, as per their likings and choice. Unless it became absolutely essential, I have avoided their commentaries and confined myself to the mere Qur'anic text. Among the very well-known English translations of George Sale, J.N. Rodwell, E.M. Palmer, M.M. Pickthal, Yūsuf 'Abdu'llāh and S.V. Mīr Aḥmad 'Ali, I have often chosen the quotations of Qur'anic verses after the comparative study of their texts. A list of such Qur'anic verses has been given at the end of the book.

The other source of reference is *Ḥadīth* (Traditions, the words of the holy Prophet Muḥammad) in which some people from time to time have mixed their own words as suited to their designs. To collect the authentic *Ḥadīths* there developed a branch of study called *'Ilmu'l-Ḥadīth* in Islamic academics. This branch was greatly expanded, each *Hadīth* was explored with regard to its source, who was its *Rāwī* (Narrator), what was his family background? From whom did he learn it? Who had directly heard it from the holy Prophet? The chain of these narrators (from the one who had directly heard it from the holy Prophet) what is to be checked is the validity of each narrator, whether or not he is false or fake on any ground. If a single link is proved fake or false, the *Ḥadīth* is rendered incredible. Within the framework of these precautions both the major sects of Islam, Shi'is and Sunnis regard their respective collections of *Ḥadīths* to be authentic and valid. The Shi'is believe in their *Kutubu'l-Arab'a* (four books) to be the authentic collections of *Hadīths*, namely *al-Uṣūl- min'al-Kāfī* by al-Kulaynī, Abū Jā'far Muḥammad-bin-Y'āqūb (d. 940 AD), *Man Lā Yahzurūh al-Faqīh* by Ibn Bābūyā, Abū Jā'far Muḥammad-bin-'Abdu'llah al-Qommī (d. 991 AD), *Tahzību'l-Aḥkām* and *al Istibsār fī Mukhtulifa fihi mina'l-Akhbār* by Shaykhu'ṭ-Ṭā'fa, Abū Ja'far Muḥammad-bin-Ḥasan aṭ-Ṭūsī (d. 1067 AD). These three scholars are collectively called 'three Muḥammads.' The Sunnis believe in their *Ṣaḥiḥu'l-Sittah* (six authentic collections) to be namely *Jām'au'ṣ-Ṣaḥīḥu'l-Bukhārī* by al-Bukhārī, Abū 'Abdu'llāh Muḥammad-bin-Ismā'īl (d. 870 AD), *Jām'au'ṣ-Ṣaḥīḥu'l-Muslim* by al-Muslim, Abu'l Ḥusain Ibnu'l-Ḥajjāj Qushayrī (d. 875 AD), *as-Sunan* by Abū Dāwūd Sulaymān as-Sijistānī (d. 888 AD), *Jām'au's-Ṣaḥīḥu't-Tirmiżī* by at-Tirmiżī (d. 892 AD), *as-Sunan* by Nasā'ī, 'Abdu'r-Raḥmān (d. 915 AD) and *as-Sunan* by Ibn Māja, Abū Īsā Muḥammad (d. 886 AD). Some also consider *Jām'au's-Ṣaḥīḥu'l-Mishkātu'l-Maṣābīḥ* by al-Khaṭīb, Walīu'd-Dīn Muḥammad-bin-'Abdu'llāh (d. 1244 AD) and Abū 'Ali Muḥammad-bin-Yażīd and *al-Muwaṭṭa* by Mālik-bin-Anas (d. 795 AD) to be authentic collections of the *Ḥadīths*. Also where necessitated the authentic books on *Fiqh* (Jurisprudence), *Tārīkh* (History) and other references of both the sects, Shi'is and Sunnis have been consulted to arrive at a proper judgment.

For me it has been a great challenge to unveil the real face of Islam. I cannot speak to a man who has a rigid mindset in advance and is not willing to listen to any other point of argument. His object is not to reach a rational fact by exchange of views, but to stick to his guns and yield to no logic, howsoever rational, convincing and strong it may be. I am not a clergy, who spends his whole life in establishing the superiority of Islam over other faiths. My pen does not 'preach', but tells the reader that instead of moaning and cribbing, we should try to understand each other's point of view, which may be useful for both. I have spent my life in the Universities studying and teaching language and literature, the universal facts and values of life as revealed in the socio-cultural context of India. So my mode of understanding religions in general and Islam in particular, cannot be like that of a professional clergy. I am fully conscious and aware of my limitations. However, I intend to introduce the facts of Islam, without compromising its basic principles, in a manner, which might be acceptable to the maximum number of people, both Muslims and non-Muslims.

As far as possible, I have made use of those sources for references, which are not controversial. Also I have not made references to sources, which are acceptable to one sect only, so that my conclusions may be broad-based and their authority may remain unquestionable. Most of the *Ḥadīths* taken by me are acceptable to both Shi'is and Sunnis. There are some differences in the theological sciences. I have placed before the readers the facts and arguments of both the sects to make them have an objective view of both sides. As far as possible, I have tried to be objective in my analysis. How far have I been successful in it, the reader will decide.

My humble endeavour is to introduce Islam and to elucidate its true place in the history of the religions of the world. The most urgent task before me has been to express what exactly afflicts us and the scientific outcome of such a study. So this book has been authored for both the general reader, who is simply unaware of Islam and also for one who has some previous knowledge of it. It is also addressed to the esteemed scholars who have expertise in Islamic religion and thought. Thus, some repetitions and obvious explanations may graciously be seen. I humbly crave their indulgence and request their patience and forgiveness to bear the same with me.

To convey the import of the technical terminology, a brief glossary has been given for the readers' convenience. For transliteration, I have tried to adhere the internationally accepted principle of having the words as pronounced in their original forms. To differentiate the complications of special diacritical marks of vowels and diphthongs is no doubt useful. But it bewilder a reader unacquainted with the 'Arabic alphabet and pronunciation. I have, therefore, allowed a few softer deviations, with a view to further simplification, for the convenience of the non-'Arabian readers. So much so, if they avoid dots, commas, symbols etc. they could know the words generally as pronounced by non-'Arabs.

In preparing a book of this nature, I have relied upon the assistance of many people, books and libraries, without whose help on particular aspects of the subject, I would have failed to convey my message. I am thankful to them all. But I shall be failing in my duty, if I do not acknowledge indebtedness to my esteemed friend and internationally known social scientist Professor R.P. Misra, who very kindly took pains in going through my manuscript and making most valuable suggestions.

I shall be highly grateful, if I could get any suggestion from you.

'Shabistan'
786, Shahganj
Allahabad 211 003 (India)
Mīlādu'n Nabī 1432 AH
21st Febraury 2011

Saiyed Jafar Reza

Contents

Chapter One

Phenomena and Perspective

Understanding Islam

To understand Islam or any other phenomenon, we must adopt an approach and methodology. A right methodology produces meaningful results. One need not be an intellectual giant to understand Islam; even an average mind following a right methodology may even surpass great geniuses. The methodology selected could however not be 'scientific' as understood and construed in the West. The 'scientific methodology' is best suited to physical phenomena that can be observed with naked eye or through various instruments. In matter of religion, particularly in Islam, one has to depend on experiential knowledge to find an appropriate methodology. While faith is a must for balanced life and living, one must know what he believes in and why. If a person claims to be a Muslim, he must know Islam. The question is how to know Islam.

Islam is a multidimensional religion. It not only defines the relationship between God and man but also the life of all that exists especially the human beings upon this earth. Qur'an itself is multi-dimensional. A number of scientific inferences have been drawn from it. Islam may be studied in two ways. Firstly, by studying Qur'an, which is the best collection of thoughts; and secondly, by studying the history of Islam, specially the changes that occurred in various periods ranging from the commencement of Prophet Muḥammad's mission to-date. The best way is to combine the two. To study Islam using either the Qur'an or the history of Islam may help in rediscovering oneself and the cultural roots of Islam and the Muslim community.

According to 'Ali Sharī'atī (d. 1977 AD) we should take guidance and help from the Islamic history to interpret and understand Islam correctly and methodically:

> "We should study the type, origin, mode, concept and particulars of God which Islam takes into consideration For example, what is Omnipotent ? Is it Merciful? Is it superior to the existing world? Is it associated with humanity? Does its aspect of Mercy overcome Its Omnipotence or *vica versa*? Generally, what type is it. What kind of God is it.......The second stage is to know the Qur'an. What kind of book is it? What problems does it consider? Does it speak more about life on earth or after-life. Does it address itself more to the individual and moral matters or social aspects. Does it refer more to the material or to the spiritual ? Finally, what problems does it consider and what form do they take.......The third stage to know Islam is to know Muḥammad-bin-'Abdu'llāh, as the prophet of this religion. The fourth stage is to study the quality of appearance of the prophet of Islam....The fifth stage of knowing Islam is through studying individuals, who form the components that built distinct and distinguished individual human beings."[1]

The socio-religious philosophy of Islam points to a constant struggle between truth and the falsehood all through human history. And this struggle continues to this day. True Muslims have always been on the side of the truth and fighting against tyrants and oppressors who tried to take Islam towards falsehood. The geographical, ethnic, national and political differences notwithstanding, Muslims all-over the world share a common belief: there is no deity other than God, the Benificent, The Merciful who sent many Messengers, the last and final of whom was Muḥammad, the Prophet. All Muslims share a common sacred scripture: Qur'an; pray five times a day facing the Ka'ba. Muslim commonly fast during the month of *Ramazān* and perform *Hajj*, if they can afford it. They are under obligation to be united and live as a family in the spirit of brotherhood and sisterhood within themselves and also with people of other faiths.

Evolution of Religious Perspective

Islam covers all the issues and dimensions of the human life, the living creatures, visible and invisible. Islam is not just a way of worship. It is also not the performing rituals. Every human activity, if performed in accordance to Divine Will, is virtue and the defiance of His Will becomes vice. The man who is subject to Divine sovereignty is neither entitled to

Heaven nor Hell, he creates his own Heaven or Hell in this world by his own free-will. Islam is another name for the crusade to safeguard human rights. But instead of being a single one time campaign, Islam, like some other great religions of the world, has waged a perpetual struggle to secure truth and justice but it also accepts some of their campaigns. For example, in the Indian perspective it gives credit to the positive human values in Jainism, Buddhism, Hinduism and in the non-Indian perspective it accepts the best of Judaism, Christianity etc.

This intellectual current started in the 6th century BC, when Greece was in political turmoil, the victorious Romans could not subdue the intellectual cross currents generated by Greek thinkers and scholars. It rather adopted and adapted their intellectual and cultural heritage. Although the boundaries of the Roman Empire (509-264 BC) extended over the whole world, Rome could not produce any great thinkers, scientists, litterateurs or artists. Romans confined themselves to the interpretation of Greek thought and civilization. As a result, the creative energy was rendered barren and a prolonged stagnancy in human thought was set in.

Then happened what was bound to happen. In the words of Nero C.C. Drusus's (d. 68 AD), the mentor Cinni: "The most contented and satisfied is the man who in seclusion makes friend of his own self !" These thoughts weakened the creative impulse in the warriors of Rome: imitation became the norm. This is how the cultural edifice of Roman Empire was built on the cultural ruins of Greek. It would rather be truer to say that in 299 BC when Socrates was killed with poison, the Greek psyche too was poisoned to death. Later, Alexander the Great dreamt of giving a new life to Greek; invaded Persia in April 330, and Darius, the last Achaemenid king, also called Codommanus, was murdered. Alexander married the daughter of Darius. But this greatest general in history became a victim of sensuous pleasures and began to dance to the tunes of hedonism and materialism.

As time passed, Alexander who had swept over the then known world, went back to his inner self and tried to open the eyes of his conscience so as to submerge the sense of defeat into the wine of oblivion. He attempted to seek peace within his inner self than the external world of pleasure. In the ancient world, Jainism and Buddhism had already initiated these thoughts. It is only partly true to say that the Greek civilization came to India when Alexander the Great invaded India, in the spring of 326. The Western thoughts had already penetrated Greek and Rome, but they failed to impress them. By the first century AD, the Roman Empire, notwithstanding, its royal glory, was on its way to fragmentation. The ordinary men and women, tired of the external glitter and glamour started looking inward, particularly when the Christian missionaries expanded their campaigns to spread Christianity. Christianity spread first in Europe and then in the rest of the world.

The oppression and exploitation unleashed by the imperial power widened the gulf between the rich and the poor. People were in search of a ruling system, which could ensure equality and restore again the dignity of Divine-human relationship. Christianity gave the needed alternative. The Christianity claimed to establish earthly kingdom of God in place of the worldly kingdom. In the court of this Divine King, all were equal: there were no rich, nor were there the poor. The Greek and Roman kings enjoyed the honour equal to the status of God. Christianity offered the doctrine of salvation and entreaty between man and God. God is the fundamental truth. He is the First and the Last. He is sovereign Lord of the Universe.

Christianity did not allow the material needs to be neglected; it tried to promote higher human values and told that the path to salvation was through tolerance, love, and the spirit to serve mankind. In the beginning Christianity was regarded as a transformed Judaism, but Jews never allowed any change in their religious system. So a conflict between the two arose. The message of Jesus Christ was based on reverence, love, sacrifice and the spirit of service, which was ready to give shelter to every sinner. On the other hand, the Judaism did not like to have any contact with the poor and downtrodden, so much so that to the Jews, it was sin to visit and enquire the health of a patient on the *Sabbath Day*. Jesus Christ declared it to be the highest virtue to serve the patient. He made it convenient for the common man to avail the charity of the heavenly kingdom. Judaism could not establish itself in conflict with Christianity, which found its way into the oppressed hearts of the common man. This struck a blow to the imperial order.

As time passed, prestige of the Church order increased. In its heyday, it emerged as a synonym of the imperial exploitation. Within the ruling structure, emerged such a centre of power, which was not accountable to anyone. The interference of the Pope in the working of the state grew so much that even the glorious kingdom had to bow down before the command of the Church. This gave rise to a sharp reaction. To subdue the reaction, the Church took to violence, which resulted in blood shedding conflict between the Church and the Crown. Yet the grip of the Church was so strong that much of the strength of European powers was lost in curbing the power of the Church. As a result, the popularity of Christianity got badly hit, frittered and diluted.

After the fall of the great Roman Empire, though the strong political system of Europe remained in power for thousand years, the religious grip of the Church became more mechanical; it crushed the potentials of individuals' creativity. There was utter confusion. The European thought rolled down from faith to reason and back to faith like a round stone.[2] Creativity was therefore at low ebb for about a thousand years. That is why the period is known as Dark Age. As the missionary campaign was based on human-Divine relationship through Christ, this trinity saved Christianity from ruin though it became the centre of mutually controversial thoughts. The influence of Judaism gradually narrowed down. It had lost the will to meet its conflict with Christianity and had to put up with its fate of leading a low-profile existence buried under the glorious Christian States, until in the 20th century because of the Holocaust – in which millions of Jews were killed in Hitler's Concentration Camps. But Palestinians' land was converted into Israel, a Jewish state.

The rise of communism in the Western world started to bring in changes in practically all walks of life. Georg Wilhelm Friedrich Hegel (d. 1831 AD) called the advent of Marxism as an accidental campaign. Bertrand Russell (d. 1970 AD) described this worldwide influence in more balanced manner. He says that the main field and source of the cultural and intellectual progress was not only Europe, rather, Europe was in deep slumber, when Islamic culture served as a lighthouse from India to Spain. The basic difference between the Christianity and Islam is that while the prolonged inertia of Greece and Rome paved the way for the growth of Christianity and made the West its centre, the rise of Islam took place in the East.

One may look at this problem from a different angle and compare the genius of 5th and 4th centuries BC with those of 15th and 16th centuries AD. Aristotle (d. 322 BC) is more of a genius of the later centuries, laying the foundations for the development of science, art and literature. How is it that a great genius failed but lesser ones awakened the human society? The Greek civilization fenced the human mind. Best of the geniuses were gathered in Athens but could not invent even a wheel, whereas an average technician of the later period registered hundred of inventions. Thomas Alva Edison (d. 1931 AD) had the philosophical ability of third hand student of Aristotle and yet discovered hidden laws of nature, which resulted in registration of a thousand large and small inventions, which could not be fed during the long period of nearly two and half thousand years by the students of the Aristotle's thought and traditions.

To my mind the essential factor responsible for European stagnancy was the use of analogical methodology of Aristotle, which was blindly followed. And the moment this analogical methodology was abandoned and changed, the culture, thought and scientific developments also changed. The change in approach being the main factor in the revolution of thinking that turned into various movements. The sociological movement changed feudalism into bourgeoisie system, which opened the well-guarded wall between the eastern Muslims and westerner Christians, through the Crusades. By the close of 13th century, the 'Arabian philosophy which was also a form of Aristotelians, tempered more or less by Neo-Platonic conceptions was transmitted to Europe, and Spain functioned as an intermediary. Avicenna (d. 1037 AD) took pain to emphasize and proved so as to include sense and imagination within the scope of deductive logic of Aristotle and also included introduction, analogy, probable arguments and methodology of science. The Islamic thought had already stagnated when al-G͟hażālī, Abū Ḥāmid Muḥammad (d. 1111 AD); who was regarded as saint and religious divine by orthodox Muslims, influenced the religious dogmas. In the name of Muslim philosophy, it remained dominant in the University of Paris throughout the 13th century. Franciscan Friars took to England, where a Latin translation of the book of Ibn Rus͟hd, Abū Walīd Muḥammad-bin-Aḥmad-bin-Muḥammad (d. 1198 AD), known among the Westerns as Averroěs (Latin: Averrhoěs) was prescribed in Cambridge University as early as 1109.

Sunni Muslims believe that the legal scholars of early period had been uniquely qualified to derive their authoritative opinion binding on the Muslims of their period and also to all future generations to come. This doctrine is usually expressed as *B'adu'l-Ijtihād* (closing of the gates of experte) of the Sunni sects, the Ḥanafīs, the S͟hāfi'īs, the Mālikīs embrace the faith of closing gates of experte, while the Ḥanbalīs reject it. Wahhābīs, the modern sub-sect of Ḥanbalīs insist on the returning directly to the old sources for making independent judgments of the issue. As a result Sunni jurisprudence has remained in the same condition as it was 800 years ago.

Shi'i Muslims hold quite different understanding of this institution. The institution of Islamic religious *Ijtihād* (literally, exertion; the process of arriving at judgment on points of religious law using reason and principles of jurisprudence) had ever continued as legal doctrine among Shi'is in every period. As every individual who does not have qualification to interpret the sources of Islamic law, may choose any of *Mujtahid* (competent religious scholar having permission to practice), who shall be *Marja' at-Taqlīd* (literally, reference point for emulation; source of authority; great religious scholar who through his learning and probity is qualified to be followed in all points of religious practice and law) and whose teachings should be observed by all. There may be different 'sources of authority' at a time, one may observe any of them. But Shi'ism does not permit imitation of a dead 'source of authority'. This is one of the facts, which has kept Islamic Shi'i jurisprudence alive and fresh throughout the ages. It is divided into two categories: *Aqlī* (reasoned, intellectual) and *Naqlī* (transmitted). Intellectual sciences include, philosophy and mathematics and transmitted ones are language, *Ḥadīth* and history.

It is noteworthy that during the periods of trials and tribulations, the learned religious theologians of Islam kept serving the imperishable cause of Islamic knowledge. They managed to store a reliable fund of Qur'anic knowledge, holy Prophet's Traditions and Islamic Laws. They safeguarded their works from the vested interests of imperial minds, which sought to change the true identity of Islam by politically motivated interpretations of Islam. This holy heritage of the pious Imāms and the learned scholars has been passing from one generation to the other. Only in the light of this heritage can the fundamental principles of Islam be ascertained.

In the study undertaken here, an attempt will be made to trace the basic aspects of Islam, identifying specially those aspects which became the formative factors in the progress of Islamic civilization. In the analysis of these essential factors of Islamic civilization, it is indispensable to trace the influence of the leading personalities of Islam. Every Muslim has sincere regard towards the holy Prophet and his Progeny. But it has been coloured by his own personality and the local culture. Here I would try to focus only on the ideological and practical aspect of Islam, which may help visualize the culture evolved as a fusion of 'Arabic, Persian and Indian-sub continental Islamic observances and then underline those elements, which serve as the guiding light for understanding the true face of Islam.

Identity of Islam

The identification of the religions has been mainly on the basis of names of its founders or the religions from where they originated. Such as religions of Israel, Christ, Buddha, Jain, Zoroast and others to their revered names and Hindu, Babylon and others to the places of their origin. But the religion of Muḥammad has a distinctive appellation. It is Islam. Its identification is solely based on its religious principles.

Islam is an 'Arabic word derived from the root word *Silm*, from which other words like *salām, muslīm, muslimīn* etc. are derived. The holy Qur'an sheds light on various aspects of its meaning by using the word *Islam* in many connotations. To mention a few as under:

(i) In the sense of peace, concord and harmony, indicating that accepting Islam would demand to live in harmony with yourself and to be at peace with all other members of the society without creating any interference in the process of social order. Some verses of holy Qur'an may be seen:

"And if they lean to peace, then leaneth thou too to it and trust in God." (*Qur'an: 8/61*)

"When you are greeted with a greeting, then greet ye with a better (*than it*) or return it." (*Qur'an: 4/86*)

"And God calleth (*you*) to the abode of peace." (*Qur'an: 10/25*)

"And if anyone from the idolaters seeketh protection from thee, grant thou protection to him till he hears the Word of God, then convey him to his place of safety; this is because they are the people who know not." (*Qur'an: 9/6*)

"(*The angels saying unto them:*) Enter ye therein in Peace, Secure." (*Qur'an: 15/46*)

"Those who spend (*in alms*) alike in prosperity and straitness, and who restrain (*their*) anger and forgive (*the faults of*) men; for God loveth those who do good (*to others*)." (*Qur'an: 3/133*)

"(*The angels*) while receiving them will say: Peace be on you; Enter ye the Garden, for what ye were doing." (*Qur'an: 16/32*)

(ii) In the sense of guidelines that one who accepted Islam has become guided and placed on the right track. Some verses of holy Qur'an are as under:

"And say to those who have been given the Book, and the unlettered (*ones;*) have ye (*too*) submitted? If they submit (*themselves to God*) then indeed they are rightly guided." (*Qur'an: 3/19*)

"And guideth whomsoever He willeth unto the right way." (*Qur'an: 10/25*)

To attain peace and security has the same implication as to attain guidance:

"Those who believe and mix not their faith with inequity, those are they for whom is security, and they are (*the ones*) guided aright."(*Qur'an: 6/83*)

(iii) In the sense of the submission imposed on creation as seen in nature in which every particle, willing or unwilling, submits to the Law of God imposed on it. Holy Qur'an orders:

"Seek they the other than the religion of God when unto Him submitteth whosoever is in the heavens and the earth, willingly or unwillingly, and unto Him they shall be returned." (*Qur'an: 3/82*)

"Celebrate His glory the seven heavens and the earth, and (*all*) those in them; and there is not anything but glorifieth Him, but ye understand not their glorification." (*Qur'an: 17/44*)

(iv) In the sense of obedience, that is, whosoever accepts Islam, accepts to be obedient to Him and surrenders to remain in compliance of His Will, prostrates to Him and never thereafter prostrates to anything other than Him:

"Say: Verily my prayers and my sacrifice, my life and my death, (*are all, only*) for God, the Lord of the worlds." (*Qur'an: 6/162*)

"And they shall tender submission unto God on that day; And shall depart from them (*leaving them in lurch*) what they were forging." (*Qur'an: 16/87*)

"Cause me die a Muslim (*in submission unto Thee*), and join me with the righteous." (*Qur'an: 12/101*)

"And bidden I am, that I shall be the first Muslim." (*Qur'an: 39/12*)

(v) In the sense of the expansion of heart to be able to induct and preserve the Words of God. The person who accepts Islam enhances his own receptivity of truth and becomes free from all kinds of narrowness and prejudices. Holy Qur'an asserts:

"Whomsoever willeth God that he should guide him aright, He expanded his breast for Islam, and Whomsoever He intendeth to leave straying, He maketh his breast straight and narrow as though he is climbing into very skies ; Thus doth God layth ignominious chastisement on those who believe not." (*Qur'an: 6/126*)

"What is he whose breast God has opened for Islam then he followeth the light from God (*like unto the hardhearted one*)." (*Qur'an: 39/22*)

(vi) In the sense of having knowledge, faith and belief in the signs of God. The person who has accepted Islam has to have faith in the holy Prophet, Qur'an etc. and all the holy Prophets preceding the last Prophet Muḥammad and the Books revealed before the last Book Qur'an with equal weight and sincerity in all of them:

"O ye who believe, Believe in God and His Prophet and Book which He hath sent down upon His Prophet (*Muḥammad*) and the Book which he hath sent down before (*him*); and whoever denieth God, and His Angels, and His Books, and His Prophets and the Last Day (*of judgment*) hath indeed strayed off, far away (*from the right path*)." (*Qur'an: 4/136*)

"And verily sent We Prophets before thee, of them there are those We mentioned unto thee; and of them are those whom We have mentioned not unto thee." (*Qur'an: 40/78*)

(vii) In the sense of an age-old religion, i.e. one who has professed Islam, is aware of the fact that essentially the religion right from Adam to Muḥammad was Islam and each prophet was an ideal Muslim for his age. This fact has been brought home through a supplication of the prophet Abraham in the holy Qur'an:

"Our Lord make us (*two*) Muslims submitting (*only*) to Thee and of our progeny (*make*) a group submissive to Thee." (*Qur'an: 2/128*)

"Abraham was not a Jew nor a Christian; but was upright man who had surrendered (*to God*), and he was not of the idolaters." (*Qur'an: 3/66*)

And this name *Muslim* has been given by Abraham as willed by God.

"The faith of your father Abraham; He (*God Himself*) named you Muslims before and in this." (*Qur'an: 22/78*)

(viii) In the sense of a perfect religion which is indispensably desirable for the human kind and God Himself grants this perfect religion the favour of His choice:

"This day have I perfected for you, your religion and have completed My favour on you and chosen for you Islam (*to be*) the Religion." (*Qur'an: 5/3*)

"Verily, the religion with God is Islam" (*Qur'an: 3/18*)

"Lay they an obligation upon Thee that they have submitted (*embraced Islam*) Say thou, Lay ye not upon me any obligation by your submission (*Islam*) rather God layeth an obligation upon you that he guideth you unto the faith if ye be truthful ones." (*Qur'an: 49/17*)

(ix) In the sense of the obligatory religion and who denies Islam shall be among the losers in the next world:

"And whosoever seeketh any religion other than Islam (*total resignation unto God*) never shall it be accepted from him, in the next world he shall be among the losers." (*Qur'an: 3/85*)

In the light of the above connotations of the word *Islam*, two basic aspects of Islamic religion come into prominence:

Firstly, the aspect pertaining to the Divine Code of Genesis and function of Nature, and

Secondly, pertaining to the Divine Code of Human Life, as per Islamic Law.

The first aspect implies the binding laws of nature in which we have no choice, willing or unwilling, we have to accept them. Our knowledge or action cannot change the essential nature of these laws. It is beyond our powers to alter their substance. For instance if Islam means peace and harmony which is its inherent property, it cannot be made other than what it is neither by action nor by attitude. If obedience and compliance to Divine Code is the nature of Islam, it cannot be mutated or denied by a faith or action contrary to its nature. If Islam is the eternal and timeless religion imposed compulsively on the phenomena of the physical nature and revealed to human free-will in order to try the wisdom of his choice, it cannot be dismissed by calling it a new or modern or a junior younger, or an immature religion. Or if God has perfected his Code in Islam no man or multitude can render it imperfect either by argument or by practice. Or to the extent a man like other creations, is bound to submit to the will of God in areas of inevitable dictates of existence such as breathing, growing, eating, sleeping, living and dying etc., he cannot undo by any powers, these inevitabilities and he is bound to be a Muslim by force as he cannot help them otherwise.

Islam being essentially the submission to the law of harmony and balance, irrespective of one's own view or action against it, its laws will have to be discovered, learned and incorporated into practice no matter we like them or not. The choice of accepting or rejecting it is entirely at the cost of one's own wisdom how he handles and wields his free-will. Islam as such can be violated by exercise of free-will but it's principle cannot be annulled by any amount of violation or revolt in words or in practice. Like life and death it is an entity which cannot be turned into a non-entity. Islam stands by itself not by other's faith in it. That is the inescapable and inexorable aspect of Islam pertaining to the inevitable submission to the laws of nature.

The other aspect of it is the Divine Code of human nature or human life or the revealed constitution of the practical norm for the individual, social and political behaviour of a perfect man, in which a man is not forced to live as demanded by the constitution. He is free to disagree with its ideology or philosophy or dismiss any of its tenets as false and untenable. He is also free to pursue no acquaintance with the meaning of Islam out of his hatred or negligence. But all these freedoms are not absolute, they are conditional, if the freedom is a precondition to afford room and space to the human free-will to make it come out with its free response to the Divine Code and make it witness to its own conduct whether it is submissive or defiant, loyal or a traitor, qualifying for reward or deserving for punishment. Thus Islam by providing freedom as a necessary condition for the trial will, actually imposes responsibility on the man to justify the use of his freedom.

An existence without an objective or an objective devoid of purity or an impure means to reach that objective can never be in the true interest of a positive life. To achieve this, Islam does not impose any restriction on the exercise of reason. The holy Qur'an not only recommends the exercise of reason but makes it compulsory as the reason leaves convincing impressions on heart and mind and makes them accept a fact without any force or fear or pressure. The honest reasoning to explore the rational grounds of a religion, makes the faith stand on an unshakable firmament.

A man checks the authenticity of his faith on two grounds *Burhān* (is evidence of fact as universally observed and confirmed) and *Jidāl* (dialectics) from universal to particular, in which the fact is reached through dialectical analysis. In *Burhān* the premise is real, self-evident and observable. The facts can be perceived by man with his cognitive faculty gifted by nature such as four is less than five or the light of the sun is hot and that of moon is cool. The facts of the objective world of nature are apprehended without contradiction. In *Jidāl,* the method is to base the reasoning on an evident fact and by comparison to other evidence arrived at by logical inference bearing the validity of a belief.

Qur'an has adopted both methods. Firstly, it has invited our attention to the wisdom of creation in heaven and earth, stars and planets, cycles of day and night and in the animal and vegetable kingdoms. Qur'an has called upon us to reflect on natural phenomena in the backdrop of established facts and the laws governing their forms and functions. Then invites to enter into logical arguments with the *People of Books* (the Jews and the Christians) in the best of the ways of argument both in substance and manner. In this way Islam has based theological reasoning and dialectics on the standard of knowledge eliminating the chances of bitterness in case of any controversy and it provides time and space for a graceful exercise of reason before admitting or refuting a theological article.

The central meaning of Islam and the behaviour of a Muslim must mutually agree. The levels of individual piety may vary from Muslim to Muslim but there can be no controversy among them about the cardinal roots and branches of the Islam. That is why the holy Qur'an has rendered the understanding of Islam as simple as may be accessible to all levels of intelligence:

> "So have we only made it (*Qur'an*) easy in thine own tongue that thou mayest give glad tidings thereby unto the pious ones, and warm by it a people (*who are*) contentious." (*Qur'an: 19/97*)

For understanding the legal aspects of Islam, the aspiration for knowledge has been strongly emphasized in numerous verses of the holy Qur'an:

> "And those possessed of knowledge, standing firm for justice." (*Qur'an: 3/17*)
>
> "O' our Lord ! Whomsoever Thou causeth to enter the (*Hell*) fire, surely Thou hast put him to disgrace. There is no for the unjust any of the helpers." (*Qur'an: 3/192*)

"He granteth wisdom to whomsoever He willeth, and he who hath been granted wisdom has been given abundant good ; and none shall mind it save those endowed with wisdom." (*Qur'an: 2/269*)

"'O mankind, your rebellion is against your ownselves, a provision for the life of (*only*) this world, then unto Us shall be your return, then will We inform you of what ye were doing." (*Qur'an: 10/23*)

In the light of these verses, it becomes clear that the unjust is basically one who refuses to recognize the power of God and gives to his own transitory powers the status of an abiding and absolute power. When he has caused all havocs, because of his wilfulness, he has lost the ground to be expiated and forgiven by God and left no room except to be condemned to God's wrath and severe punishment. The unjust is a liar, his people are deprived of the Divine guidance, God does not qualify him to get from Him and high ranks which he always accords to men who are thoroughly just and equitable.

God never likes that excess in any measure be allowed against any person from another person. In countering injustices, however, he may expiate any excessive measure if unwittingly caused in wake of fighting the unjust. The abode for the unjust is the worst place to live. Thus, oppression, injustice and the unjust are the factors of alienation in Islam. Wherever the unjust are shown be sure that Islam has no affiliation to it. On the other hand, if the one who are oppressed are shown, be sure that God's Mercy waiting to be showered on them and they deserve his Mercy. With them the Islam will be found dealing in terms of sympathy and love. The obvious reason for this is that all kinds of oppressions and exploitations are based on injustice while the grand name with which Islam is identified and laid down is the law of justice. One who has got the understanding of this law of justice has got the crux of Islam and got acquitted with real import of it.

Islam and Other Religions

Fairly liberal disposition of Islam towards other religions has a special relevance in the contemporary perspective. The common tendency of the believers of each religion is to be faithfully bound and committed only to their respective scriptures, religious founders and religious ideologies. Their liberal attitude towards other religions, at best, is confined to have only a sense of respect for other faiths. To go beyond that is not desirable.

But the spirit and ideal of other religions is to have equal reverence for all religions. Islam has picked up this sentiment and broad-based it on reasonable grounds and has emphasized to have fair regards to all the older religions.

It is necessary to refer here the verses of holy Qur'an already mentioned above regarding identification of Islam that besides the three cardinal belief of Divine Unity, Divine Prophethood and the Divine Resurrections and Day of Final Judgment, every Muslim must believe in the continuity of previous religions and all possible respect to their religious leader, already quoted in these pages that person who has accepted Islam has to have faith in all the holy Prophets preceding the last Prophet Muḥammad and the Books revealed before the last Book Qur'an with equal weight and sincerity in all of them.

We all know that the continuity of religious progress amongst the human being has been the source of awakening of human minds, which resulted in recognition of an Universal Soul say God regarding pervading and guiding all existence. Some of men were chosen by God as *Messengers of Heavens* were proclaimed as His Prophets. To know about the religious morality of Islam, it would be fitting to study the following verses of Qur'an so as to learn what Qur'an has to say about the kinships of Islam with other religions, vide Chapter *al-Baqarah* (The Cow), the verse:

> "Lo ! those who believe (*in that which is revealed unto thee, Muḥammad*) and those who are Jews, and Christians and Sābeans – whoever believeth in God and the Last Day and doeth right – surely their reward is with their Lord and there shall be no fear come upon them neither shall they grieve."
> (*Qur'an*: 2/62)

At another place the holy Qur'an clearly upholds the same spirit; almost identical to above verse:

> "Lo ! those who believe, and those who are Jews, and Sābeans, and Christians – whosoever believeth in God and the Last Day and doeth right – there shall be no fear come upon them neither shall they grieve." (*Qur'an: 5/69*)

In both these verses, one very significant fact is noteworthy. In the former verse *Sābeans* has come after Christians while in the latter

Sābeans occurs before Christians. In another place in Qur'an, it has been said:

> "Lo! Those who believe (*this Revelation*), and those who are Jews and Sābeans and Christians, and the Magians and the idolaters – Lo! God will decide between them on the Day of Resurrection. Lo! God is Witness over all things." (*Qur'an* 22/17)

In this verse *Sābeans* have been mentioned before the Christians and *Magians* (Zoroastrians) which indicates their significance as a religious cult or group. In the above verses of Qur'an, five religious-groups have been mentioned. Muslims have been addressed as *People in Faith*, (Muslims) *Margians* (fire worshippers, Aryans of Iran, Zoroastrians) and *Sābeans* (stars worshippers, Aryans of India, Hindus) Jews and Christians have been directly addressed.

The other highly influential group of the Aryans is well spread from central Asia to east Asia who may have been addressed as *Sābeans* but their existence is not clear. Historians differ, but the 10th century historian Qāzī Sa'd Undulusī has maintained that *Sābeans* are Hindus, his view is shared by 'Abu'l Fatḥ Muḥammad Shahristanī, the 12th century scholar, and by Thanau'llāh Pānīpatī, a 19th century scholar. According to Abu'l Kalām Ażād, Hindus are the religious group better and distinct from both *Sābeans* and the fire-worshippers or *Margians*.[3]

All the five religious groups mentioned above have been given recognition as religions in their own right and have been mentioned together with Islam. As such no one of these religious groups have been dismissed as devoid of Truth, nor the followers of these religions condemned as corrupt or damned. They have been bracketed with Muslims with the proviso that whoever among them will have sincere faith in God and the Day of Judgment and be righteous will get reward and grace from their Lord and no fear shall be upon them nor shall they grieve.

At another point the variance in religions, has been dealt in Qur'an in an unusual way and the difference of religion has been given a purpose of trial so that the difference may initiate a spirit of striving and excelling each other in attaining virtues and goodness, while the goal of all is to realize God, Who will show the truth of the matters in which they were disputing? God would have made them into a community of one religion, but He did not choose to unify them by compulsion because a forced unification would have deprived them of exercising their own free will, their reasons and intuition to compete each other in discovering the Truth, Qur'an says:

> "For each We have appointed a divine law and trace out way. Had God willed He could have made you one community? But that He may try you by that which He hath given you. (*He hath made you as ye are*). So vie one with another in good work. Unto God ye will all return, and He will then inform you of that wherein ye differ." (*Qur'an: 5/48*)

Affording only respect for all religions is not sufficient but respecting and protecting their places of worship is also obligatory. Qur'an has clearly pointed it out:

> "Had God not checked one set of people by means of another, there would surely have been pulled down monasteries, churches, synagogue and mosques, in which the name of God is commemorated in abundant measure. God will certainly aid those who aid His (*cause*)." (*Qur'an: 22/40*)

By ignorance some people hold that Islam calls its followers to be believers and the followers of other faith to be *Kāfir* or unbelievers. This attitude is entirely wrong. You may find that some Muslim sects who claim themselves to be pure Muslims keep passing *Fatwā* (edict) for other Muslim sects to be *Kāfir*. Refer to history and you will find sects, engaged in *Jihād* against others treating them *Kāfir*. The battle of Karbala (10th October 680) leading to the martyrdom of Imām Husain, is the most prominent of such *Jihāds*. Who does not know that the Umayyite king Yażīd-bin-Mu'āwiya was not a Hindu or the follower of any other religion other than Islam. He proclaimed to be a Muslim, who forced the holy Prophet Muḥammad's grandson Imām Ḥusain to submit to his infidelity. Imām Ḥusain refused to yield to him, and became a martyr along with his children and companions. In commemoration of this tragic event, processions are taken out every year on the occasion of Muḥarram as a mark of protest against the *Muslim Kāfirs*.

Famous scholar, as-Suyūtī, Jalālu'd-Dīn (d. 1505) has quoted the following verse of Qur'an as a sufficient proof for a corrupt Muslim to be a real *Kāfir*:

> "And God will protect thee from (*the mischief*) of men;Verilly God guideth not infidel people." (*Qur'an: 5/67*)

With regard to other religions, Qur'an has presented a fairly high standard of equity that all human beings are absolutely free to observe their own religions. No individual or group has the right to impose his religion on others by force:

> "Let there be no compulsion in religion." (*Qur'an: 2/256*)

In Islamic terminology, the people of other faiths may be divided as the *People of the Books* and others. Jews and Christians are accepted as the *People of the Books*. Zoroastrian and Hindus are also regarded as *People of the Books*, by majority of Islamic scholars. Others who have not been considered as the *People of the Books*, their religions and its leaders are also equally regarded. A few points need to be mentioned here under:

(*i*) Islam has interpreted monotheism in a consequential and literal way more than any other religion of the world, but some other religions have also the concept of God as monolatry rather than as monotheistic. The passionate importance proclaimed to Yahweh and one God, and the rejection of other gods makes truer of the monotheism of Ishrael, which became Judaic affirmation of their faith:

"Hear, O' Ishrael, the Lord is our God, one Lord." (New English Bible: Deut 6:4)

Christianity, as a monotheistic religion made triadic formulas invoking God the Father, Son and Holy Spirit: three persons and one substance. Though the doctrine of separate and absolute God was the crowning achievement of medieval times, the Jewish and Christian mysticism with a shadow of Pantheism ran through out the age.

(*ii*) It has been fundamental doctrine of orthodox Christianity that Mary was sole natural parent of Jesus Christ. She was conceived through the power of Holy Spirit. It had been universally accepted by all Christians since 2nd century, and was enshrined in Prophet Creed, based on the infamous narratives contained in Gospel accounts of Mathew and Luke. This doctrine was seriously challenged in 19th century by the liberal theologies of Protestants, who found biological problem in Biblical interpretation. It has been accepted by the Council of Chalcedom (451), which is part of the teaching of the Orthodox and Roman Catholics and also maintained by some Anglican and Luthereran theologians. However, the doctrine of Virgin Birth has remained the cardinal faith in the Roman Catholic, Orthodox, and most Protestant Churches of the world. Islam also endorses the Virgin Birth of Jesus Christ, and his position as most revered Prophet of God. Qur'an asserts that the child Jesus in the lap of her mother Mary clarified:

"He spoke: Lo ! I am slave of God. He hath given me the Scripture and hath appointed me a Prophet." (*Qur'an: 19/30*)

(*iii*) There had been a historical row among the Christian scholars over the Gospel of Judas, the holy Qur'an and Islamic history too had recorded the event in which Jew's Rabbis have been blamed for carrying a campaign against and plotting to kill Jesus. Christian sources had made Judas Iscariot a synonym for betrayal in the four accepted gospels for selling out Jesus for 30 pieces of silver. The Gospel of Judas was lost to Christianity for the past 17 centuries. The text, in the Coptic language, is a copy of an earlier Greek version. Now the Christian scholars say, even if the gospel is authentic, it appears to have been written at least a century after the death of Judas. Moreover, it is the work of a particular second century sect, the Gnostics, who were long ago declared heretical. 26-page newly discovered papyrus document tells a far different story in which Judas is a favoured disciple who was given special knowledge by Jesus and who turned him in at Jesus request.

According to Islamic sources, it was Judas, known as Tatyanus in Arabic history, who faced death on the Cross and not Jesus, whom God had 'raised unto himself ' because, when the Rabbis could no longer bear Prophet Jesus' preaching, they hatched a conspiracy to eliminate him with the help of Judas, one of his disciple. The Rabbis used Roman soldiers in their plan. The holy Qur'an did not agree with the doctrine of crucification of the Jesus Christ. It has recorded:

"And because of their saying: We slew the Messiah Jesus son of Mary, God's Messenger – They slew him not nor crucified but appeared so unto them; and lo! those who disagree concerning it are in doubt thereof; they have no knowledge thereof save pursuit of a conjecture; they slew him not for certain. But God took him up to Himself. God was ever Mighty, Wise. There is no one of the People of the Scripture but will believe in him before his death, and on the Day of Resurrection, he will he a witness against them." (*Qur'an: 4/157-159*)

(*iv*) Islam acknowledges the tendencies towards dualistic thought as <u>*Kh*</u>*ayr* (Good) and <u>*Sh*</u>*ar* (Evil) in an entirely different fashion Qur'an says:

"Every soul shall taste of death; We try with evil and (*with*) good (*by way of*) a test; and unto Us shall ye (*all*) be returned" (*Qur'an: 21/35*)

Whereas, Iranian dualism, as per Zoroastrian religious texts, *The Gāthās*, there is an opposition between two spirits – *Spenta Mainyu* (Beneficent Spirit) and *Angra Mainyu* or *Ahriman* (Distractive Spirit). Indian faith also endorsed the above dualism in a form of tendency to opposite *devas* (gods) and *asuras* (demons).

(*v*) Religion and mysticism are phenomenal. No deeply religious person is possible without a touch of mysticism and similarly no person in the deepest sense can be other than religious person but the dialogue between mystics and religious personalities has not been a happy one. Islamic scholars have divided the mysticism into two folds – *Taṣawwuf* for Islamic mysticism and *Ramżīyat* or *Sirrīyat* for general mysticism. The classic Indian formula is – *aham brahmismī* meaning – That Thou Art (Chandogya Upanisad: 6/9) which was the repeated saying: '*Anal-Ḥaqq* by famous Ṣūfī Manṣūr Ḥallāj (d. 922) for which he was punished and beheaded because Islamic mystics have a different approach to understand God.

(*vi*) The concept of sacred (or holy) has became dominant in the comparative study of various religions. Different terms from various traditions have been accepted in this regard, such as Greek *hagios,* Hebrew *qadosh,* Arabic *ḥaram* German *haminja* (luck) and Sanskrit *brahmaṇ.* The sacred power becomes great source of strength in the myth. Sometime sounds as the name of God and also does not have the common meaning; such as Hindu *om*, Budahist *om maṇī,* Parsis *hūṃ,* Jewish and Chirstians *hallelujah* and Islamic '*Allāhū.* The sacred activities include initiation, sacrifice and prayer, which have been of great significance to the believers of all religions, irrespective of their inspiration, revelation or otherwise. Most intimate essence of religions is revealed in a prayer, which is the phenomenal to all religions. Islamic payer seeks and establishes dialogue and is an act of adoration of God.

(*vii*) To be ideal great man in India, there is no condition of any religion or faith. Manu has told four signs of religion –

"*Veda* (knowledge) *smiritī* (remembrance) *sadāchār* (right conduct) and *santosh* (contentment)." (*Mansmiti: 2-12*)

The way knowledge and remembrance are accepted as the fundamental principles, is the same all religions have their respective scriptures and they too be regarded in the same way. As for the right conduct and contentment, these are regarded as ideals in every religion. In the context of Islam, if Qur'an together with other religious scriptures is accepted there remains no conflict among them.

(*viii*) Indian context is traceable at the very outset of Islam. Three Indian things namely, *kāfur* – camphor (*Qur'an: 5/76*), *żanjīl* – ginger (*Qur'an: 18/76*) and *mushq* – musk (*Qur'an: 26/83*) are mentioned in holy scripture among the holy delicious and enjoyable items of paradise. Adam is said to have descended from Heaven on Indian soil *Sarandīp* (Swarndwip or Sinhaldwip). Buddha is said to have possibly been referred to by *Bozaph.* Some believe that *Žul-kifl* might be the same as Kapilvastu. Two tombs in Ayodhya (India) are said to be those of the prophets Shīth and Job. The same belief is held regarding some tombs in Gujarat (India). The Jesus Christ is said to have spent the early days of his life in Kashmir (India), etc.

In the context of India there is a very heart-toucling *Ḥadīth* of holy Prophet Muḥammad: He said – I feel the smell of Divine fragrance from the direction of India. In the modern Indian context of Islam, it has the same inseparable relationship with India as the meaning has with word, smell has with colour, or Radiation has with heat. Now it is relevant to treat it as one among Indian religions, because it is the faith of the thousands of Muslims who were born, brought up, grew and after death became the part of the Indian soil. The Indian Muslim has his own identity among the various Muslims of the world. In his costume, food, culture and behaviour he is like all other Indians of different faiths. In the so-called Muslim countries, the Indian Muslim is called *Hindu* or *Hindi.* In fact in the modern perspective, Islam is an Indian religion as there are other religions like Hindu, Baudh, Jain and Sikh religions of India. It would be reasonable to say that after the Hindu religious community, next religious community of the majority group in India is the Muslim community.

References

1. *An Approach to the Understanding of Islām*, pp. 13-15.
2. *The Story of Philosophy*, p. 184.
3. *Jām'au'sh-Shawāhid fī'l Dakhūl Ghayr-Muslim fī'l-Masjid*, p. 55.

Chapter Two

The Cardinal Beliefs

Making of Cardinals

The cardinal faiths in Islam have complete unanimity in three principles related to God, Prophethood and Resurrection and the Last Judgment.

God is viewed as Creator, Sustainor and Restorer of the Universe. God is Unique (*Waḥid*) and inherently one. God's Nature is just, so He cannot act unjustly, because the quality of Justice is innate to the Divine Nature. Thus, the Shi'is like other Muslims believe in Divine Unity but also add Justice to Divine Nature.

The belief, in general terms, has been considered as a mental attitude of assent towards a proposition without the full intellectual knowledge of the truth but it becomes knowledge when the truth of proposition is evident to the believer, it reconstructs itself in the shape of inner attitude and conviction, if related to God or ultimate salvation. If religious traditions attain inner certainty or attitude of love conferred by God Himself, like water most soft and yielding, which can move everything, it may transfigure the human personality into a pattern of perfection through a synthetic process of the development of mind and sublimation of emotions and illumination of spirit.

The belief, as a religious trust in India, China and Japan has been different from the notions of faith in Jewish, Christian and Islamic Traditions. In Hindu (*Vedic*) traditions, the term *religion* cannot be translated for *faith* but rather to be described as cultic duties and act. Similar is the case of Egyptian religion. The belief has been alternate to *trust* (Pali *Śaddha*, Sanskrit, *Śrada*), which is described in Buddhist Eight-fold Path and also in Chinese *hsin* (confidence, sincerity and trust) is one of the five principal virtues. Some scholars are of the opinion that the Zoroastrianism and Judaism also have been important in the development of faith and belief and their prophet Zoroaster (628-551 BC) may have been first to speak of a new conscious religion for search of truth (*asha*). In Biblical Hebrew, the *faith* is mainly juridical which persons adhere to a promise with God and Ishrael. As Christianity and Islam both are rooted in the same traditions, notion of faith reflects the same viewpoint. The Christian First Letter of the Corinthians asserts the faith is a gift of God. (I.Vov. 12: 8-9), and the Letter to the Hebrews defines *pistis* (faith) as follows:

> "The assurance of things hoped for, the conviction of things not seen. (11: 1)

In Islam, the manifestation of *Īmān* (faith) in itself has been treated as favours of Heaven, which is allowed by God Himself to the deserving persons to use their choice:

> "And (*although*) it is not for any soul to believe except by God's permissions; while casteth. He incleanliness (*of infidelity*) on those who use not (*their*) sense:" (*Qur'an: 10/100*)

Belief in Islam, unlike generally accepted behaviour of assent, without the actual knowledge of the facts of the truth, has been considered as *God's permission* for those who apply their wisdom to know the facts of the truth.

Islam has legitimized and approved the rational thought for finding the solutions of his problem in two ways –

Firstly, *Burhān*: a proof premises are considered true, even if the absorbability or evidence may not be available. Such as man comprehends universal problems of existences, its origin and end. It is also known as the meta-philosophical thought as a means of spiritual realization.

Secondly, *Jidāl:* a proof based on absorbability and certain data. It has been common practice to prove the truth within the span of a particular religious principle. The holy Qur'an has applied both the above methods such as free investigation and mediation upon the principles of the existence of world cosmic order, functioning of planet, earth, animals, human beings etc. and also praises in the high eloquent language the investigation, innovation and intellectual behaviours. Qur'an has commanded for application of dialectical thought to be accomplished in the best possible manner by the persons who possess moral virtues:

> "(*Call*) with wisdom and fair exhortation, and reason (*jādil* from *jidāl*)." (*Qur'an: 16/125*)

The affirmative of faith must be based on the result of rational demonstration or dialectical wisdom and should not be customary:

> "Verily in the creation of heavens and the earth and the alternation of the night and the day and (*in*) the ships that sail in the sea with what profiteth mankind and (*in*) the water which God sendeth down from skies and enliveneth therewith the earth after its death and scattereth therein of (*every kind of*) animal, and in the changing of the winds and the clouds controlled for service between the heavens and the earth, surely there are signs for (*the guidance of*) people who understand." (*Qur'an: 2/164*)

Further, it emphasizes to ponder over as per his wisdom and intellect about the signs of the Nature:

> "A token unto them is the dead earth; We revive it, and We bring forth from it grain so that they eat thereof." (*Qur'an: 36/33*)
>
> "A token unto them is night, We strip it of the day, and lo! they are in darkness." (*Qur'an: 36/37*)
>
> "It is not (*expedient*) for the sun that it should overtake the moon, nor can the night outstrip the day; and each (*of these luminaries*) rotate on (*its peculiar*) sphere." (*Qur'an: 36/40*)

To gain the faith first and then seek proof in obedience to it, the following verses of Holy Qur'an fully establish this claim:

> "And serve the Lord till the inevitable (*al-yaqīn*) cometh unto thee." (*Qur'an: 15/99*)
>
> "(*God says*) And thus did We show Abraham (*the governing of*) the kingdom of heavens and the earth that he might be among those who are sure." (*Qur'an: 6/76*)
>
> "Nay, but the record of righteous is in *'Iliyīn* – Ah! what will convey unto thee what *'Iliyūn* is! A written record-attested by those who are brought near (*unto their God*)." (*Qur'an: 83/18-21*)

Holy Qur'an expressively assert the holy Prophets and their Vicegerents – who attain the same purification are also included in the witnesses of *'Iliyīn* and this witness is not confined to the being of the evangelical order. Holy Qur'an further says:

> "The parable of those that disbelieve is the likeness of one who shouteth to (*one*) which heareth not but a call and cry; deaf, dumb, blind (*are they*) wherefore they do not understand." (*Qur'an: 2/171*)

Once the affirmation of faith has been established, the triple principle of the enforcement becomes reciprocal factors for each others:

Firstly, *Iqrār-bil-Lisān* (Oral Declaration), to declare the faith orally in the presence of all other concerned, who become the witnesses.

Secondly, *Taṣdīq-bil-Qalb* (Affirmation by Heart), to affirm by heart that the faith accepted is actually true without any ifs and buts.

Thirdly, *'Amal-bil-Arakān* (Translated into Action), to endorse the faith by translating it into action, which was previously, declared orally and affirmed by heart. The compliance of above two conditions make him Muslim and all triple principles bestowed on him the honour of being *Mūmin* (true believer), as clarified by the holy Qur'an:

> "The wandering 'Arabs say: We believe. Say (*unto them, 'O Muḥammd*): ye believe not, but rather say: We submit (*Muslim*) for the faith hath not yet entered your hearts." (*Qur'an: 49/14*)

Prophethood is also core cardinal belief of every Muslim. The sacred scriptures which God revealed to His Prophet Muḥammad, who is the last of the series of Apostles (including Adam, Noah, Abraham, Moses, Jesus and others) and the Divine Message simultaneously consummate and abrogate the Divine revelation to earlier Apostles, The Divine Message which God revealed through angels particularly Gabriel, the Angel of Revelation, has to remain enforced till the Last Judgment, it is necessary to have authority in the human beings after the death of the holy Prophet Muḥammad, it necessitates the Imamate for maintaining the continuity in the observation of the faith. Thus, the Shi'is add Imamate after the Prophethood. Although Sunnis do not include Divine Justice and Imamate in the cardinals of faith, yet they do have faith in them. Since the Caliphate succeeded after the death of the holy Prophet, it has become the part of Sunni's belief, specially to the *Khilāfatu'r-Rāshidah* (Rightly Guided Caliphate) but Shi'is did not agree with them. Similarly, there are some differences in the faiths of both the sects regarding the Occultation and Return of Imām Mahdī. But there is complete unanimity of all Muslim sects and communities regarding Divine Resurrection and Last Judgment.

Accordingly, the following cardinal beliefs shall be discussed in the forthcoming pages:

1. The Divine Unity
2. The Divine Justice
3. The Prophethood
4. The Imamate
5. The Caliphate
6. The Occultation and Return of Imām Mahdī
7. The Divine Resurrection and Last Judgment

First of all the Divine Unity will the taken for elucidation, as it figures uppermost in the Principles of Islam (*Uṣūlu'd-Dīn*).

The Divine Unity

Allāh (God) is the foremost pivot of Islamic faith, one and unique, no partner, no equal. Etymologically, the name *God* may be probably, a contraction of 'Arabic word *al-Ilāh* (the god), which can he traced back to earliest Semitic writings where the words *Il* or *El* (with the same meaning as the god or God) have been used. *El* has been synonym to *Yahwah* in the Old Testament. But now there was *God* is most standard 'Arabic word for god or God, which also being used by 'Arabic spoken Christians for God. Qur'an's surah *at-Tawḥīd* (The Unity) takes name from its subject and reveals the nature of God in such a way that it has been called the essence of the Qur'an:

> "Say He is God, the One ! God, the eternally Besought of all! He begetteth not nor was begotten. And there is none comparable unto Him." (*Qur'an: 112/1-4*)

Islam does not content itself by mere preaching the Divine Unity but requires its adherents to believe in the divine qualities of the concept, which have been classified into two kinds – Firstly, *Ṣifāu't-Thubūtīyah* (Positive Attributes) Secondly, *Ṣifātu's-Salabīya* (Negative Attributes), which could not be attributed to God.

Positive Attribute

It is considered as the most *Asmau'l-Ḥasana* (Beautiful Names of God) are 99, to mention a few as *al-Ḥayyu'l-Qayyūm* (One and only living One and Subsisting), *al-Ḥaqq* (the Real Truth), *al-Qadīm* (the Ancient), *al-Qādir* (the Almighty), *al-'Ālim* (the Omniscient), *al-Mudrik* (the Perceiving), *al-Murīd* (the Will), *al-Mutakallim* (the Orator), *aṣ-Ṣādiq* (the Truthful), *al-'Aẓīm* (the Sublime), *al-Ḥakīm* (the Wise), *al-'Azīż* (the Omnipotent), *as–Samī'* (the Hearer), *al-Baṣīr* (the Seer), *ash-Shāhid* (the Witness), *al-Wakīl* (the Protector), *ar-Raḥmān* (the Benefactor), *ar-Raḥīm* (the Merciful) and *Ghaffār, Ghafūr* (the Constant Forgiver) etc.

According to Islamic belief, God has no beginning, no end, All Knowing, All Wise, All Justice, Ever Alive, Omnipotent, Omniscient, Independent of All Things, All Hearing, All Seeing, therefore, He has neither body nor appurtenance nor sustenance nor form, nor to be understood in terms of mass or energy, nor has He any opposite. He has no wife, no child. He has no partner, comparable to Him, Vision does not perceive Him, yet He perceives everything, hidden or manifest, born or unborn or yet to be existed. He is Sovereign, the Creator, the Sustainer, the Provider, the Determiner, the Planner. None of His Action is free from the wisdom and Divine Justice, Time cannot surpass Him nor space can exhaust Him, there is no intermediary between God and His creation, which He brought into being by his sheer command – "Be!" (*Kun*):

> " And He is Who created the heavens and the earth in Truth. In that day He saith Be ! it is." (*Qur'an: 6/73*)

Although He is everywhere, He never inhere in anything. While He is sole Creator and Sustainer of the Universe, wherein every creation bears witness to His Divine Unity and Lordship. He is Majestic and Sovereign. He is exclusively entitled to be worshipped, feared and venerated.

Negative Attributes

It is considered as the Self Repulsed qualitics, which can never he found or attributed in any way to the existence of God. They are: *al-Murakkab* (the Compound), which suggests the dependence on other component; *al-Makān* (the Accommodation) which comprehends, encompass or over; *al-Ḥulūl* (the Incarnation), which requires forms animate or inanimate, *al-Maryī'* (the Visible), as no physical eye can see ever nor imagery could be possible; *al-Eḥtiyaj* (the Need) as He needs nothing and everyone needs Him, none can assist Him or anything is beyond His reach; *ash-Shirkat* (the Association) as none could be His partner; *al-Muḥāl, al-Ḥawādith* or *Taghai'yyur* (the Changing) as He could not be undergoing change; And *aṣ-Ṣifātu'ż-Żiād* (the Qualities Additional) as He is perfect no additional qualities can be added.

The doctrine of the Divine Unity and the issues which it raises, such as the issue about relation between the essence and various attributes of God have been well debated throughout the Islamic history. In the course of events, representatives of certain theological movements, who were jurist also succeeded in converting rules to their cause and declared the rulers as *Żillu'llāh* or *Żillu's-Subḥānī* (Divine Light of God) made the rulers encourage their opponents. Thus arose some in some localities and periods as semblance of an orthodox doctrine for which, besides Shi'is and mystics were worst sufferers, because for Muslim mystics Divine Unity has pantheistic sense, all essences are divine and there is no absolute existence other than God himself. Thus, to the most Muslim scholars, the science of Divine Unity has been systematic theology, which could provide better knowledge of God. But for the Muslim mystics knowledge of God could only be obtained through religious experience and meditation.

Divine Unity, implies absolute oneness and Unity of God over the entire creation. Oneness does not have the numerical connotation since the digit *one* is limited and defined, whereas God is unlimited and indefinable. Again, the numerical substance of the figure *one* shares the numerical value of all other digits or they will be either some multiple of one or some fraction of it, whereas God the Elevated can neither he multiple nor a fraction of any entity inherent in the creation. Accordingly, the oneness of God means He is One, Unique, Peerless, Eternal without beginning or end.

Imām 'Ali has simplified the issue of Oneness of God. He explains that there are four possible assumptions with regard to the Unity of God, out of these four only two are correct. The incorrect two assumptions are, firstly, when you say: God is one ! and you have the numerical *one* in your mind, whereas God cannot be placed in the numerical unit because He transcends all numerical bounds. Imām 'Ali here called our attention to those who maintained that God is one out of three (i.e. God, Holy Ghost and Christ) and, therefore, they got deviated from the right approach to the oneness of God. Secondly, to conceive His Oneness by analogy or similitude from among the things or phenomena of the physical spiritual, temporal, spatial, mental, emotional worlds or worlds of any other dimension is illogical, because any analogy or similitude, howsoever abstract and refined in thought, cannot be absolutely free from imperfection, whereas God is absolutely free from all imperfections.

The two correct assumptions are – firstly, that you call Him *One* maintaining that He is likeable to none and nothing, and, secondly, that you call him *One* believing that His *Oneness* is not liable to division or multiplication nor admitting of any quantum-operation.[1]

Imām Ja'far aṣ-Ṣādiq, on the Oneness of God, says – His Existence is eternally self-evident. Omniscience is His-self. He was Omniscient even when there was nothing objective or subjective to be known. He was Omnicompetent even when there was nothing to be heard. He was Omniscient even when there was nothing to be seen. He was Omnipotent even when there was nothing to receive the dictates of His power.[2] Imām al-Bāqir, Imām aṣ-Ṣādiq and Imām 'Ali ar-Rezā have shared a common statement about God that He is the Light which has no trace of darkness, the Knowledge which has no trace of ignorance, and the Life which has no trace of deadness.[3]

In one of his statements, Imām aṣ-Ṣādiq says that God cannot be explained in terms of time and space, rest and motion or matter and energy, He is rather the Creator of all these dimensional, vector and material entities.[4]

Associated with the Oneness of God is the issue of *Qazā* and *Qadr* (Divine Decree and Fate). By misinterpretation of these two facts Muslim imperialism has been making justification for their injustices and oppressions. It is, therefore, pertinent to understand these terms in the light of the Holy Qur'an. The literal meaning of *Qazā* is to decree, going by Qur'an, The Divine Decree is that which dictates existence to the entire creation of the Universe, just as He decides and wills to give things their attributes and properties. Every member of creation derives its being from the same decree of God and no one has the power to counter what has been determined by the Divine Decree:

> "When He decreeth a thing. He saith unto it only. Be and it is." (*Qur'an: 2/117*)

> "When God doometh there is none that can postpone His doom and He is swift at reckoning." (*Qur'an: 13/41*)

The literal meaning of *Qadr* is almost the same as *Qazā* but for the shade of difference that *Qadr* implies the determination, specially, of physical quantity and qualities like shape, form, size, texture etc. in the things created:

> "And there is not a thing but with Us are the stores thereof. And We send it not down save in appointed measure. (*Qur'an: 15/21*)

Out of the principles of *Qazā* and *Qadr*, there started the debate among the scholars regarding the *Ikhtiyār* (free-will), whether the human being is responsible for his actions; and *Jabr* (predetermines), whether the human being is bound to do as he is predestined, he has no choice. In the initial period of Islam the scholars were divided into two camps with regard to the human accountability of his actions. One group maintained that man is helpless in choosing what he wills, he is rather made by the decree of God to choose as He wills him to choose. The other group believed that a man is free in his choice of right and wrong and he is responsible for his own action. The group which believed that man is helpless and bound with the God's will, said that man is bound to commit sin, if God has so willed and he would make virtues, if has so been decreed by God. The other group argued that in his intentions man is absolutely free and God's will does not cross the will of man, so he is absolutely responsible for his actions. Both of these extreme views with regard to the nature of human will, are ill-balanced and defective. While the first view is against the Justice of God, the other is one which delimits the power of God. Cutting across these extreme views, the *Ahlu'l-Bayt* held that a man is responsible for his actions, however, he is not completely in control of his will and he might face situations beyond his control. By giving man the faculty of reason, God has made him free to exercise his will as he pleases. Imām Ja'far aṣ-Ṣādiq's famous words of wisdom in this regard is – Neither determinism nor absolute free-will but a position between the two extremes.[5]

Imām Muḥammad al-Bāqir, Imām Ja'far aṣ-Ṣādiq and Imām 'Ali ar-Rezā have in their recurrent sayings have quoted the prophet to have said – God the Great is ever kind on his creatures. He does not force to commit sin. How can it be possible for the justice of as great Being as God to first force the man to commit sin and then punish him for no fault of him. His Greatness is absolutely above this injustice. He is absolutely free from this imperfection. Imām Ja'far aṣ-Ṣādiq says on another occasion, that He does not expect a man to perform an act which is beyond his power to act, because He is justly Omnipotent and so nothing may exist in his kingdom without a frame of Divine Justice.[6]

Some of the scholars have raised the issues relating to essence and qualities and analyzed with the example of human behaviour between the essence and qualities and between qualities themselves, and one of the consequences may be that the names and attributes of God to have no independent or hypostatic existence apart from Being and Essence of God, whereas the divine essence cannot be conceived of having qualities, which the human beings possess, which will be always limited as per human behaviour but the Divine Essence always transcends all limitation, even which in reality is a quality the Divine Essence is limitless and infinite, possesses all positive qualities. It would be incorrect, for example, to say: 'God knows everything by His Knowledge which is in His Essence.' Its correct version shall be: 'God knows everything by His Knowledge which is His Essence.'

Similarly, Sunni theologian, under the influence of Ash'arites, hold that the holy Qur'an is the uncreated, eternal Word of God, whereas Shi'is consider the holy Qur'an to have been created in time. Unlike Sunnis, Shi'is assert and say that such verses of the Qur'an as seem to imply for achieving a beatific vision of God should be understood metaphorically and not by the literal meaning, otherwise would result in attributing to God physical organs like face, hand etc. and that God has no physical form. God is beyond every quality and state. His every quality is purified from the darkness as He says:

"Nought is as His likeness." (*Qur'an: 42/11*)

Imām Ja'far aṣ-Ṣādiq has well explained – God has immutable Being. He was Knowledge Himself when there was nothing to be known. His Hearing was Himself when was nothing audible. His Vision was Himself when there was nothing visible. His Power was Himself when there was nothing over which to exercise power.[7]

Thus, it may be concluded that the positive qualities give high perfection to logical values and effects. Qualities of imperfection are reverse to such high values and effects and result in imperfection, ignorance and impatience. So holy Qur'an has related all positive quantities to God Himself, which are the part of positive attributes discussed above.

The Divine Justice

'Adl (Justice) is other pivot of Islamic faith, which is most powerful positive attribute of God. The Just is considered as the Divine Nature. God would never act in unjust manner, because of the fact that He is of Just Nature. Unjust action shall violate His own Nature, which is impossible and shall never happen. Whatever God's will, shall be just and based on Divine Justice. Ordinarily, the justice may be comprehended by *'Aql* (intellect), but not always because the human

intelligence is limited in nature and God's will is unlimited, the judgment is not completely suspended in favour of a pure voluntarism by God. Hence, greater emphasis on intelligence has been laid in Shi'i theology, whereas greater emphasis on *Irādah* (will) in Sunni on *Kalām* (dogmatics) is evident, specially predominant Ash'arite school. Thus, it may be concluded that the greater affinity of Shi'i theology with *al-'Ulūmu'l-'Aqlīyah* (intellectual science) lies in the manner of viewing Divine Justice.

The most important dimension of the Divine Justice is social justice, whereby weak is protected in conflict of interest with strong, the fear of God is tested when strong man comforts the weak. This has been religious transcending all the regional cults in viewing the principle of God's Will for justice to all human beings.

Justice is the keynote term to help explain the legal matrix of Islam, which is why it occupies the highest place in the hierarchy of human qualities:

> "God will exalt (*you in*) in ranks (*unto him*), those who believe among you, and those who have been given knowledge; and God is All-Aware of whatsoever ye do." (*Qur'an: 58/11*)

> "Say thou (*O' Our Prophet Muḥammad !*) What ! Can those who know be equal to those who know not ? Verily only the men of understanding take the warning." (*Qur'an: 39/9*)

The legal framework of Islam carries basically the structure of practical codes and gives central importance to it. Islam being essentially a practical religion, has uncommonly wide network of practical rules and regulations which theoretically operate round the basic axis of adherence to justice and avoidance of injustice in all walks of human life.

Islam was vehemently opposed to and repeatedly warned against compromising with injustice:

> "And if only those who are unjust could see (*what they will realize*) when they behold the torment, that unto God belongeth all power and verily God is severe in punishing." (*Qur'an: 2/165*)

> "There should be no hostility save against the aggressors." (*Qur'an: 2/193*)

> "And God loveth not the unjust." (*Qur'an: 3/56*)

> "And who is more unjust than he who forgeth a lie against God while he is invited unto Islam? And God guideth not the unjust people." (*Qur'an: 61/7*)

Again for the unjust:

> "And their abode shall be fire; And how bad is the abode of the unjust." (*Qur'an: 3/150*)

What could be more exalted a place for Justice than the fact that Justice is the chief representative of all the attributes of God, and it has the cardinal place in the cardinal beliefs of Islam. By using the word Justice to set it off against Injustice, Qur'an has opened many shades of the meaning of justice. Vide some verses of Qur'an in this context:

> "Verily God doeth not any injustice to people but men to their own selves do injustice." (*Qur'an: 10/44*)
>
> "God is not unjust to His servants." (*Qur'an: 22/10*)
>
> "Changeth not the word with Me nor am I (*in the least*) unjust unto (*any of*) the servants." (*Qur'an: 50/29*)
>
> "Say thou: My Lord hath enjoined justice and set ye upright your faces at (*each time and place*) of prostration, and call upon Him, being sincere exclusively unto Him in religion; even He brought you forth and unto Him shall ye also return." (*Qur'an: 7/29*)

It is Justice which is the overall objective of Prophethood. Qur'an enlightens as:

> "And for every people (*was sent*) an Prophet; and when came their Prophet, the matter between them was decided with equity and they shall not (*in the least*) be done (*any*) injustice." (*Qur'an: 10/47*)

The concept of Divine Resurrection and the Last Judgment is also infused with Justice:

> "And we shall set up the balances of justice on the Day of Judgment, so no soul shall be dealt with unjustly in the least." (*Qur'an: 21/47*)

The justice is not any abstract, academic, ideal or speculative principle. Neither it is dull and impervious to progress or limited and impractical in nature. It is rather the foundation of the whole system of social edifice. Thus, holy Qur'an alerts:

> "Verily God enjoineth justice and benevolence (*to others*) and giving unto the kindred, and forbiddeth lewdness, and evil, and rebellion; He exhorteth you that ye may take heed." (*Qur'an: 16/90*)

In elucidation of the concept of Justice, the holy Qur'an gives an outline of central activities comprising righteousness and justice:

> "It is not righteousness that ye turn your faces towards the East and the West, righteousness is rather one who believeth in God and the Last Day and the angels and the Book, the Prophets, and giveth his wealth out of love for Him to the kindred and the orphans and the poor and the wayfarer and the needy and for those in bondage; And established prayer and payeth the poor-rate; And those who fulfil their promise when they make a promise and the patient ones in distress and affliction and in the time of war, these are they who are the Truthful and these are they who are the pious." (*Qur'an: 2/177*)

In search of the meaning and implication of Islam, the central emphasis should be laid on the principle of 'live and let others live' since, bearing this principle of original Islam in mind the Islam which is supposed to have spread with sword, may be easily differentiated from the real Islam which is responsible for peace and well-being, which guideth by expanding the human sensibilities, sympathies and visions, which teaches the lesson of obedience to God and the Islam which nurturers human souls with the light of justice and fills with the energy to fight with justice as has been briefly presented in the foregoing pages. In the holy Qur'an the Wise therefore, by addressing the Jews as a nation, has called upon the entire mankind to heed the blessings and benedictions He has showered on the living humanity, putting into action, both harmony of the aspects of Islam namely the law of nature and the moral and legal law of human life:

> "And remember when Moses sought water for his people; said We, Strike thou the rock with thy staff. Then gushed out therefrom twelve springs; each people knew their (*respective*) drinking place; Eat ye and drink ye of God's provision and commit ye not evil in the earth acting mischievously." (*Qur'an: 2/60*)

The Prophethood

Risālat (Prophethood) is the second unanimous pivot of Islam, literally meaning embassy, messengership and popularly known as Prophethood, which stands for that Embassy which God employs to communicate with mankind and sends some infallible human being to act as the representative of the Divine Kingdom in human world. The Prophet is enjoined to put before mankind the Divine Law, and direct them to follow the same. It becomes most important subject of enthralling interest when studied in the context of continuity of religious progress of mankind.

Some of the oldest races, Babylonians, Hamites and Japhetics are believed to have survived after the Noah's Deluge. They must have their Prophets. Hamites who had thrown away Babylonians were also shown the doors by Assyrians, who had a positive monotheistic concept, recognizing One Supreme Personality. Prophet Abraham was of Assyrian origin, whose father or uncle Āẑar (as Shi'i believe) was evidently same as Ashshur, according to 'Arabic traditions, was creater of beautiful idols of the Supreme Personality. Many historians believe that the introduction of monarchical institution was the main cause of religious conflict between two branches of Aryans from whom Citama Zarathustra (Zoroaster) claimed to be the Prophet of God. His time, place of birth etc. have enwrapt into mystery. Another person, Darius Hystaspes, under the same name of Zoroaster revived, organized and enlarged the basis of Zoroastrian religion. Other branch of Aryans, the Vedic hymn-singers was successful in driving their polytheistic-pantheistic combined faith across the Paropamisadae, which later resulted in the shape of *Autār* (Incarnation) that the Supreme Spirit manifests Himself in various forms. And a concept of hero-god was soon found in a number of the warrior castes of Aryan in India, who were also identified with the Supreme Spirit, as the earthly existence of incarnate gods, Rama, Krishna, Durga,

Mahavira and Buddha, who may be prophets of their times, as some Islamic scholars believe. Like India the Greek myths are known today primarily from the literary epics, the *Iliad* and *Odyssey* (9th-8th century BC) were viewed by Greeks as embodying divine or timeless truth and quasi-historical legends (or sagas) of various gods and goddesses, amongst whom Hermes has been described as 'messenger of gods.' Romans were also worshippers of gods, amongst whom Jupiter (etymologically equivalent to the Greek *Zens* and Sanskrit *Dyans*) was most important being the weather god. Two other gods Mars and Quirinius and a goddess Juno were main associates of him. Roman had 15 priests of individual gods, with an elaborate priesthood system with three *Pontiffs* which may be attributed to Prophethood. In ancient China pre-Han Confucian religion laid emphasis on inspiration and divination of which prophets appeared and promised their followers the good life in the world and also in the next. In many orthodox cultures of Africa the prophets are quite common even today.

The doctrine of Prophethood leads to the recognition of a Supreme Will overshadowing the cosmos, the concept of universal soul, which is guiding, pervading and regulating all the existence. A part of the mankind proceeded forward to proclaim the duties for the call of truth amongst them (mankind itself) and his Creator, who were later called the veritable *Messengers of Heaven* and *Servants of God.*

As per Islamic doctrine the Prophets are the men, specially chosen by God, for conveying His Messages but He never speaks directly. He either sends an angel or makes him hear a voice. Islam requires recognition of all the prophets, Prophets and Messenger of Heaven, of whom some being more outstanding in their qualities. Some of Most Important Prophets are Adam, the founding father of the mankind, Noah, the saviour of mankind from deluge, also called Adam II, Abraham, the first of Hebrew patriarchs, a figure revered by three great monotheistic religions: Judaism, Christianity and Islam. His two sons Ishmael and Issac were also great Prophets. From the latter's family-tree many renowned Prophets appeared. According to Biblical account Abraham was ready to scarifice Issac as a test of his faith, but he was saved as God substituted him by a ram. But the holy Qur'an says – No, he was Ishmael not Issac. Issac's son Jacab was also great Prophet, who had 13 children of whom 10 sons were founders of various tribes of Israel. His son Joseph was most beloved person who gained favour of the then Pharaoh of Egypt. His love story has been told in Qur'an. Other Prophets of this family branch are Jonah, Job, Ezekiel (some of the scholars have identified him as Buddha), David with his Divine Psalms, Solomon. The other towering personalities of Issac's family-tree were Moses, with his Ten Commandments and Jesus Christ with his Bible. They founded two great monotheistic religions—Judaism and Christianity respectively. The family-branch of Ishmael was bestowed greatest honour because holy Prophet Muḥammad, the last prophet in this series belonged to it.

The first and foremost notable point in this regard is that human beings are not authorised to elect or select a person as their Apostle, howsoever qualified they may appear. It is the exclusive authority of God to select and appoint His Prophet by own will and His own choice. In the terminology of Qur'an it is a divine act and is termed in the holy Qur'an as *Iṣtefa* (selection) is the act by God Himself. It implies to select the best out of the existing many:

> "God Knoweth best where to place His Prophetship." (*Qur'an: 6/124*)

The second most notable point is that the Prophet never enforces any law on his own accord, neither he changes nor modifies the Divine Laws, He relates only as much as he is enjoined to relate. In keeping with this precise office of the Prophet, he has to be in strict adherence to the Divine Revelation:

> "And nor speaketh of (*his own*) inclination; It (*the wordings*) is naught but a revelation revealed (*unto him*)." (*Qur'an: 53/3-4*)

The Prophet speaks in the same language as that of the people he has been sent to, so that they may easily follow the import of his messages. Qur'an enlightens:

> "And We sent not any Prophet but with the language of the people that he might clearly explain (*Our Commandments*) unto them." (*Qur'an: 14/4*)

The obedience of the Prophet is obligatory, just as the obedience of God is obligatory. A disobedient to the Prophet is deemed out of the circle of Islam:

> "Whosoever obeyeth the Prophet, he indeed obeyeth God; and whoever turneth away We have not sent thee upon them to watch." (*Qur'an: 4/80*)

The Prophet is of necessity free from error, oblivion, and sin, he has to be infallible, of his infallibility, Qur'an states:

> "We did choose them (*for Our Prophetship*), and We guided them unto the straight (*right*) way." (*Qur'an 6/88*)

Again Qur'an states:

> "(He alone is) the Knower of the unseen, and nor doth he reveal his secrets unto any (*one else*); Save unto that one of the Prophets whom He chooseth for verily He causeth a guard to march before him; That He may know that indeed they have delivered the messages of their Lord, and He encompasseth (*by His knowledge*) all that is with them, and taketh account of everything." (*Qur'an: 72/26-28*)

In the light of these verses of Qur'an, some qualities and attributes of the Prophets have been pointed out which are not existent in the common lot of mankind and which are directly connected with unseen world of Divine control. God has distinguished them with uncommon attributes such as complete correspondence in words and actions to the Divine Revelation, devoid of error and forgetfulness and their being the most distinguished and chosen of the common mankind. The common masses are Divinely enjoined to obey and follow them. Prophets, however, are not the supernatural category of the creation, they are but human beings only, specific in respect of their obligations as Prophets:

> "And We sent not (*Prophets*) before thee but men unto whom We revealed, from (among) the people of the towns;" (*Qur'an: 12/109*)

This fact of their being the humans was the cause of their being denied the status of a Prophet by the infidels, who would argue how can a human be Prophet. Qur'an quotes their skepticism:

> "Said they – Nothing are ye but men like unto us." (*Qur'an: 14/10*)

The perfect answer to this objection from the infidels has been offered by the Prophets as recorded by Qur'an:

> "Said unto them their Prophets – (*Yes*) (*nothing*) we are but men like you but God bestoweth His favours on whomsoever He willeth of His servants; and it is not for us that we bring unto you any authority except by the permission of God." (*Qur'an: 14/11*)

This expression of Qur'an "we are but men like you" has served as a proof for a group of Islamic scholars to include the Prophets among the common folk of men. They extend their argument to a point which makes them maintain that any common human being can attain the status of a Prophet, if he rigorously pursues knowledge and purity in moral uprightness. In fact the statement of the Prophets namely "we are but men like you" is conditioned with their statement which follows the previous one namely "but God bestoweth his favours on whomsoever he willeth of his servants." Which proves that they are different from the common lot by virtue of their uncommon attributes directly in touch with the Divine Grace. The next expression of the same verse namely "And it is not for us that we bring unto you any authority or any miracle except by the permission of God" further clears their distinct status in as much as they are in perfect control of their will and emotion not to deviate for a single event or for a single moment from the Will of God. No man otherwise, can attain the control over his will such that never to let it go against the will of God and never to say or act but in utter compliance of God's command, otherwise no man having an authority and in command of miracles, has the moral restraint to ascribe his powers and authority to the revelation of God. The issue of revelation is such that no one has seen the *Lauḥ-Maḥfūz* (Preserved Tablet) nor the heavenly angels coming to earth, nor the Prophet receiving the revelations from the angel. This is only by the confidence of faith in the trustworthy Prophethood of Prophet Muḥammad who has told us honestly which is the word of God and which is of the prophet himself (his words too, however, do not spring from his self but only translate the Will of God) and which is the word of the angel. It is from the same man whose faithfulness precisely divides the words articulated from his tongue into three heads; first, *Qur'an* (Word of God), second, *Ḥadīth* (Traditions, the words of Prophet) and third *Ḥadīth al-Qudsī* (the Heaven Traditions, the holy Traditions in the words of Gabriel).

It is our faith and utter confidence in the authority of the holy Apostle Muḥammad that we accepted on the strength of his infallible character – the Unity of God, the chain of Prophets down from Adam to himself and the institution of Prophethood, the Day of Judgment as the cardinal beliefs of Islam, and we declared willingly the creedal testimony: namely "I bear witness that there is no Gods but One God the Allāh and Muḥammad is His Messenger". We do attest to Islam by words of mouth, the depth of the heart and by the involvement of the body to convert its ideology into action adopting Islam as the pattern of our life.

According to the holy Qur'an every Prophet was not the one who came with a complete code of life or Divine constitution. Only five out of the long list of the Prophets were those who came with a complete Divine Law for their respective epochs, specific to the needs of their times. The names of these five grand Prophets are Noah, Abraham, Moses, Jesus and the last and highest of all, Prophet Muḥammad. Rest of other Prophets were the exponents and followers of one of the Divine Laws, which were in force in their respective periods. The holy Qur'an informs us:

> "He hath prescribed for you the religion (*the Divine Code of life*) what He ordained unto Noah and that which we unto thee and what ordained We unto Abraham, Moses and Jesus, that: Establish ye the religion be ye not divided therein." (*Qur'an: 42/13*)

The total number of all the Prophets is said to be one lakh and twenty four thousands. There is no nation to which some Messengers, or Prophets have not been assigned to rise from among them and call them in their own language to submit to Code set for them by their Creator:

> "and there is not a people but a Warner hath gone among them." (*Qur'an: 35/24*)

It is binding for a Muslim to have faith on all of the Prophets same as it is obligatory for him to have faith in God, the Day of Judgment, the angels. Among the messengers, prophets or Prophets of God, Muḥammad is the last and the seal of messengers, prophets or Prophets and the one who came with the final Divine Law. He is the crown and apex of the chain of the Prophets and the acme of the God's messengers, through whom God has concluded his Divine Message and consummated the religion of Islam.

The Imāmat

Imām (head, leader or guide) is other pivot of Islam, after *Rasūl*. Qur'an uses the word in the same meaning:

> "And of them made We *Ai'mah* (singular, *Imām,* Heads, Leaders) to guide (*the people*) by Our command as they were steadfast (*in the calamities*); and they of Our signs were quite certain." (*Qur'an: 32/24*)

Thus, the essential conditions of *Imāmat* (Divine Leadership) are steadfastness, self-control, perseverance and the certitude in the signs of God:

> "And We made them leaders, guiding (the people) by Our command, and revealed We unto them the doing of good." (*Qur'an: 21/73*)

At this point, it becomes difficult to differentiate between *Risālat* and *Imāmat* (Imamate) because the functions of Prophethood namely to inculcate acts of goodness, establishing prayer and giving alms are also the functions of the Imamate:

> "And remember when his Lord tried Abraham with certain words then he fulfilled them. He said: Verily I make thee Imām for mankind, (*Abraham*) said: And of my offspring ? He said: My covenant reacheth not unjust." (*Qur'an: 2/124*)

Abraham was already a prophet and a messenger of God before the revelation in which he was called to face a trial, and only when Abraham came off successfully from the trial, God allowed to make him Imam of the people. This shows that the exalted rank of Imamate is not attainable by all prophets, save the chosen few among them from the time of the first prophet. Prophethood and Imamate may sometimes coexist in one individual and sometimes each in two separate individuals. Upon the last *viz.* holy Prophet Muḥammad, it co-existed in one individual. After him it got transferred to Imām 'Ali, because the existence and presence of Imām in and after the life of the Holy Prophet is imperative and indispensable mainly when the Prophethood terminated in the person of the Last Prophet leaving no room for any more Prophets to come. Whereas, the Divine Mission of the authentic guidance remained to be conducted till the last day of the human existence on earth, and this mission is not possible to be fulfilled without the presence of an infallible Imām, in every period of time after the last holy Prophet.

There has been a continuous institution of succession with figures such as Noah, Abraham, Moses, Jesus and Muḥammad have been combined in themselves in the function of the Prophethood and the Imamate, but no time has the earth been left without a Imām, who is *Hādī* (Guide) and *Ḥujjā* (Proof) of God. Thus, Imām Muḥammad al-Bāqir has said:

> "God has not left the earth, since the death of Adam, without being on it an *Imām*, guiding (*the people*) to God. He is the proof of the God to His servants and earth will not remain without the Proof of God to his servants."[8]

And Imām Ja'far aṣ-Ṣādiq said:

> "Were there to remain on the earth but two men, one of them would be the Proof of God."[9]

The Divine Light created by God, which is the inner sense of the Imamate, descended in turn upon Adam to Muḥammad and then became embodied in Fāṭimah aż-Żahrah and the Twelve *Imāms,* who are created out of the substance of the *'Illīyūn:*

> "Nay, The record of the righteous shall be in *'Illīyūn.*" (*Qur'an: 83/18*)

Etymologically the word *'Illīyūn* is said to have been derived from Hebrew *elyon,* meaning highest. *'Illīyūn* is generally considered as a synonym for highest elevated station, the *Ṣadratu'l-Muntaha* (Farthest Tree), the Seventh Heaven.

The positive attributes of the Imamate are derived from the Qur'an itself may be mentioned as under:

Āyatu'llāh: Sign of God (*Qur'an 7/9, 38/2, 101/22*)
Ṣirāṭu'l-Mustaqīm: Straight Path (*Qur'an 1/6, 6/153, 16/76*)
'Urwati'l-Wuthqa: Strongest Handle (*Qur'an 2/256*)
Ḥabl'llāh: Cord of God (*Qur'an 3/102*)
Nūru'llāh: Light of God (*Qur'an 4/174, 6/122, 7/157, 64/8*)
Ummatun Yahdūn: Guides of Men: (*Qur'an 7/181*)
Rasikhūn fi'l-'Ilm: Possessor of Knowledge (*Qur'an 3/7*)
Ulil'amr: Possessor of Authority (*Qur'an 4/59*)
Ṣādiqīn: Truthful (*Qur'an 9/119*)
Āl Yāsīn: Family of *Yāsīn*: Muḥammad (*Qur'an 37/130*)
Ullil-araḥām: Blood-relatives of the Prophet (*Qur'an: 33/6*)

The following are the necessary attributes of the Imamate:

(*i*) *The Conferment by Designation or Covenant*: His appointment is made by the *Naṣṣ* (authority of God), whomsoever He chooses him, He makes Imām without the involvement of humankind. The process sometimes may be in the *Mīthāq* or *'Ahd* (covenant) from him to next person:

> "Each Imām knows the Imām who is to come after him and so he appoints him as successor."[10]

Further, clarified Imām Ja'far aṣ-Ṣādiq:

> "Do you imagine that we place this Cause of ours (*Imamate*) with whomsoever we wish ? No! Not at all! By God! It is a covenant of the Prophet (*Muḥammad*) of God with 'Ali-Ibn-Abū Tālib, and then one man after another until finally it comes to the Lord of this Cause (*Imām Mahdī*)."[11]

The appointment of an Imām made by the authority of God should not be confused with the principle of the dynastic succession. The selection of an Imām is not based on the dynastic traditions because the first and foremost principle of the dynastic succession is to nominate the eldest son of the family. Had the foremost principle of the dynastic succession been followed, Imām Ḥusain would not have been chosen by his elder brother, Imām Ḥasan and eldest son of Imām Ḥasan would have been nominated in his place. The second principle of the dynastic succession is to nominate the son born out of the main wife. The son born out of a maid-slave is not entitled for successorship, especially when not only the eldest son from proper wife is present but other younger sons are also there. Look the case of the seventh in order of Imamate, the nomination of Imām Mūsā al-Kāẓim by Imām Ja'far aṣ-Ṣādiq completely negates the dynastic tradition in the selection of an Imām, because ā Mūsā al-Kāẓim was Imām Ja'far aṣ-Ṣādiq's fourth son born out of a maid-slave and the oldest surviving son 'Abdu'llāh al-Aftaḥ's claim was not solicited. So the people who believed in the principle of the dynastic succession made their separate groups after the nomination of Imām Mūsā al-Kāẓim. Even today the Ismā'īlī faith is instituted, as a faith apart from the Shi'i community. The description of the Ismā'īlī faith would be made later at proper place in this book.

(*ii*) *Man of Best Knowledge*: The high rank of Imamate calls for an unfaltering knowledge, vision and faith in the signs of God. And concerning the Qur'anic verses:

> "He it is Who hath sent down to thee (*O' Our Apostle Muḥammad*) the Book of it there are (*some*) verses decisive these are Basis of the Book, and others are ambiguous; But those in whose hearts there is perversity, they are after that which is ambiguous therein seeking to mislead and seeking to interpret (*to suit their selfish motives*) while none knoweth its (*hidden*) interpretation except God and those firmly rooted in knowledge; say they: We believe in it, all is from our Lord but none mindeth save those endowed with (*Wisdom*)." (*Qur'an: 3/6*)

The following Tradition illustrates this point:

> "I was with Abu'l Ḥasan ('Ali) when a man said to him: you are commenting from the Book of God some matters which you did not hear. And he said: It was revealed to us before it was revealed to the people and we commented upon it before it was commented by others. We know what is permitted and forbidden in it, we know which verse abrogates and which verse is abrogated in it, and how many verses were revealed on which night, and concerning what and whom they were revealed. We are the judges of God on His earth and His witnesses for His creation."[12]

Imām Ja'far aṣ-Ṣādiq said:

> "We are the ones who are deeply rooted in knowledge and we know its explanation."[13]

Imām 'Ali in his Tradition known as *Ḥādīth an-Nūrāniyya* said:

> "Our Lord has given to us knowledge of Great Name, through which, we want to, we would rend as under the heaven and the earth.."[14]

The Imām has, according to various Traditions, in his possession certain books, including the books of the holy Prophet Muḥammad, such as *al-Jafr* (the Divination), *aṣ-Ṣaḥīfa* (the Book), *al-Jāma'* (the Compilation), *al-Muṣḥaf Fāṭimah* (the Book of Fāṭimah), and a copy of the Qur'an, compiled by 'Ali, which he had presented to the holy Prophet.[15]

(iii) *Immunity from Sin and Error*: *'Iṣmat* (sinlessness and infallibility) is the necessary condition for the Imamate. He must be mighty forbearance in the moral construct of his character, because the goal of his office is to guide infallibly the mankind to Virtue. Any shade or measure of injustice in the character debars a man from being chosen for. The sinlessness and infallibility of Muḥammad, Fāṭimah aż-Żahrah and Twelve *Imāms* is also proven by Qur'an itself:

> "Verily, verily God intendeth but to keep off from you (*every kind of*) uncleanness O' ye the People of the House, and purify you (*with*) a thorough purification." (*Qur'an: 33/33*)

(iv) *Spiritual Guidance*: The Imām is the spiritual guide the inner truth of the religion, the '*Irfān* (wisdom). His mind, heart and body all are oriented in the light of Divine Wisdom. Their attributes are self-explanatory:

> " (*These are*) They who turn unto God (*seeking forgiveness*) who worship Him who praise (*Him*) Who fast, who bow down, who prostrate themselves (*in prayer*) who enjoin what is good and forbid what is evil, and keep (*themselves*) in God's (*ordained*) limit wherefore proclaim thou (*O' Our Apostle!*) the glad tiding unto the believers." (*Qur'an: 9/12*)

All the major branches of Sunni *Ṣūfis,* who are called as *Silsilatu'ż-Żahab* (Golden Chain), connect their linkage with Imām 'Ali for the spiritual guidance.

(v) *Divine Message through Holy Spirit*: The Imāms are assisted by God though Holy Spirit is not the same as in the case of a Prophet, in which Gabriel the archangel descends and reveals verses of the Divine Scriptures to the heart of the Prophet. Revelation through this order of Divine Revelation has been a prelude to the identity of the Prophethood. Those Prophets who were also the Imāms were not devoid of this order. But the mode of revelation as conceived in terms angels is not the only mode. Neither the suspension of this mode is the proof of the suspension of Divine Message. The formal Divine Revelation is one thing and Divine Revelation is another. The angel is not the inevitable condition for the Divine Message to be revealed. Reception or Induction of Divine Message without an angel for a Divine Prophet or Imām whose core of inner consciousness is the natural reservoir of Divine Message. The outer record of which is the holy code of Qur'an and the heart of the Prophet is the living repository of the fund of Divine Message. This Universe is shared by both the holy Qur'an and the holy *Ahlu'l-Bayt*, Qur'an is the coded form and the *Ahlu'l-Bayt* in human forms to decode and elaborate these codes.

Imām Ḥusain was asked: From what stem you gain authority? He replied softly: We rule by the authority of the House of David, and if we lack anything then the Holy Spirit sends it to us.[16] Imām Ja'far aṣ-Ṣādiq has explained it most clearly when he has said that the Prophet is who sees the Angel who comes to him with the Message from his Lord. He speaks with him just one of you would speak with your companion. And people does not see the Angel but *Waḥy* (the revelation) descends upon him and he sees the Angel in vision and the Imām hears the voice but does not see him."[17]

(vi) *Preservation of Divine Message*: After the transmission revelation and reception of Divine Message comes the issue of preservation of Divine Message, which is ensured by the existence of Imām, whose office is entrusted with it. Imamate, in fact, is the infallible instrument of God to perpetuate the original text and its interpretation in the absence of the holy Prophet. *Imāmat* (Imamate) and '*Iṭrat* or *Ahlu'l-Bayt* (Household or Progeny) are the synonymous terms centred in the same principle of perpetuation, elaboration and extension of the code of the Qur'an precisely as intended by God, the Author of this Code.

(vii) *Rationale for the Imamate*: The rationale for the necessity of Imāms from time to time till the Day of Judgment is because they fulfil the role to control and coordinate the human society: an analogy is made in human body: mind is needed to control sensory data. There are possibilities that the *Sharī'at* (Sacred Law) may be wrongly and mischiefly interpreted, which have been, unfortunately, proven in the history of Islam, the Imām is needed to give authoritative guidance on the problems of the Sacred Law. Otherwise, the people would be erring in interpreting it and God could not hold them responsible for the sin, if they were not provided true interpreters and guides by God. Since there are various verses in the holy Qur'an that are not clear and guidance is necessary and that could not be revealed by God, without someone to explain it in the times to come.

(viii) *Number of holy Imāms*: With regard to the number of holy *Imām,* there are numerous tradition of the holy Prophet – *Imāms* are twelve in number. *Imāms* are from the clan of Quraysh and *Imāms* are from my holy *Ahlu'l-Bayt*, and the last of whom is *Mahdī.* (the last saviour of the Divine Justice on earth). These traditions have been repeatedly quoted by Shi'is and Sunnis both.

The Caliphate

The issue of the Caliphate is related to the Divine Succession to the holy Prophet Muḥammad, which forms the most crucial subject in the history of Islam. This issue has given expression to the two different frames of mind with regard to the choosing of the successor. One is known as the School of Caliphate and the other is known as the Imamate School. It is indispensable to discuss these Schools before coming to any conclusion because of the fact, that Islam has well defined and well determined its own system and administrative order. Islam does not place religion and the society in separate boxes but includes the society in religion and includes the religion into the worldly thoughts.

Islam lays foundation of such a ruling system in which the God without associating with any other, is the sole, sovereign and complete ruling authority. The prophets only execute His command as His subservient on earth. The prophet, as the representative on Divine Order, has no power nor right to constitute, amend or alter the law. Only God has exclusive right to make or amend or revoke a law. This has been established as the principle Islamic right from Adam to the last Prophet Muḥammad and is meant to exist till the dooms day.

The scriptures and the laws have been revelations from time to time as required by the new situation of human history. This chain of revelation terminated in the final scripture called Qur'an and in the last and the final prophet known as Muḥammad-Ibn-'Abdu'llāh. After the holy Prophet Muḥammad, the political structure will have to be raised strictly on the instruction and guidance laid down by God.

During the lifetime of the holy Prophet no confusion, controversy or conflict surfaced in the Islamic socio-political order. The Prophet would conduct the Islamic norms in full harmony with the Divine Will. After his death, however, the issue of Divine Succession and Islamic political leadership became disputed. As a result Islam got divided into various sects. The two major sects of Islam namely Shi'a and Sunni have radically different arguments with regard to the principle of deciding the success.

The Caliphate has been called democratic by famous Sunni scholars like Abu'l 'Olā Maudūdī and an-Nadawī, Abu'l Ḥasan 'Ali Ḥasanī, and defy the universally accepted principles of democracy. Democracy, by definition is based on the principle of 'governance by the people', whereas in the Caliphate order, the verdict of God, the law of God, and rule of God, by the men chosen by God has to be accepted, as the only Islamic order, whether it finds favour with the desire of the people, or goes against their will. In this order, public has to submit his own laws and rules to the Divine Law and Divine Rules, framed by God and has to work within the framework of this Divine Law and Divine Rules. In the democratic order, political decisions are taken on the basis of the majority votes of the elected representatives of the people. Most of the decisions are taken by tbe council body of the elected people, who have to be accountable. The concept of the democracy has come into being as a product of the Greek thought.[18]

Renowned Sunni scholar and theologist Ashraf 'Ali Thānwī was deadly against including democratic thought into Islamic thought. Criticising this view, he says:

> "Some stupidly thought of stuffing democratic order into Islam, and claim that Islam does teach the democratic order. Giving arguments they quote the Qur'anic verse: 'And consult with them upon the conduct of affairs' (*Qur'an: 3/159*) But they are quite wrong. They have given up the very context of consultation and even failed to realize its place in Islam. In respect of governance the principle of consultation, the law of majority vote is simply false, otherwise there must have been the provision in Islam that none of your determination should go against the majority."[19]

The Caliphate becomes source and basis of governing the people, the culture and civilization will also be raised on the basis of those nobilities. In that case all human religions and sects will be founded on moral originality and excellences. The Caliphate selected on this ground, the religious leaders will be morally and spiritually at par with each other, and they will not remain nor need to sacrifice the principles for the public vote. The public would not show them the path of righteousness, instead they will guide mankind in perfect compliance with the Will of God. He would not follow the varied desires of the public, because he will not have to pacify the whims of his voters. He will have not to yield to the vested interests of the voters and follow their wills, even if the public will is against the basic principles of the religion and human ethics. Though people determine the religious leadership, it did not earn the right of sharing the benefits of the ruling advantages. Abu'l 'Olā Maudūdī also apprehends this liability:

> "In case of the establishment of the Caliphate by the community vote, every member of the Muslim community, equally shares the power of the Caliphate. No individual or group has right to take away the rights of Muslim participants in Caliphate, and get it monopolized in his person, nor any individual or group can claim to have an exclusive and special power of Caliphate, voted in his person or group. It is this fact which safeguards the Islamic Caliphate from turning into imperialist, oligarchy or theocracy and moulds it into democracy."[20]

The successor of the holy Prophet Muḥammad is called *Khalīfa* (Caliph) means successorship and the Caliphate of first four Caliphs is called *Khilāfatu'r-Rāshida. Rāshida* is the 'Arabic word derived from *Rāshid* which means proper guidance. In Islamic terminology *Khalīfa* has the position similar to *Imām*, explained earlier. However, the term *Imām* is more prevalent among the Shi'is for the successor of the holy Prophet and *vice versa Khalīfa* among the Sunnis.

Majority of Muslims, which consists of Sunni sect believe that after the demise of the Prophet the religious leadership was accomplished by the first four Caliphs. Their leadership is believed to be perfect in all respects by the Islamic principles, the total period of these *Khalīfas* with all honour thereto are Abū Bakr, 'Omar, 'Othmān and 'Ali is from 6th May, 632 to 28th January, 661. Some Muslims also include about a year of Imām Ḥasan's regime, till he handed over the power to Mu'āwiyah-bin-Abū Sufyyān. They regard Imām Ḥasan to be fifth rightly-guided Caliph.

With the word *Mulūkiyat* which is synonymous to imperialism, the line of demarcation can be drawn between *Khilāfatu'r-Rāshida* and the Muslim monarchy of the later Muslim empires, because *Mulūkiyat* cannot be accepted as a legitimately ordered Islamic administration. In fact it is a problem of Sunni sect. As for the Shi'is they don't accept even the *Khilāfatu'r-Rāshida* as a genuine Islamic administration. This Sunni problem can be seen in the way given below.

The *Khilāfatu'r-Rāshida* came to an end by the assassination of 'Ali, the fourth Caliph on 25th January, 661. After which the Caliphate and monarchy merged, and Caliphs were regarded and accepted as Muslim rulers of a dynasty. Five dynasties occupied the post until it was abolished by a publicly elected ruler of Turkey. The five dynastic Caliphs are as follows:

(i)	Umayyite Caliphate	661-750
(ii)	Abbāsite Caliphates	750-1257
(iii)	Qurtobite Caliphates	756-1031
(iv)	Fāṭimite Caliphates	908-1160
(v)	'Ottoman Caliphate (Turkey)	1517-1922

As a historical realism the fact remains that this *Mulūkiyat* was born out of the womb of *Khilāfatu'r-Rāshida.* All the rulers of these dynasties used to be called and regarded as Caliphs. Barring a few, the conduct and dealings of the rest of them were not in harmony with Islamic principles and laws.

It took 1400 years for the Islamic system of governance to be liberated from the grip of imperialism. In the present day, there are still Muslim states under imperial rule, and the campaign for liberation. It is believed that in the coming years entire Muslim states will be liberated from imperialism. The awareness of a new system of Islamic democracy is on the rise. It is for the future to decide how far successful the Islamic democracy proves. However, the imperial power coming to an end is definite and we can see the sign of it with our own eyes when the last emperor of Iran scared of the people's revolt against imperial monopoly left the country. The Shāh of Iran, taking all the costly jewelleries, and other royal wealth, ran away in a plane, imploring all the world for asylum and a piece of land for shelter. But he became so unwelcome, a burden on earth, that no country thought him fit for shelter. Somehow, Egypt allowed him a temporary stay but in the meantime, death made the final sweep of the last thing of the Iranian imperialism. Similar fate is hanging on the heads of remaining kings, dictators and rulers of Muslim countries for which strong revolutionary movements have already built up. May the rule of God envisaged by the holy Qur'an be established in every Muslim country. May qausi-Islamic states on the principles of modern democracy become prevalent, as being practised in some of Muslim states. But it may be safely said that the Caliphate and its intrinsic Muslim Imperialism has totally lost the creditability and it shall not last.

The Occultation and Return of Imām Mahdī

The doctrine of the Ghayāba (Occultation) and *Rij'ā* (Return) maintains that Eleventh Imām Ḥasan 'Askarī's son Twelfth Imām Mahdī Ākhiru'ż-Żamān has been concealed by God, that is why he is called *Imāmu'l-Ghāyab* (Hidden Imām). He has a large number of other titles, all indicative of specific qualifications – *Ṣāḥibu'l-Amr* (Lord of Command), *al-Mahdī* (Rightly Guided One), *al-Qā'im* (He who will arise), *Imāmu'l-'Ākhir* (Last Imam), *Imāmu'l-Muntaẓar* (Awaited Imām) etc. At Sāmarrah (Iraq), there is a mosque under which is a cave, partitioned off by a gate, called *Bābu'l-Ghayāb* (Gate of the Occultation). The area behind the gate is called *Hujrātu'l-Ghayāba* (Chamber of the Occultation) and a well at the corner is named as *Bī'ru'l-Ghayāba* (Well of the Occultation), which is believed to be placed where the Imām Mahdī disappeared. The devotees gather in the rooms of the cave and pray for his early return.

Shi'is and Sunnis both believe in Imām Mahdī, his *Ẓuhūr* (appearance) or *Qiyām* (arising) is awaiting the time decreed by God. Apart from Shi'is, the most eminent Sunni scholars like as-Suyūtī, Jalālu'd-Dīn (d. 1505 AD) in his Tafsīr *Durru'l-Manthūr fī'l-Tafsīr bi'l Māthūr* and Ibn Ḥajar, al-Haysamī, al-Makkī (d. 1567 AD) in *aṣ-Ṣawa'qu'l-Muḥriqa fi'r-radd 'alā' ahli'l Rafz wa'l Zanadiqā* and others in their commentaries have specifically mentioned the verses of the holy Qur'an in respect of Imām Mahdī. A few verses are given here:

Imām Mahdī's title of the *Baqīyyatu'llāh* (Remnant of God) has been mentioned in the holy Qur'an:

> "That which is *Baqīyyatu'llāh* unto you is good for you if ye be believers, and I am not over you a keeper." (*Qur'an: 11/86*)

Similarly, this verse mentions about the *Ṣāḥibu'z-Żamān* (the Lord of the Age):

> "And verily he shall be the sign of (*approach of*) the Hour (*of Reckoning*), doubt not then about it and follow me: this is the right path." (*Qur'an: 43/61*)

The following verses of holy Qur'an are also indicative of Imām Mahdī:

> "He perfecteth His Light, though may detested be the infidels." (*Qur'an: 9/32*)

> "He will certainly appoint them successors in the earth as He appointed Successors those before them, and that certainly He shall establish for them their religion which He has chosen for them." (*Qur'an: 24/55*)

Some specific signs of the coming of Imām Mahdī agreed upon the Traditions of Shi'is and Sunnis both[21] may be mentioned as under:

(i) Imām Mahdī will be a descendant of Prophet Muḥammad in the lineage of his daughter Fāṭimah.[22]
(ii) Imām Mahdī will bear the name Muḥammad.[23]
(iii) Imām Mahdī will be accompanied by the appearance of Dajjāl in the East.[24]
(iv) Imām Mahdī will be accompanied by the raising of the Black Standard. Tradition adds: If you see it (Black Standard) then go to it even if you have to crawl over the snow, for with it is Mahdī, the Vicegerent of God.[25]
(v) Imām Mahdī's reign will be prevailed either seven, nine or nineteen years.[26]

The best known Traditions in both Shi'i and Sunni sources, state that Imām Mahdī's reign of righteousness will fill the earth with justice after it has been filled with injustice and tyranny.[27] Tradition adds: Imām Mahdī will rule with justice. Everything due shall be returned to its owners. The roads will be safe .... He will judge among the people with the judgment of David and of Muḥammad.... At that time men will not find any poor-houses where to give their alms or to be generous because riches will encompass all.[28]

Another Tradition says: Imām Mahdī will enhance the knowledge to its last goal. It has been said in a symbolic language that all the knowledge is encompassed in 27 letters and all the messages of God have been brought in two of these letters, and so the people only know these two letters. But Imām Mahdī will bring forth the other 25 letters and will spread them among the people.[29]

It is said that Imām Mahdī will face harsh treatment as Prophet Muḥammad faced from the people of his time. They will interpret the Book of God and will bring forward proofs from it against him. He will be cursed by the people of both East and West.[30]

There are several prophecies concerning the coming of Imām Mahdī, to quote a few:

> "The Prophet Muḥammad said – There will come a time for my people when there will remain nothing of Qur'an except its outward form and nothing of Islam except its name and they will call themselves by this name even though they will be the people furthest from it. Their mosques will be full of people but they will be empty of right guidance. The *fuqahā'* (theologist) of that day will be the most evil religious leaders under the heaven; sedition and dissension will go out from them and to them will it return."[31]
>
> "Imām 'Ali has predicted the signs …and they cut open the wombs; and they follow their lusts; and they take the spilling of blood lightly; and their discernment is weak; and tyranny becomes a source of pride; and the leaders become profligate, the ministers oppressors, the religious scholars faithless and the poor deprived; and false testimony is made; immorality, lies, crime, and repression are carried out openly; and books are embellished, the mosques adorned and the minarets made tall…"[32]

Imām Ja'far aṣ-Ṣādiq's prophecies are so close to several modern phenomena and scientific inventions that some of the contemporary Shi'i scholars, like Ibrāhīm al-Mūsawī aż-Żanjānī, foresee the appearance of Imām Mahdī in the near future. For instance, the prophecies referring to television and aeroplane:

> "I heard Abū 'Abdu'llāh (Imām Ja'far aṣ-Ṣādiq) saying – The believer, in the time of the Qā'im, while in the east, will be able to see his brother in the west and he who is in the west will be able to see his brother in the east."[33]

The detailed prophecies in a lengthy Tradition of Imām Ja'far aṣ-Ṣādiq also describes the moral degrading at the time of the coming of Imām Mahdī as depicted above in the prophecies of the Prophet and Imām 'Ali, but some aspect of 'permissive society' and its secularization:

> "… and you see young men being handed over like women and women co-habiting with women and their numbers …and you see person molesting his neighbour and no-one preventing it …and you see women occupying places in the assemblies just as men do and usury is carried out openly and adultery is praised."[34]

The time is envisaged shortly before the Day of Judgment. The reign of Imām Mahdī shall see the return of Jesus Christ, Imām Ḥusain and other holy personalities. As mentioned above, Imām Mahdī will be accompanied by the appearance of Dajjal in the East. Dajjal is same as Anti-christ, the chief enemy of Christ, the concept of a mighty ruler who will appear at the end of time and whose essence will be enmity of God is, older and was taken over by Christianity from Judaism. The concept of Antichrist has been widely accepted in Christendom, and signified that this 'man of lawlessness' will obtain credence among the Jews because they have not accepted the truth. Antichrist as a perverted of men led naturally to his connection with false doctrine (I John 2:18, 4:3, II John 7). Immense similarities in the person and date of the coming of the Dajjāl or Antichrist and 'the signs of times' preceding it are upheavals in nature, pestilence, famine, wars and other disasters. Similarly, Islamic Tradition says: Before the coming of Imām Mahdī there will be red death (the sword) and white death (the plague).[35] The preachers among the Christians and Muslims have been spreading warnings in order to call the people to repentance.

There has been almost unanimity in faith between Shi'is and Sunnis regarding the birth, the occultation and return of Imām Mahdī unto the period of hundred years of the occultation. Ṣūfīs and some other Sunni sects have unanimity with Shi'is in faith regarding Imām Mahdī. However, some other Sunni sects differ on the birth, the occultation and miraculously prolonged life until the day when he will be manifested again by the decree of God. Let the issues be discussed in brief.

Surely, the birth of Eleventh Imām Ḥasan 'Askarī's son Muḥammad (Imām Mahdī Ā<u>kh</u>iru'ẓ-Żamān) was kept so secret that even the Shi'is, in general, had no knowledge about his birth in 255 HD /868 AD, so the brother of Imām Ḥasan 'Askarī's, Ja'far took the advantage of confusion remained unshakeable in his assertion that his brother had no progeny and claimed to be his successor, entered in the house of deceased Imām in order to lead the funeral prayer. At this juncture a young boy came forward and politely told him – 'Uncle, stand back ! It is more fitting for me to lead the funeral prayer for my father than you. Because he has nominated me his successor. Ja'far verified the fact and withdrew his claim. For his wrong claim he was branded *Każżāb*, the liar and when he appealed to God for forgiveness, got the title of *Tawwāb*, the repented.

The logic behind the Occultation is the similar to the birth of Twelfth Imām being kept in strict secrecy. Because, the 'Abbāsite Caliphs were thirsty of blood of the Imām and his family and wanted to finish their progeny and for that they had poisoned the Tenth and Eleventh Imāms at Sāmarrah, a cantonment.

They had been in effective Occultation, as far as their followers were concerned. Under the vigilant and hostile surveillance, the Imams rarely could meet their followers and often had to speak to some of them behind a curtain. They were usually contacted through a network called *Wikalā* (agency), which was a channel for communicating messages of the Imāms and collecting the alms for them. 'Othmān al-'Amrī had been the secretary and special agent of the Tenth and Eleventh Imāms and so effectively controlled the *Wikalā*. Thus, when 'Othmān al-'Amrī told that Abu'l-Qāsim Muḥammad is the Twelfth Imām, duly nominated by his father and has taken the Occultation, due to the threat against his life from the 'Abbāsites and also the Twelfth Imām has been kind enough to appoint him on the same position held from the periods of the Tenth and Eleventh Imāms, it must have appeared that nothing much had changed. So no dispute or confusion arose about the birth and occultation of the Twelfth Imām. It was the period of the third agent, Ḥusain-bin-Rūḥ an-Nawbakhtī, when Caliph Muqtadir (907-32 AD) was favourable to the Nawbakhtī family, which wielded considerable power at his court as ministers. During this period the religious issue was politicized and opinions took the shape of two divergent faiths.

For a believer, the miraculously prolonged life of the Twelfth Imam is no issue, because he will be manifested again by the decree of God. The occultation and the miraculously prolonged life are the parts of faiths in Islam. A few Qur'anic instances are given as under:

> Prophet Jesus Christ was not 'crucified' and "God raised (*lifted*) him up to Himself." (*Qur'an: 4/ 157-58*)
>
> Prophet Idrīs is still alive – "We exalted him to a high station." (*Qur'an: 19/57*)
>
> Khizr, who is regarded by some Muslims as the Prophet, is still alive whose meeting with Prophet Moses has been described in detail. (*Qur'an: 18/60-82*)

The Companions of the Cave – The youths seeking protection of the Lord were made to sleep for centuries in the cave. It proves, how man can be made to live long life beyond the ordinary expectation and how time could be passed without being felt, until the Day of Judgment. (*Qur'an: 18/13-22*)

However, the possibilities of the addition of fabricated stories by vested interest to the faith regarding Imām Mahdī cannot be ruled out, which has created certain confusions. With a view to prove their genuineness and creditabilities some sects and ruling elites and vested interest have also added to the fray, which have been indiscriminately incorporated in Shi'i Traditions. A few instances may be pointed out here:

Imām Mahdī's coming will be accompanied by the raising of a Black Standard in Khurāsān.[36] It appears to be fabricated for proving the genuineness and creditabilities of Sarbādarīd dynasty (1337-61 AD) the Irani rulers whose capital was Khurāsān and colour of Standard was black.

The Pure Soul (Nafs'až-Žakiyya) will be assassinated. Muḥammad an-Nafs'až-Žakiyya was a descendant of Imām Ḥasan. He was Imām of the Mughīriyya, a sub-sect of Shi'is. He was one of the chief rebels against the 'Abbāsites and was assassinated.

The sun will rise from the west and stars will appear in the east which will be as much light as moon. A number of other descriptions would not match with facts.

Between the Imām Mahdī and the Quraysh, there will only be the sword.[37] Who are the Quraysh, may be oil-rich Shaykhs !

Imām Mahdī will come with a new book and religious law.[38] It is against the unanimous basic faith of Islam that the Book of God, the Qur'an is the final verdict of religious law and shall be effectively operative unto the Day of Judgment. It appears that such a notion has been invented by Bābīs sect which had declared the abolition of Muslim religious laws in 1845 AD and thereafter enforcement of new book and religious laws !

The Divine Resurrection and Day of Last Judgment

Ma'ad (Resurrection) and *Ākhirat* (Last Judgment) is one of the three most important pivots of Islamic faith, that one who denies it, *ipso facto* is ousted from the pale of Islam and has no destiny other than eternal perdition. Eschatology has mainly three components; namely *Barżakh* (Purgatory), *'Adālat* (Judgment) and *Nijāt* (Salvation), may he found in most of the religions.

The Western prophetic religions like Zoroastrianism, Judaism, Christianity and Islam have gradually developed the concept which has rich imagery. In some primitive religions, ancient Eastern religions have also developed such beliefs. For example, in ancient Egyptian religion, a dead person's heart was judged by the God *Aubis* by placing it on a balance. If the heart was found light, it indicated that the person had comparative goodness and so the soul was allowed to go to the blessed region ruled by the God of dead, *Osiris* and if the heart was found heavy, the soul would be destroyed by a hybrid creature, *Devouress*. But in case of the Indian based religions – Hindusim, Jainsim and Buddhism, the eschatology believes in reincarnation but the concept of a Last Judgment is not absent as a stage in the career of the soul. Eventually, the soul should return to the world (or Ultimate). Jains put the soul in *bhumis*, a place where demons torture the sinner, untill any evil accumulated during the lifetime is exhausted. Whereas, Buddhism denied the existence of the World of Soul, believes in *Karma-Vacara*, the cosmic realm of five senses experienced in a variety of bodies and perceptions. In China, the Buddhist concept of realm of punishment and expiation after death was somehow modified by the Taroists.

This philosophy of soul and expiation after death has been advocated by some Muslim thinkers also. Ṣadru'd-Dīn Shīrāżī, known as Mullā Ṣadrā (d. 1640 AD) has discussed the question of soul and its becoming much more thoroughly than the earlier philosophers. Substantial intellectual proof have also been offered in the writings of Ibn Sīnā (Avicenna), Abū 'Ali al-Ḥusain-bin-'Abdu'llāh, but this is no proper place to go into the details.

The eschatology of the Western prophetic religions has similar features. 6th century BC Zoroastrian religion preached that after the death the soul waits for three nights by the grave and on the fourth day goes to the Bridge of the Requite where the deads of the dead are weighed. If the good overweigh the bad, the soul is able to cross the Bridge to heaven, *vice versa* to hell, from where after the overthrow of Ahriman, the God of demons by Ahura Mazda, the Wise Lord, all the mankind will be resurrected and the Wise Lord shall preside over the Last Judgment and restore the world to goodness. Early Judaic scholars also have emphasized the concept of Last Judgment, which has been named as the *Day of Yahweh*, the God of Israel and all nations from which kingdom of God will be inaugurated.

Christianity further developed the concept of Last Judgment, in which it will occur at the *Parousia* (the Second Coming or Second Advent of Christ in glory), where all mankind will stand before a judging God. In early Christian art the scenes of the Last Judgment with Christ as judge, the resurrection of dead, weighting of souls, they being separated for good and some damned with artistic production of paradise and hell. However, more terrible vision of the Last Judgment were produced by

Romanesque artists, with Christ as a stern judge, sometime carrying a sword and surrounded by the four mystical beast—eagle, lion, ox and winged man. In Christianity mankind can be delivered from human conditions only in the death and Resurrection of Jesus. The Roman Catholic belief in the purgatory most men at death are neither good enough for heaven nor bad enough for hell. They hold prayers on every 2nd November, (if Sunday, on 3rd November) of the faithful on earth to help cleanse these souls to fit them for the vision of God in Heaven.

Islamic doctrine of the purgatory and the Last Judgment are steps forward to the Christian doctrine of redemption. Islam is rich in its imagery and conceptual expansion of the doctrine of the Last Judgment. After death, persons are questioned about their cardinal beliefs and go through a type of purgatory, except the martyrs, whose soul immediately goes to the paradise. At the dooms day all persons will die and then resurrected to be judged as per their good deeds and evil deeds. In order to prove that the resurrection will occur, the Qur'an has used the moral and physical arguments that because not all requital is meted out in this life, a final Judgment is necessary for its completion. Those condemned shall burn into fire and those who are saved by God's mercy and forgiven for any good work by certain sinners, shall enjoy the abiding pleasures of paradise.

The Islamic doctrine of Divine Resurrection and the last Judgment has many aspects which need to be understood, such as the relationship of the body and soul, the issue of life and death, the state of purgatory, the state of life between death and resurrection, the day of resurrection and judgment, intercession shaping of a new world order etc. These aspects are briefly touched upon in following lines. With respect to the fact of *Rūḥ* (Spirit) Qur'an says:

> "They will ask thee concerning Spirit. Say: The Spirit is by command of my Lord and of knowledge ye have been vouchsafed but little." (*Qur'an 17/85*)

But if this verse is read in reference to the following verse, the relationship of the body and soul is made clear:

> "Verily We created man from a product of wet earth;Then placed him as a drop (*of seed*) in a safe lodging ; Then fashioned We the drop a clot, then fashioned We a clot a little lump, then fashioned We the little lump bones, then clothed the bones with flesh, and then produced it as an other creation." (*Qur'an: 23/12-14*)

In the Islamic concept the separation of the soul from the body is known as death but death does not mean extinction. The wise words of the holy Prophet Muḥammad are:

> "Don't think you will be extinct after dying, you will only be transferred from one place to another."

The virtuous and auspicious characters live after death and they send happy tidings to the men of faith as Qur'an points out[39]:

> "Think not of those, who are slain in the way of God, as dead. Nay, they are living. With their Lord they have provision ; Jubilant (*are they*) because of that which God hath bestowed upon them of His bounty, rejoicing for the sake of those who have not joined them but are left behind: that there shall no fear come upon them neither shall they grieve. They rejoice because of favour from God and kindness, and that God wasteth not the wage of the believers." (*Qur'an 3/169-71*)

With regard to the Purgatory, Qur'an says:

> "And we defer it only as a term already reckoned." (*Qur'an: 11/104*)

Within this intermediary period he has to taste sweet or bitter, pleasant or unpleasant, in accordance with the quality of his faith and action during his life, previous to it and thus he waits for the final day of resurrection and judgment:

> "Until when death cometh unto one of them, he saith: My Lord ! send me back; that I may do right in that which I have left behind ! But nay ! It is but a word that he speaketh ; and behind them is a barrier until the day when they are raised." (*Qur'an: 23/99-100*)

Then comes the Divine Resurrection and Day of Last Judgment. Qur'an has given detailed hints with regard to the day of judgment, here it is not intended to reproduce that detail, but only to focus the main object for which the Day of Judgment has been instituted. Qur'an has us to note:

> "Lo! Those who wander from the way of God have a awful doom, forasmuch as they forget the Day of Reckoning." (*Qur'an: 38/26*)

These were the people who regarded the life of this world to be the be all and all of human existence:

> "And they say: There is naught save our life of the world, and we shall not be raised (*again*)." (*Qur'an 6/29*)
>
> "And afterward unto Him is your return. Then He will proclaim upto you what ye used to do." (*Qur'an: 6/60*)

After all these stages are the stage of the Balance of Judgment to determine the quantum of reward and punishment in accordance with the nature and extent of one's good or bad actions. Qur'an says:

> "On the day when their tongues and their hands and their feet testify against them as to what they used to do." (*Qur'an: 24/24*)
>
> "On that day God will pay them their just due, and they will know that God, He is the manifest Truth." (*Qur'an: 24/25*)
>
> "And they say unto their skins: Why testify ye against us? They say: God hath given us speech Who giveth speech to all things, and Who created you at the first, and unto Whom ye are returned." (*Qur'an: 41/21*)
>
> "(*Then it will be said*) O ye who disbelieve ! Make no excuses for yourselves this day. Ye are only being paid for what ye used to do." (*Qur'an: 66/7*)

In this matter of reward and punishment, some luminary personalities will intercede to advocate pre-emption of various sinners. Clear indication of some distinguished personalities using their good offices to pre-empt the sinners is given in the holy Qur'an:

> "Say thou (*O' Our Apostle Muḥammad !*) God's (*alone*) is intercession altogether." (*Qur'an: 39/44*)
>
> "God! There is no God save him, the Alive the Eternal."
> (*Qur'an: 2/255*)

> "He knoweth what is before them and what is behind them, and they cannot intercede except for him whom He accepteth, and they quake of Him. (*Qur'an: 21/28*)
>
> "On the day when angels and spirit shall stay arrayed, they speak not, saving him whom the Beneficent alloweth and who speaketh right." (*Qur'an: 78/38*)

Thereafter this Universe, the galaxies, the stars and the planets this world of colour and smell whose perception we have, will disappear into extinction, because for the existence and life of everything there is a time fixed which has to expire at the point of its termination. With respect to this expiry of the age of this cosmos Qur'an says:

> "We created not the heavens and the earth and all that is between them save with truth and for a term appointed. But those who disbelieve turn away from that whereof they are warned." (*Qur'an: 46/3*)

After winding up of this set of cosmic array, a new and fresh order of Universe will be created, the detail of which are traceable in the traditions of the infallible Divine leaders. Here it is neither necessary nor relevant, instead it would be better to consider the most important of the aspects of Resurrection namely the meaning and significance of the day of last Judgment or the life hereafter.

If we refute or discredit the concept of the *hereafter*, the value and meaning of the concept of the *Divine Unity of God* and the *Divine Prophethood* would be undone and defeated, not only this but the social order as well would be despoiled because once, the provision of reward and punishment is not in existence, there would hardly remain any need to avoid lawlessness in any matter. The unbridled cravings of the self would wipe out the line demarcating between man and animal. It would leave neither a society nor a law nor the conformity to the law. It would render the human life into the brand of life in which the bestiality would become rampant.

It may be questioned: is the society which is bereft of the belief in the Resurrection, the last Judgment and the life hereafter, is necessarily a lawless one? East or West, majority of the modern governments do not give any place to Resurrection in their respective ideologies, so do they not have any law or compliance to it? The plain and simple answer to this is that whether these governments have not incorporated this concept as such, nonetheless they have derived from the Resurrection, itself the substitute of it in the form of their respective Penal Codes. This Code pronounce judgments suffer in many respects from inherent anomalies and fall short of true justice.

From the Islamic standpoint, the true and full justice can be ensured only in the Divine Resurrection, because by then the actions of every individual would have unfolded completely, and by taking into consideration all the factors, circumstances, motives etc. the full and complete sheet of the charges or rewardable services will be placed under the Divine Justice. Some religions also have belief in reward and punishment after death but Islam keeps the reward and punishment postponed till Last Day of Judgment. Looking from the external angles, it feels proper to clear the dues immediately after the end of life as the labourer has finished his work and his dues be paid off without delay. Why should he be cast in the interval between death and the day of Resurrection, spread over a period of thousands of years, but if we reflect objectively on this so-called undeclared justice, we would come to realize that the clearance of justice immediately after death would amount to killing of the very justice, because by the end of life only the sins have ceased to exist, but the effects of virtuous deeds are still in action even after the agent of that virtue has expired. So the justice cannot ignore the services of virtues still in effective operation (such as establishment of school, hospitals orphanage etc. and all the services doing good to the society), which must keep getting entered in the current account of the deceased person for years after years till the effective existence of virtuous deeds. It would remove the justice away from its natural demand, if we do not wait before the entire spell of one's action after his death has fully exhausted. It speaks of the utmost mercifulness of God to cease the account of sin at the point of death but keep running the account of virtues even after expiry of its agent.

In the hereafter code of reward and punishment, the issue of intercession (condoning of sin by the good offices of the Prophet) has been made controversial by certain scholars. With them it amounts to polytheism, if the intercession is sought from any other else than God Himself. In the first place no Muslim expects to receive the grace of intercession from any other sources than some personalities, who have the purity of the highest order because they believe that these purest of God's servants do have the desired gravity to exonerate their sins and shall but act as the intercessor before the Almighty God. On the basis of this belief they are called, the ones who believe in *the medium*. If this medium is refuted as the cardinal concept in the conceptual framework of

Islam, the need of a Divinely trained Guide is likewise annulled, because if there is no such medium to serve as a link between God and the people, who delivers God's will to the people and takes the peoples' appeal to Him, there would be no difference between them and the general community, while he is the chosen one of the Almighty. The exoneration of sins would be carried through the Guide of his community, otherwise neither there would the need of an *Ummah* nor the need of identifying them, every individual will seek to have a direct correspondence with God, which will involve him in the hazards of misguidance.

If seen profoundly, it would appear that the refutation of the concept of 'the medium' is based on the motive of undermining the status of the Prophet and undercutting the authority of his person in their concerted attempt to pull down the Prophet from his distinguished rank and make him go at par with the rank of the masses and thus repeal all the distinguished merits placing him far above the level of the masses. This was undertaken because of the selfish apprehension that if the Prophet's true portrayal is preserved then every disputed issue will have to be decided in the light of the model life-pattern of the holy Prophet Muḥammad and this would surely go against the vested interest of the malicious scholars as they have to defend the imperial stands, while the luminous life pattern of the holy Prophet has been the greatest challenge for their political survival.

References

1. *Bihāru'l-Anwār*, Vol. 2, p. 65.
2. *Bihāru'l-Anwār*, Vol. 2, p. 125.
3. *Bihāru'l-Anwār*, Vol. 2, p. 129.
4. *ihāru'l-Anwār*, Vol. 2, p. 96.
5. *Bihāru'l-Anwār*.
6. *Bihāru'l-Anwār*, Vol. 3, p. 5.
7. *Bihāru'l-Anwār*, Vol. 2, p. 125.
8. *Bihāru'l-Anwār*, Vol. 23, p. 22, *al-Uṣūl-min'al-Kāfī*, Vol. 1, p. 178.
9. *al-Uṣūl-min'al-Kāfī*, Vol. 1, pp. 178-9, *Bihāru'l-Anwār*, Vol. 23, p. 22.
10. *Bihāru'l-Anwār*, Vol. 23, p. 73.
11. *al-Uṣūl-min'al-Kāfī*, Vol. 1, pp. 227-9, *Bihāru'l-Anwār*, Vol. 23, p. 71.
12. *Bihāru'l-Anwār*, Vol. 23, p. 196.
13. *Bihāru'l-Anwār*, Vol. 23, pp. 191, 198-9.
14. *Bihāru'l-Anwār*, Vol. 26, p. 7.
15. *Tārīkhu'l-Khulafa*, p. 116.
16. *Bihāru'l-Anwār*, Vol. 25, pp. 25, 56-7.
17. *al-Uṣūl-min'al-Kāfī*, Vol. 1, p. 276, *Bihāru'l-Anwār*, Vol. 26, pp. 75-6.

18. *Selected Works*, Vol. 2, p. 81.
19. *Bayānu'l-Qur'an* 3/159.
20. *Khilāfat-o-Mulūkiyat,* p. 312.
21. For the convenience of common readers it may be pointed out that: the Shi'i sources are: *Bihāru'l-Anwār*: al-Majlisī, *al-Kāmilu'd-Dīn*: Ibn Bābūya, *Kashf al-Ghumma fī Ma'rifat al-Ai'ma:* Irbīlī, *al-Irshād fī Ma'rifat Ḥujāj Allāh 'Alā 'Ibād*: al-Mufīd, Ibnu'l-Ma'allim.
    The Sunni sources are: *as-Sunan*: Abū Dāwūd, *as-Sunan*: Ibn Māja, *as-Sunan*: Nasā'ī, *Jām'au's-Ṣaḥīḥu't-Tirmiżī:* at-Tirmiżī.
22. *as-Sunan:* Ibn Māja, p. 1367 Tr. No 4085, *Jām'au's-Ṣaḥīḥu't-Tirmiżī,* Vol. 2, p. 36, *as-Sunan*: Abū Dāwūd, Vol. 2, p. 422, *Bihāru'l-Anwār* (Urdu tr.) Vol. 11, p. 70.
23. *Jām'au's-Ṣaḥīḥu't-Tirmiżī,* Vol. 2, p. 36, *as-Sunan*: Abū Dāwūd, Vol. 2, p. 420, *al-Kāmilu'd-Dīn*, p. 648, *Bihāru'l-Anwār* (Urdu tr.) Vol. 11, p. 23.
24. *Jām'au's-Ṣaḥīḥu't-Tirmiżī,* Vol. 2, pp. 36-7, *al-Kāmilu'd-Dīn*, pp. 525-32.
25. *as-Sunan:* Ibn Māja, p. 1367 Tr. No. 4084 and p. 1366 Tr. No. 4082, *Kashf al-Ghumma fī Ma'rifat al-Ai'ma*, Vol. 3, pp. 262-3.
26. *Jām'au's-Ṣaḥīḥu't-Tirmiżī,* Vol. 2, p. 36, *as-Sunan*: Abū Dāwūd, Vol. 2, pp. 422-3, *Kashf al-Ghumma fī Ma'rifat al-Ai'ma*, Vol. 3, pp. 257, 269.
27. *as-Sunan:* Ibn Māja, p. 1367 Tr. No. 4084 & p. 1366 Tr. No. 4082 *as-Sunan*: Abū Dāwūd, Vol. 2, p. 422, *al-Irshād fī Ma'rifat Ḥujāj Allāh 'Alā 'Ibād*, p. 341 (Tr. 548).
28. *al-Irshād fī Ma'rifat Ḥujāj Allāh 'Alā 'Ibād*, pp. 343-4 (Tr. No. 552-3).
29. *Bihāru'l-Anwār*, Vol. 13, p. 187.
30. *Bihāru'l-Anwār*, Vol. 13, p. 193.
31. *Bihāru'l-Anwār*, Vol. 13, p. 152.
32. *'Aqā'idu'l-Imāmiyyau'l-Ithna 'Ashariyya,* pp. 258-9.
33. *'Aqā'idu'l-Imāmiyyau'l-Ithna 'Ashariyya,* p. 255.
34. *'Aqā'idu'l-Imāmiyyau'l-Ithna 'Ashariyya,* pp. 253-4.
35. *al-Irshād fī Ma'rifat Ḥujāj Allāh 'Alā 'Ibād*, p. 338, Tradition no. 544.
36. *as-Sunan:* Ibn Māja, p. 1367 Tradition no. 4084 and p. 1366 Tradition no. 4082, *Kashf al-Ghumma fī Ma'rifat al-Ai'ma*, Vol. 3, pp. 262-3.
37. *Bihāru'l-Anwār*, Vol. 13, p. 193.
38. *Kashf al-Ghumma fī Ma'rifat al-Ai'ma*, Vol. 3, p. 255.
39. *Bihāru'l-Anwār*, Vol. 2, p. 161.

Chapter Three

The Religious Obligations

Some Core Aspects

Islam represents a later development of the religious faculty of mankind and recognizes the true concern of man's consciousness of a Supreme Power with his sense of benefaction, which leads him to pour out the overflowing sentiments in literal words of love and gratitude or his repentance and solicitation to God. Qur'an says:

> "So when you have your Devotion, then laud God as you lauded your fathers, rather a greater lauding." (*Qur'an: 2/200*)

This is the guideline for the human beings. God never wished that the human beings should only *laud Himself*, as *the most Compassionate, the Merciful.* But *laud Himself rather a greater lauding*, of course after the lauding of their fathers, which is the logical conclusion. Because, if the fathers were not lauded, it cannot be referred to follow suit. It is the core of Islamic philosophy that Islam has given equal weightage to the obligations towards God Himself and also towards His creations in the Universe, especially human beings, which is a distinguished aspect of the Theology of Islam.

The Religious Obligations of human beings regarding their fellow beings and the cosmology have been termed as *Haqqu'l-'Ibād* (the Religious Obligations regarding the servants of God) i.e. Obligations regarding the Society. It has been specifically laid down that if an Obligation to a person remains, it could only be pardoned by the person concerned. God has relinquished His power to pardon such remains! It shall be discussed in details in the forthcoming chapter entitled 'The Universal Life-Order'.

The other part of the Religious Obligations towards God is termed as *Ḥaqqu'-llāh* (the Religious Obligations regarding God Himself) shall be dealt with here. For the believers, these religious obligations are as important as breathing. It has been significant and universal aspect of religion, whether of the primitive people or of modern philosophical thinkers of the religion. It distinguishes the phenomenon of religion from the phenomena of aesthetic feelings. Though the historians of religion, psychologists and anthropologists debate various theories and forms of the religious obligations, the core aspects remained whatever their inspirations revealed otherwise.

Islamic religious obligations emerge from its basic principles and beliefs of Divine Unity, Supreme power, unlimited love and mercy of God, the charity and brotherhood among all human beings, irrespective of the caste, creed, region or religion, the outpouring a grateful heart to the Creator, the Giver of all good and accountability for all human actions in the life, which stress on the design and order in the Universe. It is explained by the fact that every creation is endowed with a definite and defined natural pattern. Though nature allows every creation to function in a whole but also sets limits, which are the most fixed points but not as autocratic, in both the cosmology and the Theology of Islam. Qur'an says:

> "Verily everything have We have created to a determined measure." (*Qur'an: 54/49*)

Thus, the creature is limited and measured out and depends on its Creator, whose reign could not be challenged, which is unlimited, independent and self-sufficient. In order to communicate the truth, the faithful observance of religious obligations will be powerful conservation of a true religious spirit.

Islam recognizes no caste or creed or priesthood, allows no special holiness to intervene between the mankind and his Almighty God. Each soul rises to his Creator without the intervention of any other person in the shape of priest or hierophant. Every person is his own priest or hierophant. No monopoly of spiritual knowledge. The emphasis on knowing God on the basis of knowledge and science has distinguished the Islam from many other religions and bringing it into the closest affinity with the modern world of thought. The Prophet of Islam, the Divine medium of human guidance preached of the value of knowledge:

> "Acquire knowledge, because he who acquires it in the way of Lord performs an act of piety, who speaks of it, praises the Lord; who seeks it, adores God; who dispenses instruction in it, bestows alms; and who imparts it to its fitting objects, performs an act of devotion to God. Knowledge enables its possessor to distinguish what is forbidden from what is not; it lights the way to Heaven; it is our friend in the desert, our society is solitude, our companion when bereft of friends; it guides us to happiness; it sustains us in misery."[1]

Islam value the consciousness and sense of benefaction of man as the means of moral elevation and purification of mind and heart. The beauty of the morality and humanity are the elements form the supplicatory hymns in the words of the holy Prophet Muḥammad, mentioned below:

> "O' Lord! I supplicate Thee for firmness in faith and direction towards rectitude, and to assist me in being grateful to Thee, and in adorning Thee in every good way; and I supplicate Thee for an innocent heart, which shall not incline to wickedness; and I supplicate Thee for a true tongue, and for that virtue Thou knowest; and I pray Thee to defend me from that vice which Thou knowest, and for forgiveness of those faults which Thou knowest. O' my Defender! assist me in remembering Thee and being grateful to Thee, and in worshipping Thee with the excess of my strength. O' Lord! I have injured my own soul, and no one can pardon the faults of Thy servants to Thou; forgive me out of Thy loving kindness and have mercy on me; for, Verily, Thou art the forgiver of offences and bestower of blessings on Thy servants."[2]

The following two examples of the prayers of Imām Żainu'l-Ābidīn evince the highest devotional spirit and the teaching of Islam:

> "Thanks be to my Lord; He the Adorable, and only to be adored, My Lord, the Eternal, the Ever-existing; the Cherisher, the true Sovereign whose mercy might overshadow the Universe; the Regulator of the world, and Light of the creation. He is our worship; To Him belongs all worship; He existed before all things and will exist after all that is living has ceased. Thou art the adored, my Lord; Thou art the Master, the Loving

and Forgiving; Thou bestows power and might on whom Thou pleases; him whom Thou hast exalted none can lower; and him whom Thou hast lowered none can exalt. Thou, my Lord, art the Eternal. The Creator of all, All-wise Sovereign, Mighty; Thy knowledge knows everything; Thy beneficence is all-pervading; The forgiveness and mercy all-embracing. O' my Lord! Thou art the Helper of the afflicted, the Reliever of all distress, the Consoler of the broken hearted; Thou art present everywhere to help Thy servants. Thou knowest all secrets, all thoughts, all present in every assembly, Fulfiller of all our needs, Bestower of all blessings, Thou art the friend of the bereaved; my Lord, Thou art my Fortress; a Castle for all who seek Thy help. Thou art the Refuge of the weak; the Helper of the pure and true. O' my Lord, Thou art my supporter, my Helper, the Helper of all who seek Thy help........ O' my Lord! Thou art the Creator, I am only created; Thou art my Sovereign, I am only Thy servant; Thou art the Helper, I am beseecher; Thou my Lord, art my Refuge; Thou art Forgiver, I am sinner; Thou my Lord, art the Merciful, All-knowing, All-loving, I am groping in the dark; I seek Thy knowledge and love, Bestow, my Lord, all Thy knowledge and love and mercy; forgive my sins. O' my Lord, and let me approach Thee, my Lord."

"O' my Lord! Thou the Ever-praised, the Eternal, Thou art the Ever-present, the Ever-existing the Ever-near, the All-knowing. Thou lives in every heart, in every soul, all-pervading, Thy knowledge is ingrained in every mind – He bears no similitude, has no equal. One, the Eternal; Thanks be to the Lord whose mercy extends to every sinner, who provides for even those who deny Him. To Him belong the beginning and end, all knowledge and most hidden secrets of the hearts. He never slumbers, Ever-just, Ever-wakeful. He forgiveth in His mercy our greatest sins—loveth all creations. I testify to the goodness of my Lord, to the truth of His Messenger's message, blessings on him and his descendants and his companions."[3]

Each and every worshipper has amplest scope for most heartfelt devotion and humility before the most compassionate, the merciful God. Islam has, therefore, channelised the scopes of worship into the forms of some obligatory duties, which enable the individual worshipper to formulate his outpouring of devotions. Every place becomes pure and consecrated where God is faithfully worshipped:

> "It is one of the glories of Islam that its temples are not made with hands, and that its ceremonies can be performed anywhere upon God's earth or under His heaven."[4]

With a view to keep true religious spirit alive among the believers, the Islam has prescribed some practical duties, which Shi'is term as *Furū'd-Dīn* (the Branches or Offshoots of Religion) and Sunni term as *Arkānu'd-Dīn* (the Pillars of Religion). To avoid the different terms of both major sects of Islam, we shall prefer to use the term *Faraizu'd-Dīn* (Religious Obligations) because these are, actually, compulsory duties for each and every Muslim. Sunnis name it – *Shahādah* (the Profession of Faith), *Ṣalāt* (the Prayer), *Ṣaum* (the Fasting), *Žakāt* (the Religious Tax) and *Ḥajj* (the Pilgrimage) some of them also include *Jihād* (the Struggle). All the Shi'is also believed and are expected to perform as per their ability, the norms prescribed for *Ṣalāt*, *Žakāt*, *Khumus* (fifth part) *Ṣaum* and *Jihād*. Some of Shi'is also add to it – *Amr-bil-Ma'rūf* (the Enjoining of Good), *Nahy-anil-Munkir* (the Prevention and obeisance from Bad). No doubt these items are important for the believes, who accept it in one form or the other. But in our opinion appears no necessity to include in the Religions Obligations, which are the matter of action rather than that of belief. Let us explain the Religious Obligations which are accepted by both major sets of Islam.

Profession of the Faith

Shahādah or *Kalamahu 'sh-Shahadah* (profession of faith) is read or recited in two different forms among the Shi'is and Sunnis. For Sunnis it is quite simple:

> "*Lā Ilāh Ill'allāh Muḥammadu'r Rasūla'llāh.*"
> (There is no good but God, Muḥammad His Prophet.)

But Shi'is add their faith in the Imamate and read or recite as under:

> "*Lā Ilāh Ill'allāh Muḥammadu'r Rasūla'llāh 'Aliyan Ḥujjatu'llāh.*" (There is no good but God, Muḥammad His Prophet, 'Ali is Argument of God.)

Moreover, the zealous Shi'is, especially of Indian subcontinent, further add:

> "*Waṣiu'r-Rasū'llāh Khilāfathu-Bilā Faṣl.*"
> ('Ali is Trustee of the Prophet of God and his Vicegérent, without any gap.)

The inclusion of the name of Imām 'Ali infuses the faith that the Islam did not end with the life of the Prophet Muḥammad and his successor Imām 'Ali in his ministry is his representative. The two great sects, the Shi'is and the Sunnis, in which Islam stood divided at the early stage of Islamic history was based on the Divine Succession of the Prophet, which has been discussed in this book at proper place. However, the inclusion and declaration of Imām 'Ali's Trusteeship and Vicegerence of the Prophet *without any gap*, in my humble opinion, is more socio-political than that of spiritual doctrine. The reason appears to be continued suffering from persecution and assassination of the descendant of 'Ali-Fāṭimah and their followers throughout the history of Muslim rule and had also resulted into conversion of them into Sunni fold. Some of them who had not converted observed *Taqiyya* (self-protection) due to threat of flogging or imprisonment and other discomforts. So when the course of the history changed and such threats of life removed, they asserted their faith. Nevertheless 'Ali has been unanimously accepted by all Sunnis as their fourth Caliph, whereas Shi'is regard him as the first Imām. Islamic mystics start their spiritual lineage from Imām 'Ali, baring a few of Caliph Abū Bakr's lineage, yet they do believe in the doctrine of Caliphates placing Imām 'Ali at fourth position. So it was felt necessary to profess 'Ali's Trusteeship and Vicegerence of the holy Prophet without any gap.

The assertion Shi'is "without any gap" by Shi'is result into the displeasure, discontent and even sometime communal riots because the Sunnis allege it an insult to the *Khilāfatu'r-Rāshidah.* Every right minded person will say, if the doctrine of Shi'a faith is not broken by such assertions, Shi'is should stop it. I do agree with them. In most of Islamic countries, even those where Shi'is are in majority, such as Iran and Iraq, they never insist on declaring the phrase – " Ali is Trustee of the Prophet of God and his Vicegerent, without any gap." However, simply in the academic interest let us ponder over the issue whether it is actually any attempt to insult any religious personality of eminence. Take the case of Abu Bakr, the first of Caliphate. Naturally, he was Vicegerent 'without any gap.' Was 'Omar the second Caliph, the Caliph of first Caliph Abū Bakr or of the Prophet? Reply shall be that he was Caliph of the Prophet, means he was 'Caliph without any gap'. Similar is the case of 'Othmān, the third Caliph, who was also neither the Caliph of Abū Bakr nor of 'Omar but the Caliph of the Prophet. If the first-three Caliphs are the

Caliphs of the Prophet and not of their predecessor, why the fourth Caliph 'Ali in not a Vicegerent without any gap!

It is also amazing that the Sunnis keep continuously repeating the *Profession of faith* at every ritual and ceremony from the birth to death of an individual, whereas, Shi'is do not follow such restriction, although they also abide and profess like their Sunni brothers-in-faith and repeat in all the prayers. There is no basic difference in the two assertions, only the preferences are different. If one sect has laid more emphasis on one or the other item and included in the obligations, it does not imply that the other sects do not believe in that. All the sects of the Islam believe in them. The difference, *albeit*, has creeped in respect of their number. These minor differences have resulted from the elaboration of their respective emphases. By and large the same roots and branches of Islam are followed by all the sects of Islam. The basic *Kalamah* of Islam namely "I witness that there is no God but one God and Muḥammad is His messenger", is the same among all the sects.

The Prayer

Ṣalāt or *Namāż* (the prayer) the foremost pivot of the Religious Obligations of Islam, which occupies the central place in the elements of Islamic practices. This affords a medium to submit spiritually to God and seek spiritual nearness to His Lordship, *vide* some verses of the holy Qur'an with regard to it:

> "Verily I, I (*alone*), am God: There is no god but I: worship thou (*only*) Me, and establish in My remembrance." (*Qur'an: 20/14*)
>
> " Nay! Heed him not! Prostrate thou in obeisance (*unto thy Lord*) and draw yourself near (*unto Him*)." (*Qur'an: 96/19*)
>
> "And establish prayer; verily prayer restraineth (*One*) from filth and evil and certainly the remembrance of God is the greatest (*duty of the believer*)." (*Qur'an: 29/45*)
>
> "And seek ye help (*from God*) through patience and prayer; verily, it is a hard (*task*) indeed, save upon the humble." (*Qur'an: 2/45*)
>
> "What hath brought you into hell! They shall say: We were not of those who offered regular prayers (*to God*)." (*Qur'an: 74/42-43*)

Now let us see what a Muslim recites in the Prayer and how he tries to draw closer to God, the Almighty.

First heed the *Ažān* (the formal call to Prayer):

2 Calls: God is the Greatest.
2 Calls: I witness that there is no God but one the God.
2 Calls: I witness that Muḥammad is the messenger of God.
2 Calls: I witness that 'Ali is Trustee of the Prophet of God and his Vicegerent, without any gap.
2 Calls: Come to the Prayer.
2 Calls: Come to Salvation.
2 Calls: Come to the Best of Actions.
2 Calls: God is the Greatest.
2 Calls: There is no God but the God.

In the *Ažān* of the Sunni there is neither the expression 'Come to the best of Actions' nor 'I witness that 'Ali is Trustee of the Prophet of God and his Vicegerent, without any gap.' Instead in the dawn-Prayer of Sunni there is the 'The Prayer is better than sleep' which is not in the *Ažān* of Shi'is. Apart from these partial changes, the Prayer call has powerful influence to keep us getting attentive to the Greatness of God. Daily five times the Call is repeated, and in response to this call, the reciter of the prayer stands with the intention to cut himself off this world and come closer to Great Creator, the Most Compassionate.

Now, let us see what does he (Shi'a or Sunni) recite in the prayer:

The first chapter of Qur'an the *Sūrah al-Fātiḥa* with which he begins reads as follows:

> "In the name of God, the Beneficent, the Merciful. (*all*) Praise is (*only*) God's, the Lord of the worlds. The Beneficent, the Merciful. Master of the Day of Judgment. Thee (*alone*) worship we and of Thee (*only*) we seek help. Guide us (*O' Lord*) on the Right path. The path of those upon whom Thou hast bestowed Thy bounties, not (the path) of those inflicted with Thy wrath, nor (*of those*) gone astray." (*Qur'an: 1/1-7*)
>
> In the same way all the chapters or verses of Qur'an usually recited in course of the prayer, have exalted notes of guidance.

After the standing position, the prayers says:

"*Allāhu'-Akbar* (God is Great)".

Then bows down before the Greatness of God with his hands placed on his knees, and he recites:

> "Holy is my Cherisher Lord, the Greatest with His Glory."

Then he stands erect and says:

> "Heareth God whosoever declareth his Glory."

Then he says:

> "*Allāhu'-Akbar*"

And falls down in prostration and placing his forehead on the ground, he repeatedly says:

> "Holy is my Cherisher, the Lord the Highest with his Glory."

Then he goes for the second round of the same set of recitations making *Rukū'* (the bowing position) and the *Sajdah* (placing forehead on the ground in prostration).

Then he says *Tas͟hahhud* (bearing witness) saying:

> " I bear witness that there no God but the God. He is one (the only One) There is no partner of equal to him, and I bear witness that Muḥammad is His servant and his Prophet, Lord may Thy peace be on Muḥammad and his Pious Progeny."

Namāż is concluded with the *Salām* (Salutation):

> "O Lord! bestow mercy on our Divine-leader and Commander Muḥammad and his pious progeny as Thou hast bestowed mercy on Abraham and his pious progeny, Verily, Thou art the Most Praiseworthy, the Most exalted, and O' Lord shower Your blessing on Muḥammad and his holy progeny as Thou hast showered blessing on Abraham and his holy progeny, Verily, Thou art the Most Praiseworthy and the Most Exalted."
>
> The salutation of the Shi'is is much the same in which they too invoke God's blessing for the holy Prophet Muḥammad and his holy progeny.

Now, once the obligation of worshipping and praying Him is over, then he has been enjoined to struggle for a lawful earning, the holy Qur'an guides for the same:

> "And when the prayer is ended then disperse ye in the earth and seek ye of the grace of God, and remember ye God much, so that ye may be successful." (*Qur'an: 62/10*)

In order to acquaint himself with the goals and objectives of the prayer, if he reflects on the verses and other expressions recited in the prayer, it would become clear that through the course of the prayer every Muslim has his psyche implanted with the sense of the greatness of God, the obligation of worshipping and praying Him, the confirmation of his witness that Muḥammad is God's messenger, and his declaration of the holy attributes of his pious progeny, thus he undergoes a spiritual exercise five times a day to get the feedback of these vital foods for the health of his soul.

Islamic prayer is the worshipping and submitting to God. In this form of prayer the man is drawn closer to God to an extent that rising erect from the bowing position he has got awareness that God *hast heard him who has praised His Glory*. Apart from this the *Namāż* is the most effective means to make one conform to the laws of Islam. Rushing five times daily to the call of *Allāhu'-Akbar* has a semblance in the soldiers rushing for the parade in response to the call of military siren. The purpose of the parade is to brace the soldiers to keep prepared for the war. Likewise, the daily prayer prepares the individual to combat the evil forces fighting with his virtuous forces of his conscience. Through the prayer an individual fortifies the feeling of submission to God, the consciousness of duties, the habit of obedience, the moral fear of the unseen God, the understanding of the law of Islam and the lesson of integrating with the society at large. Having gathered for a pious purpose at one call, and inculcating the feeling of brotherhood and coming to know of each other's problem in life, generates a revolutionary change in the life of an individual.

The 'I : you' difference is minimized. Islamic prayer does not interfere with the normal routine of life, instead it brings about an orderliness in the normal run of the daily life. The individual has been ordained by God to rush for earning the material needs for the life, immediately after the prayer is over so as not to grow idle in the name of spirituality and fall on the mercy of others for his material needs. He has to rush for the lawful earnings as he had rushed for the prayer at the call of *Ažān.*

The Wealth Sacrifice

Žakāt (poor-rate) and *Khumus* (fifth part of wealth sacrifice) are separately numbered but because of their similar nature and objective we have preferred to discuss them jointly as the obligations of the Faith. *Žakāt* is 2.5 per cent annual tax on the capital or total assets for the poor, and *Khumus* is the 1/5 of the annual tax on net profit.

While mentioning of the articles, it may be pointed out that these two articles of Religious Obligations namely *Žakāt* and *Khumus* have to be included in the surplus gains of the material capital made during the year. Although in the Sunni *Khumus* does not figure as a separate and regular article but with the Shi'is, *Khumus* is as much an obligatory article as the *Žakāt*. The only difference between the two lies in their respective amounts.

In the holy Qur'an *Žakāt* has been mentioned frequently side by side with obligatory Prayer, so, here as well, the *Žakāt* is being taken up just after the brief introduction of *Namāž*. *Žakāt* was obligatory on the foregoing communities and is also obligatory on the Muslim community, *vide* the Qur'anic verses in this context: Talking about Abraham, Qur'an says:

> "And revealed We unto them the doing of good, and the establishing of prayer, and the giving of alms, and (*only*) unto Us did they worship." (*Qur'an: 21/73*)

About Ishmael, Qur'an informs:

> "And he was enjoining on his family, prayer and charity and was he unto his Lord well-pleasing." (*Qur'an: 19/55*)

Referring to the disobedient community of Moses, Qur'an says:

> "Said He My chastisement will I afflict with it, whomsoever, I will and My mercy embraceth unto all things, therefore soon will I ordain it (*particularly*) for those who guard (*against evil*) and pay the poor-rate and those who believe in Our signs."
> (*Qur'an: 7/156*)

Jesus Christ in his praise to God says in Qur'an:

> "And He hath made me blessed wherever I be and He hath enjoined on me prayer and poor-rate so long as I live!" (*Qur'an: 19/31*)

And Muslims have been ordered:

> "Establish ye the prayer and give ye away the poor-rate bow ye down (*while ye*) with those who bow down (*prayering*)." (*Qur'an: 2/43*)

Further, in the forthcoming verse of the same chapter, Qur'an enumerates the people whom *Žakāt* should be paid:

> "And giveth his wealth out of love for Him to the kindred and the orphans and the poor and the wayfarer and the needy and for those in the bondage; And established prayer and payeth the poor-rate." (*Qur'an: 2/177*)

Likewise, Qur'an orders in unequivocal words, the obligatory payment of *Khumus* to those entitled for it:

> "And know ye (*O' believers*) that whatever of a thing ye acquire a fifth of it is for God, and for the Prophet and for the (*Prophet's*) near relatives and the orphans and the needy and the wayfarer, if ye believe in God." (*Qur'an: 8/41*)

Then, it was again stated with additional emphasis:

> "And whatever God hath bestowed on His Prophet from them, ye pressed not against it any horse or a camel, but God granteth authority unto His Prophet against whomsoever He willeth; And God overall things is All-Powerful." (*Qur'an: 59/6*)
>
> "Whatever hath God bestowed on His Prophet from the people of the towns, belongeth unto God, and for the Prophet, and for his (*Prophet's*) kindred, and the orphans and the needy and the wayfarer, so that it may not circulate among the rich ones of you and whatever giveth you the Prophet, ye accept it,

and from whatever preventeth he, be away (*from it*) and fear ye (*the wrath of*) God; Verily God is severe in retribution." (*Qur'an: 59/7*)

From these verses it becomes clear that in both i.e. the *Žakāt* and the *Khumus* there are shares for poor, needy, orphans and the wayfarers. However, in the *Khumus* there is also the special shares for God, His Prophet and the kindred of the Prophet and these shares are not to be paid off from *Žakāt* because *Žakāt* is the *Ṣadaqa* (alm in charity) and the charity alms is unlawful to be given to God, His Prophet and his kindred, the *Ahlu'l-Bayt*.

Žakāt and *Khumus* make it obligatory on a Muslim to check the income and expenditure of his earnings in a year. He self-train himself to be lawful in his earnings and expenditures and maintain a balance between these. He learns to keep away from excessive greed on the one hand and from the excessive miserliness on the other. By including other needy ones in the income earned by his own sweat out of love to God and out of fear to His command, he proves his truth of a real Muslim in these financial trial. By obeying these orders, he earns the credentials of God and wins upon the selfish strains of his self and learns to enlarge his heart and raises above the level of purity and magnanimity of his character. Apart from the individual moral purification, it also improves one's social behaviour. It encourages an equitable distribution of wealth, it affords the poor to make up the shortcomings of his economic status and it prevents the wealth to from being locked up in few affluent families by sending it into healthy circulation to benefit each and every organ of the society.

The Fasting

Ṣaum or *Rożah* (the Fasting) is also one of the foremost obligations of faith in Islam, to the extent that the fasting has a central place in the Islamic scheme of or modes of Islamic worship. Fasting is usually mentioned after Islamic Prayer. It is obligatory to observe Fasting exceptions are a few. The God has specified to observe it daily for a month, i.e. 'the holy month of Ramazan'. This month is the month of special blessing of the Almighty God. It is obligatory on the Muslim community as it has been obligatory on foregoing communities of the pre-Islamic prophets:

> "O' ye who believe! Fasting has been ordained unto you as it was ordained unto those before you so that ye guard yourselves (*against evil*)." (*Qur'an: 2/183*)

The blessings of the Fasting are innumerable, the most valuable of them is 'so that ye may guard yourself' i.e. the moral exercise of guarding the self against evil. Guarding the self from all kinds of evil is the greatest moral virtue. In Fasting the observance of the fast takes account of the moral strength of his own self, he abstains from eating and drinking, exerts control on his desires and does not lie. These and other similar actions, which are voluntary are put under his control so that he might earn the pleasure of his Lord by strictly following his command. He spends a whole month leading a life of piety for at least 360 hours in warding off evil forces from his self. In this period the observer of the fasts makes full use of the opportunity of exercising moral and spiritual discipline on his ego. This standard of moral restraint enables him to secure an evil-free and promising future.

Fasting involves one in the first hand experience of the pangs of thirst and hunger so that if ever a hungry or thirsty man appears before him and begs of his mercy, his own experience of the thirst and hunger never allows him to refuse to help, and if he refuses, it means he is still lacking in the proper training to be compassionate towards the poor and he has not utilized the spirit of fasting as he ought to have utilized.

The Pilgrimage

Ḥajj (the Pilgrimage) in the Islamic modes of worship, is an obligation which has to be fulfilled once in the lifetime, provided he is in good health, financially capable to meet the expenses involved in the *Ḥajj*, and also has enough means to sustain the living of other members of his family during his absence from his home. If he fulfils all these conditions, he is bound to abide by the general call for the *Ḥajj*, which was made by Abraham at the command of God, the Exalted:

> "And proclaim thou unto the people the Pilgrimage (*Ḥajj*)! They will come unto thee on foot and on lean camel, coming from every remote (*high*) way. That they may witness the advantages unto them." (*Qur'an: 22/27-28*)

The rites and rituals of *Ḥajj* provides an opportunity to temporarily give up servitude to and neglectful dependence on hedonism, caprice and comfort. He undertakes this journey for the pilgrimage to the House of

God, a journey which God has asked him to see in it the advantages for himself. This pilgrimage is quite different from other journeys undertaken in life, the exclusive purpose of this journey is to seek the goodwill of God. He willingly, therefore, leaves his wife and children and home behind, submits himself to all kinds of troubles inherent in this trip, suspends his business and reaches a fixed boundary beyond which he cannot proceed without *Iḥrām,* which requires removing the stitched clothes and getting wrapped with two pieces of unstitched, clean white cloth. A piece of cloth covering the body from neck to loins, another from the waist to the feet. What is *Iḥrām?* A simple unstitched garb, just a pair of two pieces of a sheet one put on the shoulder, the other fastened on the waist, the feet wearing an open sandal assuming a saintly simplicity of body and mind. The clothes, which were on the bodies as they had set out from their homes gave an air of individual pride and social vanities have all been removed and transformed into the uniform of utter simplicity and purity, diluting all discriminations of status and social ranks. Now there is but one voice:

> "Yes here I am O' Lord, here I am, there is no partner for thee, Yes here I am."
>
> "Verily the Praise and the bounties are thine. Yes, I am here."

Now no physical or facial decoration, no incense or perfume, no ornament, is allowed. If one has put on the cloth of a mendicant, one has to be also the selfless and simple mendicant at one's heart and spirit in the path of the Lord of all mankind. A model for peace and harmony for human brotherhood, he is ordained in *Iḥrām* not to hunt or kill even an insect, nothing to say of doing any harm to human beings. None would even help or guide any hunter to his prey. He is likewise forbidden to harm even the vegetation be it just the blade of grass. If this attitude adopted outwardly the innerself will naturally catch the same colour of compassion to all creatures. Vanity and pride will take leave of the human nature. Equality and brotherhood will gradually overwhelm his nature and make to look each other as his brother or sister. The true enlightenment of the God, Universe and the man will emerge.

This is no place to give the ritualistic detail of *Ḥajj.* This may, however, be noted that whether it be the *Ṭawāf* (going seven times around the Ka'ba) or *Sa'ī* (running between two hillocks *Ṣafā* and *Marwā*) or stay in at the plain of *'Arafāt*, until sunset or proceeding to another plain (*muzalifa*) after the sunset or throwing stones on the three devils, on every point of these performances the pilgrim is constantly conscious of the Greatness of God and his own humbleness in presence of His Supremacy. Apart from its being the means of individual purification of himself the *Ḥajj* also has the effective role in influencing the social life of the community, because it is a worship performed in multitude drawn into pilgrimage from all-over the world.

Ḥajj is one of the best means of Islam to eliminate negligence. As if the universality of it imparts the message that Muslims in their collective as well as individual identity are duty-bound to remove negligence from themselves. It provides an occasion for hope and good tiding. While the magnificence of solidarity among the travellers of the House of Unity raises hope in the hearts, the refreshing of the souls through the blessing of the Divine lauding gives the good tiding of the unbolting of gate of mercy. The glory and grandeur of this unique congregation acquaints the people of the Pilgrimage with the reality of the great Islamic community, which transcends the nation, races, colour and languages. This intertwined and harmonic congregation, these tongues all chanting a single word, these bodies and hearts all marching towards the House of Unity and these men and women, old and young, rich and poor, intellectuals and illiterate, all these human beings representing various countries, nation and regions, which belong to a great unit and collective corpus called *Islamic Ummah.*

Ḥajj congregation had been the best forum to address the entire Islamic Ummah from the early days of Islamic history. Before completing the rites of the pilgrimage, the holy Prophet himself had addressed the assembled multitude from the top of the Jabal al-'Arafāt on 8th Žilḥijjah, the 7th March, 632 which is popularly known as *Ḥajju'l-Wadā'* (the Pilgrimage of Farewell). With such a message which shall ever live:

> "Ye people! listen to my words and understand the same. Know that *all Muslims are brothers unto one another*. Ye are one brotherhood. Nothing which belongs to another is lawful unto his brother, unless freely given out of good-will. Guard yourselves from committing injustice…"[5]

The message of *rising for the cause of justice* is often hearted at *Ḥajj* congregation addressing the entire Islamic Ummah that they must be completely wakeful and vigilant today, and timely action must not allow the world-devouring forces to begin a new period of colonial domination over the Islamic world. The ethical degeneration, intellectual distortion and spiritual decline would cause the defeat of the nations and disintegration of the civilizations besides the destruction of the personality of individual human beings. Unity and sympathy among the followers of the Islamic schools of thought and avoidance of sectarian and ethnic differences should be boldest slogans. Scientific endeavour, political liveliness, cultural effort and mobilization of all forces in these main arenas should be atop on the anvil of their call.

The Struggle

Jihād (the Struggle) in Islamic terminology means to strive hard in the path of God. To a certain extent, it has resemblance with *Satyāgraha* (*Satya* means Truth or God + *Āgrah* means persuasion) In both ways it is for reaching a noble goal. In so doing, the *Satyagrahī* and the *Jihādī* both encounter Truth in the absolute. By their refusal to submit to the wrong or to cooperate with it in any way, they assert the Truth. But during the confrontation with the evil, the *Satyāgrahī* must adhere to *Ahimsā* (non-violence), the Hindu philosophy of *Bhagavadgītā*. It was introduced and practiced by Mahatma Gandhi (d. 1950) and was the guiding philosophy for Indian people in their fight against British imperialism. Mahatma Gandhi in 1920 had remarkably said – If he has the option between the violence and the cowardness, his natural choice shall be the violence![6] According to Gandhian scholar R.P. Misra:

> "In the armory of the modern civilization, there is no way to gain *swarāj* (independence) except by violent rebellion or terrorism. A small group of people who considers itself the custodian of truth takes up arms and forces the majority to accept its views. The disease becomes contagious and many more aggrieved groups with imaginary or real grievances against the majority emerge and kill the people just to terrorize the government to accept their demands. Non-violence is a weapon that not only gives lasting results but also transforms the opposite party into a friend."[7]

Jihād is the part of Islamic philosophy, in which to employ violence is the last resort, if all other attempts of persuasion have failed. The blind, savage terrorism, which the Big-Powers call *Islamic Jihād* is being used as an excuse for the perpetuation of the military occupation of Islamic countries. It is always rejected and condemned according to Islamic teaching and thought. However, many so-called Muslim politicians and rulers in the name of *Jihād* have also been perpetuating awful forms of aggressions, killing and devastations which have earned considerable notoriety for this noble religion. As a result, Islam, which basically nourishes the sentiments of peace, charity, equality and brotherhood, began to be condemned as a religion spread by sword. So it is highly relevant to elucidate the Islamic standpoint with regard to *Jihād*.

In Islam, there are three forms of *Jihād* – (i) Internal, (ii) Propagator and (iii) with Armed forces. In all these forms of *Jihād*, there is an obligatory condition that each *Jihād* should be exclusively in the path of God for the sake of God and in no case for the sake of self-oriented objectives. If the *Jihād* is truly for the sake of God, the dominant motive would be to lay life to be able to earn immortality. Qur'an says:

> "And say not of those who are slain in the path of God that they are dead; Nay (*they are*) living but ye perceive not." (*Qur'an: 2 /154*)

Internal *Jihād* means to fight evil forces within your soul and self or among the members of Muslim society, which implode the inflow of virtues. This *Jihād* has nothing to do with the followers of other faiths. This is a personal, internal and among the Muslims themselves. This moral battle against the individual's own vices and those of the Muslim's own community is technically termed as *Nahy-anil-Munkir* (forbidding vice from the individual and social ethos). Qur'an has repeatedly instructed about it:

> "What! Enjoin ye upon the people righteousness and ye forget your ownselves ?" (*Qur'an: 2 / 44*)
>
> "Enjoin the good and forbid the evil." (*Qur'an: 31/17*)
>
> "And the believer men and the believer women, they are guardians to one of another; they enjoin good and forbid evil." (*Qur'an: 9/71*)

Together with this, observing and safeguarding for some virtues is also *Jihād*. An old man came to the holy Prophet to offer himself as a fighter to serve Islam and sought the permission of the Prophet to join the army. The Prophet asked if he had his parents. The old man replied, 'Yes, I do have O' holy Prophet!' The Prophet ordered him, 'Go back and serve your parents, this is your *Jihād*.'[8]

Imām 'Ali said that he had heard the Prophet say:

> "Whoever helps the members of his family in subsistence and provisions of essential things of life, God enters his name in the list of martyrs."[9]

Imām Ja'far aṣ-Ṣādiq said to 'Abdu'llāh-bin-Jandab while instructing him:

> "For a believer going out for a right job is as good as running between *Ṣafā* and *Marwā,* a ritual in the performance of *Ḥajj*. And to fulfil the need of a needy believer is as good as to have fought in Badr and Uḥad, the two great battle of Islam in which he were bathed in blood."[10]

The second form of *Jihād* is propagatory. In this *Jihād*, there is no relevance of armed struggle as the use of arms is synonymous with moral defeat. In this *Jihād* the opponents have to be prevailed with irrefutable argument based on reasons and logic. Sometimes only logical persuasion works and sometimes righteousness, sweet conduct, devoted love, benefaction and politeness in speech wins the opponent into the folds of Islam. The best example of this is the peace treaty held between the disbelievers of the Meccan Quraysh and the holy Prophet Muḥammad, which is known in Islamic history as *Ṣulhu'l-Ḥudaybia* (the treaty of Ḥudaybia) and which is called by the Qur'an as *the Manifest Victory*:

> "Verily We have caused victory for thee a manifest victory." (*Qur'an: 48 /1*)

There are clear instructions in Qur'an for the propagatory *Jihād*, vide the verses:

> "And they (*the infidels*) shall bring not unto thee any argument, but We shall bring unto thee the truth and the best explanation." (*Qur'an: 25/33*)
>
> "And call thou unto the way of thy Lord with wisdom and kindly exhortation and dispute with them in the manner which is the best." (*Qur'an: 16/125*)
>
> "Therefore declare thou (*O' Our Apostle Muḥammad!*) openly what thou art bidden, and turn thou away from the polytheists. Verily We are sufficient for thee against the scoffers." (*Qur'an: 15/94-95*)

In course of the arguments, the opponents may speak words which may be very hurting and offensive, so the Qur'an consoles:

> "And (*Recall thou O' Our Apostle Muḥammad!*) when God took a pledge from those who were given the Book; Ye shall surely make it known to mankind and ye shall not hide it; then they cast it behind their backs and brought therewith a small price; How bad (*then is what they purchase*)." (*Qur'an: 3/186*)

Bearing these verses in mind, it becomes clear that there is special significance of the propagatory *Jihād* in Islam, in which the opposite group have to be satisfied with rational, sound logic and beautiful preaching. Securing victory through knowledge and enlightenment is highly advocated and preferred to an armed victory. Because there are moments of greater patience and hardships in the path of this victory. It is just possible on certain accessions that the opponents may adopt derogatory and offending ways. But the true Muslim is required not to get infuriated by it but he is enjoined to put across his points beautifully and convince with a serious and tolerant politeness. This mode of religious propagation has been called the path of purity in the doctrine of Islam, which leaves a lasting impression on the human hearts.

The third form of *Jihād* is the armed struggle. The abuse of this form by some Muslims has been the cause for Islam being constantly put to blame. This blame, however, cannot be dismissed although as some Muslim armies, generals and kings have definitely carried out merciless acts of oppression. Some of them plundered lands while some have captured territories solely to establish their kingdoms and expand their powers. Nevertheless, looked at with the eyes of justice, it might have been a deterrent act of some Muslims, but the blame should not be put to the Muslims in general or to the Islam in particular.

There is no doubt that in Islam there is not only the sanction for the armed *Jihād* but it has also been glorified, because it takes the courage to lay one's life and wealth for the sake and cause of God. In case one fights a battle to fulfil his own ambition or, in case he is an aggressor who captures to rule a country, his armed struggle can never be called *Jihād*. This may only he ascribed to his own act and an individual conduct having nothing to do with Islam. However, the painful fact is that some groups of Muslims, under the cover of *Jihād*, have committed so heinous acts of aggression, expansion and devastation that the world at large is apt to construe it to be an Islamic armed struggle or *Jihād*. As a result of this unfortunate abuse of the sanctity of *Jihād*, Islam has been blamed to have been spread with sword. All the same, the fact is that Islam, among the world religions, is the only religion whose very name is indicative of peace, security, understanding and good-will.

In Islam it is only the last resort, when out of compulsion armed struggle is prescribed when all channels of peaceful propagation have exhausted and yet there is no permission for aggressive attack unless the Muslims are attacked for no wrong on their part and their genteel tolerance is taken to be their weakness and no mode of peaceful defence is left except the mode of armed confrontation, then, of course Islam allows the swords to be raised in self-defence as *al-Itmāmu'l-Hujjat* (the last resolve), the justification for an armed struggle has emerged, vide the Qur'anic verses:

> "And fight in the cause of God (*against*) those who fight against you but be not aggressive; for verily God loveth not the aggressors." (*Qur'an: 2/190*)
>
> "Permission (*to fight*) is given unto those upon whom war is made for they have been oppressed, and verily, to help them, God is Most Potent." (*Qur'an: 22/39*)

The armed struggle has been called *Qittāl* (killing) in Qur'an, and God has protected the lives of the believers with it:

> "And God turned back those who disbelieve in their rage, they achieved not any advantage; and God did suffice for the believers in fighting; for God is All-Strong, Almighty." (*Qur'an: 33/25*)

In the explanation of this verse, it has been said that this refers to the battle of *Khandaq* (Ditch) in the year 624 in which Muslims were saved by the sword of Imām 'Ali whose single sroke of sword averted the horrible danger by which Muslims were about to be engulfed along with their families at Medina. This stroke therefore was called to carry more weight than the entire weight of the worships made on earth and heaven.[11]

In Islam the unavoidable killing for a just cause has not been prohibited, because the armed defence and the fear of life associated with it curbs and checks the impulse of anarchy and sedition. Qur'an says:

> "Sedition and persecution is worse than killing." (*Qur'an: 2/191*)

An another place, it has been said:

> "And fight them on until there is no more persecution and religion be only for God, but if they cease, then there should be no hostility save against the aggressors." (*Qur'an: 2/193*)

Regarding the expression 'and religion be only for God' in the above verse, it would not be right to interpret that Islam has permitted to launch armed battle for the propagation or establishment of the religion of God. Islam has allowed the armed battle for curbing the persecution, mischief and sedition, because they deter and disturb the peaceful life of human beings. As for the propagation and establishment of the religion, it has given unmistakably clear injunction:

> "There is no compulsion in religion." (*Qur'an: 2/256*)

Likewise, giving clear instruction for armed *Jihād*, Qur'an says:

> "O' ye who believe! what is the matter with you that when ye are asked to go forth in the cause of God, ye are bowed down to the ground with heaviness. Do you prefer the life of this world to the Hereafter? But little is the comfort of this life compared with the Hereafter. Unless ye go forth, He will chastise you with a grievous penalty." (*Qur'an: 9/38-39*)

On the other hand, God admires greatly, those warriors who are steadfast in *Jihād*. Qur'an says about them:

> "God loveth those who fight in His way in array as if they were unbreakable metalled wall." (*Qur'an: 61/4*)

The observation of the religious injunctions and principles given above makes it clear that in Islam the basic emphasis is on the significance of an ordered and disciplined life. This order lies in bearing out human responsibilities in submission to the authority of God, the Supreme Being. In bearing out human responsibilities Islam approves no difference between Muslim and Non-Muslims. But treats them at par with each other.

References

1. *Bihāru'l-Anwār*, Vol. 1, p. 44.
2. *Jām'au's-Ṣaḥīḥu'l-Mishkātu'l-Maṣābīḥ*, Vol. 4, Chap. 15, parts 2, 3.
3. *Ṣaḥīfahu'l-Kāmilah*, pp 186-87.
4. *Our Indian Musalmans*, p. 179.
5. *Sīrat Rasūlu'llā,h*, p. 966, *al-Kāmil fi't-Tārīkh*, Vol. 2, p. 230.
6. *War and Non-violence*, p. 141.
7. *Anasakti Darshan*, Vol. 1, No. 2, July-December 2005.
8. *Anwāru'l-Qur'an*, p. 601.
9. *Jāmau'l-Akhbār*, p. 47.
10. *Bihāru'l-Anwār*, Vol. 18, p. 267.
11. *Ḥayātu'l-Ḥaywānu'l-Kubrā,* Vol. 1, p. 338.

Chapter Four

The Universal Life-Order

Man and Society

While discussing the Religious Obligations of human beings towards God, *Ḥaqqu'llāh* (the Obligations for God Himself), it was pointed out that Islam has prescribed specific Religious Obligations regarding their fellow beings and the cosmology, which has been termed as *Ḥaqqu'l-'Ibād* (the Religious Obligations regarding the servants of God). These are so strict in nature that it could only be pardoned by the person concerned and God has relinquished His power to pardon such Obligations! It has also been already discussed in the previous pages that Islam represents the continuity and progress of the religion in itself and the life-order prescribed by every prophet right from Adam to Jesus. The same life ideology will remain in practice till the day of resurrection. This is how it becomes clear that Islam is the name of life, which apart from being eternal and oldest has also been progressive. Its laws and regulations have in different periods of history been adapted to contemporary needs and requirements, and also the desire of human being to possess a felicitous life in which he can attain to the greatest extent possible the objects of his desire and be gratified. In other words, he wishes a more complete way for his needs for contuining his existence. Since all changes in Islam over the history have been made by Divine Commands and it has been by Divine Preference, the final framework of its laws, which emerged in the lifetime of the last Prophet, it cannot be altered. If anyone seeks to make changes in accordance with his own conveniences, it would be his individual act without having anything to do with Islam. It is relevant here to look into the universality of the life-order of Islam.

The fundamental point of the universal ideology of Islam is that God alone is the creator of the Universe with human being the best piece of His creation:

> "His word is truth His is the kingdom on the day when (*Spirit*) will be Breathened into forms (*Trumpet*); the Knower of the unseen and evident (*worlds*)." (*Qur'an: 6/74*)
>
> "O mankind! Be careful of your duty to your Lord Who created you from a single soul and from it created its mate and from them twain hath spread abroad a multitude of men and woman." (*Qur'an: 4/1*)
>
> "Is there any creator other than God who provideth for you with from the sky and the earth? There is no God save Him. Whither then are ye turned?" (*Qur'an: 35/3*)

Should there be an awareness of the relationship between God and the cosmos, it will help to understand the universality of the Islamic life order, which has been clarified as under:

> "And he it is who produceth garden (*of vine*) realized and unrealized, and date, palms and tilth of various (*kind of food produce*) and olives oil pomegranates, similar (*in kind*) and different (*in variety*), eat ye of its fruits when it fruit and give His (*God's*) there, on the day of its reaping, and at ye not extravagantly, verily, He loveth not the extravagant (*ones*)." (*Qur'an: 6/42*)

More than 80 per cent of Qur'an deals with nature, the sky, the stars, the rivers, the air, the water etc., also various species of animals are mentioned. Islam permits use of nature but only within limits. Trees, flowers, fruits, etc. are to be used but not extravagantly.

The human beings have certain responsibilities. They cannot destroy the beautiful creations of God. Use of nature has been permitted with certain conditions. Imām Ja'far aṣ-Ṣādiq says that before you cut a tree, you must plant a sapling at a place. You cannot cut before planting. Do not pluck the leaves said Imam, because they worship God. Do not disturb anything. You can use animals, as a food, but not in such a way that they disappear from the earth because of the overexploitation. Animal life is as important as your human life. Islam has to be seen in terms of its essence and underlying philosophies to understand its attitude towards nature.

This is the natural relationship between the Creator and the creation. Man like all other things of this Universe, has also been created by the same Creator. He is the Sustainer, the Owner, the Master. Man has the superiority by virtue of his rank in creation, so he has the right to make use of this Universe, but he is not the master or lord of this Universe. He has no right to debase, destroy or disturb the universe. He has no right to alter the life order set by the Creator of human life. He cannot claim to have created anything:

> "Have ye seen that which ye emit? Do ye create it or We the Creator? We mete out death among you, and We are not to be outdone. That we may transfigure you and make you what ye know not. And verily ye know the first creation. Why, then, do ye not reflect? Have you seen that which ye cultivate? Is it ye who foster it, or are We the Fosters? If We willed, we verily could make it chaff, then would ye cease not to exclaim; Lo! we are laden with debt! Nay, but we are deprived! Have ye observed the water which ye drink? Is it ye who shed it from the rain could or are We the shedder? If We willed We verily could make it bitter. Why then, give ye not thanks? Have ye observed the fire which ye strike out; Was it ye who made the trees thereof to grow, or were. We the grower." (*Qur'an: 56/58-72*)

The secret of the universality of the ideology of Islam lies hidden within the innate relationship between Creator and creation. It has been constantly attempted to unveil this secret, but a degree of overstatements have always led to mutual disagreement and conflict. This relationship is not that of a personal nature but that of the Master and servant. Had it been so, the Islam would have confined within *Ṣalāt* or *Namāż* (prayer), *Ṣaum* or *Rożah* (fasting), *Ḥajj* (pilgrims), *Żakāt* (poor-rate) etc. Having performed these acts as ordered by the Master, no other responsibility would have existed to be fulfilled. But Islam's notion of worship is not confined to the place of worship only, it envelops all social, moral, cultural and literary spheres of activity as economic-political activities the markets, including all areas, farms, fields and all other big and small areas of human involvement.

This is why there is no room for a life of renunciation in Islam, because it shakes off the foundation of the serving the family and causes its fragmentation. Renunciation of home and world makes a man run away from the diverse social responsibilities nor does it like human desires to be curbed. It but seeks them schematized within the framework of Divine laws. If human desires find expression on the prescribed laws, their fulfilment is at par with worship. It would be proper here to present a broad outline of the universal life-order of Islam.

Political Order

Political thinkers have made an elaborate analysis of the internal and external aspects of political order. In brief it may be stated in following terms:

(i) What would be the extent of the territories of the state?
(ii) What would be the nature of the constitution of the state – imperialist, capitalistic, dictatorial or federal character?
(iii) What would be the aim and objective of the state?
(iv) What would be the limits of the responsibilities of state?
(v) What would be the scope of individual right in the state?
(vi) What would be the basis of the sovereignty of power of the state?
(vii) What would be the mutual relation between the Parliament, judiciary and the executive of the state?
(viii) What balance would be secured between political freedom and social justice, and over above these, of the state?
(ix) Has any political system discovered the positive answer to these questions? If yes, how the same has been shaped in the political life.

There is no doubt that the political thinkers have explored minutely all the above points but it is also true that they have failed to evolve a solution comprehending all these points and made them practicalable. Some sociologists, taking Industrial Revolution, as the prime source have laid emphasis on economics as the foundation of the state after putting all political system aside, so that the benefits of the technical achievements may be made available to common people. Communists stressed on the government of the working class; however, could produce only a dictatorial state. Democracy, is well known by its definition, a form of government that is created 'by the people, for the people and of the people'. But the phenomenon of universal franchise works in its own way and often it means, doing what the people want to be done then what ought to be done. This is also an interesting fact to note that the earlier signs of dictatorial states are traceable in Kildani kingdom (1780 BC) in which the king was regarded as the representative of God on earth.

Islam's universal life order has not been framed on the basis of questions and issues raised above. Nevertheless, a satisfactory answer of all these questions and problems have been presented.

The first two questions given above deal with the boundaries of states and their constitutions which in Islamic perspective are the two forms of the same question. In the Islamic state, the boundaries are limitless. It envelops the entire cosmos, not only the globe of earth but all the imaginable stretch of time space continuance are wholly included in it. Within it is the world of galaxies, world of stars, we know today or may know tomorrow. Entire creation (not only human kind) come within the territory of Islamic rule. The second form of this question is related to constitution which in turn is related to the limitlessness of the territory of Islamic rule. As the boundaries of Islamic kingdom is boundless, the necessity of limitless and the eternal ruler is self-evident. Wherefore Islam proposes the concept of a state, which is boundless within the sovereignty of any eternal and absolute ruler. His kingdom pervades the whole Universe. Let us look into a few verses of Qur'an:

> "He covereth the night with the day, which is in haste to follow it, and hath made the sun and the moon and the stars subservient by His command. His verily is all creation and commandment." (*Qur'an: 7/54*)

The lord of this unbound kingdom is the sole Lord and absolute Ruler of this Universe without interference of any other authority or power:

> "For unto God belongeth the dominion of the heavens and earth and what is between two." (*Qur'an: 5/17*)
>
> "He unto whom belongeth the sovereignty of heavens and the earth, He hath chosen no son nor hath He any partner in the sovereignty." (*Qur'an: 25/2*)
>
> "Knowest thou not, it is God unto Whom belongeth the sovereignty of heaven and earth; and ye have not, besides God, any friend or helper?" (*Qur'an: 2/107*)

In the verse of Qur'an, it has been pointed out as to what is the nature of rulership:

> "He is God, than whom there is no other God, the sovereign Lord, the Holy One, Peace, the Keeper of Faith, the Guardian, the Majestic, the Compeller, the Superb, Glorified be God from all that they ascribe as partner (*unto Him*)". (*Qur'an: 59/23*)

This is the principle of the Divine Unity in Islam, after which come the principles related with the Prophethood and the Imamate, which have been discussed in the previous pages. Islam regards the Creator, the only Ruler without any partner. Entire Universe is subject to His sole-rulership. The Prophet is the liaison to Him who carries out his commands. The Prophet has no right or power to add or alter the Divine commands. As the command of Supreme Lord has to remain in execution till the end of the world, and the current of the Divine Prophets has terminated in Muḥammad-Ibn-'Abdu'llāh, the last Prophet, the protection, execution and establishment of the Divine Order on earth has to be looked after by the Divinely guided successors of the Prophet called Imāms or the infallible leaders. This principle makes it necessary for an Imām to be present in every age till the Divine mission is fulfilled and justice established on earth:

> "And everything have We confined into a Manifesting Imām (*Guide*)." (*Qur'an: 36/12*)

So the Qur'an enjoins:

> "O' ye who believe ! obey God and obey the Apostle and those vested with authority from among you." (*Qur'an: 4/59*)

The obedience to God, and the obedience to Prophet and Imām are not separate lines of obedience but are different form of the same obedience. In fact each one is the obedience of God Himself. He is absolutely free from error, His Prophet too is free from any impurity. So the Imams have been chosen from the Prophet's *Ahlu'l-Bayt*, whose purity has been focused in the verse of purity in Qur'an as has been discussed in previous pages.

The third point of the political order is related to the aims and objectives of the state. In the previous pages, while discussing the economic disparity in the world, it has been made clear that Islamic mission is to establish social or economic justice. There is no room for injustice and moral depravity in its order of justice. Islam presents the concept of a political order free from exploitation in which peace, prosperity and human generosity find their natural way into social structure. Compliance and faithfulness to Divine command define the relationship between God and his subjects. It is obligatory on the part of the human being to prove their excellence among God's creation by their conduct. Qur'an asserts:

> "Those if we establish them in the earth, will establish prayer and pay the poor-rate and enjoin good and forbid evil; and unto God (*alone*) is the sequel of (*all*) affairs." (*Qur'an: 12/41*)

Likewise the fourth part of the political order is related with demarking the political extent of responsibilities of the state and fulfilment of the goals. Qur'an makes clear:

> "Indeed sent We Our Apostle with clear proofs, and sent We down with them the Book and the scale, that the people may establish themselves in justice." (*Qur'an: 52/25*)

The fifth point of the political order is related with the rights of the individual. In the Islamic political order the mutual balance between the rights of the individuals over the state and the rights of the state over the individuals, has been strictly defined. The individual rights popularly called the fundamental human rights have been kept fairly vast in which no discrimination can be indulged between Muslims and non-Muslims. In the Islamic political system all members of human society have equal rights. The verses of Qur'an being quoted to show here how Islam equitably respects human being as a whole.

Fundamental Rights

1. *Right to protect life*:

"And kill ye not anyone whom God hath forbidden." (*Qur'an: 17/33*)

2. *Right to protect property*:

"And do not swallow up your property among yourselves by wrongful means, neither seek to gain access thereby to the authorities that ye may swallow up a portion of the property of men wrongfully while ye know." (*Qur'an: 2/188*)

3. *Right to protect female modesty*:

"And it is allowed for you, (*all women*) besides these that ye may seek (*them*) by means of your wealth taking (*them*) into marriage and not committing fornication." (*Qur'an: 4/24*)

4. *Right to personal and private livelihood*:

"O' ye who believe! enter ye not the houses other than your (*own*) houses until ye have sought familiarity." (*Qur'an: 24/27*)

"And spy ye not, and let not some of you backbite the others." (*Qur'an: 49/12*)

5. *Right to maintain one's religious faith*:

"No compulsion be in religion." (*Qur'an: 2/256*)

6. *Right of religious tolerance*:

"And abuse ye not those whom they invoke besides God lest they abuse God in transgression without knowledge." (*Qur'an: 6/109*)

7. *Right of expression*:

"And argue not with the people of the Scripture unless it be in (*a way*) that is better." (*Qur'an: 29/46*)

"Loveth not God, open utterance of evil in speech except by one who hath been wronged." (*Qur'an: 4/148*)

8. *Right of holding function*:

"And there may spring from you a nation who invite to goodness and enjoin right conduct and forbid indecency. Such are they who are successful." (*Qur'an: 3/104*)

9. *Right to oppose corruption*:

"The only reward of those who make war upon God and His messenger and strive after corruption in the land will be that they will be killed or crucified, or have their hands and feet on alternate sides cut off, or will be expelled out of the land." (*Qur'an: 5/33*)

10. *Right of education*:

"Thy revelations, and shall instruct them in the Scripture and in wisdom and shall make them grow." (*Qur'an: 2/129*)

11. *Right to justice*:

"And I am commanded to be just among you." (*Qur'an: 42/15*)

12. *Right of equality*:

"O' mankind! Lo! We have created you male and female, and have made you nations and tribes that ye may know one another. Lo! The noblest of you, in the sight of God, is the best in conduct." (*Qur'an: 49/13*)

On the person who enjoys the above rights beside the fundamental duties which have been bestowed on every Muslim, such as *Ṣalāt, Żakāt, Ṣaum, Ḥajj* and *Jihād* which have been detailed in the previous chapter, Islam has laid down fundamental duties and obligations which are exhaustive and obligatory.

Fundamental Duties

1. *Duty to follow instruction*:

"O' ye who believe! obey God and obey the Prophet and those vested with authority from you." (*Qur'an: 4/59*)

2. *Duty to follow the law*:

"And work not confusion in the earth after the fair ordering thereof." (*Qur'an: 7/85*)

"And those that exceed the limits ordained by God, then these are unjust." (*Qur'an: 2/229*)

3. *Duty to defend truth*:

"Go forth, light-armed and heavy-armed, and strive with your wealth and your lives in the way of God. That is best for you if ye but knew." (*Qur'an: 9/41*)

4. *Duty to maintain peace*:

"And the servant of the Beneficent (*God*) are they who walk on earth humbly; and when address them these ignorant, say *Salām* (*peace*)." (*Qur'an: 25/63*)

5. Duty to protect life:

"He who slayeth any one (*man*), without (*that being for*) murder, or for mischief in the land, (*It shall be*) as though he hath slain mankind as a whole; and he who saveth it (*a human life*) shall be as though he hath saved mankind as a whole." (*Qur'an: 15/32*)

6. *Duty to be fair in dealings*:

"And maintain ye measure with justice and do not cut short in the scale." (*Qur'an: 55/9*)

"Verily, those who eat away the properties of the orphans unjustly, they swallow (*only*) fire into their bodies." (*Qur'an: 4/10*)

7. *Duty to fellow persons*:

"Speak kindly unto all men." (*Qur'an: 2/83*)

"Is the recompense for good aught but good?" (*Qur'an: 55/60*)

"Verily (every) promise shall be questioned about." (*Qur'an: 17/34*)

"O' ye who believe ! avoid such suspicion for verily suspicions (*in*) some (*cases*) is a sin, and spy yet not, and let not some of you backbite the others; what! likest one of you to eat the flesh of his dead brother?" (*Qur'an: 59/12*)

8. *Duty to parents*:

"And goodness to parents; if either or both of them reach old age with thee, utter not unto them (*even so much as*) 'Fie' nor chide them, and speak unto them a generous word. And lower unto them the wing of humility out of compassion and say thou: 'O' My Lord ! Have mercy on them as they cherished me when I was little." (*Qur'an: 17/23-24*)

"And we did enjoin upon man concerning his parents; beareth him his mother in weakness upon weakness and his weaning taketh two years (*and*) saying: 'Be thou grateful unto Me and unto thy parents; (*and remember thou that*) unto Me is the ultimate return (*of all*)." (*Qur'an: 31/14*)

9. *Duty to Fair-Sex*:

"And of His signs is that He created for you from yourselves mates that ye may dwell (*inclined*) upto them, and caused between you love and compassion: Verily in this are signs for a people who reflect." (*Qur'an: 30/21*)

"And approach ye not adultery, Verily, it is a shameful act, and evil way (*opening to many other evils*)." (*Qur'an: 17/32*)

"Then marry those who seem good to you, two, or three or four and if ye fear that ye shall not deal justly (*with so many*) then (*marry*) one only." (*Qur'an: 4/3*)

"And if a couple among you commit it (*lewdness*) chastise them both, then if they (*both*) repent and amend, then turn ye away from them: Verily, God is Oft-returning (*to mercy*), the Merciful." (*Qur'an: 4/16*)

10. *Duty to do good to all*:

"Verily, God loveth the beneficent." (*Qur'an: 5/17*)

"And do good to parents, and to kinfolk, and to orphans, and to the needy, and neighbour close to you, and neighbour who is a stranger, and to a companion by your side and the wayfarer, and that which your right hands possess." (*Qur'an: 4/36*)

The sixth point in the political order is related to the sovereignty of the state. In the Islamic political order the sovereignty of the state has been founded on security and peace. If a person believes in the sovereignty of God over the entire Universe, he knows that there is no possibility of any other kingdom or state to exist. So the question of conflict or war for territory does not arise. Nor anyone would have the authority to cause any harm to the Divine Sovereignty. The problem of state sovereignty arises in a state where any other ruler other than God rules. Therefore, the problem of defending sovereignty has neither relevance nor meaning in the Islamic political order. Islamic concept of state and its governance are as follows:

(i) State is a part of the universe under the Lordship of God:

"God, Lord of the Worlds." (*Qur'an: 1/1*)

"Verily the earth is God's, granteth He as heritage unto whomsoever He pleaseth among His servants." (*Qur'an: 7/128*)

(ii) God is sole-owner of Universe and state is a part of it:

"His is what is in the heavens and what is in the earth and what is between them two and what is beneath the lowest of the low below the earth." (*Qur'an: 20/6*)

(iii) State is a part of Divine Sovereignty:

"He, Who is the kingdom of the heavens and earth, and has not taken He (*unto Himself*) any son, and there is not for Him any partner in the kingdom." (*Qur'an: 25/2*)

"God is the authority before and after and that day the believers shall rejoice." (*Qur'an: 30/4*)

(iv) God chooses Vicegerent for execution of His orders:

Number of vicegerents is said to be one lac twenty four thousands, who were chosen and appointed by the Lord. God's first Vicegerent was Adam, the last Muḥammad.

The seventh point of the political order is on what basis the relationship between the Parliament, Legislature and executive be determined. The reasonable solution of this problem lies inherent in the right of framing the jurisprudence in the Islamic political order, which is the exclusive right of God. He has preserved in Qur'an all the laws having given them a final shape. For any new problem requiring explanation and solution, we need not make a new law. Instead the solution will have to be traced in the words and life of the Prophet and his *Ahlu'l-Bayt* in agreement with the content of the holy Qur'an. The executive is also tide up with the Divine Law. No one has the right to amend or add to the prescribed body of Divine Laws, however emergent a situation may appear. Both judiciary and executive have been instructed in the holy Qur'an with regard to their rights and responsibilities or have been illustrated in the words and deeds of the Prophet and his *Ahlu'l-Bayt*. In this respect Qur'an has clearly stated:

> "And pursue thou not that which thou hast not the knowledge of; Verily the hearing an sight and heart all these shall be questioned about it." (*Qur'an: 17/36*)

The last point under consideration in the political order is related to the balance between the political freedom and social justice. In order to achieve this balance, different governing bodies frame various laws to generate political awareness or freedom in the citizens so that everyone may get social justice. Islam has maintained this balance through its moral code.

Economic Order

Economics is a new discipline, among the social sciences. Uptill 19th century, talking about economic matter was simply a talking point among individuals. Economics was not part of the state polity. No economist was consulted before executing any economic order. In the modern perspective, however, situation has changed. Now, economic experts, have become an important constituent of a government.

How amazing it is that Islam has laid down laws on the economic matters and problems on which decision is taken only after a boisterous debate and thorough discussion, 1400 years ago. Light will be shed on some of issues:

(i) For economic development, it is necessary to adopt industry, cultivation or other services to make a living. Any legitimate mode of earning may be adopted for sustenance of life. For all the means and modes to make a living have been created by God for human beings. Qur'an says:

"He, it is who created for you all that is in the earth." (*Qur'an: 2/29*)

"O' ye men! eat of what is in the earth lawful and good." (*Qur'an: 2/168*)

(ii) There must be a public treasury with honest treasurer, and expert book-keeper to keep its transparency:
"Said he: set me (in authority) over treasuries of land; Verily I am a (*faithful*) keeper, knowing well (*its management*)." (*Qur'an: 12./55*)

(iii) Destitute and beggars have their rights and shares in public treasury:

"And in their property was a share due to beggar and the destitute." (*Qur'an: 51/19*)

(iv) Charging interest is sternly prohibited:
"Whereas God hath decreed trade lawful and hath forbidden interest, wherefore whosoever (*after*) the admonition hath come unto him from his Lord desists, shall have what hath gone before; and his affairs rests with God." (*Qur'an: 2/275*)

(v) Gambling is filthy and outlawed. Bargaining based on speculations on lottery are prohibited:
"And (*also forbidden is to you*) what is sacrificed on altar stones (*unto idols*) and that (*which*) ye divide by consulting arrows, All these is abomination." (*Qur'an: 5/3*)

(vi) If the borrower is in trouble, he must be given a grace-time:
"And if (*any debtor*) be in strained circumstances, then let thereby respite until (*he is in*) ease; and that if ye forego it (*even the capital*) (as *charity*) it is better for you if ye only know." (*Qur'an: 2/280*)

(vii) Balance must be exercised between income and expenditure:
"And those when they spend, are neither extravagant and nor niggardly but are stationed between the two (*extremes*)." (*Qur'an: 25/67*)

(viii) The capital must not get accumulated by running into the hands of the affluent few; it must keep circulating in the market:
"O' ye who believe! verily many of the divines and the monks eat away the properties of men falsely, and obstruct (*others*) from the way of God; and those who hoard up gold and silver and spend it not in God's way; announce thou unto them a painful chastisement." (*Qur'an: 9/34*)

(ix) In the Islamic economics, payment of the tax lies within *Khumus* and *Žakāt*, which have been described in the previous pages.

The Qur'anic verses quoted above give a clear picture of the economic order in Islam, in which no one can exploit the other. Everyone to grow his wealth within legitimate means. The state will interfere only when earning of the capital is being sought to come through unfair means. There is no doubt that the economic terminology used by Qur'an is different from that of the modern times. However, to strengthen the economy in the public in general, the apparatus pointed out by Qur'an needs reflection. Would that our economists were to pay heed to it.

Social Order

The edifice of human civilization and culture is based on cooperation between a man and a woman which male-female couple brings with his existence in the family life. For this cooperation is at the root of human civilization, Islam has almost made it obligatory to institute marriage. Marriage must be made on the willingness of each partner. It must be legally solemnized in the form of *Nikāḥ,* in which the bride's free-will is primary. Only after her permission it can be solemnized by *Nikāḥ* which has been termed by Qur'an as a hard pledge taken by the bride in marriage:

> "And they (*women*) have taken from you a firm covenant." (*Qur'an: 4/21*)

Marriage forms a smallest unit of the society the onus of conducting it wisely rests to the male-partner. Qur'an instructs:

> "Men have authority over women on account of qualities with which God hath caused the one of them to excel the other." (*Qur'an: 4/34*)

The responsibility of the husband is to provide for the normal needs of his wife and their children:

> "Let him with abundance spend of his abundance and he on whom is straitened his subsistence, let him spend of what God hath given them." (*Qur'an: 65/7*)

The additional responsibility of the husband is to provide for education and training of the members of his family and save them from burning in the fire of ignorance or illiteracy:

> "O' ye who believe ! save yourselves and your families from the fire which fuel shall be men and stones." (*Qur'an: 66/6*)

The responsibility of the wife is to remain lovingly and be loyal and useful to her husband and his family:

> "The righteous women are obedient, guarding the unseen that which God hath guarded." (*Qur'an: 4/34*)

This is how the rights and obligations of the married couples have been defined:

> "These are the limits ordained by God, (*Beware!*) exceed them not." (*Qur'an: 2/229*)

Both the parties have been instructed to fully respect these limits and keep within the bound prescribed by God. However, if due to some unforeseen factors have made their marriage unsuccessful, they can separate. If the husband has right to *Ṭalāq* (divorce) her, the wife has the right to take *Khula'* (dismissal) to get separated from him. This is how both have their respective rights lent within the limits set by God. This is how Qur'an has set the guidelines on different aspects of social life.

In respect of inheritance, among the parents and other members of a family some shares are for men while others are for women:

> "For men shall be share in what their parents and kindred leave and for women shall be share in what their parents and kindred leave, be it little or much; (*It is*) a decreed (*allotment of*) share." (*Qur'an: 4/7*)

In another verse, Qur'an has described the aims and objectives of Islamic social order altogether:

> "Worship ye God (*alone*) and associate not aught with Him, and do good to parents, and kinsfolk, and to orphans, and to the needy, and neighbour close to you and naighbour who is a stranger, and to a companion by your side and to the wayfarer, and to that which your right hands presses, Verily God loveth not the proud, the boastful." (*Qur'an: 4/36*)

In following pages, an attempt has been made to introduce the original aspects of the Islamic faith and thinking. On the basis of these aspects, the correct nature of Islam may be identified. But irony of it cannot be denied that especially from the period of the third Caliph (unto 656), of the *Khilāfatu'r-Rāshidah* (except about four and half years of the rulership of the fourth Caliph 'Ali), all the aspects of social, economic and political order were not in keeping with the high ideals of the universal Islamic ethos. Although the Caliphates were seen as the successor of the Prophet yet, within a short course of time they deviated from Islamic standards and took the Caliphate to imperial expansionism. The territories of Muslim empire expanded unto Europe. Wealth got accumulated but the purity of means in acquiring wealth was largely trampled.

Islam, in the time of the Prophet, had established a social order, free from exploitation of the down trodden, while the Muslim imperialist inclination often helped evolve a capitalistic order. Islam had offered to make the capital circulate in whole society and market while it got accumulated in few hands. All those Islamic ideals of social, economic and political justice, which Islam had practically managed to structure for a exploitation – free society, gradually got transformed into an imperialistic capitalistic society which Islam had come to abolish. The learned section of this society had the obligation to resist it and present and explain the true universal ideals to the world, but it was divided into three groups – one group started supporting the capitalistic order, the other group avoided conflict and became neutral and sidelined, and the third group took resort in spirituality and turned its face away from ground realities.

Muslim imperialism, having driven into the European imperialism reached to a point, when it lost its own glory and rested on the Western imperial powers, a section of Muslim intellectuals being influenced by Western civilization, while some directly and some indirectly tried, with intellectual vigour to prove that the Western life pattern was a part of Islamic social order. For example they affirmed that Islamic political order was based on democratic principles.[1] Umayyite Caliphate was said to be based on non-religious secular principles[2] etc. These statements cannot be supported by Qur'an, *Ḥadīth*, Islamic jurisprudence and Islamic traditions. To call democratic or secular political order as the Islamic order, whereas everyone knows that these concepts are of Western origin and involve definitional problems and hence, these political ideologies cannot be construed as Islam, which is the Divinely informed ideology concluded thousands years ago.

Our attempt has been to present Islam in the right perspective of its universality as applied to various aspects of social, economic and political orders. This will help the reader to unmask the real faces of those who loudly claim to be the Islamic state in their own rights, whereas these have little to do with real Islam. They are indeed the altered faces of the imperialistic capitalistic orders with the mask of Islam. Our aim is to present original and authentic Islam and make it available to those who care to know the true Islamic order from the social, economic and political standpoints, so that they take an independent decision on natural Islamic order as a dependable guide to social justice in the world.

References

1. *Khilāfat-o-Mulūkiyat*, p. 33, *Tārīkh-i-Dā'wat-o-'Azīmat*, Vol. 1, p. 36.
2. *Some Aspects of Religious Politics in India*, p. 89.

Chapter Five

Qur'an and Ahlu'l-Bayt

The Guiding Principles

The guiding principles of Islam are inherent in the wisdom of these words of the holy Prophet Muḥammad:

> "I leave behind me, amidst you, two things of immense gravity, the *Qur'an* (the Book of God) and my *Ahlu'l-Bayt* (the Household or the Progeny of the holy Prophet Muḥammad). As long as you remain steadfast to them you will not get off the right track, these two will never get apart from each other until they have arrived at the spring of *Kauthar* (the Paradise)."[1]

Because it has dealt with 'two things of immense gravity', it is popularly known as *Ḥadīthu'th-Thaqalayn*. It has 39 narrations by Sunnis and 82 by Shi'is. By the expression 'Until they have arrived at the spring of *Kauthar*' it is evident that the attributes of the Prophet's character are fully and inclusively shared by the two grave entities namely *Qur'an* and *Ahlu'l-Bayt*. There is absolute impossibility for any difference or divergence to creep into the essential nature of those three—the Book of God, the Prophet and the *Ahlu'l-Bayt*. It is essentially required because of the popular interpretation and actual Qur'anic facts are quite different and at some places diametrically opposed, for which the only source of correct information are *Ahlu'l-Bayt,* who are authorities Divinely set up by the God and his holy Prophet.

On the basis of the tradition of the Prophet, quoted above, the following points may be deduced:

(i) The touchstone of the authenticity of Islam consists in Qur'an, in the life-pattern of the Prophet Muḥammad as well as in the words and deeds of the *Ahlu'l-Bayt*. In case there appears any discrepancy, it should be referred to Qur'an and the verdict of the Qur'an would be decisively final.

(ii) Qur'an and *Ahlu'l-Bayt* would remain the active and authentic guides till the Last Day (i.e. the Day of Resurrection). Just as no period of time will remain unprovided with Qur'an, no period of time will remain without *Ahlu'l-Bayt*. The Divinely assigned obligation of providing guidance rests on them both and they are the highest frame of reference for Islam.

(iii) It is obligatory on every Muslim to submit in obedience to Qur'an and *Ahlu'l-Bayt* as it is obligatory on him to submit in obedience to God and His Prophet. Should any Muslim ignore and leave anyone of these two namely Qur'an or *Ahlu'l-Bayt*, he will turn himself out of the original bounds of Islam.

(iv) Qur'an and *Ahlu'l-Bayt* would ever abide by Truth and their followers will remain keeping with Truth while their opponents will ever lie off the Truth.

(v) Qur'an and *Ahlu'l-Bayt* are at par with each other in their sanctity and function, the only difference is that while the one (*the Book*) is silent the other (the *Ahlu'l-Bayt*) is articulate both in words and action. Both are assigned by God to serve guidance to mankind.

It would be, therefore, in the fitness of things to study some issues related with the Qur'an and *Ahlu'l-Bayt*.

The Holy Qur'an

The 'Arabic word *Qur'an* is derived from the verb *Qarrā* meaning to read or to recite. Often spelled *Korān*, it is regarded by its believers as the true words of God, as revealed to the holy Prophet Muḥammad. In its present written form, it is accepted as the earthly reproduction of on uncreated and eternal heavenly original. As Qur'an refers:

> "And everything have We recorded in a book." (*Qur'an: 78/29*)

Many scholars have discussed; whether or not Qur'an is literal or literary. It has numerous dimensions of Islam, including philosophical teachings. Ironically, the most important dimensions of Qur'an, which are least known, its social, historic and psychological dimensions. It is because the sociology, psychology and other human science are generally not treated as science. However, there may be two ways for obtaining correct scientific knowledge of Qur'an – firstly, knowing the Qur'an as a text of Islamic thoughts and secondly, to know its history recorded at the multiple stages of growth.

Qur'an is the fundamental source of the religion of Islam. Its each and every *Ayat* reveals the Divine Wisdom or Philosophy of Islam. The principles, canons, rules and laws laid down in the holy Qur'an are the bedrock of the Islamic Jurisprudence. It is in their elucidation and elaboration that the secret of Islam lies. Qur'an elevates the religious contemplation because it asks its readers to be aware of the rationale underlying it. Qur'an exhorts to rub the faith with bright logic till the faith shines with a rational brilliance and we are firmly sure on the *Ṣirāṭu'l-Mustaqīm* (Right Path). Should one make his faith shine with enlightenment of the true awareness of God, the holy Qur'an invites him to recite attentively the verses of the Chapter *ar-Raḥmān*:

> "(*God*) The Beneficent, Taught He the Qur'an, He created man, He taught him expression, The sun and the moon follow the (*prescribed*) timings, And the herbs and trees do obeisance (*unto Him*), And the Heaven, He did raise it high, and placed the scale (*within reach*), So that ye may not transgress the scale, And maintain ye the measure with justice and do not cut short in the scale, And the earth, He has made it for (*His*) (*living*) creatures, Therein is fruit and palms having sheathed clusters, And corn with (*its*) leaves and stalks and with sweet-smelling herbs, Which then of the bounties of your Lord will ye two (*men and jinn*) belie ?" (*Qur'an: 55/1-13*)

After the revelation of the purport and meaning of this Qur'an, there remains no further need for ascertaining the right path because this is the competent Authority on mankind emanating from their Lord. In it all the clear and luminous arguments have been put together. This Qur'an is the conclusive Authority. Qur'an has it to inform:

> "And verily thy Lord well-knoweth what do enshroud their breast and what they declare. Nothing is there hidden in the heavens and the earth, but it is in the manifest Book." (*Qur'an: 27/74-75*)

At another place Qur'an says:

> "(*From*) Him is not hidden, the weight of (*even*) an atom in the heavens and nor in the earth, nor is there aught less than this and nor aught greater, but it is in the manifest Book." (*Qur'an: 34/3*)

Making it more clear, Qur'an says:

> "And perfect is the word of thy Lord in truth and justice; There is none who can change His words and He is the All-Hearing and All-Knowing." (*Qur'an: 6/115*)

In the light of these verses of Qur'an, it is clear that Qur'an is the source of the real enlightenment about God, the Book which is perfect by way of truth and justice, and in which has been preserved the smallest as well as the greatest knowledge of the entire creation – nothing is hidden from its vision and nothing lies outside its compass. This is the Book which is perfect and final and to which all arguments converge, and this is therefore the authority of Guidance for mankind and no change or modification is possible to be made into it.

There are 6235 Verses in Qur'an and 114 Chapters. According to the numerological calculations the numerological value of 114 is 6, as such the numerological value of Qur'an also is 6. The 6 is also the number of days in Divine calendar, which He has taken to arrange the creation of heavens and earth witnessed by Qur'an:

> "Verily your Lord is God who created the heavens and earth in six days." (*Qur'an: 7/54*)

On the basis of numerological calculations, some other similar features are revealed. In a catalogue of Qur'anic verses called *Mu'jamal-Mufhras li-Alfaẓu'l-Qur'ani'l-Karīm baḥashiya al-Muṣḥafi'l-Sharīf*, Muḥammad Fawād 'Adu'l Bāqī Miṣrī, the learned compiler, has also given the number of occurrence of a word of Qur'an while listing all the verses involving that word. On the basis of those numbers amazing revelations come to fore.

The word *Yaum* (day) in the holy Qur'an has occurred 365 times, and the word *Shahr* (month) has occurred 12 times. The number of months in the solar and lunar calendars are not different, but there is difference in the number of days of a year in the solar and lunar calendars. The solar year is of 365 days while the lunar year is of less than 360 days. One wonders, why the lunar calendar in Islam has been adopted which does not agree with the days of year given by the numerological hint of Qur'an. May be it is because relation of different seasons was possible only through adopting the lunar calendar as to make the months of fasting and pilgrimage come in different seasons by rotation, or because the numerological basis was perfectly sound to be given full accord. In the same Qur'an the number of the words carrying opposite meanings are same. Some examples are given in the following space:

al-Ḥayāt (life) 145 = *al-Maut* (death) 145
ad-Duniyā (present world) 115 = *al-Ākhirat* (hereafter) 115
ash-Shiyātin (the devils) 68 = *al-Malāika* (angels) 68
an-Nafa' (benefit) 50 = *al-Fasād* (loss) 50
az-Zīq (tension) 13 = *at-Tamānia* (tranquility) 13
ash-Shiddah (oppression) 102 = *as-Ṣabr* (strength of will power) 102
al-Muṣībat (distress) 75 = *ash-Shukr* (thankfulness) 75

In the holy Qur'an twenty nine Chapters begin with *Ḥurūfu'l-Muqaṭṭ'āt*, which is a complex of letters jumbled together and have no meaning in any human dictionary. These letters are said to be a mystery between the God and man. The details of such letters are given below:

Alif-Lām-Mīm = Used in 13 chapters of Qur'an
Hā-Mīm = Used in 7 chapters of Qur'an
Ṭoe = Used in 4 chapters of Qur'an
Kāf, Yē, Ṣād, Qāf,
Nūn, Rā, 'Ain and *Sīn* = Each used in one chapter

Some expert of the 'Arabic language has used these 14 letters to compose a sentence which is a guidance-generating sentence, no other sentence has been so far thought out to be composed other than this solitary sentence out of these 14 letters. The solitary sentence is this:

Ṣirạt 'Ali Ḥaqq Numassekoha
(The path of 'Ali is authentic and I adhere to it)[2]

The findings given above come within the frame of conformity with Qur'an, these could be interpreted differently but no charge of an individual subjective opinion can be laid on the person who endorses these findings.

Other areas connected with the meaning of Qur'an are translation, interpretation, and exegesis of the holy Qur'an. Translation seeks to render the 'Arabic text into other languages. Interpretation is not limited to just the explication of the words and phrases but even if the word is clear by way of meaning and yet it points to some specific fact not directly comprehended by that word, that specific meaning may be arrived at in support of sufficient proofs. At the outset of Islamic academics, the scholars of different schools of Islam were given to exploit the limited consensus of the authorities of their groups and interpret the Qur'an in accordance with the individualized beliefs of their group although these groups held mutually opposite views from each other yet the same word or verse of Qur'an would serve each one of them a different meaning.

In the exegesis of Qur'an those words which cannot be comprehended directly are elaborated to clarify their meaning. The best means of the exegesis of the holy Qur'an is the Qur'an itself together with life and traditions of the holy Prophet and his infallible progeny. But in general the exegeses have taken the colour of individual tastes and proclivities of their authors. Those who had the literary taste have emphasized on the literary merits and peculiarities of Qur'an. Those, who had the philosophical leaning have made their work rather a work of philosophy. Those who had a background of the knowledge of Physics, Chemistry, Biology, Astronomy, and Geology etc. made their exegesis to reflect the point that Qur'an is a wonderful record of the manifestation of nature. Those who were preoccupied with historical taste have focused on the events, annals and chronicles involved in reference with Qur'an. The moralists and social reformers have emphasized the ethical aspect of Qur'an. In this way every writer of the exegesis of Qur'an tries to impose his own personality on his work, that is why ar-Rāzī, Fakhu'ru'd-Dīn Abū 'Abdu'llah Muḥammad-bin-'Omar's famous exegesis of Qur'an, entitled *Mufātīḥu'l-Ghayb* (Keys of the Unseen), better known as *Tafsīru'l-Kabīr*, which runs into hundred volumes, it is the extraordinary collection of various informations has become the ridiculous object of criticism and comments – It has everything except the exegesis of Qur'an.[3]

The holy Qur'an has set three approaches to it for comprehending the Islamic realities out of Qur'an. First is *Ẓawāhiru'd-Dīn*, the literal and textual explanations. The second is the logical interpretation based on reason, and the third is the purity in devotional surrender to God.

Under the literal explanation come those Qur'anic laws and commandments which have been given in the simple unequivocal words making it possible for even the ordinary person to follow them. The laws constituting the Roots and Branches of Islam have been worded in the like manner. These may, however, be interpreted in the wider perspective of life, based on analytical reasoning.

All the laws of the Islamic *Shari'a* (the Divine Jurisprudence) may be studied in the light of logical analysis and reasoning. After this stage of rational confirmation of the Islamic laws and principles come the stage of purified devotional surrender in obedience to God. This devotional purity, through rectifying the self and illuminating the heart, elevates the spirit of the devotee to the higher realms of metaphysical origin revealing Qur'anic facts to him and overwhelming him with the Divine Light. The holy Qur'an illuminates the human world with its light. Irrespective of caste, creed, race or colour it invites mankind to reflect on its verses. It proclaims that in its verses, are the most healing source of reflection. There is no contradiction or inconsistency in it. Several traditions of the holy Prophet also speak about the high qualities of the Qur'an. Imām 'Ali introduces the book in the following words:

> "This the book of God by which you are made to see, it lends you articulation and it makes your ears listen to voice of Truth. Some of its portions explain the other portions while some testify the truth of the other portions. Qur'an does not give varying concepts of God and neither it puts its companion on a path other than its own. But you have united on the malice of your hearts and the greenery of this transitory life."[4]

Ahlu'l-Bayt

Ahlu'l-Bayt (the Household or the Progeny of the holy Prophet Muḥammad) is distinguished terminology in Islam for which no correct translation would be possible, so like Qur'an would he used as in 'Arabic language and Islamic theology. The *Ahlu'l-Bayt* is the source point from where the Imamate emerges after the death of the holy prophet Muḥammad as the continuation of the spiritual and religious doctrine of Islam.

Let us now take a brief retrospect of the term *Ahlu'l-Bayt*, which is necessary to understand aright its true significance and essence of the ethical principle involved and embodied in it. *Ahlu'l-Bayt* was not a new terminology but it was associated with the custodianship of *Ka'ba*, which *ipso facto* embodied the religious as well as socio-political headship.

Even from the pre-Islamic era, the prestige of *Ka'ba*, the chapel of Abraham and Ishmael, stood impeached among all in the 'Arabian peninsula. Every religious group and person used to send their offerings there. The custodianship of *Ka'ba* had been regarded as highest prestigious position in the society, which was conferred on the most honourable functions and privileges in life. So the custodianship of the temple of God was an object of great jealousy and rivalry among various clans. The custodianship of *Ka'ba*, the *Bayt* (house) and *Sharaf* (honour) were understood as inseparable, which is now popularly called *Ka'ba-Sharīf*. It resulted very often in combination of custodianship of *Ka'ba* with tribal leadership even extended to kingship.[5] The leaders of the clans were also called *Ḥāris-al-Bayt* (guardians of house) and these persons associated with him were called as *Ahlu'l-Bayt* (people of the house). The leading clans had also famed *Baytu'l-'Arab* (commonwealth of 'Arabia) of which at the time of the birth of the Prophet Muḥammad his grandfather was the venerable chief, which was constituted around *Ka'ba*, and met frequently as the theoretic commonwealth.

Needless to go as far back as Qossay (d. 480 AD), father of 'Abdu'd-Dār and 'Abdu'l-Manāf, from whose lineage the controversies of Umayyite and Hāshimites started, he was unrivalled supreme authority in the religion and polity. After his death, 'Abdu'l-Munāf maintained his father's influence and entrusted the most honourable religious offices of *al-Rifāda* and *al-Sikāya* of the *Ka'ba*.[6] His son Hāshim, whose unanimous historical testimony presents his great success and glory in his lifetime. For a short time after his death, this glory was shifted to his brother al-Muṭṭalib, and again shifted to 'Abdu'l-Muṭṭalib. He has been a man of initiative and energy, who enhanced his position by restoring the ancient wet of the sacred wells of Zemzem and was chief custodian of the *Ka'ba*. His successor was Abū Ṭālib, the eldest son, who brought up the holy prophet. He was the person, who was targeted along with the prophet throughout his life by the Meccans. In this background, the opposition of *Ahlu'l-Bayt* in choosing the Divine successor of the holy Prophet could easily be understood.

The holy Prophet was under the Divine Command and also best he knew 'Ali and the wishes of *Ummah* chosen. So he chose 'Ali-Ibn-Abū Ṭālib, the Prophet's words for 'Ali were:

> "Thou art to me what Aaron was to Moses."[7]

So the holy Prophet declared for common knowledge of the *Ummah:*

> "I have appointed thee (*'Ali*) my vicegerent (*Caliph*) and left Thee and Thine. O' 'Ali !, art Thou not content that thou art to me what Aaron was to Moses"[8]

Thus, if the Prophethood could be continued after the Prophet, Imām 'Ali would have been chosen for the same reason. After 'Ali, the Imamate continued and all of them were chosen amongst the *Ahlu'l-Bayt*. This issue is still alive, how the *Ahlu'l-Bayt* could be identified, the Traditions of the holy Prophet say:

> "Ibn Abbās narrates that he queried the holy Prophet as to who were hinted at by the term *Ahlu'l-Bayt* obedience to whom is binding on every Muslim, the Prophet replied, 'They are 'Ali, Fāṭimah, Ḥasan and Ḥusain."[9]

Sa'd-bin-Waqāṣ says that the holy Prophet sent for 'Ali, Fāṭimah, Ḥasan and Ḥusain and as they appeared, he addressed God saying, "O Allāh, verily these are my *Ahlu'l-Bayt*."[10]

These traditions have been repeatedly quoted by several narrators.

Qur'an and *Ahlu'l-Bayt* are inseparably unified, one illustrates the other in words and action. If found any difference between them as quoted earlier, Imām Ja'far aṣ-Ṣādiq pointed out – Confirm the authenticity of our statement to the norms of the holy Qur'an, if they agree with Qur'an, take them and if not, toss them on the face of their narrator, asserting that our Imam cannot say so.[11]

In order to understand it more closely and clearly, it would be pertinent to observe those verses of Qur'an, which are revealed in the praise of *Ahlu'l-Bayt*. The minimum number of such verses has been told to be about 300.[12] It is not practically possible here to quote all of these verses in the short space of this book, only forty well known verses of holy Qur'an are being quoted with necessary commentaries on each of them. There is a amazing Tradition that if a person memorizes forty Traditions shall be placed amongst the scholar on the day of Resurrection and the holy Prophet will recommend his case.[13]

Here, forty holy Qur'anic verses along with the Traditions are mentioned for memorizing the same. Keeping in view the authenticity and acceptability by Shi'is and Sunnis both the references of most revered scholars and theologists of the respective sects are being made along with their Qur'anic exegesis:

1. "Verily, verily God intendeth but to keep off from you (*every kind of*) uncleanliness O' ye *Ahlu'l-Bayt* (the People of the House), and purify you (*with*) through purification." (*Qur'an: 33/33*)

   In the explication of the above verse many narrators of traditions including *Umhātu'l-Mūminīn* (wives of the Prophet) Umm Salmah and 'Ā'isha and the Sa'd-bin-Waqāṣ, Abū Sa'īd Khużrī, Wāthqa-bin-Asqa', Ma'qal-bin-Yasa', Anas-bin-Mālik, Aḥmad-bin-Ḥanbal, Ibn 'Abbās and Abu'l-Ḥamrah, Aḥmad Tirmizī, Ibn Shībah, Ibn Jarīr Ṭabarī, Abū Ḥātim, al-Ḥākim, Baqīhī, Daylāmī, Ibn Abī Shibah, Jalālu'd-Dīn Suyūtī etc, all most revered names in Sunni scholars have strongly asserted that the term *Ahlu'l-Bayt* specifically refers to 'Ali, Fāṭimah aż-Żahrah, Ḥasan and Ḥusain.[14]

2. "Verily God and His angels bless the Prophet ! O' ye who believe ! send ye blessings on him and ye greet him with a salutation worthy of the respect (*due to him*)". (*Qur'an: 33/56*)

   In this verse, the believers are enjoined upon to send their blessings to greet him with salutation worthy of the respect. The phrase 'worthy of the respect' has been clarified by the Prophet himself who said that this praise asks you to include my *Ahlu'l-Bayt* in your greetings to me. To send blessing and greet *Ahlu'l-Bayt* along with the Prophet is not only the part and parcel of the daily prayers, without which all prayers will be void[15], but the person shall be condemned to Hell.[16] There is complete unanimity over the fact that the above verse of the holy Qur'an relates to the *Ahlu'l-Bayt.*[17]

3. "And unto him who disputeth with thee therein after the knowledge hath come unto thee, Say! (*O' Our Apostle Muḥammad!*) (*Unto them*), Come ye, let us summon our sons, and (*ye summon*) your sons, and (*we summon*) our women and (*ye summon*) your women and (*we summon*) ourselves and (*ye*) yourselves and then let us invoke and lay the curse of God on the liars !" (*Qur'an: 3/60*)

   This verse refers to the event of *'Mubāhila'* (the spiritual contest) which took place in the year 631 against the Christians of Najrān. A deputation of sixty Christians came to the Prophet and discussed about the personality of Jesus as the son of God, when the Christians did not agree to any amount of reasoning, then this verse was revealed enjoining upon the Prophet to take

Ḥasan and Ḥusain in places of his sons and Fāṭimah aż-Żahrah in place of his women and 'Ali in place of his self and call the Christians to the spiritual contest. Although in the verse the pronoun used is for the plural (in 'Arabic grammar for plural at least 3 are required), but in place of these plural ; 'selves' only 'Ali, in place of 'women' only Fāṭimah and in place of 'sons' only Ḥasan and Ḥusain were included, which testifies that only these individuals comprise the list of *Ahlu'l-Bayt*, and besides them no other individual, howsoever great on any ground, was included in the list of *Ahl-Al-Bayt.*[18]

4. "And make me of *Waraṯhati* (the heirs) of the garden of Bliss" (*Qur'an: 26/85*)

   The word *Waraṯhati* (heirs) in the above verse implies that there are characters of such excellence that they have been awarded the ownership of paradise. Again in the Traditions reported by the narrators Imām 'Ali has been said by the Prophet to be the distributor of the paradise, Fāṭimah aż-Żahrah has been said to be the sovereign Lady of the paradise. And Imām Ḥasan and Imām Ḥusain are the overlords of the youth of the paradise.[19]

5. "He hath let loose two seas that flow together meeting each other." (*Qur'an: 55/19*)

6. "Come forth out of the two, pearls and corals" (*Qur'an: 55/22*) In the above verses the expression 'two seas' refers to Imām 'Ali and Fāṭimah aż-Żahrah and 'pearls' and 'corals' refer to Imām Ḥasan and Imām Ḥusain.[20] At several other places the spiritual creation of the *Ahlu'l-Bayt* has been hinted in the holy Qur'an, such as the following.

7. "God is the Light of the heavens and the earth; the similitude of His Light is as a niche in which is a lamp, the lamp is in a grass; The glass is as it were a star shining bright, lit from a blessed olive tree, neither eastern nor western, the oil whereof almost gloweth forth (*of itself*), and (*even*) though fire touches it not; Light upon light: God guideth unto His Light whomsoever He willeth." (Qur'an: 24/35)

Saiyed Farmān 'Ali (d. 1915 AD) in his exegesis of Qur'an has reported on the authority of famous Ṣūfī Ḥasan Baṣrī (d. 728 AD), and Abu'l-Ḥasan Nāżlī a<u>sh</u>-<u>Sh</u>āfi'ī, that by 'niche' is meant Fāṭimah Żahrā, by 'lamp' are meant Ḥasan and Ḥusain, by 'a blessed olive tree' is meant Abraham, by 'neither eastern nor western' is meant their being neither Jews nor Christians, by 'the oil whereof almost gloweth forth (*of itself*)' is meant their affluence in knowledge, by 'Light upon light' is meant one Imam after another, and by 'God guideth unto His light' is meant the belief in their lordship and the love due to them.[21] Nūru'-llāh Shūshtarī[22] and 'Obaydu'-llāh Amritsarī[23] have also similar statements.

In elucidation of the same continuity of the Divine Light is the tradition of *an-Nūr*, in which the holy Prophet has said: "Myself and 'Ali are created with one and the same Light."[24]

8. "(*The lamp is lit*) In houses which God hath permitted to be exalted and His name be mentioned therein, declare glory unto Him in the mornings and evenings." (*Qur'an: 24/36*)

It has been reported by Jāru'llāh al-Żamakhasharī, 'Abdu'llāh al-Bayzāwī, Jalālu'd-Dīn Suyūtī and several others that when the Prophet recited this verse among his companions present there, one of them asked him which house was meant by that 'house', the Prophet replied 'the houses of the prophets'. On hearing this Caliph Abū Bakr, pointed to the house of 'Ali and Fāṭimah and asked the holy Prophet Muḥammad: Is that house included in those houses? The Prophet said: Of course, Rather this house is the noblest of all those houses.[25]

9. "And (*while needing it for themselves*) they give away food, out of love for Him, to the poor and the orphan and the captive." (*Qur'an: 76/8*)

10. "(*Saying*) We feed you only for God's sake, we intend not of you any recompense, nor (*even*) thanks (*thereof*)." (*Qur'an: 76/9*)

The whole chapter of *ad-Dahr* (the Time) of which two verses have been quoted as above, is in the appreciation of the unbeatable excellence of the sacrifice of *Ahlu'l-Bayt*. Each verse of this Qur'anic chapter testifies their surpassing merits. The above verses mention about a episode worthy of attention: Invoking God's order to fulfil a vow of keeping fasts, if their sons Ḥasan and Ḥusain come off the fever they were suffering from, 'Ali and Fāṭimah fasted for three days, on each day at the time they were about to break their fast, a poor on the first day, an orphan on the second and a captive on the third day appeared on their doorstep and they would handover all the breads they had for their breakfasts to each one, on each day, and remained pleased to be hungry and break their fasts by water only. This feeding to the needy at the cost of intense hunger was made purely out their love to God and love to the needy humanity. Then on the third day this verse was revealed in appreciation of 'Ali, Fāṭimah aż-Żahrah, Ḥasan, Ḥusain and the maid-servant Fizza, the great Abyssinian lady, who always spoke in the verses of Qur'an, as reported by the scholars on the authentic sources. This is the verse of the holy Qur'an in which God feels proud of the excellence of the self-sacrificing extent of *Ahlu'l-Bayt.* [26]

11. "Say thou (*O' Our Apostle Muḥammad*): I demand not of you any recompense for it (*the toils of the apostleship*) save the love of (*my*) relatives." (*Qur'an: 42/23*)

Thus, the adoration and love of the *Ahlu'l-Bayt* has been made obligatory on every Muslim, as enjoined by the holy Qur'an. In all these verses quoted above, the *Ahlu'l-Bayt* have been praised collectively.[27]

12. "O' ye who believe! Obey God and obey the Apostle and *ulil amr minkum* (those vested with authority from among you)." (*Qur'an: 4/59*)

The above verse relates to the obedience of the persons who have been vested with authority amongst the human being from God. The scholars have mentioned that the expression *ulil amr minkum* are the Twelve Imāms originated from the *Ahlu'l-Bayt* whose obedience has been mandatory for every Muslim, after the holy Prophet Muḥammad.[28]

13. "And enjoin prayer on thy followers, and adhere thou steadily unto it." (*Qur'an: 20/132*)

When the above verse was revealed, the Prophet Muḥammad made his routine for 8-9 months to come at the doors his *Ahlu'l-Bayt* and call for the prayer.[29]

14. "Verily, Verily your guardian is (*none else but*) God and His Apostle (*Muḥammad*) and those who believe, those who establish prayers and pay the poor-rate, while they be (even) bowing down (*in prayer*)." (*Qur'an: 5/55*)

This is one of verses in which *Ahlu'l-Bayt* have been praised individually. It would be appropriate, first of all, to see the verses in which Imām'Ali has been appreciated for one or other of his services to Islam. Each and every word and action of Imām 'Ali had been in full conformity with the holy Qur'an, His deeds enjoy the full approval of the holy Qur'an. There is the perfect correspondence between 'Ali and Qur'an. If Qur'an is *'Hudau'l-Muttaqīn'* (the Guide for the God-fearing people), Imām 'Ali too is *'Imāmu'l-Muttaqīn'* (the leader of the God-fearing people).

The above verse relates to an incident when Imām 'Ali gave his ring to a needy person on his call while he was (even) bowing down in performing the prayer of God. It has been recorded by many scholars.[30] According to ar-Rāzī, Fakhru'd-Dīn Abū 'Abdu'llāh Muḥammad-bin-'Omar this verse was revealed in respect of the *Wilāyah* (Guardianship) of 'Ali.[31]

15. "What make ye the giving of drink to the pilgrims and maintenance of the Sacred Mosque, equal to the one who believeth in God the Last Day (*of requital*) and striveth in God's way? They are not equal in God's view; and verily God guideth not the unjust people." (*Qur'an: 9/19*)

'Abbās-bin-Muṭṭalib, the uncle of the Prophet Muḥammad, prided over others by saying that he is superior to others as he supplies water to the pilgrims, Ṭalḥā-bin-Shaybah claimed his superiority to 'Abbās, saying that he held the keys of the *Ka'ba*, just then Imām 'Ali passed them and said that he was superior to both of them for it was he who was the first to believe, the first to offer prayer with the Prophet of God and fought in the way of God. When the matter was referred to the Prophet for his verdict this verse was revealed.[32]

16. "Is then he who knoweth that what hath been sent down unto thee from thy Lord is truth, like unto him who is blind (*void of knowledge*)? Will bear in mind only those possessed of understanding." (*Qur'an: 13/19*)

Imām 'Ali's knowledge and understanding is the widely acknowledged fact with both his friends and rivals. There are many Traditions of the Prophet in which Imām 'Ali's knowledge and understanding has been recorded. The commentaries of the Qur'an also acknowledge that this verse relates to Imām 'Ali.[33]

17. "(Fight *against*) those who fight you but be not aggressive; for verily God loveth not the aggressors." (*Qur'an: 2/190*)

    Imām 'Ali's warriorship for the cause of God is the most renowned quality he is known by the famous Tradition of Angel:

    Lā Saif Illā Žulfiqār wa lā Fatā Illā 'Ali (No sword is better than *Žulfiqār* (the sword of double-edged) and No youth is better than 'Ali.[34]

18. "Enter ye the house by their doors." (*Qur'an: 2/189*)

    Here the word 'doors' receives its meaning from the Prophet's following Traditions:

    "I am the city of knowledge and 'Ali is its door, one who intends to come to me should come by the door."[35]

    "When all the doors opening in the Mosque were closed, the only door of the house of Imām 'Ali was allowed to remain open in the Mosque."[36]

19. "And among men there is one who selleth his self (*soul*) seeking the pleasure of God; and verily, God is affectionate unto His (*faithful*) servants." (*Qur'an: 2/207*)

    It is general consensus that the above verse was revealed in appreciation of Imām 'Ali's risking his life to save the Prophet Muḥammad on the night of Prophet's exodus from Mecca to Medina.[37]

20. "So their Lord did respond to them (*saying*) 'I will not suffer the work of any of you that worketh, to be lost, be he male or female." (*Qur'an: 3/194*)

    This verse was revealed when Imām 'Ali and the ladies of the house of the Prophet left Mecca on the occasion of exodus from Mecca and reached Ṣaḥnān, a place between Mecca and Medina and stayed there for a day and a night. During the course of the whole expedition they kept reciting names of God in His glory and Hymn, on which this verse was revealed.[38]

21. "Those who spend their wealth by night and (*by*) day, secretly and openly, for them shall be their reward with their Lord, fear shall not be on them nor shall they grieve." (*Qur'an: 2/274*)

    It has been unanimously recorded that the above verse was revealed when Imām 'Ali, having in all only four Dirhams on his person, gave all in charity, one by night, one in day, one secretly and one openly.[39]

22. "And said they, *Ḥasabana Allāh wa ne'mul wakīl* (God is sufficient for us) and the most excellent Protector is (*He*)." (*Qur'an: 3/172*)

While retreating from a place Ḥamratu'l-Asad, Abū Sufyyān, the chief of the enemies' army, had threatened to attack the following year 624 at Badr. The challenge was accepted by Imām who said *Ḥasabana Allāh wa ne'mul wakīl*. These words of Imām 'Ali were revealed as verse in praise of his perfect faith in God, and the battle of Badr did prove his words to be literally true. This shows the perfect concord between Imām 'Ali and Qur'an.[40]

23. "Who when misfortune be falleneth them, say, *Innā lillāh wa innū ilayhe rāj'ūn* (Verily, we are God's and verily unto Him shall return.)" (*Qur'an: 2/156*)

It relates to the incident that the news of the martyrdom of Ḥamża was conveyed to Imām 'Ali, he said: *Innā lillāh wa innū ilayhe rāj'ūn.* God was so pleased with this sentence that He made it part of Qur'an and now every Muslim repeats it, whenever, he hears a bad news.[41]

24. "This day have I perfected for you your religion and have completed my favour on you." (*Qur'an: 5/4*)

It relates to the famous incident of K̲humm, which has already been discussed in the previous pages. According to the account given in Ibn Hanbal, a Sunni collection of *Ḥadīt̲h* and the holy Prophet convened an assembly of the people accompanying him and took Imām 'Ali's hand and said:

"Of whomsoever I am Lord (*Mawlā*), then 'Ali is also his Lord. O God! Be Thou the supporter of whoever supports 'Ali and the enemy of whoever opposes him."[42]

25. "Say thou (*O' our Apostle Muḥammad*), sufficient is God a witness between me and you, and he with whom is the knowledge of the Book." (*Qur'an: 13/43*) The scholars have said that the expression 'with whom is the knowledge of the Book' refers to Imām 'Ali.[43]

26. "Indeed successful are the believers."(*Qur'an: 23/1*)

Here the term 'believers' specify those who love Imām'Ali. The holy Prophet says:

" 'Ali is from me and I am from 'Ali and he helps every believer."[44]

When Imām 'Ali was wounded during his prayer. He had pronounced:

"O' God ! I am successful."[45]

27. "Said He:This is right way unto Me."(*Qur'an: 16/76*)

The scholars have mentioned that this verse is in respect of Imām 'Ali.[46]

28. "Verily those who believe and work good deeds the Beneficent (*God*) will appoint love for them." (*Qur'an: 19/96*)

Imām 'Ali's love has been enjoined by God upon the believers as he is one of the *Ahlu'l-Bayt* and love born for him generates 'Faith' and 'good deeds.'[47]

29. "And He is Who hath created man of water, and made him related in blood and in wedlock." (*Qur'an: 25/54*)

This verse refers to Imām 'Ali's relationship with the Prophet as his brother and his son-in-law.[48]

30. "And it shall be judged between them with justice." (*Qur'an: 39/75*)

This verse refers to the Imām 'Ali's 'justice' which was personified in him as amply illustrated throughout his life.[49]

31. "What, is he whose breast (*heart*) God hath opened for Islam then he followeth the Light from God (*like those who are hard-hearted*) ?" (*Qur'an: 39/22*)

Ibn Aḥmad Kalbī has recorded that 'those whose heart has been opened by God for Islam' refers to 'Ali and Ḥamża and by the 'hard-hearted' are meant Abū Lahab and his posterity.[50]

32. "Demanded a demander, the chastisement inevitable." (*Qur'an: 70/1*)

When the Prophet declared at Ghadīru'l-Khumm the *Wilāyat* (Mastership) of Imām 'Ali, one Hāriṯh-bin-No'manu'l-Fahrī blamed the Prophet for having declared so without the permission of God and said that if the Prophet was true, in proof of this truth he be chastised by God. No sooner he said it then a stone-piece came down on him and passed all the way from his head to bottom leaving him dead.[51]

33. "And verily they who are the guilty ones, use to laugh at those who believe." (*Qur'an: 83/29*)

Ar-Rāzī, Fakhru'd-Dīn has reported that once Imām 'Ali happened to pass by the Hypocrites, who ridiculed him. Even before Imām 'Ali would reach the Prophet, God revealed the above verse.[52]

34. "By the witness and the witnessed." (*Qur'an: 85/3*)

Hereby 'witness' is implied the Prophet and by 'witnessed' is implied Imām 'Ali.[53] There are several verses in reference to the merits of excellence of the Prophet's highly beloved daughter Fāṭimah, the pious wife of Imām 'Ali. To avoid detail, only two verses are being given here. In the first verse, Fāṭimah, her husband Imām 'Ali and her mother-in-law Fāṭimah daughter of Asad, are indicated for their piety, devotion and moral excellence.

35. "And soon will give thee thy Lord that thou shall he well pleased !" (*Qur'an: 93/5*)

Once the Prophet called at Fāṭimah's home and found that she was grinding flour in the stone-mill and on her body was the sheet of camel's shin, the Prophet thereupon said to her: to be able to earn happiness in the next life hereafter learn to be accustomed to the pains of righteous living in this life. On this came the above verse.[54]

There are verses of Qur'an bearing indication to the excellence of Imām Ḥasan and Imām Ḥusain, jointly called Ḥasnayn, the maternal grandsons of the Prophet and the sons of 'Ali and Fāṭimah:

36. "Verily, we have granted to thee (*O' Our Apostle Muḥammad*) The *Kauthar* (Abundance)." (*Qur'an: 108/1*)

This verse was revealed when the deviated 'Arab Qurayshites started to make taunting remarks on the Prophet for his having no alive male issue, a son to carry out his mission after him. The revelation of this verse was meant to tell them that Imām Ḥasan and Imām Ḥusain were to be announced the sons of the Prophet and the chain of their families would flourish a great deal and through them, the Prophet's family would spread widely to keep going with his mission. The descendents of the Prophet's family are called *Saiyed*, plural *Sādāt*.

37. "And fight (*endeavour*) ye in (*the way of*) God as it behoveth you to fight (*endeavour*) for Him. He hath chosen you and hath not laid upon you any hardship in religion." (*Qur'an: 22/78*)

    The second Caliph 'Omar is the narrator of the Tradition, in which the holy Prophet Muhammad has been reported to have said that in this verse the *Jihād* of Imām Ḥasan and Imām Ḥusain against the Umayyites has been pointed out.[55]

38. "Verily your possessions and your children are only a trial and verily God it is (*He*) with Whom is a great recompense." (*Qur'an: 64/15*)

    Once the Prophet was delivering sermon in the mosque, when Imām Ḥasan and Imām Ḥusain entered the mosque, their feet got entangled with their cloak-ends and they fell on the floor, the Prophet stopped his sermon, got down from the pulpit, raised them up from the floor, got back to the pulpit and recited the above verse.[56]

39. "And neither heaven nor earth shed a tear over them; nor were they given a respite." (*Qur'an: 44/29*)

    Once Imām 'Ali had to pass through the land where Imām Ḥusain's martyrdom was to take place as told by the Prophet. Imām 'Ali said: This is the land where Ḥusain will meet his martyrdom, and in sympathy with the agony, pain and tortures with which he will be slaughtered, the earth will cry and shed tears as well as the heaven, vide the above verse of the Qur'an.[57]

40. "Then strive together towards all that is good. Wheresoever ye are, God will bring you Together. For God has power overall things." (*Qur'an: 2/148*)

    Revered companion of the Prophet, Salmān Farsī is reported to have said: Once I came to the Prophet and found that Ḥusain was sitting in his lap and the Prophet was kissing his eyes and his face and was saying to Ḥusain: you are Saiyed and son of a Saiyad, you are Imām and son of a Imām, you are the Divine

Proof and the son of a Divine Proof and you are the father of nine Imāms, the ninth of them will be the Mahdī.[58] With regard to the above verse of the Qur'an, the commentators of the Qur'an maintain that this verse is about the Twelfth Imām Mahdī, the Proof of God's Divine Order and Guidance.[59]

Keeping in mind the above quoted verses of Qur'an, it may easily be said that there is clear correspondence and parity between the Qur'an and *Ahlu'l-Bayt*. The guiding principles and religious doctrine in Qur'an have found their living counterpart in *Ahlu'l-Bayt*. They are the practical norms and role-models of the theoretical injunctions of the Qur'an, the sequel of Qur'an sent by the same Sovereign Authority which has revealed his words, If the God appoints a man of perfect and sinless character as his spokesman both in words and action, how otherwise any ruling authority would be apt to act as a dictator. The Prophet's life, a paragon of piety, truth and justice, extended into and preserved in the life of the Prophets' *Ahlu'l-Bayt*, is a great challenge of excellence to all mankind.

References

1. *Jām'au's-Ṣaḥīḥ al-Muslim*, Vol. 2, p. 229, Tradition no. 2270, *Jām'au's-Ṣaḥīḥu'l-Mishkātu'l-Maṣābīḥ* Vol. 3, p. 254, Tradition no. 5878, Vol. 3, pp. 256-7, Tradition nos. 5890-91, *al-Bidāyah w'an-Nihāyah,* Vol. 5, p. 209, *Żakhayiru'l-'Uqbā*, p. 16, *Fuṣūlu'l-Muhimmah*, p. 22 *al-Khamāys*, p. 30 *aṣ-Ṣawa'qu'l-Muḥriqa fī'r-radd 'alā' ahli'l Rafz wa'l Zanadiqā,* p. 147, *Kanzu'l-Ummah-fī-Sunnatu'l-Aqwāl-w'al-Alfāẓ* Vol. 1, p. 44 *al-Mustadraku's-Saḥiḥayn*, Vol. 3, pp. 109, 533.
2. *Anwāru'l-Qur'an*, p. 16.
3. *ath-Thaqāfatu'l-Islāmia* (Urdu tr:*Tārīkh-i-Afkār-o-'Ulūm-i-Islāmī*), Vol. 1, p. 35.
4. *Nahju'l-Balāghah*, Sermon no. 131.
5. *aṭ-Ṭabaqātu'l-Kabīr*, Vol. 1, p. 74.
6. *aṭ-Ṭabaqātu'l-Kabīr*, Vol. 1, p. 85.
7. *Jām'au's-Ṣaḥīḥ al-Muslim,* Vol. 1 Tr. 2262.
8. *Sīrat Rasūlu'llāh*, p. 904, *al-Kāmil fī't-Tārīkh*, Vol. 2, p. 215, *al-Mukhtaṣar fī Akhbāru'l-Bashar*, p. 85.
9. *Yanābia'u'l-Muwaddah,* p. 311.
10. *Jām'au's-Ṣaḥīḥu'l-Mishkātu'l-Maṣābīḥ* (Urdu tr.) Vol. 2, Tradition no. 5842.
11. *al-Uṣūl-min'al-Kāfī*, Introduction.
12. *Yanābia'u'l-Muwaddah* 239.
13. *Muwaddatu'l-Qurba,* p. 34.

14. *Jām'au's-Ṣaḥīḥ al-Muslim,* Vol. 2 Tr. 2304, *Jām'au's-Ṣaḥīḥu'l-Mishkātu'l-Maṣābīḥ* Vol. 3 Tr. 5843, *Mushkilu'l-Āthār,* Vol. 2, pp. 267, 323, *Arjaḥu'l-Maṭālib,* p. 64, *Yanābia'u'l-Muwaddah,* p. 87, *Nūru'l-Abṣār fī Akhaż al-Thār,* p. 101, *aṣ-Ṣawa'qu'l-Muḥriqa fi'r-radd 'alā' ahli'l Rafz wa'l Zanadiqā,* pp. 85-89, *Iżālatu'l-Khulafā,* p. 260. *Muwaddatu'-l Qurba,* p. 34, *Munāqīb Ahlu'l-Bay,* pp. 48-110, *Anwāru't-Tanżīl,* p. 341 *Mufātīḥu'l-Ghayb al-mushtahir bi'l Tafsīru'l-Kabīr,* Vol. 6, p. 783, Vol. 7, p. 469.
15. *ad-Durru'l-Manthūur fī'l-Tafsīr bi'l Māthūr,* Vol. 5, p. 323, *aṣ-aṣ-Ṣawa'qu'l-Muḥriqa fi'r-radd 'alā' ahli'l Rafz wa'l Zanadiqā,* p. 88, *al-Musnad:* Aḥmad,Vol. 6, p. 323.
16. *Anwāru't-Tanżīl,* p. 343.
17. *Jām'au'l-Bayān fi Tafsīru'l-Qur'an,* Vol. 22, p. 30, *Mufātīḥu'l-Ghayb al-mushtahir bi'l Tafsīru'l-Kabīr,* Vol. 25, p. 226, Vol. 7, p. 469, *Rūḥu'l-Ma'ānī fī Tafsīru'l-Qr'anu'l-'Aẓīm wa'l Sab'āu'l-Mathanī,* Vol. 22, p. 72, *Tafsīru'l Qur'an,* Vol. 3, p. 506, *-Gharā'ibu'l-Qur'an wa'l-Raghā'bu'l-Furq'an,* Vol. 22, p. 30, *Lababu't-Tāwīl fī Mā'nī –at-Tanzīl,* Vol. 5, p. 226, *Tārīkhū'l-Baghdād,* Vol. 6, p. 216, *Jām'au's-Ṣaḥīḥul-Bukhārī,* Vol. 6, p. 12, *al-Mustadraku's-Saḥiḥayn,* Vol. 3, p. 148.
18. *Anwāru't-Tanżīl,* Vol. 1, p. 118, *Mufātīḥu'l-Ghayb al-mushtahir bi'l Tafsīru'l-Kabīr,* Vol. 2, p. 107, *al-Kāmil fī't-Tārīkh,* Vol. 2, p. 112, *Riyāzu'l-Munẓarah fī Fazāyilu'l-'Ashrah,* Vol. 2, p. 218, *Arjaḥu'l-Maṭālib,* p. 56, *Muwaddatu'-l Qurba,* p. 34.
19. *Kanżu'l-'Ummāl-fī-Sunnau'l-Aqwāl-w'al-Afā'l,* p. 107, *Muwaddatu'-l Qurba,* pp. 84-85.
20. *Anwāru'l-Qur'an,* p. 45.
21. *Tarjima-i-Kalām-i-Ilāhī,* pp. 565-66.
22. *Aḥqāqu'l-Ḥaqq,* p. 171.
23. *Arjaḥu'l-Maṭālib,* p. 96.
24. *Muwaddatu'-l Qurba,* p. 79.
25. *Durru'l-Manthūr fī'l-Tafsīr bi'l Māthūr,* Vol. 5, p. 50, *Anwāru't-Tanżīl,* p. 295 *Arjaḥu'l-Maṭālib,* p. 94.
26. *al-Kashshāf 'an Ḥaqāyiqu'l-Tanżīl,* Vol. 3, p. 239, *Anwāru't-Tanżīl,* p. 451, *Yanābia'u'l-Muwaddah,* p. 87, *Tafsīr-i-Qur'an,* Vol. 7, p. 607.
27. *Anwāru't-Tanżīl,* p. 387, *al-Kashshāf 'an Ḥaqāyiqu'l-Tanżīl,* Vol. 3, p. 67, *Mufātīḥu'l-Ghayb al-mushtahir bi'l Tafsīru'l-Kabīr* Vol. 7, p. 406, *Arjaḥu'l-Maṭālib,* p. 337, *Yanābia'u'l-Muwaddah,* p. 86.
28. *Mufātīḥu'l-Ghayb al-mushtahir bi'l Tafsīru'l-Kabīr* commentary on verse 4/59, *Yanābia'u'l-Muwaddah,* pp. 96, 394, *aṣ-Ṣawa'qu'l-Muḥriqa fi'r-radd 'alā'ahli'l Rafz wa'l Zanadiqā,* p. 120, *Arjaḥu'l-Maṭālib,* p. 83.
29. *Anwāru't-Tanżīl,* p. 270, *Tafsīru's-Ṣāfī,* p. 292, *Arjaḥu'l-Maṭālib,* p. 321.
30. *Tafsīru's-Ṣāfī,* Vol. 2, p. 130, *Arjaḥu'l-Maṭālib,* p. 80, *Riyāzu'l-Munẓarah fī Fazāyilu'l-'Ashrah,* Vol. 2, p. 218.
31. *Anwāru'l-Qur'an,* p. 267.
32. *Durru'l-Manthūr fī'l-Tafsīr bi'l Māthūr,* Vol. 3, p. 219, *Arjaḥu'l-Maṭālib,* p. 65, *Rawā'hu'l-Qur'an,* p. 215.
33. *Tafsīru's-Ṣāfī,* p. 234, *Rawā'hu'l-Qur'an,* p. 228, *Aḥqāqu'l-Ḥaqq,* p. 165.

34. *Tafsīru's-Ṣāfī*, p. 55, *Nūru'l-Abṣār fi Akhaž al-Thār*, p. 148, *Muwaddatu'-l Qurba*, p. 58.
35. *Jām'au's-Ṣaḥīḥu'l-Mishkātu'l-Maṣābīḥ*, Vol. 3 Tr., 5844, *Yanābia'u'l-Muwaddah*, p. 113.
36. *Jām'au's-Ṣaḥīḥu'l-Mishkātu'l-Maṣābīḥ*, Vol. 3 Tr. 5834, *Iżālatu'l-Khulafā*, p. 262.
37. *Durru'l-Manthūr fī'l-Tafsīr bi'l Māthūr*, Vol. 2, p. 179.
    Mufātīḥu'l-Ghayb al-mushtahir bi'l Tafsīru'l-Kabīr, Vol. 2, p. 189.
    Gharā'ibu'l-Qur'an wa'l-Raghā'bu'l-Furq'an, Vol. 1, p. 202.
    Tafsīr-i-Qur'an, Vol. 1, p. 273, *al-Musnad:* Aḥmad,Vol. 1, p. 331.
    Nūru'l-Abṣār fi Akhaž al-Thār, p. 77, *Yanābia'u'l-Muwaddah*, p. 75.
    Tārīkhu'r-Rusūl wa'l-Mulūk, Vol. 2, p. 224, *al-Kāmil fī't-Tārīkh*, Vol. 2, p. 38, *Tārīkhu'l-Khamīs*, Vol. 1, p. 367.
38. *Tafsīru's-Ṣāfī*, p. 97, *Tarjima-i-Kalām-i-Ilāhī*, p. 119, *Iżālatu'l-Khulafā*, Vol. 2, p. 280.
39. *Durru'l-Manthur fī'l-Tafsīr bi'l Māthūr*, Vol. 1, p. 363, *al-Kashshāf 'an Ḥaqāyiqu'l-Tanżīl f*, Vol. 1, p. 286, *Anwāru't-Tanżīl*, p. 125, *Mufātīḥu'l-Ghayb al-mushtahir bi'l Tafsīru'l-Kabīr*, Vol. 2, p. 528, *Gharā'ibu'l-Qur'an wa'l-Raghā'bu'l-Furq'an*, Vol. 1, p. 278, *Tafsīr-i-Qur'an*, Vol. 1, p. 273, *al-Musnad:* Aḥmad, Vol. 1, p. 331 *Yanābia'u'l-Muwaddah*, p. 76, *Fatḥu'l-Bayān fī Mqāṣidu'l-Qur'an*, Vol. 1, p. 362.
40. *Tafsīr-i-Ṣāfī*, p. 95, *Tafsīr-i-Qur'an*, Vol. 2, p. 102, *Aḥqāqu'l-Ḥaqq*, p. 166.
41. *Tafsīru-i-Ṣāfī*, p. 49, *Aḥqāqu'l-Ḥaqq*, p. 172, *Tarjima-i-Kalām-i-Ilāhī*, p. 36.
42. *al-Musnad:* Aḥmad, Vol. 4, p. 281, similar Traditions in the same book, Vol. 1, pp. 84,118,119, 331, Vol. 4, pp. 367, 370, 372, Vol. 5, pp. 347, 366, 419, *as-Sunan*: Ibn Māja, Vol. 1, p. 43.
43. *Arjaḥu'l-Maṭālib*, pp. 84-86, *Rūḥu'l-Ma'ānī fī Tafsīru'l-Qr'anu'l-'Aẓīm wa'l Sab'āu'l-Mathanī*.4, p. 203, *Rawā'hu'l-Qur'an*, p. 231, *Muwaddatu'-l Qurba*, pp. 51, 59.
44. *Jām'au's-Ṣaḥīḥu'l-Mishkātu'l-Maṣābīḥ* Vol. 3 Tradition nos. 5829, 5830 and 5831.
45. *Tārīkh-i-A'imma*, p. 201.
46. *Anwāru't-Tanżīl*, p. 222, *Tafsīru's-Ṣāfī*, p. 224, *Rawā'hu'l-Qur'an*, p. 233. *Labābu't-Tāwīl fī Mā'nī-at-Tanzīl*, Vol. 1, p. 17.
47. *Jām'au's-Ṣaḥīḥu'l-Mishkātu'l-Maṣābīḥ* Vol. 3 Trs. 5827.
48. *Arjaḥu'l-Maṭālib*, p. 91, *Rawā'hu'l-Qur'an*, p. 333, *Yanābia'u'l-Muwaddah*, p. 97, *Aḥqāqu'l-Ḥaqq*, p. 160.
49. *Tafsīru-i-Ṣāfī*, p. 396, *Rawā'hu'l-Qur'an*, p. 456.
50. *Arjaḥu'l-Maṭālib*, p. 96, *Riyāzu'l-Munẓarah fī Fazāyilu'l-'Ashrah*, Vol. 2, p. 207, *Anwāru'l-Qur'an*, p. 955.
51. *Kashifu'l Bayān fī Tafsīru'l-Qur'an* verse 70/1, *Anwāru'l-Qur'an*, p. 1164.
52. *Mufātīḥu'l-Ghayb, al-mushtahir bi'l Tafsīru'l-Kabīr* verse 83/29.
53. *Anwāru'l-Qur'an*, p. 1213.
54. *Durru'l-Manthūr fī'l-Tafsīr bi'l Māthūr*, Vol. 6, p. 361.
55. *Durru'l-Manthūr fī'l-Tafsīr bi'l Māthūr*, Vol. 4, p. 371.
56. *Anwāru'l-Qur'an*, p. 1147.

82. Tārīkh-i-'A'imma, p. 357.
83. *The Shi'ite Religion*, p. 218.
84. *Muqaddima-i-Tafsīr-i-Qur'an*, pp. 87.
85. *al-Milal-wa'n-Nihal*, Vol. 1, p. 154.

Chapter Six

The Prophet and His Successors

The Last Prophet Muḥammad

The last of the series of the Prophets of God, Muḥammad (in full: *Abu'l Qāsim* Muḥammad, son of 'Abdu'llāh, son of 'Abdu'l-Muṭṭalib, son of Ḥāshim, son of 'Abdu'l-Munāf, son of Qossay) was born on the Friday, 17th Rabi' I, in the First year of the Era of the Elephant, or the 20th August 570[1] in Mecca. Expired while praying God in the noon of Monday, and 28th Ṣafar 11 AH, or 25th May 632 in Medina and buried at the place of his death. The cause of his death is said to be slow poisoning given to him at the battle of Khaybar in the year 629.[2]

Qossay (d. 480), a descendant of Fihr was known as the 'Master of Mecca', and gradually of the entire Hijāz. He made various rules for proper governance of the people and introduced tax system. He rebuilt the Ka'ba, the sacred shrine and also erected a palace, the *Daru'n-Nadwā* (the Council Hall), where the transactions of public business were performed. He arranged food and water for the pilgrims who came from different parts of the Arabia to worship at Ka'ba. He was succeeded by his eldest son 'Adbu'd-Dār but upon his death a dispute broke out among his grandsons and the sons of his brother 'Abdu'l-Munāf dividing various clans, their allies and neighbours themselves on either side. The dispute was settled in dividing the position of profit and prestige among themselves: *Sikāya* (the intendance of the sacred wells of Zemzem) and *Rifāda* (the administration of poor-rates) were instructed to 'Abdu'-ash-Shams son of 'Abdu'l-Munāf, whilst the *Ḥijāba* (the guardianship of the keys of the Ka'ba), *Nadwā* (the presidency of the assembly), *Diyat* (the civil and criminal magistracy), *Sifārah* (legation), *Khaymmuh* (the guardianship of council chamber), *Liwa* (the custody of the standard), *Khāżina* (the administration of public finance and *Ażlam* (the guardianship of the dividing arrow through which they believed to get the judgment of god/goddess remained in the hands of the family of 'Adbu'd-Dār.

'Abdu'l-Munāf had during his lifetime designated his eldest son 'Abdu'-ash-Shams as his successor and he succeeded him without any dispute. 'Abdu'-ash-Shams, who was comparatively a poor man, transferred the authority to his brother Hāshim son of 'Abdu'l-Munāf. A man of great consequence as well as riches among the Quraysh. Umayya a Roman slave boy, who was the personal servant of 'Abdu'-ash-Shams.[3] Upon the death of his master, Umayya's family seriously disputed the succession and transfer of the authority to Hāshim by his brother 'Abdu'-ash-Shams and claimed to being the real descendants of 'Abdu'-ash-Shams. This so-called successor of 'Abdu'-ash-Shams, Umayya, is the founder of Umayyite clan.

Despite such unequal, unjust and uncanny distribution, the celebrated son of 'Abdu'l-Munāf, Hāshim (d. 510 AD), the founder of Hāshimite clan, rose on the basis of personal character and had been most revered in masses for providing food to the strangers, who congregated during pilgrimages in Mecca. He also founded the custom of sending Quraysh in two carvans, one in winter to Yemen and other in summer to Syria and so was called Father of Commerce. Hāshim was succeeded by his brother Muṭṭalib (d. 520 AD), surnamed *al-Fāiz* (the Generous), who was also succeeded by his nephew Shayba son of Hāshim, better known as 'Abdu'l-Muṭṭalib. Unfortunately, the envious and malignant Umayyites could not digest the rise of Hāshimites and became their blood thirsty rivals. In these hostile circumstances, when an orphan of Hāshimites, Muḥammad raised the issues relating to justice and equality, the Umayyites felt every position of profit and prestige going out of their hands and so opposed them tooth and nail.

Muḥammad was born after the death of his father 'Abdu'llāh and so was at first under the care of his paternal grandfather, 'Abdu'l-Muṭṭalib, who gave the infant to a wet nurse Ḥalīmā from a nomadic tribe for a better climate for heath and spent some time in the desert life. At six Muḥammad lost his mother, Āmina of Żuhrā clan and at eight his grandfather, so he was taken under the care of his uncle and the new head of the Hāshimite clan, Abū Ṭālib and his wife Fāṭimah daughter of Asad, who bestowed their love and affection, as a result of which Muḥammad also regarded them as his own parents and grew up in their house. Fāṭimah used to feed him, wash and dress him like her own child. Abū Ṭālib never allowed him to be away from his eyes and even after his reaching the age of adolescence used to keep him in his company on journeys by caravans. Muḥammad also responded in the same fashion and when his cousin 'Ali son of Fāṭimah and Abū Ṭālib was born, he took him under his care and he was like a son unto him.

Around year 595 AD, when Muḥammad was accompanying his uncle Abū Ṭālib in a journey, a rich woman Khadījah of Asad clan requested him to take charge of merchandise which resulted in a very high profit. Greatly impressed by his honesty and skill, she offered marriage. She was 40 and he was 25. Muḥammad saught permission of his uncle Abū Ṭālib, who not only consented but also recited the *Nikāh* and made the couple husband and wife. The marriage has been a turning point in the life of Muhammad. As per the then 'Arab custom, minor did not inherit so the orphan Muḥammad had no share in the properties of his father or grandfather but the marriage with Khadījah brought sufficient capital to promote mercantile activities on the scale commensurate with his high abilities. Khadījah has been the most notable figure and an exemplar among the womanhood of Islam. She and her daughter Fāṭimah, the 'lady of light' occupy a distinguished position in the estimation of Islam. Khadījah bore Muḥammad four children i.e. three sons – Qāsim, on whose basis he is called *Abu'l Qāsim* (father of Qāsim), Ibrāhīm and 'Abdu'llāh alias Ṭayyab and Ṭāhir. All the sons died in infancy and the only daughter Fāṭimah servived. Some add names of more daughters, Ruqqayya, Żaynab and Umm Kulthūm, who were daughters of Khadījah from her first husband, other scholars say they were daughters of Hāla, sister of Khadījah and brought up by her. It is notable that while the Prophet Muḥammad has said so many good words for Fāṭimah but nothing about these ladies. Fāṭimah aż-Żahrah, the 'lady of light' was married with Imām 'Ali, who had two sons Ḥasan and Ḥusain and two daughters Żaynab and Umm Kulthūm are most distinguished figures in the history of Islam.

Seen in the socio-religious context of the then 'Arabia, the significance of the prevailing polytheistic religion was that the gods were ascribed power of fecundity or revenge against enemies and their idolatry has been called the *Jāhiliyah* (Age of Ignorance). The most notable point in the present context had been their 'terrorism' and then the specifically 'Arabian character of the ties of blood and family *esprit de corps* afforded protection against partisan and injustice but other clans, especially strangers were, exposed to all types of oppression. They were robbed, not only of their goods and chattels but also their daughters and wives. In this atmosphere of lawlessness and crimes, when the institutions of the *Diyat* (the civil and criminal majesty, and also the *wehrgeld*, the price which a murderer pays to the family of victim, if they so consented) and the *Sifārah* (the legation) had totally collapsed in the hands of Umayyites and their men. At the instance of an energetic youth of 25, Muḥammad, the descendants of al-Hāshim and al-Muṭṭalib and some members of Zuhra and Taym clans, bound themselves by a solemn oath to defend each and every human being, irrespective of the caste, creed and region, whether stranger, free or slave from any wrong or injustice to which he might be subjected in Meccan territories and he shall obtain redress for him from the oppressors. It was composed mainly of four persons – Fazl, Fāzal, Muffazzal and Fuzayl, collectively *Fuzūl* (plural of above), so this chivalrous league was named *Ḥilfu'l-Fuzūl* (League of *Fuzūl*). It was founded by Muḥammad in 595 AD, shortly after his marriage and, which continued unto half a century.[4]

Muḥammad's scrupulous refinement, austerity of conduct and behaviour, gentle disposition, severe purity in life, ever ready to help downtrodden, poor and deprived of basics of life and his commitment towards them had kindled hope in their life and earned for him the designation of *al-Amīn* (the Trustee).[5] The people kept their valuables with him, having best faith in his trusteeship. In 605 AD when Muḥammad was thirty-five, the Quraysh decided to reconstruct Ka'ba but in the course of work a dispute arose among them on the issue as to which clan would get the privilege of placing *Ḥajaru'l-Aswad* (the sacred Black Stone) to it right place. The dispute seemed likely to lead to big bloodshed. Muḥammad was unanimously chosen as judge and his judgment happily settled the issue to the satisfaction of all concerned.[6] Until the age of forty, Muḥammad had gained a widespread reputation for wisdom and trustworthiness. He never worshipped idols which was a common religious practice in Mecca. However, occasionally, he did *Khalwah* (spiritual retreat) in which he prayed and discoursed secretly with God.

About 610, at the age of forty in the cave of *Ḥira* (the Tihamah mountain region, near Mecca), when Muḥammad was in spiritual retreat, God chose him as Prophet with a mission of propagating His religion. The first and unique message conveyed to holy Prophet Muḥammad is an universal command for all mankind in every part of the globe for all times to come:

> "Read thou (*O' our Prophet Muḥammad!*) In the name of the Lord Who created (*Every thing in the Universe*) He created man from a clot. Recite (*thou O' Our Prophet Muḥammad*!) And thy Lord is the Most Honourable! (*He*) Who taught (*to write*) with Pen. (*He*) taught man what he knew not!" (*Qur'an: 96/1-5*)

It is most amazing that in a society which was totally illiterate and only 17-18 persons were in a position to somehow read and write in the entire 'Arabian peninsula, such an orde. of God emphasized that Islam is the religion of 'reading' and 'reciting'. Pen is most powerful tool of knowledge, ignorance and illiteracy has no place in Islam.[7]

After the first revelation from God, the Prophet returned to his house and told his wife Khadījah what had occurred. She and 'Ali declared their acceptance of the faith. Then, the Prophet invited the people of his clan to a party, which has been named by the historians as *Da'watu'l-Žul-'Ashīra* (Feast of the Families). The holy Prophet told them that God has chosen him to declare himself Prophet with a mission of propagating His religion. He also promised whosoever extend his helping hand would be his natural successor. He was faced with distressing and painful reactions. 'Ali promised his humble assistance and the Prophet nominated him for the position. The famous historian Abū Ja'far Muḥammad Jarīr Ṭabarī has recorded the event. Thus:

> "The Prophet of God said, 'O clan of 'Abdu'l-Muṯṯalib, I know not if any 'Arab before me has brought to you a gift better than this in which there is all good for this world as well as for the world hereinafter. God has commanded me to call upon you to come to this gift. Whoever among you will offer to share my burden so that he may become my brother, my will-bearer and my successor among you. After this invitation, all had held a silence. No one supported the call of the Prophet, except 'Ali who got up and said to the Prophet, although I am the youngest in this gathering, my eyes are the smallest, my belly is bigger, my shin is thinner, but 'O Prophet of God I am ready to assist you share your burden. The Prophet, held 'Ali by his shoulder and announced: 'He is my brother, bearer of my will, and my successor among you. You listen to his words and obey his commands."[8]

Necessity forced him henceforth to preach the Message of God secretly among the people close to him, which enabled some men and women to choose the path of those upon whom God had bestowed His favours. They were his beloved servant, and former slave Żayd, his uncle Abū Ṭālib and his old friend Abū Bakr, etc. Some dispute Abū Ṭālib's faith in Islam but it is also evident from the poetry composed by him in the praise of the Prophet that Abū Ṭālib was the follower of Islam. Morever, he was sole protector of the Prophet Muḥammad during the period of insurgency, his wife Fāṭimah daughter of Asad had nourished the Prophet like her son.

At the end of third year God commanded the Prophet:

> "O thou (*O' Our Prophet Muḥammad!*) covered under thy mantle! Arise (*thou*) and warn (*mankind*)." (*Qur'an: 74/1-2*)

Whereupon, Prophet Muḥammad began to throw his heart and soul into his preaching in public. He told them in burning words which stirred the hearts of the listeners to abandon their evil ways and abominations. He explained to them the nature's tremendous laws of day and night, the problems of life and death, the growth and decay and how the creations manifest the power of their Creator and attest to the sovereignty of God. And also that all human beings are equal, exceptions and gradation could only be made on the basis of sanctity in his life. He asked them not to discriminate on the basis of caste, creed, wealth, manpower etc. The Meccan took these messages most horribly and Muḥammad instead of being called the most trusted, honest and the man of wisdom, was declared a wizard, a poet and even insane. Quraysh with all possible hatred and hostility at their command began mocking and insulting him and persecuting the poor newcomers to Islam, who were mostly the humble folk unable to defend themselves. On the advise of the Prophet Muḥammad in 615 most of them emigrated to Abyssinia, a Christian country, from there also the Meccan tried to get Muslims expelled but the king could not agree to their request.[9]

Meccan were sad that despite the emigration of some persons and the cruel persecutions of newcomers, the Muslims were growing in number day by day. Failed in their attempts, Meccan proposed a compromise to the Prophet, offering to accept his religion, if he would so modify it as to make room for their gods and intercessor with God and they would regard him as their king, promising him wealth, power and best of the fair sex. The Prophet replied them using metaphorical language, that if they were to put the sun in the palm of his right hand and the moon in the palm of his left hand, he would not turn away obeying the Unique God or refrain from performing His mission.[10]

The failed Meccan went to his uncle Abū Ṭālib offering him best of their young men in place of Muḥammad with all that he desired, if he allowed them to kill Muḥammad. Abū Ṭālib refused and condemned them.[11] In about 616 AD Umayyite clan-chief Abū Sufyyān, his brothers-in-law 'Utbah and Shībah, Saham clan chief Abū Jahl and other Meccan clan chiefs caused a document drawn to the effect that none of their clan would have any interaction, sell or purchase and completely boycott the Hāshimite clan, because it was protecting Muḥammad. The document was deposited in Ka'ba.[12] The Prophet and uncle Abū Ṭālib, along with other members of Hāshimite clan took refuge in the *Sh'obu'l-Abū Ṭālib* (the mountain pass of Abū Ṭālib) for three years, during which none had any dealing or transaction with them and the Hāshimite did not dare to leave their place of refuge. After three years the social boycott lost momentum, not only because of harm it did to their economic interest but because the 'Arabs deeply believed and respected the kind of wisdom and knowledge that Muḥammad clearly had. Some of them grew weary of the boycott of old friends and neighbours and managed to have the document reconsidered and when it was brought from the Ka'ba, it was found that all the writing has been eaten by the white ants, except *Bismika-Allāh-Hummah* (thy name, O God). Astounded by the happenings they lifted the ban.[13]

The Prophet was again free to go about the city but the opposition to his Preaching was made more rigid. The Prophet Muḥammad went to the city of Ṭā'if, but his mission was not taken there kindly and he returned wounded.[14] But God was kind enough that a group of twelve men, in the summer of 621, during annual pilgrimage season came to Mecca from Yathrib, more than two hundred miles away, met the Prophet Muḥammad of whom they had already heard, gladly embraced Islam and returned to their native place.[15]

Islam was growing and expanding from day to day, the Meccans continued inflicting all kinds of pressure and tortures, striking and beating, insulting, ridiculing and defaming Muslims and also the Prophet Muḥammad. This scenario turned worse when Prophets wife Khadījah, and uncle Abū Ṭālib, who stood like a rock in his protection died in about 619 AD and another uncle Abū Lahab, who joined with his arch enemy clan Umayyites, because of his wife who was of that clan, succeeded as the head of Hāshimite clan. He was only Hāshimite who bitterly opposed and made it his business to torment would the Prophet Muḥammad and his wife picked thorn bushes and strew them in the sand, where she knew that the Prophet was sure to walk barefoot. In the whole Qur'an their case is the only one, among the opponents of the Prophet, who are denounced by name. All the five verses denouncing Abū Lahab (*Father of Flame*) read as under:

> "May perish both hands of Abū Lahab. Shall avail him not his wealth nor what he earneth. Soon shall he burn in flaming

fire. And his wife, the bearer of firewood, Upon her neck shall be halter of twisted rope." (*Qur'an: 111/1-5*)

The only consideration which had prevented Quraysh from killing Prophet Muḥammad was the fear of the blood-vengeance of Hāshimites to which clan his family belonged but now the head of the clan was himself after his head. The Prophet waited for God's command, which came at length in the night appointed for his murder by Quraysh. It was July 16, 622. The slayers had surrounded the house from all sides. The Prophet gave his cloak to 'Ali, bidding him lying down on the bed so that the slayer looking in night think their target was there, left the house along with Abū Bakr for Yathrib. After travelling for many days by unfrequented paths reached a suburb of Yathrib, where the people of the city were going every morning, watching till the heat drove them to shelter. It was a Jew who saw him first and called out Muslims in a derisive tone that he whom they were waiting had at last arrived. It was forenoon of the Friday, September 24, 622, when the Prophet reached Yathrib safely, thus, became famous as *Medīnah'ur-Rasūl* (the city of Rasūl) and *Medīnah'ul-Munawwara* (the illuminated or par excellence city). Imām 'Ali, who was left in Mecca for returning the valuables of some Meccans, which they had kept in the trust of Prophet Muḥammad, after completion of job, emigrated from Mecca, with the family of the Prophet, women and children on foot hiding themselves in the day time and travelling only at night, lest they may fall into the hands of Meccans, reached Medina some months late. Most of other Muslims residing in Mecca, who had been in a position to emigrate had already sold their properties and shifted to Medīna.

Emigration was not just a historical event, it was transfer of a primitive tribe from one place to another, affecting the life. But it had deep philosophical and social implications too, which can be seen in all the twenty-seven civilizations, we know. The emigration had resulted in the development of the civilizations and a primitive tribe became civilized and gave rise to a higher culture. The other most important implication was geographical in nature. Medīna was different from rocky, inflexible and barren Mecca. Medīna was an oasis where date palms and cereals grew and agriculture had already been developed by the inhabitants, which changed the psyche of the immigrants of Mecca.

The Prophet was gifted a piece of land to built a house for him and later a mosque also. It was a free gift from two orphan brothers. The Prophet Muḥammad affectionately agreed to receive the payment of the value. The construction was simplest with walls of brick and earth and the roofs of palm leave. A portion of the mosque was also allowed for residential purpose for those who had no shelter of their own. The Prophet used to preach and pray standing on the bare ground or leaning against a palm tree and the Muslim devotees heard him bent in unison with the soul-stirring words.

The purity and nobleness of Prophet Muḥammad and his earnestness and fiery enthusiasm for the Truth he preached brought various persons, tribes and clans of the Yat͟hrib and surrounding areas, rallying round the standard of Islam and formed the nucleus of Islamic commonwealth. The Hās͟himites of Medīna, later named as *Ansār* (the Helpers) were ready to scarifice anything to their brothers-in-faith, and those who had forsaken their birth-place the ties of kith and kin and every tie of home for the sake of Islam, were later named as *Muhājirīn* (the Emigrants). In order to unite the helpers and the emigrants into closer bonds, the Prophet established brotherhood between them in practical shape, as a result of which they found themselves together in sorrow and happiness and also distributed their properties equally with their brothers-in-faith. The Jews, who may be said to be the third party, had close business relations with the Quraysh͟ite Meccans, extended half-hearted welcome, to the holy Prophet Muḥammad, they were, however, inclined to look with favour on the preaching of Islam on the basis of their faith in the promised Messiah. Now the greatness of the Prophet Muḥammad can be seen from the fact, that he granted a charter to the people, which is most relevant even today. It reveals his real greatness not in his own age but all ages, as no one of that age could even dream to pull down the existing fabrics of the society and take the task of reconstructing a State, a commonwealth and introducing a society based on universal humanity.

Ibn His͟hām has carefully preserved in his biography of the holy Prophet Muḥammad the document, which reads as under:

> "In the name of the most merciful, compassionate God."

Commenced the first charter of the freedom of conscience:

> "Given by Muḥammad, the Prophet, to the Believers whether Quraysh͟ite of Yat͟hrib, and all individuals of whatever origin who have made common cause with them, all these shall constitute one nation."

Further, puts certain norms for payment of the *Diyat* (the wehrgeld price, which any homicide pays to the family of the victim, if they so consented) by different clans, and fixing some important duties of Muslims among themselves, the Charter proceeds, thus:

> "The state of peace and war shall be common to all Muslims, no one among them shall have the right of concluding peace with, or declaring war against, the enemies of his co-religionist. The Jews who attach themselves to our commonwealth shall be protected from all insults and vexations, they shall have equal rights with our own people to our assistance and good offices: the Jews of various branches of 'Auf, Najjār, Ḥārith, Jashm, Thalāba, Ans and others domiciled in the Yathrib, shall form with the Muslims of composite nation; they shall practice their religion on as free as Muslims; the *clients* (the protected) and allies of the Jews shall enjoy the same security and freedom; the guilty shall be pursued and punished; the Jews shall join the Muslims in defending Yathrib (Medīna) against all enemies; the interior of Yathrib shall be a sacred place for all who accept this Charter; the *clients* and allies of Muslims and Jews shall be as respected as the patrons; all true Muslims shall hold in abhorrence every man guilty of crime, injustice, or disorder: no one shall uphold the culpable, though he were his nearest Kin."

Further, there are some provisions of internal administration of the state and it concludes with:

> "All future disputes between those who accepted this Charter shall be referred to The Prophet of God."[16]

It was about April 627, The Prophet sanctioned a Charter, to the monks of the monastery of St. Catherine (near Mount Sinai) and to all Christians, which may be mentioned as one of the noblest monuments of enlightened tolerance, which secured to Christians privileges and immunities, which they could not possess even under the sovereigns of their own creed. This Charter, unique in nature, declared:

> "That any Muslim violating and abusing what was therein ordered, should be regarded as a violator of God's testament, a transgressor of His commandments, and a slighter of His faith."

The Prophet along with his followers monitored the strict adherence of the Charter to the effect that:

> "To protect Christians, to defend their Churches, the residences of their priests and to guard them from all injuries. They were not to be unfairly taxed, no bishop was to be driven out of his bishopric, no Christian was to be forced to reject his religion; no monk was to be expelled from his monastery, no pilgrim was to be detained from his pilgrimage. Nor were the Christian Churches to be pulled down for the sake of building mosques or homes for the Muslims. Christian women married to Muslims were to enjoy their own religion and not to be subjected to compulsion or annoyance of any kind on that account. If Christian should stand in need of assistance for the repair of their Churches or monasteries, or any other matter pertaining to their religion, the Muslims were to assist them. This was not to be considered as taking part in their religion, but as merely rendering the assistance to their need, and complying with the ordinances of the Prophet, which were made in their favour by the authority of God and this Prophet. Should the Muslims be engaged in hostilities with outside Christians, no Christian resident among Muslims should be treated with contempt on account of his creed. Any Muslim so treating a Christian should be accounted recalcitrant to the Prophet...... etc."[17]

Needless to emphasize that if the Charters cited above could be reciprocated by Jews and Christians to the Muslims and the *vice versa*, it would immediately result in global peace and harmony. These are guidelines for every religions of the world. It was because of this generous attitude of Prophet Muḥammad that the religion of Islam spread so rapidly. Various scholars, representing different religious clans and creed came to the holy Prophet to discuss various aspects of religion and society. Prophet received them with great honour and affection, usually took off his shoulders the cloth sheet and spread it on the earth for the guests and discuss the issue. The kindness of the Prophet even for the enemies soon converted them into most devoted followers.

The Meccan infidels were burning with revenge. They made formidable preparation to pounce upon Muslims and succeeded in obtaining the help and assistance of other tribes and clans including Jews of the Hejar, who had desisted from the charter cited above. They were unrestrained in their harassment of the Muslims with the help of *Munāfiqūn* (the hypocrites, who actually did not believe in Islam, but mingled with Muslims) created hardship every day until finally the matter led to war.

There were altogether over eighty major and minor battles, in most in which Muslims had been victorious, amongst them Badr (624 AD), Uḥud (625 AD), Khandaq (627 AD), Khaybar (629 AD) and Ḥunayn (630 AD) were the battles, in which the Prophet Muḥammad personally participated. If we look at the typology of these wars, all of which have been fought in close vicinity of Medīna, it becomes crystal clear that the war were imposed on Muslims and they fought in self-defence. In these wars less than two hundred Muslims and more than a thousand infidels were killed. Mostly of Muslims' victory was through the efforts of Imām 'Ali, who was the only person, who never turned away from the battles. Most of the stalwarts of enemies, especially Umayyites, were killed by Imām 'Ali, which resulted in personal enmity of Umayyites towards him and his descendants.

Kind hearted holy Prophet Muḥammad was grieved to see the war captives corded, when produced before him for final verdict, amongst them was his uncle 'Abbās. The merciful Prophet ordered the release of the war captives after paying a meagre sum as a token fine. No compulsion for being converted to Islam. Similarly, a tormenting incident had happened, when a poor Bedouin was brought by the Quraysh as a captive to Mecca! Muḥammad had recognized her with tears of joy, she was none else than his caretaker mother, Ḥalīmah of Sa'd clan, during his early infancy. He obtained her from Quraysh after some payment and made an ample provision for the rest of her life. The Prophet himself paid for release of his uncle 'Abbās, whose descendants established 'Abbāsite Caliphate and ruled for about five centuries and vexed every type of oppression, tyranny and finally assassination of them. But it was most torturous for the Prophet in the battle of Uḥud to see the barbarously mutilated body of his brave uncle Ḥamża, slain in yaw battle. The wife of Abū Sufyyān, Hindah, had shown the greatest ferocity in the savage vengeance, tearing out the heart of Ḥamża and making bracelets and necklaces of the ears and noses of the slain Ḥamża. The holy Prophet was profoundly sorrowful and wept bitterly as an ordinary human being.

But in total contrast to his enemies, this Man, above all human beings, when victoriously entered Mecca, where he was hunted out of his place of birth and had been stoned out at various places, pardoned, each and every person, including Abū Sufyyān and declared natural equality and brotherhood of mankind. Mecca regained its past glory, the most holy city of Islam, *Mecca al-Muaẓẓamah* (the revered Mecca), centres upon *al-Ḥaram* Mosque and sacred well Žemžem located inside and in the central courtyard is Ka'ba, the holiest shrine of Islam. Mecca is the city where *Ḥajj* pilgrimage is performed.

Now, the mission of the Prophet Muḥammad was achieved and people steeped in barbarism, utter darkness, degrading and sanguinary superstition have been inspired to believe in one sole God of truth and love. At a time when the hosts of 'Arabian peninsula came flocking to join the faith of Islam, the prophet felt that his task was accomplished, the holy Prophet Muḥammad received the message of God:

> "When God's succour and triumph couseth. And thou seest mankind entering the religion of God in troops. Then hymn the praises of thy Lord, and seek forgiveness of Him. Lo! He is ever ready to show mercy." (*Qur'an: 110/1-3*)

In the light of the above Qur'anic verses, the farewell pilgrimage of Mecca could be visualized. On 23rd February, 632, the Prophet Muḥammad left Medina an immense concourse of Muslims, whose numbers are estimated to be from ninety thousands to one lac forty thousands. This pilgrimage had been called by historians and scholars as *Ḥajjatu'l-Balāghah* (the Great *Ḥajj*) or *Ḥajjatu'l-Islam* (the *Ḥajj* of Islam) and more popularly *Ḥajjatu'l-Wada'a* (the pilgrimage of farewell). Before completing the rites of the pilgrimage, the holy Prophet addressed the assembled multitude from the top of the Jabal al-'Arafāt on 8th Žilḥajjih, the 7th March, 632, in such words which shall ever live in the hearts of all genations of Muslims:

> "Ye people! listen to my words, for I know not whether another year will be vouchsafed to me after this year to find myself amongst you at this place....
>
> "Your lives and property are sacred and inviolable amongst one another until ye appear before the Lord, as this day and this month is sacred for all; and (*remember*) ye shall have to appear before your Lord, who shall demand from you an account of all actions ....
>
> "Henceforth the vengeance of blood practised in the days of paganism (*Jāhilyah*) is prohibited; and all blood-feud abolished ...
>
> "Ye people! listen to my words and understand the same. Know that *all Muslims are brothers unto one another*. Ye are one brotherhood. Nothing which belongs to another is lawful

> unto his brother, unless freely given out of good-will. Guard yourselves from committing injustice…
>
> "Let him that is present tell it unto him that is absent. Haply he that shall be told may remember better than he who hath heard it…."[18]

After each sentence the holy Prophet Muḥammad stopped and his words were repeated in a stentorian voice by the Muslims present, so that made clear that whatever was said was heard by the entire assembled host. This practice was again repeated while returning from the pilgrimage, the Prophet halted at a place called *Khumm* and convened an assembly of the people accompanying him and made a long sermon to the huge gathering and then raised Imām 'Ali aloft with his arms and made this vital announcement. The following is the account given in Ibn Ḥanbal, a Sunni collection of *Ḥadīths*:

> "We were with the Apostle of God in his journey and we stopped at *Ghadīru'l-Khumm*. We performed the obligatory prayer together and a place was swept for the Apostle under two trees and he performed the mid-day prayer. And then took 'Ali by the hand and said to people: 'Do you not acknowledge that I have a greater claim on each of the believers than they have on themselves?' And they replied: 'Yes!' and he took 'Ali's hand and said: 'Of whomsoever I am Lord (*Mawlā*), then 'Ali is also his Lord. O God! Be Thou the supporter of whoever supports 'Ali and be the enemy of whoever oppose him.'
>
> And 'Omar met him ('Ali) after this said to him: 'Congratulations, 'O son of Abū Ṭālib! Now morning and evening (i.e. forever) you are master of every believing man and woman."[19]

This wishing of Caliph 'Omar has been mentioned by many historians. Many 'Arab poets said *Qaṣīdāhs* by way of congratulating Imām 'Ali and celebrating the occasion of the announcement of his *wilāyah*. The couplets of the famous 'Arabic poet Ḥassān-bin-Thābit became very popular. And thus, made announcement of his *Khalīfāh* in favour of Imām 'Ali.[20] In the past too, Imām 'Ali was nominated as his Vicegerent on the occasion of *Da'watu'l-Žul-'Ashīra*. This was second occasion. Since the succession of the Prophet is the deciding factor between Shi'is and Sunnis, it has already been dealt with in detail at the appropriate place in the preceding pages. But it should be clearly borne that the Imām 'Ali's nomination as the Vicegerent was not based on the personal liking but on the criterion of merit and excellence.

With respect to being the best of Companions of the Prophet, every Shi'is and majority of Sunnis, specially the *Ṣūfīs*, regard Imām 'Ali to be the best after the Prophet Muḥammad. Books are replete with traditions in the appreciation of the various aspects Imām 'Ali's excellences. In founding the Caliphate, all the four Caliphs, from a practical consideration, were the highly placed companions of the Prophet, who were also respectable for their being in close relationship with the Prophet. But, of them all, Imām 'Ali's was of the highest order in the knowledge, the valour, the moral nobility and the superiority of clan. He had to his merit an additional edge, because all the participants of the battle of Badr (624 AD) were regarded to be distinguished, and he was the victor of Badr and, therefore the most distinguished.

The conduct of the holy Prophet Muḥammad was, however, directly against any kind of the nepotism, he never allowed the family relations and personal liking to be the criterion of merit and excellence. An objective observation would show that the Prophet Muḥammad always kept his relations back from available benefits and rewards and put them forward in moments of fear and material loss. When her daughter Fāṭimah who was dearer to him than his life, came to request for a maid-servant to assist in the hard labour of grinding mill, the Prophet sent her away by telling her, how to mutter on the string of leads, the greatness, praise and glory of God, and told her to say 34 times *Allāhu'-Akbar* (God is Great), 33 times *Alḥamdū'-Lillāh* (Praise is due to God) and 33 times *Subḥān-Allāh* (God is all perfection). This specific muttering, on the string of beads is known as *Tasbīḥu'l-Fāṭimah* (Rosary of Fāṭimah), which is practiced even today after the daily prayers.

In the battle of Badr in 623, the arch-opponents of Islam, 'Atbah, Walīd and Shībah, respectively the maternal-grandfather, the maternal-uncle and the brother of Mu'āwiyah-bin-Abū Sufyyān and also Ibn Rabī'h, the renowned merciless warrior of his time, all in representation of the Quraysh clan, challenged the Muslims to fight and there were among the Muslims the men who could be sent to combat them, but the Prophet sent the closest of his relations namely 'Ali his cousin, Ḥamża and 'Obayda, his uncles, who smashed their vanity and made them lick the dust. 'Ali and Ḥamża returned victorious, while 'Obayda was severely wounded.

The backbone of Islamic economic system is *Żakāt*, the payment of which is obligatory for every Muslim, accordingly a portion of every one's capital enjoined by the law of poor-due gets distributed among the needy Muslims, and would remain ever in practice, the only exception in this law of poor-due is that it has been made *Ḥarām* (unlawful) for Fāṭimah aż-Żahrah, the beloved daughter of Prophet Muḥammad, and her family. It means that the Prophet's own family cannot get any share out of the poor-due fund. This was made so, lest Islam should become a property of inheritance, and the people of Prophet's gynecology should get used to earn their living without due labour. The Prophet used to prefer for his family, devotion to God, purity of self, sacrifice, and a life of contentment in moderation, and he consistently used to pray God:

> "O Lord, the livelihood of the people of my family be just in keeping with their needs."[21]

The last year of the life of the Prophet Muḥammad was spent in Medina, where he settled the organization of provinces and tribal communities, which had entered in Islam and had become the part of Islamic federation. He visited sick, followed each and every bier that met him, participated in a slave's dinner, mended his own clothes, milk his goats and met the people and tell them high traditions. His physical heath and strength had rapidly failed.

The holy Prophet Muḥammad in his last days called for pen and paper which was refused, is famous as the *Wāqiyau'l-Qirṭās-wa'l-Qalam* (Episode of Pen and Paper). Imām al-Bukhārī, Abū 'Abdu'llāh Muḥammad-bin-Ismā'īl (d. 870 AD), the most trusted Sunni Traditionist, has given the account of it:

> "When the Prophet's illness became serious, he said: 'Bring me writing materials that I may write for you something, after which you will not be led into error.'
>
> 'Omar said: 'The illness has overwhelmed the Prophet. We have the Book God and that is enough for us.'
>
> 'Then the people differed about this and spoke many words. And he (the Prophet) said: 'Leave me! There ought not be quarrelling in my presence.'
>
> And Ibn 'Abbās went out saying: The greatest of all calamities is what intervened between the Apostle and his writing."[22]

At the age of 63, while praying God earnestly in whisper, the spirit of this great Man took flight to the blessed compasionship of high. After the departure of the Prophet, 'Ali did not participate in the election in which Abū Bakr was made the first Caliph. Neither Imām 'Ali could do so. Should any one expire in a family, its members are concerned with the funeral rites of the deceased and never leave him to settle the matter of election along with the aspirants of Caliphate. Although the responsibility of the funeral rites of the departed Prophet was equally obligatory on all Muslims but the most trusted and closest companions of Prophet were too keen for the issue of election to heed their moral and human obligation to attend the funeral rites of the Prophet. These were the companions who had defied the command of the Prophet to join the army under commandership of Usāmah-bin-Żayd and had argued with prophet a few days before his death.[23] It was only after the issue of the Caliphate was *willy nilly* settled in *Saqīfaụ'l-Banīu's-Sa'da* (Terrace of Sa'da clan) that they thought of joining the last rites of the Prophet. Having come after two days, they disputed as to where should be the place of burial of the Prophet. As a result of all these the Prophet could be buried only after two days of his death.[24] 'Ali, 'Abbās and others performed the funeral rites of the Prophet Muḥammad.[25]

The holy Prophet Muḥammad was extremely simple in his dress, belongings, habits and mode of life. Often, went without a meal, some dates and water were the source of nourishment. For several months no fire could be lighted in his house for scantiness of means. God had given him the key to the treasures of this world, but he never used it for him or his family. He had the mind of the Teacher, with highest intellectualism, progressive ideals, innovative and most modern thought. Fourteen centuries have passed after him but the time has enhanced his concept of life, human relationship, equity, peace and love to all. The holy Qur'an denotes the essence of his personality:

> "And that man hath only for which he maketh effort." (*Qur'an 53/39*)

Faithful ever remembers with grateful heart and tears:

> *Rūḥī Fidaka yā Rasūl Allāh*
> (May my life be thy sacrifice, 'O Prophet of God).

Fāṭimah aż-Żahrah, *the Lady of Light*

Fāṭimah aż-Żahrah (Fāṭimah, the resplendent), the most loving daughter of the Prophet Muḥammad has special significance in Islam. According to the chapter *Nūr* (the Light) of holy Qur'an she is symbolic of tree and fruits, the analogy of the *Kalamahu'sh-Shahadah. Kalamahu'sh-Shahadah* (profession of faith) has been said to be like a blessed tree, which refers to the chosen geneology of the Prophet Abraham in whose progeny were numerous prophets, including Moses, Jesus and Muḥammad. In the same chapter in the verse of the *Nūr,* the word *Mishkāt* (the Chandelier) stands for Fāṭimah aż-Żahrah and *Miṣbāḥ* (the Lamp) stands for Ḥasan and Ḥusain. A description of this has been made in the previous pages, so no more details again.[26] However, some of the Traditions of the Prophet may be mentioned hereunder:

> "Fāṭimah is the Head of the womenfolk of the Paradise."[27]
>
> "Fāṭimah is a piece of myself and one he who pained her, pained me[28] and who pained me, pained God and who pained God, his place shall be Hell."[29]

"*Ummu'l-Mūminīn* 'Ā'isha said, I found no one superior to Fāṭimah, except her father, the Prophet."[30]

The Lady of the Light, Fāṭimah aż-Żahrah (in full: *Khātūnu'l-Jannah* Fāṭimah aż-Żahrah, daughter of *Ummu'l-Mūminīn* Khadījah daughter of Khawaled of Asad clan and the holy Prophet *Abu'l Qāsim* Muhammad, was born on the Friday, the 20th Jamādi II, in the 45th year of the Era of the Elephent[31], or 614 in Mecca. Expired while praying God in the noon of Wednesday, 3rd Jamādi II, 11 AH or 26th August, 632 in Medīna and buried in al-Bāqī' cemetery, ignoring her last wish to be buried by the side of his father the holy Prophet Muḥammad.

Arabs are known for their pride, pugnacity, peculiar sense of honour, and the wonderful force and patience for vindictiveness. Their tearful custom was burying alive of the female children, which was most prevalent in the tribes of Quraysh and Kindah with many other nations of antiquity, observed, on the form of sacrificing the children to their gods. Islam prohibited all inhuman practices and imposed severe punishments, brushed aside all the complexes in a single stroke in the famous declaration of the Prophet: Paradise is at the foot of the mother.

Islam enforced as one of the essential teachings, the respect of the womenfolk. It was a routine practice by the Prophet Muḥammad to come daily morning at the doors of his daughter and calling out aloud: O' Lord! bestow Mercy on my *Ahlu'l-Bayt.* Whenever his daughter Fāṭimah called upon him, the Prophet Muḥammad would stand up in her respect, kiss her forehead and offer his seat to her.[32] Every Muslim, male or female, in their love and reverence for all the pure, true or and the noblest ideal of human conception in a holy women, proclaimed her the Lady of

Paradise, the representative of womenfolk and the Lady of Light for she was the embodiment of all divine elements in womanhood.

Daughter of the Great Lady, the sole companion, helper and the first wife of the Prophet Muḥammad, *Ummu'l-Mūminīn* Khadījah when Fāṭimah married Imām 'Ali, the Prophet's cousin on Friday, 25th May, 624, she was only 9 years old. Their sons Ḥasan and Ḥusain are the grandsons of the Prophet. A third son Muḥsin died in infancy. Żaynab and Umm Kulthūm were the other daughters. Though the married life of 'Ali and Fāṭimah was of a short period of eight years; Fāṭimah died due to unbearable shocks after the demise of her father within six months. But during the said period the couples presented exemplary ideals of uninterrupted sunshine of faithfulness and happiness.

In the early years of Islam women continued to occupy an exalted position. Fāṭimah was tall, slender, and endowed with great beauty, for which she was called *aż-Żahrah*, the beautiful. She was most brilliant, accomplished and virtuous lady. Her sermons and aphorisms were the index to her strength of character and nobility of mind. She was noted for her learning, her virtues and strength of character. Fāṭimah was a lady covered with the orbits of *ar-Rāsikhūn-fi'l-'Ilm*. She was a good commentator and interpreter of the holy Qur'an. She was expert in Islamic *sharī'a*. The womenfolk used to take her guidance in various issues facing them. It is notable that during the lifetime of the Prophet, Fāṭimah avoided involvement in political affairs but after the demise of her father, the Prophet Muḥammad, she had a sharp clash with the first Caliph Abū Bakr and whenever she took part in the crucial discussions regarding the succession of the Prophet, her eloquent reasoning and presentation of facts, made her opponents speechless. It was her intellectual heritage and training that her daughter Żaynab shielded her youthful nephew 'Ali, mostly known as Imām Żainu'l-Ābidīn from Umayyites after the butchery of Karbala. Fāṭimah's maid-servant Fizzah, to whom she had distributed the household work in the ideal way that would be completely free to take rest on every alternative day and Fāṭimah would do all the household work in her place.

Caliph Abū-Bakr

The name of first Caliph was 'Abdu'llāh alias 'Atīq. The virginity of his younger daughter 'Ā'isha has given him popularly known name *Abū Bakr* (Father of the Virgin). Because she was the only virgin wife of the Prophet; all other wives were married previously to other persons. Thus, Abū Bakr was the father-in-law of the Prophet. He was also called *Siddīq* (upright). He was contiguous in genealogy with the holy Prophet Muhammad, after seven predecessors. He was born in 573 in Mecca and died on 23rd August, 634 in Medīna and buried adjacent to the grave of the Prophet Muḥammad.

Caliph Abū Bakr belonged to the Tayam clan, which was one of the minor clans of ruling merchant tribes of Quraysh of Mecca. He was close friend of the Prophet Muḥammad, Abū Bakr purportedly was one of the first few to convert to Islam. Some believe, he was first among the male Muslims, but this view is doubted by a majority of Muslim historians. However, his prominence is marked clearly by many other factors. He was who accompanied the holy Prophet at the time of *Hijrat* (emigration) to Medīna and was with him in the cave. He would lead a simple life. He was great gynecologist of his time. By his efforts prominent men had come into the Islamic faith, like 'Othmān, the third Caliph, Sa'd-bin-Waqāṣ,'Abdu'r-Raḥmān-bin-'Auf, Żubayr-bin-'Awām etc. Through his benign efforts, some notable figures like Bilāl al-Ḥabashī and 'Ammār al-Yāsir were rescued from the slavery and torture of their masters. These tortures became more inhuman when the slaves had taken to Islam. In this way it may be said that even if there had been no other distinctions in Abū-Bakr, Islam would remain indebted to him for these distinctive services.

Caliph Abū Bakr was one of the closest companions and advisors, specially conducting the holy pilgrimage to Mecca in 631 and also leading the prayer in Medina during the last illness of the Prophet. He was made first Caliph of *Khilāfatu'r-Rāshida* on the demise of the Prophet Muḥammad on June 8, 632. Both Sunni and Shi'a sources agree that Imām 'Ali was urged by persons like his uncle 'Abbās and Abū Sufyyān of Umayyite to set himself as alternative leader, even to the extent that Abū Sufyyān offered to fill Medīna with armed men to enforce 'Ali's claim.[33] But Imām 'Ali refused to split the community.

However, the conflict between the Prophet's family and the first Caliph became evident when the beloved daughter of the Prophet, Fāṭimah aż-Żahrah advanced her claim for *Fidak*, which was her personal property and was refused by the first Caliph[34], though a written document of the Prophet was also available. Also shocking events was the incident when 'Omar (later the second Caliph) with some others with fire in their hands marched to the House of Fāṭimah demanding 'Ali's pledge for his allegiance to Caliph Abū Bakr and threatend to burn the house, if he refused.[35]

Another most shocking happening was the incident in which his military General Khālid-bin-Walīd raped the beautiful wife of the chief of

Novīrah clan, Mālik and also killed him. 'Omar vehemently opposed it and took the issue with the Caliph Abū Bakr but he pardoned him on the ground that Khālid was great warrior.[36]

During his about two years rule (632-634 AD) the relationship between the Caliph Abū Bakr and *Ahlu'l-Bayt*, the family of the holy Prophet Muḥammad could not be cordial; it had gone to such extent that Fāṭimah aż-Żahrah, daughter of the holy Prophet made her last will that these people should not be allowed in her burial ground.[37] These incidents were most shocking for the noble hearted Abū Bakr himself. So in his last days he was a terribly sorry person and used to wring his hands expressing the dejection of mind.[38]

Caliph Abū Bakr, on his death bed, nominated 'Omar to succeed him. He also secured pledges from various important persons in favour of his nominated-to-be Caliph 'Omar.[39] Caliph Abū Bakr is also credited for bringing central 'Arabia under the control of his Caliphate. Then he took direct expansion of political boundaries up to Iraq and Syria. Raids from the north were followed by reprisals in the land watered by the two great rivers the *Dajla* (Tigis) issuing from the mountains of Armenia and the *Furāt* (Euphrates) taking the rise in the height of Taurus, rolling down towards the Persian Gulf. Many flourishing settlements had existed by the sides of these famous rivers, such as Nineveh, the seat of the mighty Assyrian monarchs, Madain, the Capital of the Persia, the ancient Babylon, the ancient Circesium (now Kirkessia), Hira, Kūfa and several others. These conquests opened the eyes of the neighbouring governments to the gravity of a danger and encouraged the newly formed Muslim Caliphate, resulting the chain of military conquests.

Caliph 'Omar

The second Caliph was 'Omar son of Khaṭṭāb, also called *Fārūq* (one who distinguishes between right and wrong), belonged to 'Adī clan of Quraysh, contiguous in genealogy with the holy Prophet Muḥammad, after eight predecessors. His daughter, Ḥafṣah was married previously to some other person, then to the Prophet in 625 and hence, was the father-in-law of the Prophet Muhammad. He was born in 586 AD in Mecca and died on November 3, 644 in Medina and buried adjacent to the grave of the Prophet Muḥammad.

'Omar began as an enemy of Islam but about 615 became Muslim. Before him 21 women and 45 men had already professed Islam.[40] He was nominated and appointed by the first Caliph Abū Bakr to succeed him as second Caliph, which took place on 23rd August, 634, when 'Omar was of 48. He was stern, just, farsighted, fully versed and highly fitted to handle the unruly 'Arabs. Keeping in view the other future claimants of the Caliphate, he posted them as chief commanders giving a standard in their hands for an expedition into land of God. Most of them had fought against the holy Prophet Muḥammad before the fall of Mecca. Tempted by the rich soils, they had joined the army of Caliphate, previously of Caliph Abū Bakr and now of Caliph 'Omar. On the 30th instant Yermuk fell to Muslims by defeating the Romans with fearful slaughter.

Caliph 'Omar had never approved ferocities of Khālid-bin-Walīd, insult fully deposed him from chief command and appointed Abū 'Obaydah in his place, who one by one capitulated Syrian cities like Damascus, Hem, Hama (Epiphania), Kinnisrin (Chalcis) Aleppo etc. and reached in front of Antioch, the capital of Roman East and the rival of Constantinople. Another army under 'Omar-bin-'Ās was successful in Palestine. After a siege of some duration the capitulation of Jerusalem was made in presence of the Caliph 'Omar himself. An expedition into land of Pharaohs cleared the country of the Byzantines. The Romans of Egypt took refuge in Alexandria which fell in the hands of Muslims. The entire Egypt, up to Libya in the north and Abyssinia in the south became under Muslim domination and immediately other countries were conquered. A new sovereign of Persia, under the ambitious Yezdjard with a large army battled at Nehawand, at the foot of the Elburz. It decided the fate of Asia and has been called by the historians *Fatḥu'l-Fatūḥ* (the victorty of the victories).

About Caliph 'Omar, Jalālu'd-Dīn Suyūṭī (d. 1505 AD) has commented that he has not found anyone more innovative and modern in his thinking and aptitude than him.[41] Caliph 'Omar never framed or compiled no jurisprudence, but 18th century Indian scholar Shaykh 'Abdu'l-Ḥaqq Muḥaddith (d. 1762 AD) has collected and compiled a book named *Fiqahu'l-'Omar* ('Omar's Jurisprudence). According to him his innovations in Jurisprudence are about in a thousand cases.[42] In some cases he has been more advanced to his counterparts. For example:

Caliph 'Omar allowed *Ṭalāq* by husband in single space and time through declaring *Ṭalāq* thrice, whereas Qur'an has effected a check upon any type of indiscrimination in the matter of marital life and limited the revocable *Ṭalāq* to only twice giving the final chance to reunion and finally after third *Ṭalāq*, they could be separated:

> "Divorce (*shall be lawful*) only twice then (*you should*) either keep her in fairness or send her away with kindness." (*Qur'an: 2/229*)

> "So if he hath divorceth her (*for a third time*), then she shall not be lawful unto him until she wedeth another husband; and if (*also*) divorceth her, then there shall be no sin on either of them if they think that they shall (*be able to*) keep (*themselves*) within the limits ordained by God; these are the limits ordained by God (*which*) He maketh them clear for a people who understand." (*Qur'an: 2/230*)

Caliph 'Omar banned the inter-religion marriage with the woman of the *People of Scriptures* i.e. Jews, Christian etc. whereas the Qur'an permits:

> "And so are the virtuous women of the believers and virtuous women of those who received scripture before you (*lawful for you*), when ye give them their marriage portions and live with them in honour." (*Qur'an: 5/5*)

Caliph 'Omar's Jurisprudence has not been accepted by many scholars. Imām 'Ali was also critical of his judgments. He not only acceded to 'Ali's suggestion but went to the extent to say:

> *Laulā 'Ali Lahlakā 'Omar*
> ('Ali saved 'Omar from disaster)[43]

But, to be fair, Caliph 'Omar's strong moral fibre, with great energy was especially fitted for the leadership of unruly 'Arabs known for their pride, pugnacity, and the vindictiveness. He dealt the helm with iron hand and severely repressed the tendency of luxury and vice. His first act, after re-organizing the internal administration was to dispatch reinforcements to help the Muslim troops in their conquest expedition of Persia and after the capture of Holwan, a peace treaty was concluded with Persian king but it could not work for long and Muslim forces captured the entire Persia after a war.

Caliph 'Omar's principles of legal affairs and his practices, controlled general polity and administration of the conquered land, established the *Dīwān* (Finance Department) for administration of revenue, consolidated rules for the governance of the provinces, which became the basic structure of Islamic empire. His ten years reign (634-644 AD) transformed the 'Arabic principality into a world power. Looking at the splendid personality of Caliph 'Omar one may come to note his strict adherence to Islamic laws, selfless outspokenness and matchless ability to rule. He had the extraordinary knowledge and natural wisdom to foresee the things which would normally take many years to happen.

His practical wisdom and foresight may be witnessed in his insisting upon the holy Prophet to put Abū Sufyyān to death, because he had known it beyond doubt that Abū Sufyyān's entry into Islamic fold was not motivated by religious feeling but a strategy to harm Islam from inside.[44] Once he had told 'Abdu'llāh-bin-'Abbās about making 'O<u>th</u>mān as his successor:

> "If I make 'O<u>th</u>mān my successor, he would make the Umayyite clan ride on the shoulders of Muslims and this will go against the Will of God. By God, if I did so it will turnout exactly so, Muslims will rebel and kill him."[45]

His prophecies regarding Abū Sufyyān and 'O<u>th</u>mān proved literally true. Similarly his prophecy about 'Ali also proved true. He had said:

> "By God, you will never make 'Ali Caliph, because, by God, if you were to do so, 'Ali will not rest until he has established you on the path of truth, whether you like it or not."[46]

Who can doubt in the truism of this prophecy! He has a number of feathers in his cap. Caliph 'Omar was assassinated by a personal slave for personal reasons. The bitterness between the Caliphate and *Ahlu'l-Bayt* had been minimized during his reign and Imām 'Ali was one of the chief advisers but ignoring Imām 'Ali's claim, Caliph 'Omar appointed a council of six members to decide the leadership issue after his death. Though Imām'Ali was also kept as a member, the committee was constituted in such a way that Imām 'Ali could not be made Caliph this time too, but if he shows dissent should be beheaded. This had been made one of the condition and the committee was constituted in such a way that Imām 'Ali would surely dissent. Its two members Sa'd-bin-Waqāṣ and 'Abdu'r-Raḥmān were cousins and supporters of 'O<u>th</u>mān (later third Caliph). 'Abdu'r-Raḥmān was the brother-in-law of 'O<u>th</u>mān. Ṭalḥa and Żubaiyr were personal friends and aspirant for themselves. Two conditions were also laid down. In case of disagreement in choosing unanimous Caliph surface, then the late Caliph 'Omar's son 'Abdu'llāh, be opted as additional member, who was bound to vote in favour of 'Abdu'r-Raḥmān and the person showing his dissent should be beheaded, who could it be, as per strategy, no one else but 'Ali!

But the total planning took another turn. 'Abdu'r-Raḥmān skilfully offered Caliphate to Imām 'Ali with the condition that he will follow the path shown by his two predecessors. Imām 'Ali replied, if their path is same as the Prophet, Scripture and God, I shall abide, otherwise not. 'Othmān agreed to this condition and was made Caliphate.

Caliph 'Othmān

The third Caliph 'Othmān son of 'Affān of Umayyite clan. Because of being wealthy merchant was called *Ghanī* (opulent) and *Žun-Nūrayn* (a man of double light, meaning doubly son-in-law) on the presumption that two of the daughters of the Prophet, one after other were married to him, though it is proved beyond doubt that those ladies were never the daughters of Prophet, but the daughters of his first wife Khadījah from her previous husbands. Hence some call him son-in-law of the Prophet, also contiguous in genealogy with the holy Prophet Muḥammad, after five predecessors. He was born in Mecca and died on June 17, 656. in Medina buried in the cemetery of Jews, after three days of his assassination because the rebels had obstacled his proper burial.

Caliph 'Othmān's Umayyite clan was the bitterest enemy of Hāshimites, to which the holy Prophet Muḥammad belonged and so the holy Prophet also faced highest hostility. But 'Othmān under the influence and persuasion of Abū Bakr accepted Islam and became the first convert of high social and economic standing. He is allegedly credited for establishing the official version of the holy Qur'an, though it has existed in various versions. He was made third Caliph by the intrigues of his brother-in-law, 'Abdu'r-Raḥmān, which has already been discussed in the previous pages. After considerable debate and discussions for several days, he was made Caliph on 7th November, 644. But his accession to the Caliphate proved to be total disaster, for which famous Sunni scholar and the founder of Jama't-i-Islami Movement, Abu'l 'Olā Maudūdī pleads:

> "He did not have all those merits which his predecessors had been gifted with, therefore, in the period of his Caliphate, religious corruption had found their way into the administrative order as a whole."[47]

However, while coping the odds and difficulties, he never lost sight of his ultimate aim, the expansion of Muslim kingdom. He continued the conquests which had steadily increased the size of Islamic empire. He kept the armies busy. The incursions of Turks in Tranoxiana led to conquest of Balkh. Later Hirāt, Kābul and Ghażnī were also captured and Kirmān and Sīstan were subjugated. In Africa, Tripoli and in the Mediterranean Cyprus were also conquered and so on.

The advent of 'Othmān as the third Caliph was as good as the monopolization of Umayyite clan on Islamic kingdom. The mischievous character of Umayyite clan Abū Sufyyān had become old. Deprived of inner vision, now he had lost also his outer eye-sight. Walking with a stick he came down to congratulate 'Othmān on his Caliphate and explained to him: "I am witness to the fact that there is no such things as Hell and Paradise and no such thing as *Qiyāmah* (Catastrophe) that is going to happen; all is humbug of the Hāshimite to deceive the world. Now that the crown has come your way, play it like a ball."[48]

'Othmān just after his accession to Caliphate fell under the influence of his family and Umayyite clan. Marwān and his father Ḥakam, who were expelled by the Prophet himself for breach of trust and were further driven off by the first two Caliphs Abū Bakr and 'Omar were honourably taken back. Marwān was made his secretary and principal advisor in all affairs.

All the trusted Governors appointed by his predecessor Caliph 'Omar were removed from their positions and new incumbents were installed, in which were the persons like his half-brother Walīd-bin-'Uqbah, condemned by Qur'an.[49] Caliph 'Othmān displaced Sa'd-bin-Abī-Waqāṣ, the governor of Kūfa, and replaced him with Walīd-bin-'Uqbah. Thereafter he gave away this post to his half-brother Sa'īd-bin-'Āṣ, condemned drinker.[50] His other choice 'Abdu'llāh-bin-Abī-Saraḥ, for whom the Prophet had ordered that if he was found taking shelter within the sacred-cloths of Ka'ba, where everything is saved and even the grass could not be plucked, but 'Abdullah-bin-Sa'd-bin-Abī-Saraḥ be slaughtered. Dismissing 'Omarū-bin-'Āṣ the governor of Egypt, he appointed Abī-Saraḥ's grandson, 'Abdu'llāh, who was Caliph 'Othmān's brother by way of sharing the breast milk of the same wet nurse.[51] Displacing the governor of Baṣra, Abū Mūsā Ash'arī and replacing him with his maternal cousin 'Abdu'llāh-bin-'Āmir.[52]

Mu'āwiyah-bin-Abū Sufyyān had got governorship in the very ruling period of Caliph 'Omar itself. He raised the status of Mu'āwiyah and a number of other provinces were given under his governorship.[53] His ruling territory was expanded by annexing Syria, Hamas, Palestine, Jordon, Lebanon etc.

To be brief, all the territories of Islamic empire were given in the hands of Umayyite clan. Caliph 'Othmān designated his cousin Marwān-bin-Ḥakam the Chief Secretary in the Capital and thus established his influence and power. In this way his clan Umayyite swayed power over the entire area from Khurāsān (modern Iran) to northern Africa, and the Chief Controller of the Islamic State and the principal executive at the Central Office at Medina was his own cousin and son-in-law Marwān-bin-Ḥakam.[54]

Caliph 'Othmān used the *Bayt-al-Māl* (State Exchequer) as his personal property. The bounty earned from the conquest of various countries were distributed amongst the Ummayites in preference to others. Some of the cases of beneficiaries from State Exchequer, without any justification, were of the family and clan of the Caliph 'Othmān are mentioned as under[55]:

(i) The *Fidak*, the personal property of the Prophet Muḥammad for which his daughter Fāṭimah aż-Żahrah had made claim before the first Caliph Abū Bakr and was refused and had been made the part of the State Exchequer was given by Caliph 'Othmān to his son-in-law Marwān in addition to a sum of five Lakhs from the State Exchequer.

(ii) When Caliph 'Othmān married his next daughter to Ḥārith-bin-Ḥakam, brother of Marwān, he was given one lakh as dowry from the State Exchequer.

(iii) Marwān's father Ḥakam was also gifted one lakh from the State Exchequer.

(iv) Noxious Abū Sufyyān was awarded two lakhs from the State Exchequer.

(v) Walid son of 'Uqbah, half-brother of the Caliph 'Othmān, who was declared transgressor by Qur'an, was offered one lakh from the State Exchequer.

(vi) 'Abdu'llāh-bin-Khālid was given the sum of four lakhs from the State Exchequer, etc. etc.

These are some of the cases where awardees were from Umayyite clan and close relations of the Caliph 'Othmān. Here, no speciousness of language could help in conniving the corruption and nepotism, which has been vehemently criticized and condemned by the famous Sunni scholars, like Ibn Ḥajar Ḥaythmī al-Makkī, Badru'd-Dīn 'Ayni, Ibn Qudāma, Abu'l 'Olā Maudūdī[56] etc.

The weakness of Caliph 'Othman and wickedness of his favourite created great ferment among the people. By 650 AD rebellion had broken out. The rebels besieged 'Othmān in his house and after severed days of desultory fighting, he was killed. The prophecy of the Caliph 'Omar appeared cent per cent true that 'he would make the Umayyite clan ride on the shoulders of Muslims' and 'Muslims will rebel and kill him.'

Caliph 'Othmān's most favouriste was his own cousin and son-in-law Marwān-bin-Ḥakam, who became fourth Caliph of Umayyites in 685 AD. But the founder of Umayyites Caliphate was Mu'āwiyah-bin-Abū Sufyyān (d. 680 AD). The regime of Mu'āwiyah is not regarded by the majority of Sunni Muslims as a Caliphate in Islamic sense but regards his regime as the beginning of the Muslim imperialism. The way Caliph 'Othmān made his clan to dominate the Islamic state, prepared the ground and transformed the Caliphate into Imperialism. This has been discussed in detail in the history of Islam.

This was made possible in the regime of second Caliph 'Omar who had obliged all clans (except the Hāshimites) by appointing them on important positions. He appointed Mu'āwiyah-bin-Abū Sufyyān from the Umayyite clan as the governor of Syria. After a year of the martyrdom of Imām 'Ali (28th January, 661) Mu'āwiyah turned Islamic Caliphate into a despotic and dynastic state. He, having won over despotic authority, would publicly and proudly declare:

> "I am the first of the kings."[57]

Many Muslim would wish peace to him by addressing him as *Ahlu'l-Mulk* (Lord of State). After securing the power with sword, Mu'āwiyah made a speech at Medīna, in which he said:

> "By God, while handing the reign of exclusive power, I was not unaware of the fact that you will not be happy about my having got this authority and you don't like it. In this regard whatever is there in your heart, I know it fully well. But with the power of my sword I have now subdued you and got it firmly in my hand."[58]

Again, in his victory trip to Iraq, Mu'āwiyah said the same in a more clear phraseology:

> "O my subjects, it is not to make you say prayer, and pay poor-due or keep fasts, that I have faught with you. All I wished was to rule over heads in which I have achieved the success. Now, say prayer, if you pleased or say it never, if you pleased, keep fast or keep it never as you please. I have to do nothing

with these things. Prayer or no prayer is your right. All I am concerned with is that you will have to regard me as your ruler and *Sultān* in every condition whatever."[59]

A contrary state of things erupted in Islam where imperial interests were being advanced in the name of Caliphate. Imperialism, however, did neither match the divinely organised leadership of Islam, nor Muslim paid to these self-styled Caliphs the respect duly payable to the religious leadership. They were regarded only as rulers who had forced their authority on Muslim nation. Should any individual or group refused to submit, the rulers sought to crush them. Thousands of people went into submission to these rulers on account of fear of life and property, greed and vested interests. On the other hand in the prevailing situation Qur'an and *Ahlu'l-Bayt* were sidelined and a group of Muslims began to take these very rulers to be the models of Islam. Eventually, what happened was that the rulership marched ahead of Islam, and Islam followed the steps of the rulership!

Imām 'Ali

The first and grand Imām of the series of the twelfth Imāms and Fourth in the order of Caliphate, the emeritus and the excellent soul in knowledge and virtue, next to the holy Prophet Muḥammad, his cousin and son-in-law, *Abu'l Ḥasan*, 'Ali son of Hās͟himite parents, Fāṭimah-bint-Asad and Abū Ṭālib. He was born on the 13th Rajab, in the Era of the Elephent 30, or in 600 AD within the four walls of Ka'ba' the revered house of God in Mecca. Martyred while leading the prayer of God and left two days after for Heavens on Tuesday, 21st Ramazān, 40 AH or 28th January, 661 in the mosque of Kūfa and buried at Najaf (Iraq).

Imām 'Ali's father, Abū Ṭālib was the chief of Hās͟himite clan and was real brother of 'Abdu'llāh, father of the holy Prophet Muḥammad, who were sons of 'Abdu'l-Muṭṭalib and Fāṭimah daughter of 'Omaro of the Mak͟hżumī clan. Prophet Muḥammad regarded Abū Ṭālib and his wife Fāṭimah, daughter of Asad, father and mother of 'Ali, as his own parents and under whose care in their house he grew up from his tender age, and when the members of the Qurays͟hite had united to oppose the holy Prophet Muḥammad and frustrate his mission, then Abū Ṭālib himself and along with his family had stood like a iron wall to all challenges and faced all distress to protect the Prophet and support and facilitate his mission.

When Imām 'Ali was born, Prophet Muḥammad took his cousin under his care and he was like a son unto him. He used to live with him, used to sleep with him and feed, wash and dress him and even carried him on outings, whenever went out, so naturally Imām 'Ali was brought up right from his childhood to his youth under the guardianship of the Prophet Muḥammad.

Imām 'Ali was 10 years old when the revelation of God was announced by the holy Prophet Muḥammad, he had inducted Islam in constant exposure with the Prophet Muḥammad from the very beginning he accepted Islam and remained his lifelong devoted follower and also risked his life by sleeping in the bed of the Prophet Muḥammad, when enemies has gathered to assassinate the Prophet. The holy Prophet Muḥammad could emigrate to Medina in 622 AD. 'Ali left Mecca, only after he restored all the properties of merchants of Mecca to their respective owners that they had entrusted to the *Amīn* (truthful) Muḥammad.

Imām 'Ali displayed rare courage in battles, became renowned as warrior during Islam's struggle for survival, often leading the Islamic army. He was also one of the Prophet's scribes and chosen to lead several important missions. When the hostile Meccans fully demoralized finally surrendered to Islam without any fighting or battle, it was Imām 'Ali who smashed the pagan idols in the Ka'ba, the foremost shrine in Mecca.

A man of the look of great amiability and kindness, soft gray eyes, ruddy complexion, reasonable height, with a flowing bread, extremely strong, inclined to the stoutness, 'Ali was 21, when the Prophet Muḥammad married him to his only daughter Fāṭimah aż-Żahrah in the year 631 AD. Out of this unique wedlock of the infallible couples, were born Ḥasan and Ḥusain, that the progeny of the holy Prophet Muḥammad, the *Saiyeds* descend. A third son Muḥsin who died in infancy and two daughters Żaynab and Umm-Kul<u>th</u>ūm.

Imām 'Ali is revered by the Shi'is as only true successor of the holy Prophet Muḥammad, because he was unequivocally twice nominated as his successor first on the occasion of the *Da'watu'l-Żul-'A<u>sh</u>īra*[60] and also while he was returning from his 'farewell pilgrimage to Mecca.'[61] Most of Sunnis believe that the nomination was for spiritual succession and not for all matters. So a conflict arose resulting into the split in Islam as Shi'is and Sunnis. It is the attachment to Imām 'Ali that the Shi'a community is popularly referred to as *Shi'ianu'l-'Ali* (the Followers of Imām 'Ali).

Imām 'Ali became the Fourth Caliph of *Khilāfatu'r-Rāshidah*, after 24 years of the death of the Prophet Muḥammad and was martyred after

4½ years of his Caliphate. Imām 'Ali was invited by the Muslims to accept the Caliphate after the murder of the third Caliph 'Othmān, which he accepted very reluctantly after long hesitation and faced great difficulties due mostly to the corrupt state of affairs, when he had inherited. Imām 'Ali was ranked as Caliph on 23rd day of June, 655, at a general meeting held at Medina in the Prophet's mosque where nearly all Muslims pledged allegiance at the hand of Imām 'Ali.[62]

Soon after the accession to the Caliphate, Imām 'Ali based his rule on the Islamic ideals of justice and equality, which was a blow to the interest of the Quraysh aristocracy, which, had highly grown due to various conquests. Umayyite clan was by birth the adversary to the Hashimites clan to which belonged the Prophet Muḥammad and Imām 'Ali. Umayyites were highly apprehensive of Imām 'Ali having been chosen as the successor of the Prophet. All the wealth taken and used in personal pleasures and luxury in the ruling period of Caliph 'Othmān, was threatened to be checked and confiscated, so its future looked dark. So Mu'āwiyah-bin-Abū Sufyyān made a huge army by bringing together Umayyites and the pseudo-Muslims and occupied some areas by setting up a battle front against Imām 'Ali.[63] But some of them mounted difficulties and unrest against him and forced him to fight against the rebellion which resulted in the battles of Jamal, Siffin, Nahrwan etc.

They organised several battles against the Caliph and were defeated. The first rebellion was led by the daughter of the first Caliph and widow of the Prophet, *Ummu'l-Mūminīn* 'Ā'isha, known as battle of *Jamal* (camel). Second rebellion was led by Mu'āwiyah-bin-Abū Sufyyān, a kinsman of 'Othmān was on the verge of being crushed by the army of Imām 'Ali but he was forced to accept arbitration of a friend. Again Imām 'Ali was forced to war by *Khawārijīs* (Seceders). They were killed but one of them struck with a poisoned sword on Imām 'Ali, while he was praying in the Mosque of Kūfā, which resulted in his death after two days.

Chivalrous, humane, and forbearing, Imām 'Ali was a ruler who had come before his time, whose forbearance and magnanimity were misunderstood, and his humanity and love of truth was twisted by the enemies of Islam to their own advantage. But the accounts of his valorous deeds are still remembered and recited with enthusiasm among the people. Ever ready to succour the weak and to redress the wrongs of the injured, though facing heaviest odds, during the short span of the reign for four years as Caliph, he worked for the uplift of the masses, consolidation of the state, creation of a Central Bureau and re-introduction of Islamic governance. He made it possible by turning various divisions of public service departments into Public Finance, Army, Central Secretariat, Judiciary and Provincial Offices etc.

There is the consensus among all Muslims about his highest status in knowledge, devotion, purity, holiness, spiritual attitude and multi-dimensional nobility. It is noteworthy that while the Muslim militia under the reign of Caliphate was busy in the extension of territorial limits of the kingdom, Imam 'Ali's endeavour was to give an intellectual turn to the newly developed energy of the people. Imām 'Ali and alumnus-cousin 'Abdullāh-bin-'Abbās delivered weekly lectures on philosophy and logic, history, traditions, rhetoric and law, whilst others dealt with other subjects, in the public mosque at Medīna. Thus, it formed the nucleus of the intellectual movement which displayed itself in such great force in later times.[64]

In creating a Central Bureau, he intended the training of the crude 'Arabs for becoming educated and cultured persons – 'Abdu'r-Raḥmān Sulmī for training them the correct recitation of the holy Qur'an, 'Abdu'l-Asswad Dawelī for teaching 'Arabic language, grammar and syntax, 'Omar-bin-Salmah for 'Arabic prose, 'Obaydah-bin-Ṣāmit for poetry and logic, Kumayl-bin-Żiyad for teaching Mathematics, Engineering and Astronomy, 'Abdu'llāh-bin-'Abbās for making the principles of rhetoric and administration. For himself he retained philosophy of religion, ethics, commentary of Qur'an and Tradition of the Prophet.

Talking of the merits of Imām 'Ali, 'Abdu'llāh-bin-'Abbās had said that Imām 'Ali had four such distinctions in which no one else could be his equal. Firstly, he was the first in 'Arabs and non-'Arabs to say prayer along with the prophet of Islam. Secondly, he was the commander of army in all the battles fought in the lifetime of the Prophet Muḥammad. Thirdly, when other companions of the Prophet Muḥammad would flee for life and leave the Prophet Muḥammad behind, he would remain steadfast and guard the Prophet with utmost courage and faithful valour. Fourthly, he remained by the Prophet Muḥammad at his death-bed and after his death, he performed his funeral rites and set his body in the grave.

Likewise the statement of Imām Muhammad-bin-Idrīs a<u>sh</u>-<u>Sh</u>āfi'ī (d. 819 AD) in praise of Imām 'Ali is well-known, he says:

> "What words can I use in praise of the man who had combined in him three such merits with three opportunities which no mortal can combine in his person. Extreme charity

> with extreme poverty, highest valour with highest wisdom and marvellous work-efficiency with unbound knowledge."[65]

Imām 'Ali was the paragon of all virtues bearing an ideal human personality. A lot can be said in his praise. All that this humble can say is that God had put together all divine attributes to be manifest in him at the highest level. In the single life of Imām 'Ali, the Almighty compressed an exhaustive experience and achievement of a thousands lives. Every experience was without a parallel in its originality, novelty and relevance. Each act he performed and word he uttered was an outlet for a ceaseless variety of new chapters of thought and ideas.

Imām 'Ali's socio-political discourses, religious sermons, important letters and thought-provoking sayings have been collected and compiled by revered scholar ash-Sharīf ar-Razī (d. 1015 AD) in a book entitled *Nahju'l-Balāghah* (the Road of Eloquence) which is well known in 'Arabic literature and so in the commentary by Abī al-Ḥadīd (d. 1258 AD).

Imām Ḥasan

The second in the order of Imamate, Imām Ḥasan was the eldest son of Imām 'Ali and Fāṭimah aż-Żahrah, the daughter of holy Prophet Muḥammad, popularly called son of holy Prophet and *Saiyed* (the (Venerable Leader) as he was the progeny of the holy Prophet Muḥammad. He was born in the night of Friday, 15th Ramazān, 03 AH, or Febraury 28, 625 in Medīna. Martyred by poison on Thursday, 28th Ṣafar, 50 AH, March 27, 670 in Medīna and buried in al-Bāqi cemetery next to his mother, Fāṭimah aż-Żahrah.

Ḥasan in Hebrew *Shabbar*, meaning to embellish, was the son of Aaron and the holy Prophet Muḥammad had already declared: ' O' Imām 'Ali, art thou not content that thou art to me what Aaron was to Moses'[66], so he named him Ḥasan and when second child of Imām 'Ali was born, he named him Ḥusain, after *Shabbīr*, second son of Aaron, meaning small Ḥasan.

They were brought up by the holy Prophet Muḥammad in his own household. The early years of the two brothers were spent in close and consistent touch with the holy Prophet Muḥammad right unto the end of his life. There could be no doubt that he had greatest fondness for Ḥasnain, the holy Prophet used to caress and kiss them, not only because of blood-relations but faithful Muslims believe, it was in response to the will of God. The Prophet Muḥammad, as given in the Qur'an, does not even speak except as willed by God:

> "It (*the wording*) is naught but a revelation revealed (*unto him*)." (*Qur'an 53/3-4*)

So whatever the holy Prophet Muḥammad said or did about Ḥasnain was in keeping with the will of God. He had been widely quoted as saying:

> "Ḥasan is *Saiyed* (chief), who will bring peace among two in fighting groups of Muslims."[67]
>
> "Ḥasan and Ḥusain are chief of the youth of paradise."[68]
>
> "He who has loved Ḥasan and Ḥusain, loved me and he who has hated them has hated me."[69]

It was in keeping with the will of God, for instance when on the eve of Eīd, the two children desired to wear new clothes, as Muslims believe, the *Janitor of Paradise* (a distinguished Angel) descended from Heaven with new clothes for Ḥasnain priding himself to be their tailor. While preparing to go to the mosque, the children told the Prophet Muḥammad that other children were going on camel; they didn't have a camel and how could they go to the mosque. The holy Prophet Muḥammad, then, put them on his shoulders and said 'I am your camel'. 'But there is the nose-string with their camels', said the children. The Prophet Muḥammad asked them to hold his hair locks into their hands. Then the children told him, 'The camels make camel-cry but our does not do so.' Then the Prophet Muḥammad made the sound of camel-cry with his mouth. Some of the revered companions of the Prophet offered to take at least one of the two children on their shoulder, but the Prophet declined. One companion said to the children, 'What a fine carriage!' 'Nay, say what a fine rider', asserted the holy Prophet.[70]

On another occasion the Prophet was making sermon in the mosque when Ḥasnain appeared in the mosque. Rushing to their grandfather, their feet got tangled in the floor-sheet. The Prophet Muḥammad interrupted his sermon, climbed down the pulpit went to the children, raised them up in his lap, went back to the pulpit, started sermon while keeping them in his lap.[71] There are numerous episodes of this nature whereby the holy Prophet Muḥammad tells his companion to realize the love and significance Ḥasnain have in the eyes of God and the Prophet. Then he enjoins his companions to love Ḥasnain and note his significance and states the Traditions in praise of Ḥasnain and their value in Isalm. The revered companions were witness but of no avail after the death of the Prophet Muḥammad.

Imām Ḥasan was thirty-seven years old when Imām 'Ali, the fourth *Rāshdūn* Caliph was assassinated at Kūfa in 661. He was chosen as fifth *Rāshdūn* Caliph in succession to his father 'Ali a few days later without any dissent, except from Syrians under Mu'āwiyah-bin-Abū Sufyyān, whose secret agents spread false propaganda and liberal bribes, the army melt away and rebelled against Imām Ḥasan, and a part of it went over to the Syrians. His own tent was plundered, he himself was wounded. In this situation what Ḥasan decided was the only realistic course of action to avoid senseless bloodshed.

Imām Ḥasan was outstanding in generosity, tolerance, morality and non-violence. But by that time political power had become the arbitrator of leadership in Islam rather than religious merit or precedence. Mu'āwiyah-bin-Abū Sufyyān knew well that mere seizer of power and military victory would not be justified, until Imām Ḥasan was regarded as Caliph.

Mu'āwiyah proposed to Imām Ḥasan, if he could agree handing over the Caliphate to him, he would be happy to offer generous terms such as general amnesty for Shi'is, abolishing regular cursing against Imām 'Ali in the most abusive words from the official pulpits, large financial settlement and the Caliphate shall revert to Imām Ḥasan (in case of his death to Imām Ḥusain) on the death of Mu'āwiyah-bin-Abū Sufyyān.

Be it borne in mind that since the martyrdom of Imām 'Ali in 661 until that time, two principles of establishing divine polity had assumed the forms of a religious faith among the Muslims. One, the principle of selecting the Caliph by the vote of allegiance; and two, the principle of Imamate in which the Imām is divinely appointed in the same way as a Prophet is appointed. However, in both of these systems no one stands as candidate but he is accorded the leadership of Muslims. Imām Ḥasan was the head of the Muslim nation by both of these principles. In order to forestall the fragmentation among Muslims, after the death of Mu'āwiyah-bin-Abū Sufyyān.

Imām Ḥasan handed over the rulership to Mu'āwiyah, within a few months of his succession to Caliphate on Tuesday, 29th July, 661 through a written treaty on the condition that after him he would hand it over to the younger brother Imām Ḥusain who was already the Imām next to Imām Ḥasan. Had the terms of the treaty been observed both principles would have come together and under the leadership of Imām Ḥusain, the Divine polity as guided by Qur'an would have been established.

Mu'āwiyah crushed the paper of treaty under his feet saying that all he meant by the treaty was to secure the power and rule the masses; he had no obligation to fulfil the terms of the treaty. Imām Ḥasan on the other hand, kept living by the terms of the treaty, yet Mu'āwiyah got him poisoned.[72]

It was Mu'āwiyah who transformed Islamic polity into dynastic polity and made his son Yażīd-bin-Mu'āwiyah-bin-Abū Sufyyān his successor. After this, the Islamic order of the rulership came to an end and the dictatorial imperialism was adopted in the name of Islam.

Imam Ḥusain, *Saiyed-ush-Shuhadah*

The third in the order of Imamate, Imām Ḥusain was the younger brother of Imām Ḥasan, the second son of Imām 'Ali and Fāṭimah aż-Żahrah, the daughter of holy Prophet Muḥammad, popularly called son of holy Prophet Muḥammad and through his offspring the progeny of the Prophet Muḥammad.

He was born in the fourth year of Prophet's emigration on Thursday, the 3rd of Sha'bān 4 AH or 10th January 626 at Medīna. The holy Prophet Muḥammad took him on his lap, said *Ażān* into his right ear and *Aqāmat* into his left ear, and put his tongue into the mouth of the child to suckle, which served as the first food of Imām Ḥusain. He was martyred at Karbala on 10th Muḥarram, 61 AH or 10th October, 680.

No one else could share these genealogical distinctions with Imām Ḥusain, save his real elder brother Imām Ḥasan. Being one of the prominent members of the *Ahlu'l-Bayt*, he is entitled for all Qur'anic verses and Prophets' Traditions addressed to *Ahlu'l-Bayt* in glorifying their ranks and status over and above all Muslims. Imām Ḥusain was 10 months 17 days younger than his elder brother Imām Ḥasan. As stated earlier, the two brothers were so similar in piety and purity of nature and conduct that they were also collectively called by a single name Ḥasnain.

In order to establish the truth of Islamic cause and the devotion to it, against the pseudo Islamic power, he came along with the members of his family and his companions and all laid their lives and attained martyrdom. Imām Ḥusain, for this glorious martyrdom, is popularly known as *Saiyed ush-Shuhadah* (Leader of Martyrs). His revolutionary martyrdom, his courage, steadfastness, perseverance and sacrifice for a noble cause left deep impression in the world history. To keep mourning for these victims of the oppressive rulership, and keep their deeds alive is the unforgettable goal of the life of a Muslim.

Imam Ḥusain was still a small child of 6 years and 6 months when the Prophet died (May 25, 632) and he was deprived of the shelter and warmth he enjoyed in the life of the Prophet. Then after only 3 months and 6 days, his mother Fāṭimah aż-Żahrah too died on 26th August, 632. These two deaths, one after the other, were not just deaths but the severest blow to Muslims in general and to Ḥasnain, the young children in particular. A shocking event as it was, the first Caliph Abū Bakr was in deep agony and he repented his failure not to have asked the Prophet Muḥammad about various problems arising after his death. He would also repent his failure not to concede to the Prophet's daughter Fāṭimah aż-Żahrah, when she came over to his court with her claim to her property be quested to her in his own writing by her father.[73]

Events encountered in childhood leave deep impressions on the tender minds of children, which get all the more deepened in course of time. The extraordinary brain of Imām Ḥusain was not only storing these events in his mind but also reflecting on the consequences and dimensions of these events. His eyes had witnessed the painful scene when his reverend mother Fāṭimah aż-Żahrah, who apart from being the most affectionate daughter of the Prophet Muḥammad, was herself the noblest of all ladies in her spiritual purity and piety and in whose glorious character were revealed many verses of Qur'an and the Prophet had eulogized her in his Traditions, and whose respect was so lofty in his eyes that whenever she would appear before him, he would stand up in her honour. Imām Ḥusain witnessed that the same Fāṭimah aż-Żahrah appeared as a plaintiff and her appeal was turned down. After her death, this hostile attitude towards the Prophet's progeny subsided a little in the middle of the regime of the second Caliph 'Omar (634-44 AD).

Thereafter came a period when the situation became so bad that every tom, dick and harry of Umayyite clan became the ruling Lords over Muslim nation. In the regime of the third Caliph 'Othmān (644-56 AD), numerous remarkable events took place; like the monopoly of the ruling power by one Umayyite clan, revolt of the masses against it, murder of Caliph 'Othmān and the eventual come back of the Caliphate to Imām 'Ali, which could not be tolerated by Umayyite clan who went on fighting one battle after another against Imām 'Ali, widening network of conspiracy, monopolization of power by Mu'āwiyah-bin-Abū Sufyyān under the nose of the rightly-guided Caliphs, regular cursing against Caliph-cum-Imām 'Ali in the most abusive words from the official pulpits and in the very midst of these hostile conditions, while leading the morning prayer on the 19th day of the venerable month of the Ramazān,

Imām 'Ali was attacked resulting in his martyrdom three days later on 28th January, 661.

Imām Ḥusain had lived under the holy shelter and care of his father Imām 'Ali for 29 years and 5 months and 7 days. Imām 'Ali was confidentially buried at the dead hour of night in Najaf in an atmosphere charged with gloom. The reason of keeping secret the place of his burial, was that if it were discovered, his body would have been exhumed and made the object of severe revenge in accordance with the practice of the brutal 'Arabs of pre-Islamic era against their enemies.[74]

Imām Ḥusain's about 30 years of life was spent in getting the light of knowledge and nobility of conduct from his father. The erudite like Imām 'Ali, learned-theologist, interpreter of Qur'an, equitable, generous, expert in Divine polity and social science and matchless in manhood and valour, if a man of his excellence, enlightens and grooms a person, then what less can be thought of the able recipient of knowledge from him. If a careful observation is made of Ḥusain's conduct, every step in his life would seem as if it were Imām 'Ali in action.

If the greatest tragedy of Islamic history namely Karbala (10th October, 680), in which Imām Ḥusain sacrificed his family, relatives and friends is thoughtfully studied, it will make it clear beyond doubt that in this battle, his message was that of peace and harmony among the people and security for all. The principles of setting apart the truth from falsehood, is not confined only to Islam, it is universally accepted by all human beings, who proclaim to follow a Divine Faith; be they Christian, Jews, Hindu, Buddhist, Sikh or of any other religion or faith. Imām Ḥusain's message is to make truth distinct from non-truth using the doctrine of your faith.

Imām Ḥusain added: Do try to realize what is humanly expected of you? While living in the society, do undertake to execute your social responsibilities. Do respect the ways of developing human culture. Never go back to corruption, once you have come out of it. Do have courage to oppose the factors which tend to make hell of this earth through exploitation. Put them to end even if you have to part with your life. If you will sacrifice this mortal life for an immortal cause you will attain immortality and enter the Divine realm of everlasting grace, as indicated in Qur'an:

> "And say not those who are slain in the path of God that they are dead; Nay (*they are*) living, but ye perceive not." (*Qur'an 2/154*)

Imām 'Ali-Ibnu'l-Ḥusain, *Imām Żainu'l-Ābidīn*

The fourth in the order of Imamate, Imām 'Ali-Ibnu'l-Ḥusain was the eldest son of Imām Ḥusain and Shahr Bānū, the daughter of Yezdegerd III, the last Sāsānid king of Persia[75], and in him was perpetuated the house of the Prophet Muḥammad. He was born on Friday, the 15th of Jamādī I, 38 AH or 19th October, 658 at Medīna. Martyred by poison on Friday, 25th Muharram, 95 AH, or 19th October, 714 in Medīna and buried in al-Bāqī'h cemetery next to his uncle Imām Ḥasan and grand mother Fāṭimah aż-Żahrah.

'Ali-Ibnu'l-Ḥusain was better well-known as Imām *Żainu'l-Ābidīn* (Decor of the Pious) and *Saiyedu's-Sajidīn* (Ahead of all Prostrates). He had been known without his equal for his contentment at fate and Divine decree and for the high attitude of the worship to Lord.

He was present at the time of the tragic event of Karbala but in extremely indisposed condition of health, nevertheless, he got up to assist his father, Imām Ḥusain but Imām did not allow him to go to the battle field. After the martyrdom of Imām Ḥusain he was made prisoner and taken from Karbala to Kūfa, and from Kūfa to Damascus (Syria). Being too weak to walk with heavy iron cuffs in hands and fetters in feet and with pointed yoke round his throat, he was being brutally dragged and flogged throughout the long passage of his miserable journey. All the same he stood firm with the hope and strength of his conviction and his absolute trust in God.

When the ailing son of Imām Ḥusain was brought before 'Obaydu'llāh, governor of Kūfa, he ordered for his killing and, thus, put an end to the progeny of Prophet Muḥammad. But he saw Żaynab, the celebrated daughter of Imām 'Ali and Fāṭimah aż-Żahrah and grand-daughter of the Prophet Muḥammad, who was determined to die with her young nephew, the tyrant was struck with great fear. All women, children with young Imām 'Ali in the same condition were sent to Damascus, the then capital of Muslim empire, the soldiers of their escort carrying on the top of their lances the heads of the martyrs were produced before Yażīd-bin-Mu'āwiyah-bin-Abū Sufyyān, the then Muslim ruler. The young Imām presented the stand of his father Imām Ḥusain so effectively that Yażīd-bin-Mu'āwiyah, held his breath and the whole crowd of Yażīd-bin-Mu'āwiyah's court was simply spell bound at the confidence, force of logic and elegance of the speech of a young ailing prisoner.

If a historian could stand at the horizon of post-Karbala era, he would find that the Paganism was once more triumphant and its reaction against Islam was cruel, terrible and revolting. There was a thrill of horror throughout Islam; and sad revulsion of the feeling which eventually endangered the salvation of the faith. It had resulted in the contemporary depravity, which was flowing from the Umayyite court of Damascus. Beside the butchery of Karbala, the flower of the Medīnite chivalry and the revered Companions of the Prophet Muḥammad, perished in the disastrous fight at Ḥarra, where a desperate battle took place. The holy city which had sheltered the Prophet Muḥammad, and which had been sanctified by his life and ministry, was deceitfully deserted and could never recover her prosperity and glory. Its best men were either killed or fled to safe places. A few who could save their life who had to acknowledge themselves the slave of Yażīd-bin-Mu'āwiyah, and the same was branded on their necks. It was the high wisdom of Imām Żainu'l-Ābidīn that he, his family and followers were spared from this ignominy. Big question was: how to re-establish the doctrine of Islam among the totally demoralized and frustrated people. This arduous task could only be possible by Imam Żainu'l-Ābidīn, which may be numerated as under:

(i) *To create self-confidence among demoralized people*

Imām Żainu'l-Ābidīn re-established the doctrine and essence of Islam by creating self-confidence among the demoralized people in a language so simple and sweet that every man could easily understand. It is popularly known as *aṣ-Ṣaḥīfah-al-Kāmilah-as-Sajjādia*, which contains the highest esoteric doctrines and it is through its reading that man emerges with greater courage, stronger will and purer mind. It records that the mind and spirit of morphology is an integrated part of religion. Form is not less essential than substance. The religion for national culture is the skin and the skeleton that preserves a fruit with its juice and taste. We cannot squeeze religion and hope to bottle and keep the essence of religion. The holy figures are necessary for any culture, spiritual foundation and function, as a life giving inspiration and guide.

(ii) *To re-establish the institution of learning and knowledge*

Imām Żainu'l-Ābidīn revived, in Medīna, the school of learning and knowledge which was established and flourished under his grandfather Imām 'Ali and continued by his father Imām Ḥusain. He equipped numberless students with knowledge and adorned them with faith in his span of life. He bought slaves from the market, educate them, until they became learned scholars, then he made them free to pursue a respectable way of life. He has the honour and credit of being the writer, next to Imām 'Ali, of the exegesis of Qur'an he has rightly proclaimed: what is not in Qur'an, is nowhere.

(iii) *Institutionalized the message of the martyrdom of Karbala*

The event of Karbala had the deepest and most painful impact on Imām Żainu'l-Ābidīn. He had made the propagation of the message of Karbala, the exclusive goal of his life. He institutionalized the message of the martyrdom of Karbala which in course of time became the guiding force in the name of *Azādārī* or *Tāziādārī* (commemoration ceremony) and became the inseparable part of Islamic religious life, especially for Shi'is.

(iv) *To maintain and preserve the rights of Imamate*

The last person among the progeny of the Prophet Muḥammad was Imām Ḥusain, who was asked by Yażīd-bin-Mu'āwiyah for his *Bai'yat* (pledge allegiance), resulting into the battle of Karbala. None of the Caliphs could dare to ask for pledge of allegiance from Imām Żainu'l-Ābidīn and his successors. The people, by then, had realized that the Caliphate has been usurped from the Progeny of the Prophet Muḥammad, so after the death of Yażīd-bin-Mu'āwiyah, a Hāshimite 'Abdu'llāh-bin-Żubayr, could capture Hijāz, Irāq and Khorāsān, in the name of the progeny of the Prophet Muḥammad, though he was arch enemy of them. Similarly, Mukhtār established himself in Iraq and from there hunted the murderers of Imām Ḥusain's people in the battle of Karbala and systematically pursued and killed them like vermin. He offered the reign to Imām Żainu'l-Ābidīn, who politely declined but expressed his pleasure when the head of Ḥurmulah, the killer of Imām Ḥusain's six months child 'Ali Asghar was presented to him, by the envoy of Mukhtār, Imām thanked him and ordered to celebrate the day as Eīd. No doubt, it was most successful judicial skill of Imām Żainu'l-Ābidīn that the rightful claim of the progeny of the Prophet over the Caliphate were made brightly clear to stand for future.

Imām Muḥammad al-Bāqir

The fifth in the order of Imamate Imām Muḥammad al-Bāqir was the eldest son of Imām Żainu'l-Ābidīn and Fāṭimah, daughter of the Imām Ḥasan, second in the order of Imamate, so he joined in himself two lines of descent: Imām 'Ali and Fāṭimah aż-Żahrah and thus perpetuated the house of the Prophet, Muḥammad. He was born on Sunday, the 1st Rajab, 57 AH or 10th May, 677 at Medīna. Martyred by poison on Thursday, 7th Żilḥijjah, 114 AH, or 29th January, 734 in Medīna and buried in al-Bāqī' cemetery next to his father and other members of the progeny of the Prophet.

Imām Muḥammad al-Bāqir strictly followed the 4-point practical strategy of his father Imām Żainu'l-Ābidīn by creating self-confidence amongst demoralized Muslims, re-establishing the institution of learning and knowledge and institutionalizing the message of the martyrdom of Karbala. He himself was the witness of the tragedy of Karbala as a child of 5 years. His extraordinary brain had encountered events leaving deepest impressions on the tender mind, which got all the more deepened in course of time. His aim of life had become the propagation of the cause of Karbala.

Imām Muḥammad al-Bāqir followed the policy of maintaining and preserving the rights of Imamate over Caliphate. Thus, like his father, he was politically quiescent and refrained from openly putting forward his claim to the Caliphate. In the past when his father Imām Żainu'l-Ābidīn had returned to Medīna after being released from the prison of Damascus, a conflict arose because his uncle and half-brother of Imām Ḥusain, Muḥammad al-Ḥanafiya made a claim on Imamate, because of the fact that Imām Ḥusain had nominated him his deputy while leaving Medīna for the cause of God. But after verifying the fact that Imām Ḥusain has finally made *Naṣṣ* (specific designation of the Imām by his preceding Imām) in the favour of Imām Żainu'l-Ābidīn, the noble hearted Muḥammad al-Ḥanafiya withdrew his claim and maintained his pledge of allegiance to Imām Żainu'l-Ābidīn throughout his life. But after his death his son Abū Hāshim had renewed the claim of his father which resulted in the form of a sect called Kīsānī, which was named after the Kīsān, a slave of Muḥammad al-Ḥanafiya who had masterminded the episode.

Imām Muḥammad al-Bāqir is also known as *Bāqiru'l-'Ulūm* (breaker of new grounds of knowledge). He was perfectly informed of all branches of the knowledge. He developed the school of learning and knowledge, which flourished under his successors. He expanded the traditions of opening the centres of learning like his father Imām Żainu'l-Ābidīn. The scholars of different schools of thoughts liked to attend his lectures in order to enlarge their knowledge. Complex issues of the Islamic theology and its various dimensions received ample attention. His natural generosity opened the door for all sects of Muslim to acquire knowledge and were welcomed to attend and participate in his learned lectures.

It is reported that the then Umayyite Caliph Hishām had summoned Imām Muḥammad al-Bāqir and his son Imām Ja'far aṣ-Ṣādiq to Damascus and debated with them the issue, whether Imām 'Ali possessed *'Ilm'l-Ghayb* (knowledge of unseen). The Caliph himself and the *Ulama* of his court made various arguments but miserably failed. It was with the consultation of Imām Muḥammad al-Bāqir that the Islamic state could release its own coins minted under his supervision for the first time.[76]

Imām Muḥammad al-Bāqir has authored a commentary on Qur'an, which has been referred to by Ibn Nadīm in his famous work *Fehris*. Based on this commentary, Abū Baṣīr Yaḥyā-bin-Qāsim Asadī and other commentators have quoted many of his wise sayings. Imām Muḥammad al-Bāqir was married with Umm Farwah, the granddaughter of the forst Caliph Abū Bakr, so Shi'is and Sunnis both have special reverence for the father and son. Beside the Sūfīs of *Silsilatu'ẓ-Ẓahab* (Golden Chain), those of Ṭayfūriyya and Khwajagān their spiritual lineage from Imām Muḥammad al-Bāqir and whose sayings made *'Irfān* (mystical knowledge) acceptable to Shi'i *Ulama*, who have been opposed to Sūfīsm.

Imām Ja'far aṣ-Ṣādiq

The sixth in the order of Imamate, named Ja'far and the appellation *aṣ-Ṣādiq* (the veracious) *aṭ-Ṭāhir* (the pure one) and *al-Fāzil* (the excellent), was the eldest son of Imām Muḥammad al-Bāqir and Ummu'l-Farwah, daughter of Qāsim, son of Muḥammad, son of Caliph Abū Bakr, so he combined in himself two lines: from the paternal side his genealogy goes back to the Prophet Muḥammad and from the maternal side to the first Caliph Abū Bakr, who was grandfather of his mother and so distinguished genealogy from both sides. He was born on Friday, the 17th Rabī' I, 83 AH or 20th April, 702, at Medīna. Martyred by poison on Tuesday, 15th Shawwāl, 148 AH, or December 4, 765 in Medīna and buried in al-Bāqī' cemetery next to his father and other members of the progeny of the Prophet Muḥammad.

The life of Imām Ja'far aṣ-Ṣādiq consist of two phases. In the first phase the Umayyite rule was in its last legs, facing internal turmoil, Imām Ja'far aṣ-Ṣādiq was relatively free from the persecution of the authorities. He quietly taught Islamic thought to his numerous pupils irrespective of their sectarian faith and succeeded in establishing the considerable reputation. In the second phase of his life when 'Abbāsites came to power, especially during early half of the reign of al-Manṣūr (754-65 AD), he was summoned on the several occasions and put in prison.

There were some political activities in a few members of the progeny of the Prophet Muḥammad also. The half-brother of Imām Muḥammad al-Bāqir, Żayd had started advocating more politically active role and with a view to attract more people, he was ready to accommodate some faiths of the majority of Muslims too. He revolted in 740 AD against Umayyite rule and was killed. Similarly, in 744 AD 'Abdu'llāh, (a descendant of Ja'far aṭ-Ṭayyar, brother of Imām 'Ali) revolted and killed. But the revolt in 762 AD by grandson of Imām Ḥasan, Muḥammad, popularly known *an-Nafs aż-Żakiyya* (pure soul) received great deal of Shi'is support against 'Abbāsite but could not get through. Imām Ja'far aṣ-Ṣādiq maintained the policy of his father and grandfather. Even when the political leader of the 'Abbāsite revolt, Abū Salama, reportedly offered him the Caliphate, Imām Ja'far aṣ-Ṣādiq declined it.

At a glance it appears that if the claim of the progeny of the Prophet Muḥammad over the Caliphate had been continued, Imām Ja'far aṣ-Ṣādiq should extend his support to the above revolts and at least must accept the offer of the political leader of the 'Abbāsite revolt, Abū Salama. But if the objective analysis of the facts is done, the results would tell that the sagacious Imām was circumspect beyond imagination. None of these revolts could be successful in bringing the derailed vehicle of Islam on right track. Except Abū Salamah, who was killed after the revolt, all others were killed during the insurgency.

It would not be an exaggeration to call Imām Ja'far aṣ-Ṣādiq as 'Father of Islamic Jurisprudence'. There are five Schools of Islamic Jurisprudence. Shi'is have a single School of Jurisprudence named after its compiler and interpreter Imām Ja'far aṣ-Ṣādiq. Shi'is are also called Ja'fariyya sect, being the followers of the school of Imām Ja'far aṣ-Ṣādiq in theological laws. Sunnis have four Schools of Jurisprudence named after their respective compilers and interpreters, such as Ḥanafī School of Jurisprudence of Imām Abū Ḥanīfa (d. 767 AD), Mālikī School of Jurisprudence of Imām Mālik-bin-Anas Asḥabī (d. 795 AD), as<u>h</u>-<u>Sh</u>āfi'ī School of Jurisprudence of Imām Muḥammad-bin-Idrīs as<u>h</u>-<u>Sh</u>āfi'ī (d. 819 AD) and Ḥanbalī School of Jurisprudence of Imam Muḥammad-bin-al-Ḥanbal (d. 855 AD). The first two founders of Sunni Jurisprudence, Imām Abū Ḥanīfa and Imām Mālik were direct disciple of Imām Ja'far aṣ-Ṣādiq. Imām Abū Ḥanīfa had also privilege of sitting with other pupils in the classes met by Imām Moḥammad al-Bāqir. Imām Abū Ḥanīfa who is followed by the majority of Sunni sect, prides on being the disciple of Imām Ja'far aṣ-Ṣādiq from whom he had learned the subtle issues of Islamic Jurisprudence. He used to say that the period of his life which he spent in his patronage was the real life, rest is *raigān* (waste).

Ad-Damīrī has reported an interesting episode in which Imām Ja'far aṣ-Ṣādiq had several questions to him, the purpose was to inform Imām Abū Ḥanīfa that the way he used to derive inference on the basis of analogy and guess was not correct. One of these questions was why four witnesses are required for adultery, while only two witnesses are required for a case of murder. When Imām Abū Ḥanīfa could not guess the correct answer Imām Ja'far aṣ-Ṣādiq explained to him that in the case of murder the criminal is one so only two witnesses are essential while in an adultery there are two criminals so the essential number of witnesses is four.[77]

Another founder of the School of Sunni Jurisprudence, Imām Mālik-bin-Anas Asḥabī (d. 795 AD) was also his disciple and was evidently closely associated with Imām Ja'far aṣ-Ṣādiq and transmitted Traditions from him. Imām Shāfi'ī (d. 819 AD) was the direct pupils of Imām Mālik and received instruction in Ḥanafī Jurisprudence from Muḥammad ash-Shabiyānī, who was disciple and colleague of Imām Abū Ḥanīfa (d. 767 AD). Imām Ḥanbal (d. 855 AD) has been no compiler and interpreter of any new Jurisprudence, he is best known as Traditionist. Besides other scholars who, later on, became the founders of other Muslim School of Jurisprudence, were also his disciples, prominent among them being Imām Sufyyān-bin-'Uiniya (d. 813 AD), Imām Sufyyān Thūrī (d. 777 AD), Imām Shu'bah-bin-Ḥajjāj (d. 776 AD) and Imām Fuzayl-bin-Ayāż (d. 802 AD). All of them were proud of being the alumnus of Imām Ja'far aṣ-Ṣādiq. The number of his students had gone up to 4000, many of them turned out to be great scholars.

In the Ja'fari School of Theology, *Naṣṣ* and *'Ilm* have fundamental value. *Naṣṣ* implies the nominating of one Imām by another Imām and *'Ilm* implies comprehensive knowledge peculiar to an Imām. It was Imām Ja'far al-Sadiq, who established that *Taqiyya* (concealment of faith when it causes life to be threatened) is a Qur'anic theological principle.

In addition to the knowledge of theology, he also developed the knowledge of *Ramal*, *Jafr* and *Jam'iā,* the occult, the sciences of numbers. On the subject of *Jafr* many writers have quoted his name for his contribution in their occult sciences. One of his numerous alumnus, Jābir-bin-Ḥayyan (d. 803 AD), known as Gabber in the western world, is the first scientist among Muslims. His contribution in Chemistry and Physics had been recognized by western scientists. Gabber used to assert that he had been taught Physics and Chemistry by Imām Ja'far aṣ-Ṣādiq. Imām Ja'far aṣ-Ṣādiq had exhaustive knowledge of various sciences, such as Astronomy, Medical Science, Botany, Zoology etc.

Apart from the Shi'is, Imām Ja'far aṣ-Ṣādiq, has a general respect among the Sunni scholars and highly popular among the common Muslims. All lines of the Muslim mystic schools regard him as their spiritual guide including those few Ṣūfīs who regard Caliph Abū Bakr as the spiritual guide. Majority of Ṣūfīs regard Imām 'Ali as their top spiritual guide.

Imām Mūsā al-Kāẓim

The seventh in the order of Imamate, named Mūsā and the appellation *al-Kāẓim* (the forbearer) and *'Abdu'ṣ-Ṣāleḥ* (the pious slave of God), was fourth son of Imām Ja'far aṣ-Ṣādiq and Ḥamīdah-Muṣaffāt, appellation *Lūlūt* (pearl) a Barbariyan (Spanish) slave-girl.[78] He was born on Monday, the 7th Ṣafar, 128 AH or 10th November, 745, at Medīna. Martyred by poison on Sunday, 25th Rajab, 183 AH, or 4th September, 799 in Ba<u>gh</u>dad and buried in the cemetery of Quray<u>sh</u>, which is now contained in the double shrine of Kāẓimayn.

Imām Mūsā al-Kāẓim's life was got significant in more than one way. His nomination as an Imām sheds light on some important aspects of the process of Imām's selection that the fourth son of Imām from a maid-slave gets Imamate and the claim of the oldest surviving son Abdu'llāh al-Afṭaḥ was not solicited. It completely negates the dynastic tradition in the selection of an Imām. It was purely on the basis of *Naṣṣ*, already explained in the earlier pages. However, the claim of some people on the basis of dynastic tradition that the eldest son Ismā'īl, should be made Imām has caused division in the Shi'is community, instituting the Ismā'īlī faith. The announcement of Imām Mūsā al-Kāẓim as the successor of Imām Ja'far aṣ-Ṣādiq was popularly accepted by majority of Muslims and it was established that the designation of Imam was not made on dynastic basis.

Imām Mūsā al-Kāẓim was the best person of his time. His appellations, meaning one who controls one's rage and the pious slave of God truly reflect his purity and righteousness of his nobility of character. He was extremely generous, sweet in nature and exceedingly devoted to God. The degree of forbearance and endurance was such that out of his 55 years of life, he spent most of his time in the prisons of the Abbāsite Caliphate, yet he never made a complaint of it.

But whenever some serious problem forced the then Caliph to seek his help in resolving of the crisis, Imām Mūsā al-Kāẓim was sent for and he came to the royal court in iron chains and hand cuffs of the prisoners. He solved the problem and went back to the prison in the very chains and fetters of the prisoner. This went on unless he was poisoned in the very prison to put an end to his life. At the time of burial, it was required to remove the iron chains off his body, the flesh pealed off, as the iron-chains had cut deep into the flesh below the skin for being laid on body for so long a time. So he had to be buried along with the chains and fetters.

As mentioned earlier, the Islamic mystics regard Imām Ja'far aṣ-Ṣādiq as their spiritual head along with Imām Mūsā al-Kāẓim. The famous Ṣūfī saint Shaykh Shaqīq Balkhī (d. 770 AD) has described many of his miracles. Another Ṣūfī saint Shaykh Bashar Ḥāfī (d. 840 AD) had confessed his sins and repented on the hand of Imām Mūsā al-Kāẓim. The reason why he is called *Ḥāfī* (bare-footed) is that he came to Imam bare-footed for repentance. Imām Mūsā al-Kāẓim had 37 children from whom originates the genealogy of most of Saiyeds, who held their respective places of merit in Islamic history. Beside his son Imām ar-Rezā, the most notable among them was Saiyad Razī *'Ilmu'l-Hudā* (d. 1015 AD) who has been a great thinker, erudite, theologist and writer of eminence. He is mostly remembered for his valuable compilation of the scattered sermons, letters and saying of Imām 'Ali in a book entitled *Nahju'l-Balāghah*, famous in 'Arabic literature. The humble writer of the present book too has the honour of belonging to his family tree.

Imām 'Ali ar-Rezā

The eighth in the order of Imamate, named 'Ali and the appellation *ar-Rezā* (the acceptable to all) and *Shāh-i-Khurāsān* (King of Khurāsān), was the eldest son of Imām Mūsā al-Kāẓim and a Persian slave-girl Najmah-Khīzrān, appellation *Ummu'l-Banīn* (mother of sons). He was born on 11th Ziqadah, 148 AH or 29th November, 765, at Medina and martyred by poison on 17 Safar, 203AH, or 23rd August, 818 in Ṭūs (Khurāsān) of Iran and buried near the tomb of 'Abbāsite Caliph Hārūn ar-Rashīd.

Apart from his personal excellence was also the fact that the Abbāsite Caliph al-Māmūn ar-Rashīd (809-13 AD) had made him his heir-apparent to the Caliphate, under the title of *ar-Rezā min Ālul Muḥammad* (the acceptable among the children of Muḥammad—shortly *ar-Rezā*). Hence, he is called in history as *ar-Rezā*.[79] Caliph al-Māmūn had also given his daughter Umm Ḥabība in the marriage and decreed to the effect that green colour was to be used thereafter, which distinguished the house of Imām 'Ali, instead of black colour which symbolized the 'Abbāsite. A brother of Imām ar-Rezā was appointed governor of Kūfa and another Presiding Officer of annual pilgrimage. Imām ar-Rezā's name was also added in inscription on coins which read: "The King of God ar-Rezā and the Faith, al-Māmūn, Amīr and Caliph of the Faithful, and Imām ar-Rezā, the Imām of Muslims."[80] In Khurāsān there was general approval, so a great Darbār was held on Friday, March 21, 816, but in the Baghdad this news created so much consternation that they deposed al-Māmūn as the Caliph and proclaimed his uncle Ibrāhīm-bin-Mahdī who held the position for two years. It could only be settled after the death of Imām ar-Rezā within a few years, so al-Māmūn forced him to take poisoned grapes and thus he got him secretly killed.[81]

The description of his coming over to Khurāsān, of pouring over of public welcome on him, of designating him as his heir-apparent by the Caliph al-Māmūn all have been given in detail in the books of Islamic History. His polemical dialogues with the scholars of different religions and his eventual victory is also on record. As a result, the debating opponents yielded to his sound logic and embraced Islam. All the contemporary learned scholars realise the extraordinary knowledge of Imām ar-Rezā. Many poets have composed eulogy in his honour, notable among them are Debal al-Khazaī and Abū Nawās.

All these circumstances are self-explanatory. Caliph al-Māmūn, son of a Persian mother, had defeated and killed his half-brother Caliph al-Amīn whose mother was an 'Arabian and was successful in capturing the power. 'Arabian were under the influence of Ash'arīs, a form of Sunnis, whereas most of the contemporary Persians were Mu'tażilīs, much closer to the Shi'i faith. Caliph al-Māmūn himself was a Mu'tażilī, so some of the historians who could not differentiate between the Shi'is and Mu'tażilīs have mentioned him Shi'a, which is untrue. It was a part of political strategy of the time for the Caliph to appease the Shi'is and get their favour. Nothing could be more beneficial than getting Imām 'Ali ar-Rezā included in the ruling groups. It appears that Imām ar-Rezā was fully aware of the *pros and cons,* so while leaving his family behind in Medīna on February, 816, he performed the *Naṣṣ,* which implied nominating one Imām by another Imām to make his five year old son to be the Imām next to him, who is known as Imām Muḥammad at-Taqī so that the continuity of Imamate would be maintained. Imām ar-Rezā risked his life fully knowing that the offer of heir-apparentship to him was just a cover to carry on the plan of ruling the masses.

Imām had highest degree of wisdom, and a cautious and sagacious comprehension of political reality. Political maturity calls for historical understanding but one should not remain a prisoner of the past. One has to create a new methodology to solve problems, quietly and silently. It would be presumptuous on my part to draw conclusions but keeping in mind the contemporary sources, it appears that Imām ar-Rezā had taken a prudent decision while accepting to be al-Māmūn's heir-apparent. It appears to be a two-fold strategy – firstly, to confirm the policy of Imām Żainu'l-Ābidīn that the claim of the progeny of the Prophet over the Caliphate would stand for future; and secondly, in pursuance of Imām Ḥasan's policy to forestall the fragmentation among Muslims, after the death of the contemporary ruler (caliph al-Māmūn). The Caliphate would thus combine in the Imamate, with Imām ar-Rezā as head of the Muslim nation by both of these principles.

Imām ar-Rezā has been great littérateur and profound scholar. Among the books attributed to him are *Ṣaḥīfahu'r-Rezā, Ṣaḥīfahu'r-Rizāvia, Ṭibbu'r-Rezā* and *Musnad Imām ar-Rezā.* Some of these books have been published. In the city of Mashhad (Iran), within the premises of the Mausoleum of Imām ar-Rezā, a grand museum and library of rare materials has been opened. Nearby, there is also the Imām ar-Rezā University, which is very impressive in its own way.

There is also special significance of Imām ar-Rezā in the school of mysticism. The spiritual chain starting from Imām'Ali to Imām ar-Rezā is known among the Ṣūfīs as *Silsilatu'ž-Žahab.* One of its main branches gave rise to the branch of Khwaja M'arūf Karkhī which in turn gave rise to many other branches like Saqtiyya, Junaydiyya, Qādiryyia and Chishtiyya etc.

Imām Muḥammad at-Taqī

The ninth in the order of Imamate, named Muḥammad, the appellation *at-Taqī* (the God-fearing) and *al-Jawād* (the generous), was the only son of Imam 'Ali ar-Rezā and a Nubian slave-girl Salīkah or Reḥāna. He was born on Tuesday, the 10th Rajab, 195 AH or 27th March, 812 AD, at Medīna. Martyred by poison on Thursday, 29th Ziqadah, 220 AH, or 28th November, 835 in Baghdad and buried in the tomb of his grandfather Imām Mūsā al-Kāẓim. The grave is now contained in the double shrine of Kāẓimayn.

After a year in 835 AD of martyrdom of the eighth Imām, ar-Rezā, the Caliph al-Māmūn went to Medīna and was highly impressed to see Muḥammad at-Taqī, the only son of Imām ar-Rezā. He was still a very young boy. Caliph al-Māmūn brought him along with him to Baghdad. He told the people in his court about the great knowledge of the young Imām Muḥammad at-Taqī. Upon this the contemporary scholars started polemical debate with him. All of them were prevailed upon by the extensive knowledge of Imām. Among them was Yaḥyā-bin-Ak<u>th</u>am, the chief jurisprudent of his time.[82] al-Māmūn gave his daughter Ummu'l Fazl in marriage.

Having lived at Baghdad for an year, Imām Muḥammad at-Taqī came back to Medīna where he taught and enlightened people of the theological wisdom of Islam and trained them in Islamic ethics. People in great number used to visit him in order to discuss and learn about the complex issues of theological matters. His *sayings* run into thousand, and are collected in various books. After al-Māmūn, al-Mu'taṣim became the Caliph. He was highly jealous of Imām Muḥammad at-Taqī's widening popularity because of his knowledge and charitable character. So he secretly got him poisoned to death.

Imām 'Ali an-Naqī

The tenth in the order of Imamate, named 'Ali and the appellation *an-Naqī* (the distinguished) and *al-Hādī* (the guide), was the eldest son of Imām Muḥammad at-Taqī and a Moroccan slave-girl Samānah-Mag<u>h</u>ribiyya or Sūsan or Darah. He was born on 15th Žilḥijjah 214 AH or 5th March, 828, at Medīna. Martyred by poison on Monday, 3rd Rajab, 254 AH, or 27th June, 868 in Sāmarrā and buried in the twin shrine called 'Askariyān in Sāmarrā (Iraq).

Abbāsite Caliphate who were anxious to destroy the order of Imamate, so on the basis of the *Naṣṣ,* an-Naqī was made Imām in the tender age of 6 or 7 years. Caliphate mischievously planned to exploit his tender age and to seem overtly to be generous to the child, but covertly seeking to end his life, he appointed an scholar 'Obaydu'llāh Junaydī, who had extreme grudge against the Imamate, to be the tutor and mentor of tender aged Imām 'Ali an-Naqī. So that people may not get to see him and he may mould the tender mind of the child into his faith. But he failed in his efforts and had to confess that even in his tender age, Imām 'Ali an-Naqī was for more knowledgeable in theology and other disciplines.

Imām 'Ali an-Naqī lived for 29 years in Medīna. His house was crowded with people seeking knowledge. Apprehensive of this crowd, his house used to be searched by the royal soldiers to humiliate him, though never any objectionable article was traced in his house. But the contemporary Caliph Mutawakkil (847-61 AD) forced him to leave Medīna for Sāmarrā (Iraq). In course of time he was poisoned to death in Sāmarrā.

Imām Ḥasan al-'Askarī

The eleventh in the order of Imamate, named Ḥasan and the appellation *al-Hādī* (the guide) and *al-'Askarī* (named after a place in Sāmarrā where he lived) was the eldest son of Imām 'Ali an-Naqī and a slave-girl Ḥadīthah or Sūsan or Umm Ḥabīb or Salīl or Ḥarabiyya. He was born on Friday, the 8th Rabī'i II, 232 AH or 1st December, 846, at Medīna. Martyred by poison on Sunday, 8 th Rabi'i I, 260 AH, or 1st January, 874 in Sāmarrā and buried in the twin shrine called 'Askariyān in Sāmarrā (Iraq).

Being the reverent father of the Imām of the last epoch, Imām Ḥasan al-'Askarī commands special regards among the Muslims. He was nominated Imām by his father Imām 'Ali an-Naqī as per *Naṣṣ*. He succeeded his father and shouldered his responsibilities at the age of 22 years. He devoted his life in educating and imparting knowledge together with his devotion to God. He was without parallel in various branches of knowledge. He knew many languages which he used from time to time. He is reported to have talked in Turkish to Turkish soldiers, in Persian to Iranian soldiers and in Indian language to the Indians.[83]

Imām Ḥasan al-'Askarī is also said to have dictated an exegesis of holy Qur'an. Based on his exegesis, Ḥasan-bin-Khālid Barqī prepared a detailed commentary on Qur'an which runs into 120 volumes. But his exegesis of Qur'an published at present is not regarded by many scholars as his original work.[84] Imām Ḥasan al-'Askarī preferred to lead a peaceful life nevertheless he too was poisoned to death and became a martyr. He was buried next to his father in Sāmarrā. Three years before his martyrdom, his only son Muḥammad al-Mahdī was born whom he had nominated, as per *Naṣṣ*, to be the twelfth and last Imām.

Imām Muḥammad al-Mahdī

The twelfth in the order of Imamate, *Abu'l Qasim* Muḥammad is remembered by appellations like *al-Mahdiu'l-Ākhir'ż-Żamān* (the guide of the last epoch), *Imāmu'l-Aṣr-wa'ż-Żamān* (the commander of time and age), *al-Muntaẓar* (the awaited), *al-Ḥujjat* (the proof), *al-Qā'im* (the one will arise), *al-Baqīyyātu'llāh* (the remnant of God), was the only son of Imām Ḥasan al-'Askarī and a Roman princess made captive and sold as a slave-girl, Narjis K͟hatūn, also called Sūsan, Reḥanah and Mariyam. He was born on Tuesday, the 15th S͟ha'ban, 256 AH or 18th July, 870, at Sāmarrā (Iraq).

According to the belief of the Imāmiyya sect no age can remain without an Imām. Hence, Imām al-Mahdī is called the Divinely enlisted guide of the last age. The principle of *Mahdawiyyat* (Mahdism) is commonly believed by all sects of Islam, but the Imāmiyya community cherishes special faith in the existence and coming of the *Imām al-Munṭazar* (the Imām who is eagerly awaited). There is no great difference between the Shi 'as and Sunnis with regard to the Imām al-Mahdī. Both believe that before the *Qiyāmah* (final Catastrophe), a Divine Government will be established on earth based on perfect justice under the premiership of Imām al-Mahdī. The only difference is that some of Sunnis believe that Imām al-Mahdī was not born and will be born at the appropriate time and place.

Looking at the different periods of Imamate, the Imām of a particular period, should hold the Islamic power and become the ruling authority. But the truth-abiding Imāms rejected every opportunity to do so. The reason for this abdication was the fact that, it would have become an imperial dynastic rule, in which the royal pleasures became the upper-most objective. The Imāms of the respective periods proved that the so-called Islamic rule was only to enjoy material pleasures. They expressed their unhappiness on the rot set the ruling classes. The respective Caliphs subjected the contemporary Imāms to various kinds of tortures but the Imāms never turned away from their objectives and responsibilities. They braved all tortures and faced all plots, while at the same time continued imparting and training of Islamic principles both by words and actions.

As mentioned in the previous pages, although several dignified and pious men of the Imām 'Ali's genealogy like Imām Żainu'l-Ābidīn's son Żayd (d. 740 AD), Yaḥyā-bin-Żayd (d. 740 AD), Muḥammad al-Nafs al-Żakiya (d. 763 AD), Ibrahīm-bin-'Abdu'llāh al-Maḥaz (d. 763 AD) raised sword against these exploiting rulers but there was no change in the principled nature of Imāms. They never supported the rising of the above-mentioned men. This was to such an extent that Abū Muslim K͟hurāsānī offered to overthrow the Umayyite regime and give the ruling power on a platter to Imām Ja'far aṣ-Ṣādiq but he refused it out-rightly.[85] Had he accepted it, then Abū Muslim K͟hurāsānī and his associates, would have tried to cash in and served their own interests as is normal in the politics. There is no room for advancing selfish interests in a Divinely ruled government. This is how a state rulership gets established but the truly Islamic rule could not come in powers. It was the establishment of a true Islamic ruling order for which every Imām in his respective would strive, suffer tortures and even lay down his life until all the eleven Imāms right from Imām 'Ali to Imām Ḥasan al-'Askarī were put to martyrdom.

It may be noted that capturing the leadership of the ruling power by declaring one-self as the self-selected Caliph had never been accepted by the Muslim world. On the contrary, Muslim gave their support by actively struggling against such moves. But the majority kept aloof from active campaign. Some gave the rank of Imamate to those who raised their voice against the corrupt ruler. For example Imām Żainu'l-Ābidīn's son Żayd is regarded as Imām in his own right as he moved an armed struggle against the unjust Umayyite rulers until his martyrdom. This gave birth to Żaydiyya sect in the same way as some people regarded Abū Muslim Khurāsānī to be an Imām.

References

1. There is difference of opinion regarding the actual dates of birth and death. Sunnis are not unanimous on the dates of birth and death and say 3rd or 9th or 12th of Rabi' I as date of birth and say 2nd or 12th of Rabi' I, as date of death. Some also dispute the names of month as Muḥarram, Ṣafar, Rajab or Ramazān. But majority of them believe and observe 12th of Rabi' I as the Birth Anniversary of the holy Prophet. However, Shi'is believe and observe 17th of Rabi' I in the First year of the Era of the Elephant, or the 20th August, 570 as true date of birth and 28th Ṣafar 11 AH, or 25th May, 632 as date of death. Since these dates believed and observed by Shi'is are based on family tradition, they have more creditability, hence mentioned here. *Ḥayātu'l-Muḥammad*, pp. 120-1, *Sīratu'n-Nabī*: Shiblī, Vol. 1, p. 34. *Kanżu'l-Ansāb*, p. 29, *The Spirit of Islam*, p. 7.
2. *'Aqā'idu'sh-Shaykh Ṣadūq*, p. 88 (Urdu tr. *Hadiyā-i-Jā'fariyą̄*, Muḥammad 'Aejāz Ḥasan, Delhi, 1928.
3. *Jām'ans-Saḥiḥ al Muslim* Vol. II, p. 251, Tradition No. 2431 *Kanżu'l-Ansāb*, p. 26, *Yake AżShākh-i-thamarbār*, p. 27.
4. *aṭ-Ṭabaqātu'l-Kabīr*, Vol 1, p. 82.
5. *Sīrat Rasūlu'llāh*, Vol. 1, p. 115, *aṭ-Ṭabaqātu'l-Kabīr*, Vol 1, p. 76.
6. *aṭ-Ṭabaqātu'l-Kabīr*, Vol 1, p. 93, *Sīrat Rasūlu'llāh*, Vol. 1, p. 124.
7. *Mutālia'i-Qur'an*, p. 645.
8. *Tārīkhu'r-Rusūl wa'l-Mulūk*, Vol. 1, p. 89 similar Traditions in *al-Musnad:* Aḥmad, Vol. 1, pp. 11, 159, *al-Mustadraku's-Saḥiḥayn*, Vol. 3, p. 32, *Labābu't-Tāwīl fī Mā'nī-at-Tanzīl* 5/106, *Kanżu'l-Ummah-fī-Sunnatu'l-Aqwāl-w'al-Alfāz*, Vol. 6, pp. 396-97, *al-Mukhtaṣar fī Akhbāru'l-Bashar*, Vol. 1, p. 116, *Tārīkhu'l-Khulafa*, p. 65.

9. *Tārīkh-i-Islam,* p. 83.
10. *Sīrat Rasūlu'llāh,* Vol. 1, p. 89.
11. *aṭ-Ṭabaqātu'l-Kabīr,* Vol. 1, p. 134.
12. *aṭ-Ṭabaqātu'l-Kabīr,* Vol. 1, pp. 139-40.
13. *aṭ-Ṭabaqātu'l-Kabīr,* Vol. 1, p. 140.
14. *aṭ-Ṭabaqātu'l-Kabīr,* Vol. 1, p. 142.
15. *aṭ-Ṭabaqātu'l-Kabīr,* Vol. 1, p. 146.
16. *Sīrat Rasūlu'llāh,* pp. 341-343.
17. *al-Kāmil fi't-Tārīkh,* Vol. 2, p. 143, *Tārīkhu'r-Rusūl wa'l-Mulūk,* Vol. 3, p. 72.
18. *Sīrat Rasūlu'llāh,* p. 966, *al-Kāmil fi't-Tārīkh,* vol. II, p. 230.
19. *al-Musnad:* Aḥmad, Vol. 4, p. 281, similar Traditions in the same book, Vol. 1, pp. 84,118, 119, 331, Vol. 4, pp. 367, 370, 372, Vol. 5, pp. 347, 366, 419, *as-Sunan*: Ibn Māja, Vol. 1, p. 43.
20. *Madārijul-Nabūwat,* p. 182.
21. *Jām'au's-Ṣaḥīḥul-Bukhārī,* Vol. 3, p. 298 (Tr. 1376).
22. *Jām'au's-Ṣaḥīḥul-Bukhārī,* Chapter 40, Vol. 1, p. 41.
23. *Tārīkhu'r-Rusūl wa'l-Mulūk,* Vol. 3, p. 188, *al-Kāmil fi't-Tārīkh,* Vol. 2, p. 120, *Madārijul-Nabūwat,* Vol. 2, p. 488.
24. *Hayātu'l-Muḥammad,* p. 54.
25. *Sīratu'n-Nabī,* Vol. 2, p. 814.
26. *Tarjima-i-Kalām-i-Ilāhī,* pp. 565-66, *Aḥqāqu'l-Ḥaqq,* p. 171, *Arjaḥu'l-Maṭālib,* p. 96.
27. *Jām'au's-Ṣaḥīḥul-Bukhārī,* Vol. 2, p. 258, *Muwaddatu'l-Qurba,* p. 101.
28. *Jām'au's-Ṣaḥīḥul-Bukhārī,* Vol. 2, p. 258 (Tr. 947), *Jām'au's-Ṣaḥīḥ al-Muslim,* Vol. 2, p. 238 (Tr. 2349).
29. *Yanābia'u'l-Muwaddah,* p. 276.
30. *Yanābia'u'l-Muwaddah,* p. 277.
31. *Bihāru'l-Anwār,* Vol. 3, p. 14.
32. *Yanābia'u'l-Muwaddah,* p. 275.
33. *Ansābu'l-Ashrāf,* Vol. 1, p. 588, Tr. 2.
34. *'Iqdu'l-Farīd,* Vol. 2. p. 253, *Tārīkhu'r-Rusūl wa'l-Mulūk,* Vol. 3. p. 198 *Kanżu'l-'Ummāl-fī-Sunnau'l-Aqwāl-w'al-Afā'l,* Vol. 2. p. 135 *Jām'au's-Ṣaḥīḥul-Bukhārī,* Vol. 3, p. 346, Tradition No. 1625.
35. *Ta'wīlu'l-Mukhtalifu'l-Hadīth,* Vol. 1, p. 14, *Tārīkhu'r-Rusūl wa'l-Mulūk,* Vol. 3, p. 198.
36. *Tārīkhu'r-Rusūl wa'l-Mulūk,* Vol. 2, p. 119.
37. *Tārīkhu'r-Rusūl wa'l-Mulūk,* Vol. 3, p. 533.
38. *Tārīkhu'r-Rusūl wa'l-Mulūk,* Vol. 2, pp. 254-67.
39. *al-Mukhtaṣar fī Akhbāru'l-Bashar,* Vol. 1, p. 159, *Tārīkhu'r-Rusūl wa'l-Mulūk,* Vol. 2, pp. 240-53.
40. *Tārīkhu'r-Rusūl wa'l-Mulūk,* Vol. 3, p. 239.
41. *Tārīkhu'l-Khulafa,* p. 101.
42. *al-Fārūq,* p. 245.
43. *al-Isti'āb fi Mā'rifatu'l-Aṣḥāb,* Vol. 2, p. 453 (Tr. 2015).
44. *al-Istibsār fī Mukhtalifa fihi mina'l-Akhbār,* Vol. 3, p. 166.

45. *al-Isti'āb fi Mā'rifatu'l-Aṣḥāb*, Vol. 2, p. 467.
46. *Kanżu'l-'Ummāl-fī-Sunnau'l-Aqwāl-w'al-Afā'l*, Vol. 3. p. 158.
47. *Tajdīdu'-Aḥyāi'-Dīn*, p. 341.
48. *al-Kāmil fī't-Tārīkh*, Vol. 3, p. 46.
49. *Minhāj as-Sunna an-Nabawiyyā*, Vol. 3, p. 176,: *al-Bidāyah wa an-Nihāyah*, Vol. 7, p. 155, *al-Isti'āb fi Mā'rifat al-Aṣḥāb*, Vol. 2, p. 603.
50. *Murūju'ż – Żahab-wa'l-M'adinu'l-Jauhar*, Vol. 2, pp. 263-65.
51. *al-Mukhtaṣar fī Akhbāru'l-Bashar*, Vol. 1, p. 167.
52. *al-Mukhtaṣar fī Akhbāru'l-Bashar*, Vol. 1, p. 167.
53. *al-Bidāyah w'an-Nihāyah*, Vol. 8, p. 124.
54. *Khilāfat-o-Mulūkiyat*, p. 99.
55. *Khilāfat-o-Mulūkiyat*, p. 99.
56. *Khilāfat-o-Mulūkiyat*, pp. 96-107.
57. *al-Bidāyah w'an-Nihāyah*, Vol. 8, p. 135.
58. *al-Bidāyah w'an-Nihāyah*, Vol. 8, p. 135.
59. *At-Tarikh*, Vol. 2, p. 191.
60. *Tārīkhu'r-Rusūl wa'l-Mulūk*, Vol. 2, p. 217.
61. *Madārijul-Nabūwat*, p. 182.
62. *Tārīkhu'r-Rusūl wa'l-Mulūk*, Vol. 3. (iii) p. 37.
63. *Tārīkhu'r-Rusūl wa'l-Mulūk*, Vol. 3. (ii) p. 239.
64. *A Short History of the Saracens*, p. 47.
65. *ar-Risālah*, p. 35.
66. *Sīrat Rasūlu'llāh*, p. 897.
67. *Jām'au's-Ṣaḥīḥul-Bukhārī*, Vol. 2 Tradition No. 927.
68. *as-Sunan*: Ibn Māja, Vol. I, p. 44.
69. *as-Sunan*: Ibn Māja, Vol. I, p. 51.
70. *Jām'au's-Ṣaḥīḥu'l-Mishkātu'l-Maṣābīḥ* Vol. 3, p. 260 Tr. 5910.
71. *Jām'au's-Ṣaḥīḥu'l-Mishkātu'l-Maṣābīḥ* Vol. 3, p. 260 Tr. 5876.
72. Khwāja Ḥasan Niẓāmī states that this was the first murder historically well established and undisputed of which Mu'āwiyah-bin-Abū Sufyyān was guilty and no ancient or historical and legal analysis can deliver Mu'āwiyah of this guilt, *Muḥarram Nama*, p. 174.
73. *Tārīkhu'r-Rusūl wa'l-Mulūk*, Vol. 2, pp. 254-57.
74. *al-Kāmil fī't-Tārīkh*, Vol. 3, p. 156 *al-Mukhtaṣar fī Akhbāru'l-Bashar*, Vol. 1, p. 181.
75. Abu'l-Aswad, famous Arabic poet says:
    'Thou youth whose maternal grandfather was king of Kisrā (Yezdegerd) and grandfather was Hāshim, would be finest amongst all youth of the world,' *al-Uṣūl-min'al-Kāfī*, p. 255.
76. *Ḥayātu'l-Ḥaywānu'l-Kubrā*, Vol. 1, p. 63.
77. *Ḥayātu'l-Ḥaywānu'l-Kubrā*, Vol. 2, p. 86.
78. *Jilā'u'l-'Uyūn*, p. 270.
79. *A Short History of the Saracens*, p. 265.
80. *The Shi'ite Religion*, pp. 318-9.
81. *al-Kāmil fī't-Tārīkh* Vol. 6, p. 119, *Murūju'ż – Żahab-wa'l-M'adinu'l-Jauhar*, Vol. 9, p. 23, *Islāmī 'Ulūm kā Ta'rruf*, p. 260.

57. *Tarjima-i-Kalām-i-Ilāhī,* p. 792.
58. *Muwaddatu'l-Qurba*, p. 90.
59. *Anwāru'l-Qur'an*, p. 913.

Chapter Seven

The Communities and Sects

Some Guiding Principles

Firqa is an 'Arabic word, its plural is *Firaq* meaning sects, differences. Qur'an has warned against discrimination and separation between the people and has repeatedly laid emphasis on their unity and warm-heartedness. The insistence on unity and amiability is not limited to Muslims only. Its first step is to maintain peace and unity with *Ahlu'l-Kitāb* (the people of the revealed Books). Some have restricted it to Jews and Christians, but others have included Zoroastrians, Hindus and all the claimants of the Divine Book:

> "Say; O' People of the Book! come to a Word Common between us and you." (*Qur'an: 3/63*)

In the second step a general unity and geniality with the whole mankind based on the Qur'anic logic that the entire mankind hail from the same origin because:

> "O mankind! fear your Guardian Lord, who created you from a single person." (*Qur'an: 4/1, 6/98, 7/189, 39/6*)

According to Islamic faith all the prophets totalling one lakh and 24 thousands have invariably focused on unity and co-existence without conflict with the mankind as a whole:

> "The same religion has He established for you as that which He enjoined on Noah, the one which we have sent by inspiration to thee and that we enjoined on Abraham. Moses,

> and Jesus namely that ye should remain steadfast in religion and make no division therein." (*Qur'an: 42/13*)

Qur'an has made it rather clear that those who create divisions have nothing to do with Islam, vide the verse:

> "As for those who divide their religion and break up into sects, thou hast no part in them in the least." (*Qur'an: 6/159*)

Qur'an instructs to be away from those who create divisions:

> "And hold fast all together, by the cable, which God (*Stretche, out for you*) and be not divided among yourselves." (*Qur'an: 3/ 103*)

Then in another place Qur'an orders to proceed on straight path and keep away from all those paths, which create divisions:

> "Verily this is my Way leading straight: follow it. Follow not (*other*) paths, they will scatter you about from His path." (*Qur'an: 6/153*)

To save from these scattering, the holy Prophet Muḥammad had provided the directive principle underlying the *Hadīthu'th-Thaqalayn*: "I leave behind me, amidst you, two things of immense gravity, the *Qur'an* and my *Ahlu'l-Bayt* ...". *Hadīt͟hu'ṯh-Ṯhaqalayn* has already been discussed in the earlier chapters, it also enjoined the Muslims to remain firmly adhered to both Qur'an and *Ahlu'l-Bayt*, so that they might not be led astray. This *Ḥadīṯh* has been discussed in detail at due place. But this is a mockery of Islam that the men in power, specially in the dark period of the Umayyite Caliphate made a pile of fabricated *Ḥadīṯhs* to eclipse the authenticity of *Ahlu'l-Bayt* as shown in the Prophet's word's and deeds. With the result the *Ḥadīṯhu'ṯh-Ṯhaqalayn* too was altered, in which the focus on *Ahlu'l-Bayt* was replaced with the ideal of Prophet's life only, as if there were differences between the two! This fabrication of *Ḥadīṯh* took Jalālu'd-Dīn Suyūṭī (d. 1505) to write a book entitled *L'alīu'l-Maṣnū'ah* (Artificial Pearls) in which he has laboured to sort out the genuine *Ḥadīth* from the spurious ones after a thorough analysis. It is not possible here to talk extensively on the issue of original and counterfeit *Ḥadīṯh*; suffice it to say here that the purpose to produce counterfeit *Ḥadīṯhs* was to cause rift and division in Muslims and make the question of successorship of the Prophet, a controversial subject. The separatist group was even successful in its move. The historian ash-Shahrastānī, Abu'l-Fatḥ Muḥammad (d. 1153 AD) maintains that basically the cause of sectarian division is the issue of appointing the successor of the Prophet. Not so many swords were drawn out of sheath for any religious matter as in the matter of appointing the successor of the holy Prophet Muḥammad.[1]

About the number of Islamic sects, a *Ḥadīth* of the Prophet Muḥammad is usually quoted, to prove that there would be 72 sects, but on the basis of a different reading:

> "There would be 73 sects" – "all would go to Hell except the one who would go to Heaven."

Considering that the number is not definite, it rather signifies the magnitude of divisions. If it were literally a fixed number, the fact of cropping up of new sects in different times would be negative. In fact the number of sects and subjects, over the last 14 hundred years have increased to hundreds. What seeds of dissention has this number 72 or 73 sowed may be imagined. An interesting aspect of this is that every sect regards itself to be the only sect which will go to Heaven, while rest are regarded damned for Hell.

While looking at these sectarian difference, it should also be observed that there have been attempts to end disunity and bring unity between the Sunni and Shi'a sects. For example the introduction of Shi'i theology in al-Aẓhar University in Egypt, the provision of a cordial atmosphere by Islamic Democrat Iran for all sects to still explore and highlight the grounds of unity among them, as also the books as: *'Adāwatu'l-Islamia-i'la-Waḥdatu'l-Ahlu'l-Sunnah-wa'l-Imamiyya* by Abu'l Ḥasan al-Khanīzī, *Lā Sunnah Lā Shia* by Muhammad Ali al-Żа'bī, *Shi'a-i 'Alawīyya Shi'a-i Ṣafavīyya* by 'Ali Sharī'atī etc. may be mentioned in particular.

There are two extreme stands usually taken in sectarian differences. One: putting all issues of difference from parts to whole under objective analysis, without allowing any subjective emotions or bias, so as to reach the truth. Second: allowing sectarian bias and fidelity to dominate and admitting no difference of opinion. Both these stands are the extremist. One extremely flexible, the other extremely rigid. By way of principle, when an issue or problem is addressed, the difference between the interpretation of meaning and knowledge of the subject is very natural and unavoidable. But it is not necessary that differences cause separation, because the basis is the search for truth, faith and fidelity to facts. But, if the same is based on communality, personal ego and ignorance then, even the ordinary or small difference is sufficient to cause groups and division. The disputes which surfaced just after the death of the Prophet, arose from these extreme positions.

As expressed by al-Ash'arī, Abu'l Ḥasan-bin-Ismā'īl (d. 935 AD) the main cause of dissension was appointment of the successor to the Prophet Muḥammad. He has described in detail how Caliph 'Omar played the role of making Caliph Abū Bakr acceptable as the first Caliph. He has also touched upon other events specially the murder of Caliph 'Othmān.[2]

Ash-Shahristānī, Abu'l-Fatḥ Muḥammad (d. 1153 AD) has described those events more elaborately.[3] According to him dispute had surfaced in the very lifetime of the Prophet. At the same time the *Munāfiqūn,* the hypocrites, outwardly Muslim, inwardly dangerous enemies of Islam, while remaining within Islam, had started playing foul with it. For example 'Abdu'llāh bin Sabā or Marwān bin Ḥakam or events connected with his father, on account of which he and his father were driven out of the Medina, were the product of division and dispute. Ash-Shahristānī (d. 1153 AD), has counted ten crucial disputes after the death of the Prophet Muḥammad[4]:

1. The Prophet Muḥammad asking for pen which was refused, when he was on his death bed.
2. The Prophet Muḥammad ordering his companions to join Osāmā's army under his commandment and defiance of command of Abū Bakr, 'Omar and other Qurayshites.
3. After the death of the Prophet Muḥammad, the denial of his death by Caliph 'Omar arguing that Prophet cannot die.
4. Dispute raised about the place of burial of the Prophet Muḥammad.
5. The problem of selecting the successor of the Prophet, in which one group maintained that the Prophet Muḥammad had already appointed Imām 'Ali as his successor, while the other group supported the election of Abū Bakr as the successor.
6. The issue related to the *Fidak*, a property bequeathed to his daughter by the Prophet Muḥammad, which was denied by Abū Bakr, when she claimed to get it as her right.
7. War of Abū Bakr against those who refused to pay *Żakāt*.

9. Abū Bakr's nominating 'Omar as his successor by the statement of will. The role of the council for appointing 'O<u>th</u>mān as the third Caliph.
10. Pitching a full-blooded battle of *Jamal* against Imām-cum-Caliph 'Ali by 'Ā'isha, Ṭalḥā and Żubayr.

There is no doubt that as time passed more differences were cropped up. On the whole the disputes were of fundamental nature and if they are analyzed, we may find three important causes:

Firstly, Differences in the basic articles of the Faith

The two major sects of Islam namely Shi'a and Sunni are formed on different interpretations of two basic articles of faith namely *Imāmat* and *<u>Kh</u>ilāfat*. Each has sub-sects within it.

Secondly, Political Differences

Keeping in mind the ten disputes mentioned by a<u>sh</u>-<u>Sh</u>ahristānī one may clearly senseout the political motives behind them. In course of time, political differences got enmeshed in religious ones and thus emerged different movements; such as Movement of 'Arab Chauvinism, <u>Sh</u>u'ūbī Movement, 'A<u>sh</u>'arī Movement, Mu'tażilī Movement and recently Wahhābī Movement etc.

Thirdly, Contemporary Differences

Differences born under the compulsion of a historical situation or because of some selfish stand taken by an individual, disappeared with the end of those situations or individuals. For example; <u>Kh</u>awārij, Murji'īs, Jabriyya, al-Qādriyya etc.

Important sects of Islam are being introduced in the following pages:

The Shi'i Community

Shi'ī is an 'Arabic word, whose root according to 'Arabic grammarians is *Shi'a*. This word is used in Qur'an in 12 forms of its derivatives:

<u>Sh</u>ī'a	(*Qur'an: 19/69*)
Ta<u>sh</u>ī'a	(*Qur'an: 24/19*)
<u>Sh</u>ī'i	(*Qur'an: 15/10*)

Ashiyā'akum	(*Qur'an: 54/51*)
Beashya'ihim	(*Qur'an: 34/54*)
Shī'atihī	(*Qur'an: 28/15*) (twice), 37/83
Shī'an	(*Qur'an: 6/65 and 159, 28/4, 30/32*)

The number 12 has a specific significance for Shi 'as for they have faith in the 12 Imams. So they are called the *Ithnā-'Asharī* (Twelvers).

In one of the verses referred above, Qur'an says:

> "And verily from his (*Noah's*) Shi'a was Abraham." (*Qur'an: 37/83*)

The time interval between Noah and Abraham is said to be 2640 years.[5] It proves the logic that it is never necessary to be a contemporary of someone in order to become his Shi'a. To be Shi'a means to be attached by faith to someone which is possible after any interval of time. The literal meaning of the word *Shi'a* is – friend, helper, follower, religious order, group and adherent. *Shi'a* is equally used both as a singular and plural as also both as masculine and feminine. By way of definition the community is called *Shi'is*, which is identified with *Ahlu'l-Bayt*, Prophet's infallible progeny and Imām born in that progeny. Ibn Khaldūn, Abū Żayd 'Abdu'r-Raḥmān (d. 1406 AD) has said:

> "In dictionary the meaning of the word *Shi'i* is friend and follower, from the earliest time to the present, the theologian have used, this word for the followers of 'Ali-Ibn-Abū Ṭālib."[6]

Shi'is' existence is established since the very lifetime of the Prophet Muḥammad.[7] We come across a dialogue between Caliph 'Omar and Salmān Fārsī, the celebrity companion of the Prophet Muḥammad, regarding whom he has said: "If there are ten degrees of truth, Salmān has all ten degrees of truth." The instant dialogue shows that in the life-time of the Prophet, Salmān Fārsī (d. 657 AD) was regarded as the Shi'a of *Ahlu'l-Bayt*. The dialogue goes like this – Caliph 'Omar asked Salmān Fārsī, 'Why did you oppose Caliph Abū Bakr ?' Salmān Fārsī replied, 'I am the Shi'a of *Ahlu'l-Bayt,* in my life, in this world, and after my death, I am the opponent of every person who is their opponent.'[8] This fact is supported by the statement of a famous anti-Shi'a scholar and writer of Syria, Muḥammad 'Ali Kurd (d. 1953 AD), he writes:

> "In the very lifetime of the Prophet, a group of his distinguished companions was famous for its spiritual attachment to 'Ali such as Salmān Fārsī whose statement was, 'We had pledged allegiance to the Prophet, that we shall be well-wishing to Muslims, be respectful and be obedient to 'Ali and keep faithfully attached to him.' Likewise, Sa'īd Hažarī used to say that five things had been instructed to act upon. Out of them four were acted upon, while the fifth was dropped. When he was asked what was that fifth one, he said it was 'Ali-Ibn-Abū Ṭālib's successorship. When questioned, 'Was it essential to accept it?' He answered, 'Yes, it was essential like those four things.' This belief was shared by the Prophet's other esteemed companions like Abūžar Ghaffarī, Ammār-bin-Yāsir, Ḥužayfa-bin-al-Yamānī, Khuzayma-bin-Thābit *Žūshahadatayn*, Abū Ayyūb Anṣārī, Khālid-bin-Sa'īd, Qays-bin-'Abādah."[9]

Qāzī ash-Shūshtarī, Nūru'llāh (d. 1707 AD) has written that Shi'is of Imām 'Ali enjoyed distinguished status in the lifetime of the Prophet Muḥammad. Their number went unto thousands hailing from different clans. Qāzī ash-Shūshtarī has written biographies of 100 highly notable persons among them. This refutes the anti-Shi'is propaganda that after the death of the Prophet, the followers of Imām 'Ali were only three or four.[10] In the opinion of Abū Bakr Sirāju'd-Dīn the Shi'is and the Ṣūfīs were the same but their sphere was wider later on.[11]

The facts given above indicate that the *Shi'is* as a group or friends and followers of Imām 'Ali did exist in the very lifetime of the Prophet Muḥammad. Apart from the *Shi'is of Ahlu'l-Bayt,* there were various small groups also called Shi'is by way of their allegiance either to some clan or some individuals.

An-Naubakhtī, Abī-Muḥammad al-Ḥasan-bin-Mūsā (alive in 940-1 AD) is of the view that after the death of the holy Prophet Muḥammad, Muslims were divided into three major groups – the Shi'is of Imām 'Ali, the Shi'is of Caliph Abū Bakr, and the Shi'is of Sa'd-bin-'Obayda, who were also called *Hāshimīs*, the descendants of the Prophet's grandfather, Hāshim; *Muhājirīn*, the emigrants of Mecca; and *Anṣār,* the sacrificing natives of Medīna; respectively.[12] During the rule of Caliph 'Ali (656-61 AD) other groups of the Muslims merged with the Shi'is of Imām 'Ali. But Umayyites, who were the hereditary enemies of Hāshimīs, were not willing to accept the leadership of Hāshimīs at any cost. The people of Umayyites formed a separate group of their own and named it as the

Shi'is of 'Othmān. They fought as such against Imām 'Ali and also against Imām Ḥusain in Karbala.[13]

Most of the so-called scholars, who are given highest honour even at present by those who have imperial mentality, make no difference between Shi'is and *Khawārij, Żanādiqa, Ghulāt, Mu'tażilīs, Malāḥida* etc. They treat these synonymous. But in fact each term stands for a different path or sect. For Shi'is they popularly use the abusive word *Rāfizī.* Their source book is by and large the books of those Sunnis who are given to use the word Shi 'as in very derogatory manner, such as *Khawārij* (who driven out of Islam), *Żindiqa* (the followers of the ancient religion of Persia), *Ghulāt* (the one who exaggerate in religious matters), *Mu'tażilīs* (the separatists) *Mulāḥida* (the Heretics) and *Rāfzī* (a pure abusive term meaning, dissenter and swindlers). Mulla Aḥmad Thathwī, whom Emperor Akbar had entrusted with writing the book, *Tārīkh-i-Alfī* (the Islamic History of Thousand Years), has opined that Sunni's all books are replete with insulting and abusing terms against Shi'is.[14]

This hostile conduct is also because the Sunni authors alleged in their writings that the originator of Shi'is sect was a Jew called Ibn-Sabā, who formed the Shi'a sect to divide the Muslims. So the Shi'is are oftener referred to as *Sabā'iyya,* the followers of Ibn-Sabā. But there is no scarcity of genuine and honest Sunnis scholars. They have fully established the fact that the episode of Ibn-Sabā is a pure fiction. No one of this name ever existed in history. However, the deadly-prejudiced Sunni writers continue to refer Ibn-Sabā as the founder of Shi'a sect and keep calling Shi'is as the *Sabā'iyya.* On this subject, the renowned Sunni scholar Ṭah'ā Ḥusain (d. 1973 AD) of al-Ażhar University of Egypt, in his research work writes:

> "I think those who make an elaborate and exaggerated theme of Ibn-Sabā, are extremely unfair both to themselves and to the history. First of all we catch sight of the standard classic works of early scholars which are also the authorize source books for the scholars of the later period, have absolutely no mention of Ibn-Sabā."[15]

At another place, he writes:

> "The disagreement of the genuine historians with the validity of the name of Ibn-Sabā and *Sabā'iyya,* mirrors the validity of the fact that Ibn-Sabā is a pure myth and invention. He was fictitiously invented when Shi'is sect was confronted with other

> sects. The adversaries of Shi'is sect wanted to discredit Shi'aism by identifying it with Jewish elements. All these were the situations of a very horrible designs, myth making and misleading measures whose sole purpose was to humiliate the Shi'is."[16]

The five sects among the Shi'is have been given by a<u>sh</u>-<u>Sh</u>ahristānī (d. 1153 AD) as – *I<u>th</u>nā-'A<u>sh</u>arī* or *Imāmiyya*, *Sāb'iyya* or *Ismā'īlis*, *Żaydiyya*, *Kaysāniyya* or *Hā<u>sh</u>imiyya* and *'Alawiyya.*[17] At present among the main sects of the Shi 'as community are *I<u>th</u>nā-'A<u>sh</u>arī* or *Imāmiyya, Sāb'iyya* or *Ismā'īlī, Żaydiyya* and *'Alawiyya.* The *Kaysāniyya* or *Hāshimiyya* has faded away. An introductory note on these sub-sects is given below:

I<u>th</u>nā-'A<u>sh</u>arīs or Imāmiyyas

I<u>th</u>nā-'A<u>sh</u>arī in 'Arabic means twelve. Those who believe in twelve Imams are called *I<u>th</u>nā-'A<u>sh</u>arī* or *Imāmiyya. Imāmiyya* means the followers of Imāms. A large majority of Shi'is community is *I<u>th</u>nā-'A<u>sh</u>arī* or *Imāmiyya*, so much so that the very word Shi'a has become synonym of *I<u>th</u>nā-'A<u>sh</u>arī* or *Imāmiyya.* Other sub-sects of Shi'is are known separately by their own respective names. As we have already discussed the doctrine of Imamate and the twelve Imams early in this book, we need not repeat it here.

I<u>th</u>nā-'A<u>sh</u>arīs or *Imāmiyyas*, regards 5, 12 and 14 as holy numbers. The number 5 stands for *Panjatan*, five holy luminaries namely, the holy Prophet Muḥammad, Imām 'Ali, Fāṭimah aż-Żahrah, Imām Ḥasan and Imam Ḥusain. By the number of 14 they signify the fourteen infallible souls whom God has kept intact and untouched by any sin or error and they are the Prophet Muḥammad, his daughter Fāṭimah aż-Żahrah and the 12 Imāms from his holy progeny including the first Imām 'Ali.

The Imamate

The twelve Imams from the progeny of the Prophet Muḥammad carry special significance as they are believed to have been Divinely blessed with knowledge, devotion, purity, piety, patience and saintliness, par excellence. The names in chronological order of these Imams, regarded with reverence by the Muslims in general[18], and Shi'is in particulars, are given below:

First	:	Imām 'Ali-Ibn-Abū Ṭālib: (600-61 AD)
Second	:	Imām Ḥasan: (625-70 AD)
Third	:	Imām Ḥusain: (626-80 AD)
Fourth	:	Imām Żainu'l-Ābidīn: (658-713 AD)
Fifth	:	Imām Muḥammad al-Bāqir: (677-734 AD)
Sixth	:	Imām Ja'far aṣ-Ṣādiq: (702-65 AD)
Seventh	:	Imām Mūsā al-Kāẓim: (745-99 AD)
Eighth	:	Imām 'Ali ar-Rezā: (765-818 AD)
Ninth	:	Imām Muḥammad at-Taqī: (812-35 AD)
Tenth	:	Imām 'Ali an-Naqī: (828-68 AD)
Eleventh	:	Imām Ḥasan 'Askarī: (846-74 AD)
Twelfth	:	Imām Mahdī Ā<u>kh</u>iru'ż-Żamān: (870 AD-Till the Day of Judgment)

The Occultation

The first occultation period of last and hidden Imām Mahdī Ā<u>kh</u>iru'ż-Żamān (873-940 AD) is known as *<u>Gh</u>aybatu'ṣ-Ṣug<u>h</u>rā* (Short Occultation). In this period the Imām had his four representatives, each made direct contact with the Imām, received the instruction from him and conveyed it to the believers. The period after that is known as *<u>Gh</u>aybatu'l-Kubrā* (Greater Occultation) in which the facility of making direct access to him through the representatives was stopped. The names of the four representatives were as follows:

First *Nā'ibu'l-Imām*:	'O<u>th</u>mān-bin-Sa'īd: (873-93 AD)
Second *Nā'ibu'l-Imām:*	Muḥammad-bin-'O<u>th</u>mān: (893-917AD)
Third *Nā'ibu'l-Imām*:	Ḥasan-bin-Rauh: (917-37 AD)
Fourth *Nā'ibu'l-Imām*:	'Ali-bin-Muḥammad Sāmarrī: (937-40AD)

These special Deputies of the Twelfth Imām in his short occultation period (873-94 AD) are also known as *Nā'ib* (Deputy), *Wakīl* (Advocate), *Safīr* (Ambassador), *Bāb* (Gate) etc. These titles imply to be assistant to the contemporary Imām. The fourth Nā'ibu'l-Imām, 'Ali Sāmarrī brought the following written instruction and message from the *Hidden Imām*:

> "Do not appoint anyone to your position after you. For the second occultation has come and there will not now be a magnification except by the permission of God and thereafter a

long time has passed, and hearts have hardened and the earth become filled with tyranny."[19]

Re-establishing the Doctrine

With a view to re-establish the doctrine of Islam, it appears necessary to understand again this apparently arduous task in the light of four-point guideline prescribed by Imām Żainu'l-Ābidīn which may be numerated to create self-confidence among demoralized people, to re-establish the institution of learning and knowledge, to maintain and preserve the rights of Imamate and institutionalize the message of the martyrdom of Karbala. These points have already been discussed in details at the appropriate places, and hence need no repitition. However, these issues were again addressed in the changed perspective of the occultation of the Twelfth Imām Mahdī Ākhiru'ż-Żamān. The holy figures were necessary for cultural, spiritual development regeneration life giving inspiration and guide. To create self-confidence among the people, the exegesis of Qur'an and *Ḥadīth* were compiled by Imām Żainu'l-Ābidīn, so that the claim of the Progeny of the holy Prophet over the Caliphate is ensured, and admitted. But there is no match to the institutionalized message of the martyrdom of Karbala.

The eleventh century AD has been called *the Shi'i century*[20], during which the Buyid were in control of Iraq and Iran, the Hamādānīs ruled over northern Syria and Fāṭimīds reigned over Egypt, southern Syria and the Ḥijāz. Despite having a freehand they never tried to impose the Shi'i ideology on the persons of other faiths. However, the Shi'is made substantial inroad on the Muslim masses through emphasizing to love the Prophet Muḥammad and his pious progeny. During the Buyid era some important incidents took place, which later developed as popular religion of the Shi'is. Mu'izzu'd-Dawla Daylamī, under the Buyid regime, instituted two great Shi'is commemorations in 351 HD/962 AD in Baghdad: firstly, on the martyrdom of Imām Ḥusain, the 10th day of Muḥarram, the day of the butchery of Karbala (Iraq), in which the noblest spirit of time was martyred and with him perished all the members of his family, the pious companions of the Prophet Muḥammad and others, causing a thrill of horror throughout Islam. Secondly, the festival of *Ghadīru'l-Khumm* on 18th day of Żilḥijjah, now popularly known as *Eīdu'l-Ghadīr* among the Shi'is, commemorating the nomination of Imām 'Ali as his successor, by the holy Prophet Muḥammad at *Ghadīru'l-Khumm*.

It was during the Buyid era that public mourning for Imām Ḥusain, the members of his family, the pious companions of the Prophet Muḥammad and others were initiated. Their shrines were built and the custom of pilgrimage to these shrines established. The custom of commemorations on the martyrdom of Imām Ḥusain, in course of time has become a guiding force in the name of *'Ażādārī* or *Tā'żiādārī* and also the inseparable part of the Islamic religious life, especially for Shi 'as.

Apart the Shi'is countries like Iran and Iraq, *Tā'żiādārī* was given much encouragement and regards in India. The speciality of Indian *'Ażādārī* has been that Sunni and Shi'is both observe it in their respective ways. Hindus not only respect it but some participate in it. A few Imambaras were built by Hindus. There are some Hindu poets who have composed poems and *Marthiyas* (elegies) on Imām Ḥusain. The Indian sub-continent, which consist of India, Pakistan and Bangladesh, has highly enthusiastic tradition of commemoration for a period of two months eight days every year, whereas, it is not prevalent in Iran and Iraq. Afghanistan's Shi'is mostly live in Mazār-i-Sharīf and its adjacent areas, where they do *'Ażādārī* with geat zeal. In the most of the 'Arabian countries the ruling class is against such commemoration ceremonies but the areas where some Shi'is live, they perform it silently and where they are in majority bring out processions.

The commemoration ceremonies on the martyrdom of Imām Ḥusain are observed in various forms as per Indian traditions, in all parts of the world, where Shi'is community has been settled.[21] In European countries England is main centre and especially London, where the commemoration is observed in big way. Muslims in Germany, France and Italy also observe. In Spain these commemoration ceremonies are called *Ḥusainiya.* In United States New York, New Jersey, Washington are the centres. South American countries Brazil, Bolivia, Argentina and Colombia's Muslim also observe '*Āshūrah* (the tenth day of Muharram, the day of the martyrdom of Imām Ḥusain). Canadian Shi'is observe the martyrdom of Imām Ḥusain and organize various functions. In African countries: Fez, Mequineza, Morocco and Egypt are important centres. Countries like China, Japan, Thailand, Borneo (Kalimantan), Myanmar, Sri Lanka etc. also commemorate the martyrdom of Imām Ḥusain as per their traditions.

Indonesians call the month of Muḥarram as *Sura*, which may be folk-form of 'Arabic word '*Āshūrah*, which evidences their attachment to the *Ahlu'l-Bayt* but unfortunately the nation is presently in the grip of Wahhābīs, who have been deadly opposed to observing the martyrdom of

Imām Ḥusain, so various restrictions were imposed from time to time but in vain. They have been blushed aside by the people of the Island Java, who enthusiastically observe the martyrdom of Imām Ḥusain with their folk-traditions. They cook meal in red colour, prepare soup and distribute among needy ones. They dress their children as images of the holy Imāms. Likewise, the people of Island Sumatra call the Muḥarram as the month of Imām Ḥasan and Imām Ḥusain. In the north of Sumatra, cities of Atjeh and Benkulu, the commemorations are marked with distinction. Similarly, other most important centres of *'Azādārī* are: Bukhara, Tashkent, Samarkand, Andijan (Uzbekistan), Baku (Azerbaijan), Dushanbe (Tajikistan), Turkistan (Kazakhstan), Khiva (Tukmenia) Yerevan (Armenia) etc.

Institution of Jurisprudence

The development of the institution of jurisprudence, the *Ijtihād*, helped in authentic interpretation of theology. Shi'is believe that the door of *Ijtihād* remain open for interpretation. They regard it as symbolic of a scientific pursuit, so that the theological thought may not become static or stagnant, and all new issues may be addressed timely and consistently.

The transmission of *Ḥadīth* by al-Kulaynī, Abū Jā'far Muhammad-bin-Y'āqūb (d. 940 AD) and Ibn Bābūya, Abū Ja'far Muḥammad-bin-'Abdu'llāh al-Qommī (d. 991 AD) enabled the Shi'is to obtain knowledge directly from the Tradition of the Imāms. The complexities of life and time threw up new problems such as the influence of the Mu'taẓilīs, to which many Shi'is felt concerned. Al-Mufīd, Ibn al-Ma'allim, Shaykh Abū 'Abdu'llāh Muḥammad (d. 1022 AD) and his pupil 'Alamu'l-Hudā Sharīfu'l Murtazā Mūsāwī (d. 1044 AD) and also his pupil Shaykhu'ṭ-Ṭā'fa, Abū Ja'far Muḥammad-bin-Ḥasan aṭ-Ṭūsī (d. 1067 AD) not only countered the influence of the Mu'taẓilīs but gave a fresh approach to the jurisprudence, resulting al-Ḥillī, Muḥaqqiq Najmu'-Dīn Abu'l Qāsim Ja'far (d. 1277 AD) making *'Aql* (reason) its central feature. Aṭ-Ṭusī. Khwāja Naṣīru'-Dīn (d. 1274 AD) developed *Shi'i Kalām*: dogmatic, speculative theology, so as to incorporate philosophical concepts. *Shahīdu'l-Awwal* Shamsu'd-Dīn al-'Āmilī (d. 1384 AD) sacrificed his life for giving new interpretation of jurisprudence. Shaykh Ja'far Najafī (d. 1812 AD), who is better known for his book *Kāshifu'l-Ghiṭā* (uncovered of error) removed various cobweb from the interpretations of the jurisprudence.

The concept of the *Mujtahid* (pl. *Mujtahidīn*) as competent authority in jurisprudence) being the *Nā'ibu'l-Imām* has become the basic authority and influence. There is only a Tradition known as *Maqbūla* (accepted as reliable) of 'Omar-bin-Ḥanẓala, states the Tradition of Imām Ja'far aṣ-Ṣādiq:

> "Let them agree to having him give judgment for I (*Imām Ja'far aṣ-Ṣādiq*) have made such a person *Ḥākim* (judge) over you."[22]

Shi'i scholars al-Karakī, Muḥaqqiq-ath-Thānī Nūru'd-Dīn 'Ali (d. 1533 AD), *Shahīd-ath-Thānī* Shaykh Żainu'd-Dīn (d. 1558 AD) and al-Khu'ī, Āyatu'llāh Saiyed Abu'l Qāsim Mūsāwī, the present *Marjau't-Taqlīd*: reference point for emulation for all Shi'is, have argued in favour of *Mujtahid* being general representative of the Twelfth Imām Mahdī Ākhiru'ż-Żamān. Imām Khomeinī (d. 1989 AD), the founder of the Islamic Republic of Iran, has taken the same argument to its logical extension and stated that only the government by a *Faqīh* (expert in Islamic jurisprudence) is permissible and developed the concept of *Wilāyatu'l-Faqīh,* that government belongs by right to those who are learned in jurisprudence.

Some Shi'i Faiths

The Shi'i faith and thought have been given in the foregoing pages where the Cardinal Beliefs and Religious Obligations of Islam have been discussed. The main area of doctrinal difference between Shi'is and Sunnis is that of Imamate and Caliphate. Besides there are serious differences between them in the principles of jurisprudence of the issues like *Ijmā'* and *Ijtihād*, *Tawallā* and *Tabarra* etc. Let us share some basic information:

Ijmā': literally means, to agree or to resolve – in Shi'is thought is possible only by the consensus of all the clergies. According to Shi'i principles like *Qiyās* (analogical reasoning), *Istiḥsān* (lenient interpretation) and *Masāilu'l-Mursala* (expedient issues) do not help reach an authentic judgment, so it is not wise to act upon them. But according to Sunnis these three principles are the constituent elements of *Ijmā'*. Similar is the case with *Taqlīd* (emulation) and *Ijtihād.*

Ijtihād: literally means, exertion–the process of innovative exegesis to arrive at judgment on points of religious law using *'Aql* (reason) and *Uṣūlu'l-Fiqh* (principles of jurisprudence), and to reach authentic interpretation. As has been made clear in the foregoing pages that in the Shi'i belief, Imām is regarded as *Manṣūṣ-mina'-llāh* (Divinely ordained and appointed rank). The use of reason is essential in all except the ritualistic injunctions. Ritualistic injunctions relate to mode of worship, like the components of such as sitting, standing, lowering, prostrating in *Ṣalāt* or *Namāż*. The problem related with a ritualistic matter like *Namāż* should be resolved by a clergy.

There are two principles of *Ijtihād,* to reach authentic interpretation:

Firstly, If there is no explicit instruction given by God in a specific matter *Mujtahid*, the learned scholar having studied sufficiently and achieved the level of competence necessary to obtain *Ijāżah* (permission, the certificate) permitting a pupil to transmit his thought or testifying his ability to exercise and practice *Ijtihād* make earnest effort to find instruction about that matter. The instruction thus found may vary from *Mujtahid* to *Mujtahid*. Anyone *Mujtahid* may be followed. No *Mujtahid* may be held wrong for the expression of his individual finding. This principle is known as *Taṣwīd* (convenience), based on the principle of all the four schools of Jurisprudence of the Sunnis.

Secondly, if it is not essential to follow the *Mujtahid,* every person is fully qualified to exercise his own judgment. Of course if he is ignorant of the science and application of Islamic jurisprudence he will have to follow a *Mujtahid,* whose reputation in knowledge is well established and who can be followed without hesitation. The expert opinion of the *Mujtahid* is applicable only between him and his followers.

To follow the instructions of a *Mujtahid* is allowed only in the practical and applied matters of the religion, as it is forbidden and unlawful in Cardinal Faith and Religious Obligations. They have to be accepted only after serious contemption and reasoning on individual basis.

Tawalla is to be in love with the Prophet and his pious progeny. The difficulty arises with extremes, holding doctrines that the persons loved are so heretical as to put those holding them outside Islam.

Tabirra is to be detached emotionally from the enemies of the Prophet Muḥammad and his pious Progeny. A few enthusiastic Shi'is feel no wrong in openly condemning and using abusive terms for the enemies of the Prophet and his pious family, but the large majority of Shi'is is against this. The reason of those who use abusive terms is their emotional reaction to the conduct of Mu'āwiyah-bin-Abū Sufyyān and other Umayyite caliphs who used to publicly condemn Imām 'Ali and hurl volley of abusive words on him, a practice which went on for many years.[23] So they argue, why not pay them in the same coin and by their own standards! A Sunni theologist as-Sarkhasī, Abū Bakr-bin-Aḥmad (d. 1106 AD) has mentioned that once a man who used to abuse Imām

'Ali was brought before him. His followers strongly felt that the man should be killed but Imām 'Ali left him free and asked his Shi'is not to condemn him in return if they so liked.[24] Enlightened Shi'is follow Imām 'Ali's behaviour. They maintain that using abusive words is against the sanctity of ethics and Imam's action can never go against this sanctity. So the use of abusive language can never be justified on any ground. It has been reported in *Nahju'l-Balāghah* that when the news of publicly cursing and abusing Imām 'Ali by the Syrian caliph, Mu'āwiyah-bin-Abū Sufyyān and his court reached him, he said:

> "I can never like it for you that you start abusing. If you unveil their deeds and present their conduct as it really is, then it would be a proper way of retaliation. Instead abusing them you pray God to protect us and them and bring between us and them a state of reform and rectification and lead them from depravity to righteousness so that the ignorant of truth may get to identify truth and turn away their faces from the deviants and mischief mongers."[25]

The Schools of Ithnā-'Asharīs or Imāmiyyas

There is no difference among Ithnā-'Asharīs or Imāmiyyas in so far as the basic principles and its practical off-shoots are concerned. All the schools of the Ithnā-'Asharīs or Imāmiyyas are the followers of the Ja'fari Jurisprudence. The difference lies in their approach to the rights and responsibilities of the *Mujtahid* and *Marjau't-Taqlīd*, for reference point for emulation; grand *Mujtahid,* who through his learning and probity is qualified to be followed in all points of religious practice and law. This has resulted into three schools of Ithnā-'Asharīs or Imāmiyyas – *Uṣūlīs*, *Akhbārīs* and *Shaykhīs*. Their vast majority belong to Uṣūlīs. However, a small number of Imāmiyyas still belong to Akhbārī and Shaykhī schools, who have played their important role in the history of Shi'i thought but very little has been researched on these minority schools.

Uṣūlī School

They are named on the basis of their insistence to adhere to certain *Uṣūl* of the jurisprudence, which will be discussed in the following pages in comparison to the Akhbārīs. However, the famous Shi'i canonical books of *Ḥadīths* could only be written towards the end of fourth to tenth and subsequent centuries by the revered three Muhammads, i.e. al-Kulaynī (d. 939 AD): *al-Uṣūl-min'al-Kāfī,* Ibn Bābūyā (d. 991 AD): *Man Lā Yahzurūhu'l-Faqīh* and Shaykhu'ṭ-Ṭā'fa (d. 1067 AD): *Tahzību'l-Ahkām* that al-Ḥilli, Ibn al-Muṭahhar (d. 1325 AD) authored numerous books particularly on the *Uṣūlu'l-Fiqh,* which established the role of *Mujtahids.* He introduced *Diraya,* the methodology and terminology of the critical study of *Ḥadīth* literature. Shi'i jurisprudence came to be based on four pillars: *Qur'an* (The Book), *Sunnah* (The Tradition), *Ijmā'* (The Unanimity) and *'Aql* (The Wisdom). Keeping in view the unreliability and uncertainty of many of the *Ḥadīths* due to fault of their narrators, the reasoning was made the central feature and to arrive at the legal decision, its process was called *Ijtihād* in which the process of arriving at a judgment on the basis of *Uṣūlu'l-Fiqh* was prescribed, apart from several books on various aspects of Uṣūlī Shi'i thought. The list is too long to be given here.

Akhbārī School

It crystallized out as a separate school in the wake of the writings of Muḥammad Amīn Astarābādī (d. 1623 AD). The Akhbārī School achieved greatest influence in Iran during the Safavids (1501-1722 AD) and was crushed by the *Uṣūlī Mujtahids* during the Qajar era (1794-1925 AD). The differences between Uṣūlīs and Akhbārīs in their respective approaches are as follows:

Sources of Jurisprudence: (i) The Uṣūlī School believes in four sources *Qur'an, Sunnah, Ijma'* and *'Aql*. But the Akhbārī School believes in only two sources to be authentic – Qur'an and *Sunnah*, (ii) Uṣūlī School interpret Qur'an and *Ḥadīth* with the literal meaning of words, implied meaning and meaning based on reasoning. Akhbārī School do not use reasoning, but includes the meaning explained by Imāms to interpret Qur'an and *Ḥadīth*, (iii) Uṣūlī School doesn't regard all contents of *Kutub-Arb'a* (four books) to be authentic collection of *Ḥadīths*, namely *al-Uṣūl min al-Kāfī, Tahzību'l-Ahkām, al-Istibsār fī Mukhtulifa fihi mina'l-Akhbār, Man Lā Yahzurūh al-Faqīh* to be absolutely authentic. They say that some *Ḥadīths* of these books are unauthentic. But the Akhbārī School regard all *Ḥadīths* to be authentic, (iv) Uṣūlī School regard authentic only those *Ḥadīths* which have been stated only by Imams and reached the common man through Shi'i scholars of high credibility in knowledge and character. But Akhbārī School give credit even to those stated by Sunni scholars, (v) Uṣūlī School classify *Ḥadīths* into four categories – *Ṣaḥīḥ* (correct), *Ḥasan* (fine), *Muwaththaq* (proved authentic), and *Zaīf* (weak). But Akhbārī School classify into two categories only – Correct and Weak.

Religious Interpretation: (i) Uṣūlī School believes in interpretation. Akhbārī School reject it, (ii) Uṣūlī School employs *Ẓan* (strong presumption) to take decision in matters not directly found in Qur'an and *Ḥadīths*. But Akhbārī School accepts only those decisions about which Imam's *Ḥadīths* are available, (iii) Uṣūlī School believes that the verdict of the *Mujtahids* should be accepted. But Akhbārī School doesn't accept it.

Authority on Islamic Jurisprudence: (i) Uṣūlī School put them into two groups – *Mujtahid* (Interpreter) and *Muqallid* (followers) Akhbārī School believe only in the group of *Muqalladīn*, (ii) Uṣūlī School believes in the right of the *Mujtahid* to give edict on the basis of his specialization in Jurisprudence within the framework of Islamic law. But the Akhbārī School believes that the right of giving edict is confined to Imām, (iii) Uṣūlī School doesn't accept to follow the edicts of a clergy who has died but emphasize the necessity of a living *Marjau't-Taqlīd*, but for Akhbārī School the dead clergy is as good as a living one.

Shaykhī School

The Shaykhīs support the Uṣūlīs, but differ in few other matters in the field of jurisprudence are *Furū'* (peripheral elements). The Shaykhī School, however, has almost disappeared in course of time. Akhbārīs, too, are few and far between. The Shaykhī School was founded by Shaykh Aḥmad-bin-Żainu'd-Dīn al-Aḥsā'ī (d. 1826 AD), on the simplest level of analysis, as a further development of the *Ḥikmat-i-Ilāhī* of Iṣfahānī school, in which the achievement of the *Ḥikmat* (Wisdom) considered the aim of philosophy. Apart from other details, it is important to mention that they divide the *Ḥukama* (Philosophers) into two categories – Firstly, the *Masha'īyūn* (periaptic philosophers) who believe that the wisdom may be achieved through intellectual efforts and rational process. Secondly, the *Ishrāqīyūn* (illuminationist philosophers) who consider that the true wisdom could only be achieved under the spiritual discipline, the cleaning the soul from all defilements and acquisition of the virtues. Shaykhī School's chief endeavour was to harmonize reason and religion. They considered that between the physical world and the spiritual world, there exists an intermediary world, the *Hūrqalyā* or *Huvarqalyā,* stated to be originated from Hebrew, Greek or Syrian. It is also identified as *Barżakh* (isthmus or purgatory) in Islamic theology. Every human being in the physical world has two bodies, one in physical shape and the other in the *Hūrqalyā.* Imām Mahdī and cities of Jabulsa and Jabulqa, where he is supposed to have lived, all exist in the realm of the *Hūrqalyā.* The Shaykhī School has similar innovative theories regarding God, the Prophet, the Imamate, nature of world and eschatology. In course of time *Nakhshabīs*, *Bābīs* or *Bahā'īs* etc. came to fore, but on account of their beliefs and conduct were thrown out from Islam.

At present Ithnā-'Asharī or Imāmiyya emphasize the Uṣūlī School. Because of the oppression of the Muslim rulers on Shi'is, they began to live in *Taqiyya.* As a result their children in course of time became cut-off from the real faith of their forefathers and the number of Shi'is collective went on receding. Nevertheless, their number at present is told to be over 200 million, who live in all those parts of the world where Sunni Muslim live. The Shi'is population is specially concentrated in Iran, Iraq, India, Pakistan, Syria, Lebanon, Bahrain, Saudi 'Arabia, Afghanistan, Middle East, Australasia, Russia, Europe, America and Western Africa etc. Apart from Iran and Iraq they are in minority but in specific areas of some countries, they also form majority.

Ismā'īlīs or Sāb'iyyas

Sāb'iyya is an 'Arabic word, derived from *Saba',* which means the seven, so *Sāb'iyya,* the seveners, just like the *Imāmiyya* who are, *Ithnā-'Asharī,* the twelvers, believing in Twelve Imāms. They are popularly known as Ismā'īlīs, because of their allegiance to Ismā'īl as seventh Imam, after Imām Ja'far aṣ-Ṣādiq, instead of Imām Mūsā al-Kāẓim, as the Imāmiyyas believe.

Ismā'īlīs or Sāb'iyyas, the seveners, have got a special significance for the *Seven.* They believe that number *seven* is associated with the number of grand Divine Esoteric – such as seven heavens, seven earths, seven skies, seven seas, seven constellations of stars, seven colours, seven notes of music, seven minerals etc.

Similarly, Ismā'īlīs emphasize the circle of seven grand Prophets and grand Imāms. They believe in seven for two categories of Divine Messengers – the *Nāṭiq* (vocal) or the Prophet, who brings the revelation of truth. The Prophet throughout his life must have another person as the *Asās* (foundation), who is also said the *Ṣāmit* (silent). After each Prophet there are six Imāms followed by the seventh who initiates a new circle and rank as the Prophet. *Seven Nāṭiqs* or the Prophets are – Adam, Noah, Abraham, Moses, Jesus Christ, Muḥammad and Ismā'īl – and *Seven*

Ṣāmits are – Shith, Sam, Ishmail, Aroan, Shamun, 'Ali and Muḥammad-bin-Ismā'īl.

Ismā'īlīs also believe that there are seven manifestations of the Divine Embassy on earth. Therefore, out of his entire creation, God has made the seven most choicest of his creation, as the Imāms whose names are Imām 'Ali-Ibn-Abū Ṭālib, Imām Ḥasan, Imām Ḥusain, Imām Żainu'l-Ābidīn, Imām Muḥammad al-Bāqir, Imām Ja'far aṣ-Ṣādiq, and his son Ismā'īl. It is Ismā'īl himself, the *Imāmu'ż-Żamāna* as well as the contemporary Imām of this period. In the Imāmiyyas this rank is for *Imām Mahdī Ākhiru'ż-Żamān*, the Divine Guide of the last period, whose Imamate will persist now for every age to come until the Last Day.

There is no difference of belief between Imāmiyyas and Ismā'īlīs with regard to the mode and principle of Imām's appointment. Both regard the Imām to be pinpointed and appointed exclusively by God. Like the Imāmiyyas, Ismā'īlīs also believe that the earth cannot go without a living Divine emissary on it, in every period of its existence, the presence of one or the other living Imām is essential.

Ismā'īlīs have well organized hierarchy, known as *Ḥudūdu'd-Dīn*, which is correlated with cosmic entities in the religious sphere to be as: (i) the *Prophet* with Universal Reason, (ii) the *Asās* (foundation) with Universal Soul, and then in order, (iii) the *Imām* (literally means, the one who stands in front; designated religious leader), (iv) the *Bāb* (literally means, the gate; designated contact-person to the *Imām*) or the *Ḥujjat* (literally means, the proof; a high position person), and (v) the *Dā'ī* (literally means, the Claimant, the Emissary); *Nā'ibu'l-Imām* (means, Deputy Imām). *Dā'īism* has three stages – *Dā'īu'l-Māzūn*, *Dā'īu'l-Mukāsir* and *Dā'īu'l-Mustajīb*. They are also called *Balāgh*, *Muṭlaq* and *Maḥṣūr*.

There are *nine* phases of education in the Ismā'īlīs – In the *first* phase curiosity is kindled, and interest created for its solution. Some elementary principles are also told in this phase. In the *second* phase faith in the Imamate is instructed. In the *third* important articles of Ismā'īlī faith are told in which the significance of the *seven* number and things connected with this number is discussed. In the *fourth* phase seven most noble men are mentioned. In the *fifth* phase the significance of the number Twelve is emphasized as in one evidence twelve *Dā'ī* were maintained. In this phase, obedience to *Dā'ī* or *Shaykh* is instructed. In the *sixth* phase the rational and philosophical background of the religious laws are explained. In the *seventh* phase specially the knowledge of *Jafar* (science of numeric) is imparted. In the *eighth* phase the organs of the human body and their relation to human soul is explained. The *ninth* phase is related with *'Ārifīn*, the men of perfect accomplishment.

The propagation of Ismā'īlī faith by the *Dā'īs* passes through three stages – In the first step is *Mukāsir*, the second is *Māzūn* and the third is *Dā'ī*. The *Mukāsir* has the good knowledge of other religions. By making a comparative presentation, he tries to convince others of his faith. But he does not argue himself; he only refers to the *Māzūn* who argued and proved through comparative analysis of different religions that the Ismā'īlī principle of faith is the most rational. If it caused confusion in the mind of the other man who requests for the *Māzūn* to guide him. The *Māzūn* sends him to the *Dā'ī* who invites him to new faith. These three steps are still in practice.

Ismā'īlīs regard Imām 'Ali to be the bedrock of the Muslim Ummah, more than just an Imām and believe him to be *Asās* or *Asāsu'l-Imāmt* (Founder of Imamate). In this way the chain of Imamate in the Ismā'īlīs, starts with Imām Ḥasan. This faith is based on the following *Ḥadīth* of the Prophet Muḥammad:

> "Ḥasan and Ḥusain are the Imāms and their father is more honourable than them."[26]

The Ismā'īlīs share the history of I<u>th</u>nā-'A<u>sh</u>arīs and recognize the Imāms up to and Imām Ja'far aṣ-Ṣādiq (d. 765 AD) as their own. After him they diverge. Ismā'īlīs maintain that after Imām Ja'far aṣ-Ṣādiq, Imamate was transferred to his eldest son Ismā'īl on account of which they refer themselves to be Ismā'īlīs.[27] According to other sects of Islam as well as that of I<u>th</u>nā-'A<u>sh</u>arīs the Imamate was given to Imām Mūsā al-Kāẓim, the fourth son of Imām Ja'far aṣ-Ṣādiq, after his death who was alive at that time. I<u>th</u>nā-'A<u>sh</u>arīs and other sects believe that the very question of Ismā'īl's Imamate does not arise, as he had died in the very lifetime of his father.

According to Ismā'īlīs, the eldest son of Imām Ja'far aṣ-Ṣādiq, Ismā'īl did not die, rather he has gone behind the scene and will reappear as and when wished by God. Some believe him to be the *Imām Ā<u>kh</u>iru'ẓ-Ẓamān*, who will appear in the time preceeding the Dooms Day.[28] A subsect of Ismā'īlīs believe in the death of Ismā'īl (d. 145 AD), say that he had appointed his son Muḥammad al-Ḥabīb, to be Imām after him[29], who was fourteen years of age and continued to live in Medīna under the care of his grandfather Imām Ja'far aṣ-Ṣādiq. As this nomination was made confidential so Muḥammad al-Ḥabību'l-Attam is appellated as *Imāmu'l-Maktūm* (undisclosed Imām), who is the last Muḥammad of the order of Imamate. The chain of Ismā'īlīs Imamate as well as the *Dauru's-*

Sitar (veiled period) started from Imām Muḥammad al-Ḥabību'l-Maktūm (d. 798 AD).

Dauru's-Sitar is a period in which the Shi'is were exposed to calamities perpetrated on them by the Abbāsite Caliphs, who were no less than the Umayyites in torturing the Shi'is but were all the more cruel for them. In the Abbāsite Caliphate the Imāms of the I<u>th</u>nā-'A<u>sh</u>arīs or Imāmiyyas were kept prisoners and then secretly poisoned to death. It was not possible for the Shi'is to openly propagate their faith, so from Medīna Imām Muḥammad al-Ḥabību'l-Maktūm went to Kūfa, where his son 'Abdu'llāh was born. He also went to Sabur and Far<u>gh</u>āna, where he died. His tomb was there, but the Fāṭimid Caliph Mu'tażż-bil'llāh (866-9 AD) is said to have transferred his remains to Cairo. He was successful in bringing some of the I<u>th</u>nā-'A<u>sh</u>arīs into his fold, and also some astray sects, especially <u>Kh</u>aṭṭābiyyas and its branches—Bażī<u>gh</u>iyyas, Mufazzaliyyas, <u>Gh</u>urābiyyas and 'Umayriyyas or 'Ijliyyas.

After Imām Muḥammad al-Ḥabību'l-Maktūm there were two more Imāms known as the veiled Imāms – Imām 'Abdu'llāh ar-Razī (d. 825 AD) and his son Imām 'Abdu'llāh at-Taqī-wa'l-<u>Kh</u>ayr (d. 854 AD) with whom the chain of the veiled Imāms terminated. It is from them that the chain of the *Fāṭimīnu'l-Miṣr* (Fāṭimid Caliphs of Egypt), the Successors or Caliphs from the Fāṭimid clan in Egypt, started.

Imām 'Abdu'llāh ar-Razī, after the death of his father Imām Muḥammad al-Ḥabību'l-Maktūm, had shifted from Far<u>gh</u>āna to Daylām. From there he came to Salāmiya along with a tradesman and settled there. He handed over the obligations of the propagation of religion to his brother Muḥammad's son Ḥusain. One of his brothers came over to India of that time up to Qandhār, by whom Indians became familiar with Ismā'īlīs.

Imām Aḥmad-bin-'Abdu'llāh at-Taqī-wa'l-<u>Kh</u>ayr, also called Imām Aḥmadu'l Mūfī was an erudite person of his time. He was keenly interested in propagating the Ismā'īlī faith. He founded an organization namely *Anjumanu'l-A<u>kh</u>wān-uṣ-Ṣafa* in Baṣra (Iraq) and had authored many books on Unity of God, Qur'an, *Ḥadī<u>th</u>s* etc. which are famous as *Risaelu'l-A<u>kh</u>wān-uṣ-Ṣafa*. He nominated his son Imām Husainu'ż-Żakī al-Muqtadā al-Mahdī (d. 909 AD), who had great interest in disseminating the ideology of Ismā'īlī faith. He sent two special exponents of Ismā'īlī faith, Ḥasan-bin-Faraḥ and 'Ali-bin-Fazl to Yemen to propagate it. They achieved extraordinary success there. Within a short period of two years, they managed to openly preach their faith. Got a castle built in La'-Adan, formed an army and began to capture cities of

Yemen one after the other. Abu'l Qāsim put Sīnā under his rule and become famous as Manṣuru'l-Aiman.

Imām Ḥusainu'ż-Żakī, who was the last veiled Imām, sent many propagators of Ismā'īlī faith to different countries, such as, Yemen, Bahrain, Sindh (India), Egypt, Morocco and Tunis etc. He declared his son 'Obayd'ullāh to be Imām Mahdī and began to manage his appearance. Imām 'Obayd'ullāhu'l-Mahdī was only eight years old when his father expired. At his death-bed Imām Ḥusainu'ż-Żakī made a will – "You are Imām Mahdī, you will have to go to far off countries, where you will have to face much sufferings."[30]

Imām 'Obayd'ullāhu'l-Mahdī wanted to go to Salāmiya, but the 'Abbāsite administration made him prisoner in Tunis. This place is famous today by the name of Mahdīya seaport. The news of the arrest of Imām 'Obayd'ullāhu'l-Mahdī reached the great Ismā'īlī Abū-'Abdu'llāh Shi'ī. He attacked Kariwān, defeated Abbāsites, and got Imām 'Obayd'ullāhu'l-Mahdī released from the prison, put him on a horse, took the bridle in his hand and walked while making the slogan, "Whose slave I am, he is that Master!"

This event is of 909 AD. *Fāṭimīnu'l-Miṣr* had ten Imāms:

First Imām	'Obayd'ullāhu'l-Mahdī	(909-34 AD)
Second	Imām al-Qāim bi-amr-Illāh	(934-46 AD)
Third	Imām al-Manṣūr bi-amr-Illāh	(946-53 AD)
Fourth	Imām al-Mu'iżż li-dīn-Illāh	(953-75 AD)
Fifth	Imām al-'Ażiż b'Illāh	(975-96 AD)
Sixth	Imām al-Hākim bi-amr-Illāh	(996-1021 AD)
Seventh	Imām aẓ-Ẓāhiru'l-'Azāz-dīn-Illāh	(1021-36 AD)
Eighth	Imām al-Mustanṣir b'Illāh	(1036-94 AD)
Ninth	Imām al-Musta'lī b'Illāh	(1094-1101 AD)
Tenth	Imām al-Amr bi-Aḥkām-Illāh	(1101-30 AD)

All these ten personalities were simultaneously the Imāms, the Caliphs and the Kings. After the last Caliph of Fāṭimid dynasty, known as Imām al-Amr bi-Aḥkām-Illāh, firstly Afzalu'l-Malik, then 'Abdu'l Majīd Maimūn, who took the name *Ḥāfiz,* held the office in trust but were not designated as Imām. Fāṭimid Caliphate remained established up to 1171 AD until Sultān Ṣalāḥu'd-Dīn Ayyūbī finished it. They were as under:

Eleventh	Caliph al-Ḥāfiẓ li-dīn-Illāh	(1130-49 AD)
Twelfth	Caliph aẓ-Ẓāfir bi-amr-Illāh	(1149-54 AD)
Thirteenth	Caliph al-Fāiż bi-naṣr-Illāh	(1154-60 AD)
Fourteenth	Caliph al-'Āzid li-dīn-Illāh	(1160-71 AD)

The foundation of a strong Shi'i Caliphate, even if Ismā'īlīs not Imāmiyyas, was just like a gland in the throat of 'Abbāsites, who had captured the Caliphate in the name of restoring it to its real claimants, the descendants of Fāṭimah-'Ali, the *Ahlu'l-Bayt.* 'Abbāsites were counterfeitly propagating to be themselves included in *Ahlu'l-Bayt.* In 1011, after hundred years the Fāṭimid dynasty was founded, the 'Abbāsites issued a manifesto that Fāṭimid are not the descendants of Fāṭimah aż-Żahrah-cum-'Ali-Ibn-Abū Ṭālib, the *Ahlu'l-Bayt,* but they descended from some Daisan, a dualist who had died four hundred years before Islam.[31]

Arab historians are divided in this respect. While al-Maqrīzī and Ibn Khaldūn support the legitimacy of Fāṭimid, Ibn Khallikān, Abu'l Fidā and as-Suyūṭī refute. Over two hundred genealogies exist on the point and all mention the lineage of Imām 'Ali to Imām Ismā'īl and Imām Ismā'īl to Imām al-Mahdī! The reign of Imām al-Musta'lī b'Illāh was highly disturbed and fragmented. The tenth Fāṭimid Caliph Imām al-Amr bi-Aḥkām-Illāh was killed by Nizārīs, the other outfit of Ismā'īlīs. The historians are divided whether he left any son.

The first sub-group of Ismā'īlīs were Durūz, who deified their Imām al-Hākim bi-amr-Illāh and also from the mainstream of Ismā'īlīs and formed a distinct group in Syria which has survived to the present day. But the main religious divide among the Ismā'īlīs came after Imām al-Mustanṣir b'Illāh about the nomination of his successor. He had two sons al-Nizār and al-Musta'lī. Al-Nizār was the elder and al-Musta'lī was the younger son. The nomination controversy gave rise to two sub-sects, whose followers are called Nizārīs and Musta'līs respectively.

Musta'līs:

Musta'līs recognize twenty-one Imāms as under:

(i) *al-Attimmah* (the Finals) – Imām Ḥasan to Imām Ja'far aṣ-Ṣādiq = five,
(ii) *al-Mastūr* (the Veiled) – Imām Ismā'īlī to Imām Imām Husainu'ż-Żakī = five,
(iii) *al-Khulafah* (the Vicegerents) – Imām 'Obayd'ullāhu'l-Mahdī to Imām Abu'l Qāsim Ṭayyab = eleven.

They are also called *Ashhad* (the Witnesses). It is compulsory for each believer to abide by the *Bai'at* (oath of allegiance). Its special ceremony is called *Mīthāq* (Agreement).

The Musta'līs lay their significance in the fact that their Imām was the duly recognized last Caliph of Fatimid dynasty, known as Imām al-Amr bi-Aḥkām-Illāh (d. 1130 AD). He was only five years old when his father Imām al-Musta'lī b'Illāh died in 1101 AD. In the meantime, the Musta'līs believe that Imām al-Amr bi-Aḥkām-Illāh had a son, Abu'l Qāsim Ṭaiyib, who was two years some months old. Ṭaiyib became Imām and went behind veil at the age of four and from him again began the *Dauru's-Sitar*. The twelfth Imām of the Ith̲nā-'Asharīs, Imām Mahdī Āk̲h̲iru'ż-Żamān, too, went behind veil in the very same age of four years. The veiled period began once again from Imām Ṭaiyib. 'Abdu'l Majīd Maimūn Ḥāfiz, the grandson of Imām al-Mustanṣir b'Illāh, was entrusted with the state affairs only, the *Dā'ī* Ibn Madian was made the *Bāb* to the Imām Abu'l Qāsim Ṭaiyib, and a council of *Dā'īs* was also constituted.

Since the death of the Imām al-Musta'lī b'Illāh in 1101 AD, the control and direction of religious *Dā'wat* (literally means, feast; propagation) passed to Queen Ḥurra (d. 1138) of Yemen, who had the rank of the *Ḥujjat*. Her tomb in the Yemen is still a shrine for pilgrimage. She was assisted by al-K̲h̲aṭṭāb Ḥamadānī and *Dā'īs* Lamak and Yaḥyā both sons of Malik. Queen Ḥurra had appointed Zuaib-bin-Mūsā as her successor. He had the rank of the *Dā'īu'l-Muṭlaq* (in absolute charge). The centre of the Musta'lī Ismā'īlīs was formely in Yemen, but in 1539 AD, the 24th *Dā'īu'l-Muṭlaq* Yūsuf-bin-Sulaymān (d. 1567 AD) shifted the centre from Yemen to India and settled in Siddhpur in Bombay province (now Maharastra, India) but a sub-centre continued in Yemen with his wife's nephew Sulaymān-bin-Ḥasan as *Dā'ī*. After 26th *Dā'īu'l-Muṭlaq* Dāwūd-bin-'Ajab S̲h̲āh (d. 1591 AD), there arose a dispute again in the nomination of the next *Dā'ī*. Some began to call his son Dāwūd Burhānu'd-Dīn to be *Dā'ī*, while some regarded Sulaymān-bin-Ḥasan as the *Dā'ī*. This gave rise to two more sub-sects of the Ismā'īlīs – Dāwūdī and Sulaymānī. Sulaymān came to India to present his case before the court of Emperor Akbar who came to the conclusion that Dāwūd Burhānu'd-Dīn was right. Sulaymān died in India in 1597 AD and Dāwūd Burhānu'd-Dīn in 1612 AD. Strange as it is the graves of both Dāwūd and Sulaymān are built face to face in Ahmedabad.

The *Dā'īu'l-Muṭlaq* of the Sulaymānīs continue the old Yemenite traditions, whose representative in India is called *Manṣūb* (Accusative) and his headquarters is at Baroda. The *Dā'īu'l-Muṭlaq* of the Da'udis lives at Surat (Maharashtra) whose headquarters is famous by the name *Dyorhī* (Threshold). Both the branches use the title *Sayyadna* for their respective *Dā'īu'l-Muṭlaq*. But the Dāwūdīs also add *His Holiness*

Sardār. Dāwūdīs have their own *Madarsa* (School), known as *Dars-i-Sayfī,* named after the famous *Dāwūdī Dā'īu'l-Muṭlaq* of the foregoing years, His Holiness Sardār Saiyedna Ṭāhir Sayfu'd-Dīn. Their current *Dā'īu'l-Muṭlaq* is His Holiness Sardār Saiyedna Burhānu'd-Dīn whom the followers call *Saiyedna Ṣaheb* or *Mulla Ji Ṣahib*. He is Fifty-second *Dā'īu'l-Muṭlaq* in this sect. In India the Musta'lī Ismā'īlīs are called *Bohrās* whose community profession is business. They are mainly concentrated in Gujarat, Malwah and Deccan. A small group of Bohrās, who had separated themselves from the period of Dāwūd Burhānu'd-Dīn (d. 1612 AD), have the religious allegiance to Ja'far Shīrāzī are called *Ja'farī Bohrās* and have converted to Sunni faith.

Nizārīs

The followers of Nizār, the eldest son of Imām al-Mustanṣir b'Illāh, rejected the succession of his younger son al-Musta'lī b'Illāh as Imām. According to them, Imām al-Mustanṣir b'Illāh had already nominated his eldest son Nizār to be next Imām after him. Nizār was away from Egypt at the time of the demise, so it was conspired to enthrone al-Musta'lī b'Illāh as the tenth Caliph of Fāṭimid dynasty. His accession has no religious sanctity. The followers of Nizār are called *Fidaī'* (pl. *Fidā'īn*) in Iran and *Khojā* in India. *Fidā'īn* were so named because of their activities during Alamut rulers. *Khojā* is equivalent of Khwāja, the master or lord, the term used for old merchants of Sind port.

The Nizārī Imāms have been subject to the tyranny and hardship for centuries. Nizār was accused to be rebel against the throne; was captured; and imprisoned with his two sons. No record is available to indicate the period of his imprisonment but it may be seventy years between 1094-1165 AD. During this period of darkness when even his shadow had refused to walk with him, Ḥasan-bin-Ṣabbāh championed Nizār's cause and broke all connections with the Musta'lī line. Ḥasan-bin-Ṣabbāh is one of the most controversial figures in the history, who is called *Shaykhu'l-Jebel* (elderly chief of mountains) and founded a new sect *al-Bāṭinī'in* (the Secretistics), which will be dealt with at the appropriate place in this book. But there is no doubt that Ḥasan-bin-Ṣabbāh was completely loyal to Imām Nizār, who gave his son al-Hādī under his protection. Ḥasan-bin-Ṣabbāh nurtured al-Hādī with affection and devotion in the fort of Alamut and married him, when he was mature. A son was born. Kīya Buzurg Umīd, the successor of Ḥasan-bin-Ṣabbāḥ exchanged the son of al-Hādī with his own son, so that the grandson of Imām Nizār could be safe. al-Hādī's son was named as Ḥasan *'alā-*

žikrihi's-salām or *žikrihi's-salām* alone. Later rulers of the Alamut were also favourable to Nizārīs.

Because Nizārīs records are scarce being largely destroyed after the capture of Alamut by Hulagu Khan in 1256 AD, the traditions of the sect indicate the first three names after the Imām Nizār. They are al-Hādī son of Imām Nizār, al-Mahdi or al-Muhtadī and al-Qāhir.[32] Thus, the fifth Nizārī was Imām Ḥasan *'alā-žikrihi's-salām* (d. 1166 AD). The chain of Nizārīs Imamate as well as the *Dauru's-Sitar* started from him and the *Ḥujjat* or a designated *Dā'ī* carried on *Dā'wat*. He was succeeded by his son Imām Muḥammad (d. 1211 AD), then his son Imām 'Alāu'd-Dīn Muḥammad (d. 1247 AD). The last Imām and ruler of Alamut, Imām Ruknu'd-Dīn Khurshāh (d. 1256 AD), sensing the danger to his family and community, sent his son Shamsu'd-Dīn, seven years boy to a place of safety and security in Azerbaijān with his uncle. Azerbaijān and its vicinity had been centre of Nizārīs for about two centuries. Shamsu'd-Dīn lived there in concealment as a *Żardoż* (embroiderer), so he is popularly known as Shamsu'd-Dīn Żardoż, who was twenty-eighth Nizārī Imāms. There had been fifteen Nizārī Imāms between him, other Persians and Imām Abu'l Ḥasan 'Ali Shāh.

Imām Abu'l Ḥasan 'Ali Shāh (d. 1780 AD) had been a active person. He was the resident of Qomm (Iran) and ruler of Kirmān (Iran) during the reign of Zand kings. He was succeeded by his son Khalīlu'llāh, also known as Saiyed Kahakī, because of residing at Kahak, near the Mahallāt in the district of Qumm. He was greatly revered by his followers. He and many of his followers were killed in 1817 AD at Yezd, by a mob blasted by a jealous Ithnā-'Asharīs. Qajari king Fatḥ Shāh (1797-1834 AD) sensing the deadly vengeance of the Nizārīs, administered severe punishment to the guilty ones and richly rewarded the young Imām Ḥasan 'Ali Shāh, son of the deceased Imām by giving him the district of Qumm and Mahallāt in addition to his inherited estates and crowned him with the title of Āghā Khān and also married his daughter to him. Fortune smiled on him during the reign of Qajāri king Fatḥ Shāh but after his death in 1834 AD the situation changed to such an extent that the Persian Imamate of Nizārīs came to an end.

The first Āghā Khān, Āghā Hasan 'Ali Shāh came to India in 1840 AD. His arrival in Sind coincided with the military success resulting in the annexation of the province to India. He was awarded by the British with the hereditary title of His Highness. He made his *Darkhānā,* the headquarters at Bombay. He was succeeded by his son (d. 1884 AD), then his son Sultān Muḥammad Shāh, alias Imām Āghā 'Ali Shāh Āghā Khan III. He was awarded the title of Sir by the British. He had been

President of Commonwealth for several years, and also the President of Muslim League. He died in Geneva at the age of 80. As per his nomination, Prince Karīm Khān (b. 1936 AD), his grandson succeeded him at the age of twenty-one. He is Imām Āghā Karīm 'Ali Shāh Aghā Khān IV; fiftieth Imām in the series of Nizārī Ismā'īlis. Educated at the University of Harvard, his occultation of the Imamate was held at a big ceremony at Dar-es-Salam, the capital of Tanzania (East Africa). He is the *Imāmu'l-Aṣr-wa'l-Żamān* of Nizārī Ismā'īlis. Thus, the system of nomination of the Imām is still on and Imām is called *Āghā Khān*.

As the part of the Shi'as community, Ismā'īlis irrespective of any difference as the Musta'līs or Nizārī boldly faced the oppressive and suppressive attitude of the Umayyites and 'Abbāsites and played effective and important role in the propagation of the Shi'is principles of faith. In the course of this struggle, action and reaction some new communities also came up from among them such as Qarāmiṭa (Carmathians), Bāṭinī'in or Ta'līmiyya etc. Since these small communities acquired separate positions in the later periods, they will be discussed separately.

Ismā'īlis forms part of the larger Shi'is community, and their number runs into millions. They are widely spread in the whole world and the system of their religious propagation is strong and active. Compared to the Ithnā-'Asharī Shi'is, Ismā'īlīs have been highly organized and more active.

Żaydīyyas

The nomenclature of the Żaydīyyas is associated with the name of Żayd (d. 740 AD) who was the son of the fourth Imām Żainu'l-Ābidīn and the brother of the fifth Imām Muḥammad al-Bāqir. He fought against the unjust Umayyite Caliph Hishām and was martyred in 743 AD. Żayd was the matchless learned figure of his time and was the teacher of Imām Abū Ḥanīfa, the founder of the Ḥanafī School of Sunni faith.[33] Imām Muḥammad al-Bāqir was not in favour of any political revolt, so the followers of Żayd cut-off from Shi'i community. After the death of Imām Żainu'l-Ābidīn Shi'is were divided into two subsects. One group which regarded Imām Muḥammad al-Bāqir as the true Imām nominated by his father Imām Żainu'l-Ābidīn, the second group which followed Żayd, because he showed courage to rise against the unjust and oppressive Umayyite Caliph. The reason for counting the Żaydīyyas into Shi'i community is simply because they were together in the belief of Imamate up to Imām Żainu'l-Ābidīn. Otherwise they are totally different from each other in their thought and faith. In contrast with the Shi'is, they are more adjusted with Sunni.

Żaydīyyas started new chain of Imamate from Żayd onwards. Imām Żayd raised his revolt in January 740 AD but was unsuccessful and was killed in Kūfa (Iraq). His son Yaḥyā fled to Khurāsān (Iran) and started a revolt there but was killed in 743 AD. Muḥammad-bin-'Abdu'llāh *Nafs-aż-Żakiyya* (the pure soul), a descendant of Imām Ḥasan claimed the Imamate and rose in rebellion against the 'Abbāsites and was killed in 762 AD. His Imamate was transferred to Muḥammad-bin-Qāsim (d. 834 AD), one of the descendants of Imām Ḥusain, who lived in Talaqan and died in prison. Ibrāhīm-bin-'Abdu'llāh-al-Mahaz (d. 763 AD) and Yaḥyā-bin-'Omar (d. 864 AD), a descendant of Imām Ḥusain was also unsuccessful in his revolts. But the same year, 864 AD, Ḥasan-bin-Żayd succeeded in founding the Żaydīyya state in Tabaristān in north Irān and ruled for a long period.

Idrīs-bin-Abdu'llāh-bin-Ḥasan-ath-Thānī (d. 791 AD) had escaped into the western Mauritania, with the help of Berber tribes, accepted him as their chief and Imām, established a powerful kingdom which flourished for two hundred years (789-985 AD) in the North Africa. They have been called by the historians as Idrīsites who were Żaydīyyas in faith. After the disintegration of the Idrīsites rule, they scattered and the followers of this faith spread in different countries of Asia and Africa. Żaydīyyas Imāms are still present in North Yemen.

Imām Żayd is said to have studied under Wāṣil-bin-'Aṭā, the founder of the *Mu'tażilīs*. A number of Żaydīyyas had been members of Mu'tażilī movement and under their influence have also incorporated some of their faith. Żaydīyyas had propounded the doctrine of *Imāmatu'l-Mafżūl* (leadership of the inferior), under which while believing that Imām 'Ali was far ahead in knowledge and virtue, they testify the remaining three Caliphs. In the faith of both, Sunnis and Żaydīyyas, the relative excellence of Imām or Caliph in knowledge and character is not essential. An ordinary person may be elected in the presence of a more qualified person in knowledge and moral purity.

Stretching the same logic in case of their Imām Żayd, the Żaydīyyas believe in his Imamate in spite of their belief that Imām Muḥammad al-Bāqir was far ahead of Imām Żayd in knowledge and moral purity. Żaydīyyas maintain that Imām 'Ali was more learned, brave and morally sound than any other companion of the Prophet and was entitled most of all to be the Imām or Caliph. The election of the older companion was merely to curb this conflict, by virtue of his age and respectable personality, which could prevail upon the differences and control controversies in order to protect the interest of Islam. They justify the Caliphate of Caliph Abū Bakr and Caliph 'Omar on the basis of this logic, but they keep mum on the lavish favour Caliph 'Othmān granted for the members of his own clan.

Żaydīyyas believe like Sunnis that Imamate or Caliphate is based on the vote of the Muslim masses, they however have a difference with Sunnis who limit the election of a Caliph to the Quraysh clan only as a sufficient condition for qualifying in the Caliphate election. Żaydīyyas believe that Imām can only be from the family tree of Fāṭimah aż-Żahrah.

For the Żaydīyyas the main and essential qualification for Imamate is to achieve control of power through the arms, this qualification leaves all other qualifications behind. As for *Fiqh* Żaydīyyas confirm to the Ḥanafī School rather than the Ja'fari School of Islamic law. The reason behind this is also political because Imām Muḥammad al-Bāqir refused to support Żayd in his revolt against the Umayyite Caliph while Imām Abū Ḥanīfa did support him. Żaydīyyas are called *Rawāfiz* on account of their being included in the Sunni sect. *Rawāfiz* is an 'Arabic term and is the plural form of *Rāfizī* which means the group or person who deserts his leader and guide. Ignorant of this context, Sunni scholars call every Shi'is as *Rāfizī*, although this ridiculous nickname was used originally for the Żaydīyyas, who had deserted Shi'is.

Subsequently, the Żaydīyyas were divided into four sub-divisions, as a result of the difference of opinion regarding the nomination of Imam:

Muḥammadiyyas: It was a group of followers of Muḥammad-bin-'Abdu'llāh, *Nafs-aż-Żakiyya,* who considered himself beyond the pale of death, and said that he was in concealment and would return to fill the earth with justice.

Jārūdiyyas – It was named after the founder Abu'l Jārūd-bin-Żiyād. They held that sufficient descriptions had been given by the holy Prophet to recognize Imām 'Ali and all should have recognized him. They, therefore, considered the persons sinful in failing to recognize Imām 'Ali.

Sulaymāniyyas or Jarīriyyas: It was named after the founder Sulaymān-bin-Jarīr. They held that the choice of Imām is the matter of consultation. First two caliphs had been in error in failing to follow Imām 'Ali but it did not amount to sin. They attacked the third Caliph 'Othmān.

Butriyyas or Ṣālihiyyas: They were two groups named after their respective founders, Kathīr an-Nawa al-Abtar. They endorsed the views of *Jarīriyya* regarding first two caliphs and keep the third caliph in abeyance. They followed *Mu'tażilīs* in theology and Ḥanafīs in jurisprudence. However, in some cases prefer ash-Shāfi'ī or Shi'i.

Muhaddithīs: It was a group of the *Murji'īs,* who were also known as Żaydīyyas who got political favours for their allegiance to Imām Mūsā al-Kāẓim and Imām 'Ali ar-Rezā but after the death of the latter. returned to their former faith.

Hāshimiyyas or Kaysāniyyas

This sect came into existence because Imām Ḥusain (d. 681 AD) had entrusted his younger brother Muḥammad Ḥanafia with the responsibility of looking after the affairs of Medina as he left Medina for Iraq. Muḥammad Ḥanafia was the son of Imām 'Ali from his second wife Khaulah, who was from the Ḥanafia clan, which is why he was known as Ibn Ḥanafia. He had a personality equipped with glorious attributes. So after the martyrdom of Imām Ḥusain at Karbala, the Shi'is of *Ahlu'l-Bayt* took him to be their Imām. But afterwards, when Imām Żainu'l-Ābidīn having been released from Yazīd-bin-Mu'āwiyah's prison, returned to Medīna, Muḥammad Ḥanafia, having confirmed that Imām Ḥusain had nominated his son Imām 'Ali popularly known as Żainu'l-Ābidīn next to him, left his claim for Imamate and swore allegiance to Imām Żainu'l-Ābidīn and never again raised his claim for Imamate. But after the death of Muḥammad Ḥanafia, his devotees took his son Abū Hāshim 'Abdu'llāh to be their fifth Imam.[34] On this ground the name of this sect became *Hāshimiyya* and because this move was spearheaded by a slave of Imām 'Ali called Kaysān and because of his efforts, it was accomplished, so this sect is called *Kaysāniyya* also.

Abū Hāshim 'Abdu'llāh was poisoned to death by the Umayyite Caliph Hishām-bin-'Abdu'l Malik (d. 705 AD). As he had no issue, he appointed Muḥammad-bin-'Abdu'llāh, as his successor Imām, before he died. The father of this Muḥammad, 'Abdu'llāh was the son of 'Abbās-bin-'Abdu'l Muṭṭalib, the uncle of the Prophet. 'Abdu'llāh-bin-'Abbās was honoured for his knowledge and moral purity. He had also the honour of being the disciple of Imām 'Ali. He was one of the main sources of narrating numerous Traditions of the Prophet Muḥammad.

This family background proved extraordinarily helpful for Muḥammad-bin-'Abdu'llāh. He himself was a knowledgeable man and a sharp judge of the trend of time. He multiplied his followers and supporters. He made Kūfa (Iraq) the centre for propagation and expansion of his sect. Kūfa had been the Capital of Imām 'Ali's caliphate and his Shi'is were in majority there. He died in 722 AD. He had three sons namely Ibrāhīm, 'Abdu'llāh and Ja'far. Ibrāhīm became Imām and he took up to complete the work of his father with full zeal, but was murdered by Marwān II (d. 781 AD), the Umayyite Caliph. He was succeeded by his younger brother 'Abdu'llāh, who fought a battle with the support of Abū Muslim Khurāsānī in 749 on the bank of the river Zāb, between Mosul and Arbela, at a village called Kushaf against the Umayyite Caliphate and defeated it. He founded the splendid 'Abbāsi kingdom in the name of Abu'l 'Abbās 'Abdu'llāh as-Saffāḥ in 750 AD, which flourished for about 500 years.

Hāshimiyyas too were started by Shi'is, who provoked the Muslims against the atrocious rule of the Umayyite dynasty and asked them to avenge the blood of Imām Ḥusain. Having captured the ruling power, they killed the Shi'is of *Ahlu'l-Bayt* one by one. All kinds of atrocities were let loose on them. They were subjected to torture, and their six Imāms from the *Ahlu'l-Bayt* (Imām Ja'far aṣ-Ṣādiq, Imām Mūsā al-Kāẓim, Imām 'Ali ar-Rezā, Imām Muḥammad at-Taqī, Imām 'Ali an-Naqī and Imām Ḥasan 'Askarī) were kept in prison and poisoned to death. The repeated act of 'Abbāsites in putting the Imāms in prison and getting them poisoned and killed became also the cause of the occultation of the twelfth and last Imām. In the hostility of Hāshimites against *Ahlu'l-Bayt,* they went far ahead of the Umayyites' atrocities.

After establishing their Caliphate, the Hāshimiyyas were in no way Shi'i in behaviour and conduct, rather they were bent on finishing and destroying Shi'is, under their influence. The Iraqis who used to be Shi'is, were detached from Shi'i ideology and faith. Among the law-experts of Kūfa, Imām Abū Ḥanīfa (d. 767 AD) and Sufyyān Thūrī (d. 778 AD) who were nourishing Shi'is ideology in the beginning, founded their own schools of theology parallel to the Shi'i theology under the influence of the 'Abbāsite reign. Ḥejāz, which used to be the centre of *Ahlu'l-Bayt,* before the 'Abbāsites became the victim of great turmoil. 'Abbāsites brought even the Żaydīyyas into their folds and in due course of time both merged in the Sunnis mainstream. But the merger could not remove the contradictions within the faith, resulting in the Hāshimiyyas being divided into different sub-sects:

Karibiyya or *Khashabiyya*: It was named after the founder Abū Karib az-Zarīr. They believe that Ibn al-Ḥanafiyya had not died but was concealed on the mount Rawza and would return to fill the earth with justice. The drawing of swords during the occultation of Imām was forbidden and they used to fight with the *Khashab* (sticks), and so were called *Khashabiyya.* Famous 'Arabic poets al-Ḥimyarī and Kuthayyir belonged to this sub-sect.

Janāḥiyya: It was named after the founder 'Abdu'llāh-bin-Mu'āwiyah, one of the descendants of Ja'afar Ṭayyār, brother of Imām

'Ali, who rose in revolt against 'Umayyites in 744. They believed in the incarnation of God, transmigration of souls and allegorical interpretation of Qur'an. The incarnation of God in a succession the Prophets and Imāms passing eventually thorough Ibn al-Ḥanafiyya and Abū Hāshim to 'Abdu'llāh-bin-Mu'āwiyah.

Bayāniyya: It was named after the founder Bayān-bin-Sam'ān at-Tamīmī. They maintained that the divinity passed from Imām 'Ali to his sons and though Abū Hāshim to Bayān. They believed in anthropomorphism with respect to God.

'Alawiyyas

Alawiyyas are one of the living sects of Shi'is, who exaggerate the belief about Imām 'Ali and maintained him to be Divine. Their amazing arguments are that: if 'Ali is named *Yadu'llāh,* because 'Ali's hands are the hands of God, he is called *Lisanu'llāh,* because his tongue is the tongue of God and when he is maintained *'Ainu'llāh,* because his eyes are the eyes of God and so on, precisely, his name 'Ali is the name of God, then what would be objection in his being the God!

The religious faith of 'Alawiyyas is based on following verse of Qur'an:

> "And the one for whom God does not make light, there is no light for him." *(Qur'an: 24/40)*

They also have their interpretation of *Ḥadīth an-Nūr* (the Tradition of Light) about the above verses of Qur'an, which does not agree with the common belief of the Shi'is. The *Ḥadīth an-Nūr* is the statement of the holy Prophet Muḥammad, which goes as follows:

> "God has created me and 'Ali with same *Nūr* (Light)."[35]

'Alawiyyas have no uniform set of beliefs, rather they form a loose network. During the lifetime of Imām 'Ali, there were persons saying to him – 'Ali thou art God. Imām 'Ali even caused some of them to be burned.[36]After the assassination of Imām 'Ali, they said, 'Ali has not died, he is alive in the clouds and would return to fill the earth with justice.[37]

Though refuted by renowned Sunni scholar Ṭah'ā Ḥusain of al-Ażhar University of Egypt that the episode of Ibn Sabā has no *locus standi*[38], some of Sunni scholars still believe in it. According to them Ibn-

Sabā has his own claim to be Prophet of 'Ali, who is God; it is also the faith of 'Alawiyyas, they assert. Nevertheless, the *'Ulyāniyyas* or *'Alyā'iyyas* named after 'Ulyān (or 'Alyā)-bin-Ibn Žirā as-Sadūsī (or az-Zāwsi or al-Asadī) also called *az-Zammiyya* (the blamer), who appeared around 800, maintained that 'Ali was God and Muḥammad his apostle. Muḥammad was to be blamed because he was sent to call the people to 'Ali but he called for himself. Similarly, *Isḥāqiyyas* or *Hamrawiyyas* who have been named after Isḥāq-bin-Muḥammad an-Nakha'ī al-Aḥmar (d. 802 AD) of Kūfa. They had the faith that both Muḥammad and 'Ali were Divine and shared the Prophethood. *Muḥammadiyyas* or *Mīmiyyas,* championed by al-Fayyāz, were the counterpart of *'Ulyāniyyas* or *'Alyā'iyyas* and believed in the Divinity of Muḥammad.

'Alawiyyas are also included in *Ghulāts* community. *Ghulāt* is derived from 'Arabic word *Ghul,* which literally means enthusiastic and strong. This refers to that group of Shi'is, which has exaggerated belief about Imām 'Ali and *Ahlu'l-Bayt*. Since some branches of the Ismā'īlīs, sect such as *Qarāmiṭa* (Carmathian) *al-Bāṭinī'in* or *Ta'līmiyya* (Secretist) were accused of being armed terrorists, and the *Ghulāts* were the extremists in their beliefs, so they too were put under the Ismā'īlī sects. However, the fact of the matter was just the opposite. The origin of the exaggerated ideology of the *Ghulāts* may be traced outside Islam. The source of such beliefs may be traced in the bi-theistic Irani religion, Jewish mysticism, Egyptian and Mesopotamea cultural currents as well. It is greatly similar to the Christian mysticism. Their Islam sees Imām 'Ali to a large extent and prophet Muḥammad to some extent in the form of Jesus Christ.[39] The exaggerated belief about Jesus Christ is found in the second century.

Most of the *Ghulāts* have, by now, disappeared. According to their thinking, Muḥammad, 'Ali, Fāṭimah, Ḥasan and Ḥusain, who are known as *Panjatan* among the Shi'is, are collectively placed on divine throne. None of them is believed to have died but they assume occultation as and when necessitated. The followers of Muḥammad-bin-Nuṣayr an-Namīrī, whose follwers are called *Nuṣayrīyyas* or *Namīrīyyas* and sometimes 'Alawīyyas have considerable variation in their faith and teaching. They are often erroneously called *Ahlu'l-Ḥaqq*, who had originated from amongst the tribes in the Qarā-Quyūnlū empire in 15th century AD. With a loose network in their belief, they are most numerous among the Kurds in west Iran, north Iraq (especially around Sulamāniyya and Kirkūk), south-east Turkey and among the Turkomāns. The person responsible for the establishment of the sect was Ḥusayn-bin-Hamadan al-Khasbi

(d. 957 AD or 968 AD), who under the patronage of the Hamadanid dynasty greatly extended the influence of the sect to Aleppo.

The *'Ulyāniyyas* or *'Alyā'iyyas,* who are also known as *'Ali Ilāhīs* or *'Aliyu'llāhīs* have survived to the present day, are now popularly called *'Alawiyyas.* Although the follower of this sect were being hanged and put to death for centuries by the Muslim rulers, they could not be finished. After First World War the French attempted to set up a separate *'Alawiyyas* state centred on Lattakia but later this was abandoned. At present there are several million followers of this ideology; they are spread from Lattakia (Syria) to Antakia (Turkey). They are politically dominant in Syria under the President Ḥāfiz al-Assad.

The Sunni Community

The majority of Muslims belong to Sunni Community whose full name is *Ahlu'l-Sunnat-wa'l-Jamā't*, the people of tradition and group. This naming makes it clear that in this sect, it is essential to have faith in the life-pattern of the holy Prophet Muḥammad, and the collective model of the companion of the Prophet Muḥammad in general and *Khilāfatu'r-Rāshida* in particular. The making of the holy Prophet's *Sunnat* and the *Sunnatu'l-Jamā'tu'l-Ṣaḥāba* (words and conduct of the holy Prophets' Companions) as the bed-rock of Sunni faith was initiated by 'Abdu'r-Raḥmān-bin-'Auf who was the brother-in-law of the third Caliph 'Othmān-bin-'Affān, and was also the convener of the selection committee constituted by the second Caliph 'Omar to select the third Caliph after his death.

'Abdu'r-Raḥmān was interested in 'Othmān-bin-'Affān to be selected the third Caliph, so he placed such a condition which could in no way be acceptable to 'Ali-Ibn-Abū Ṭālib. He said to 'Ali – Give me word that you will always act upon Qur'an, the Prophet's Traditions and Traditions of the two preceding Caliphs Abū Bakr and 'Omar. The reply of 'Ali to this demand still adorns the pages of Islamic history, he said – I am committed to Qur'an and the Prophet's Traditions, if the *Sunnat* of the two preceding Caliphs were in harmony with Qur'an and the Prophet's Traditions, there is no need to make any additional condition and I will abide by it, but if their Sunnah is other than Qur'an and Prophet's Traditions, then it must not be accepted by any Muslim.[40]

'Ali was deprived of the Caliphate while 'Othmān took oath as per proposal of 'Abdu'r-Raḥmān-bin-'Auf. This event took place on the 1st Muḥarram 23 or 7th November 644[41], so the same date may be called foundation date of the *Ahlu'l-Sunnat-wa'l-Jamā't*. Caliph 'Othmān became the first *Ahlu'l-Sunnat-wa'l-Jamā't*. But this name could not get currency in his time. The followers of 'Othmān were called *Shi'anu'l-'Othmān* or *Ummavīs*, the followers of Ummayyite clan. But their opponents used to call them *Nāṣbī,* meaning the betrayer. The name of the Sunni sect *Ahlu'l-Sunnat-wa'l-Jamā't* became current for the first time during the reign of the 'Abbāsite Caliph al-Manṣūr (754-75 AD), and then in the reign of Hārūn al-Rashīd (786-809 AD).[42] At present it is called in brief the *Sunni sect*. We, too, will refer to it only by addressing it as Sunni sect.

The religious identity of Sunni sect is not traceable before the 'Abbāsite Caliphate (750 AD), whereas, by that time, other sects of Islam like Shi'is, Ṣifātiyyas, Jabriyyas, Murji'īs, and Mu'tażilīs, not only had come into existence but heated debates on various theological issues among them used to be held from time to time. The founder of the Sunni school of theology, Imām Abū Ḥanīfa was himself educated by Shi'is, emerged out of them, and was a Shi'i by the tradition of his family. His grandfather Żoṭā, was among the great devotees of Imām 'Ali.[43] When the Abbāsites made Kūfa (Iraq) as their capital, the Shi'is as a result lost one of their centres. The people of Kūfa had to go into *Taqiyya* (concealment of real belief). Some of them started supporting 'Abbāsites. From among the disciples of Imām Ja'far aṣ-Ṣādiq, besides Imām Abū Ḥanīfa, Imām Mālik-bin-Anas Asḥabī, Imām Sufyyān Thūrī, Imām Sufyyān-bin-'Ainiyya, Imām Sho'ba-bin-Ḥajjāj, Imām Fuzayl-bin-Ayāz etc., cutting off from their religious mentor and spiritual teacher, Imām Ja'far aṣ-Ṣādiq and occupying special places in different schools of Islamic theology became the founders of their respective schools of jurisprudence. The framing of the articles of faith and religious principles of the Sunni sect could get accomplished in the hands of Imām Abū Ḥanīfa. Famous Sunni scholar Abu'l 'Olā Maudūdī (d. 1979 AD), had admitted that Imām Abū Ḥanīfa is the first man who, having written *al-Fiqhu'l-Akbar* has established Sunni ideology *viz-a-viz* other Islamic sects.[44]

The Sunnis in spite of having faith in the religious leadership of all the Twelve Imāms of *Ahlu'l-Bayt*, from Imām 'Ali to Imām al-Mahdī, also uses the title of Imām for any learned figure in theology and jurisprudence. They also use it for any distinguished person of a religious community, sect, religion, in reference of a branch of knowledge etc. such as, *Imāmu'l-Islam, Imāmu'l-Ahlu'l-Sunnat, Imāmu'l-Hind, Imāmu'l-Ḥadith* etc. The founders of the four Sunni schools of jurisprudences are also called *Imām*.

It has been discussed in the foregoing pages that the main difference between the Shi'is and Sunni sects is about the mode of appointing Imām or Caliph. In addition to this, some other issues also come up, like the definition of Imām, the difference between Imām and Caliph, *Kufr*, the effect and consequence of sin. Since Imām Abū Ḥanīfa had moved over to Sunnism *en route* Shi'aism, so the dominant tendency of his thought and faith is conciliatory.

As he had gone a long way on Shi'is and Imāmiyyas faith before going over to Sunnism, he has admitted the greatness and superiority of the Imāms in *Ahlu'l-Bayt* which made him take a conciliatory attitude. He kept Imām 'Ali closer to his heart than other Caliphs.[45] He kept theological principles similar to those of Shi'a sect. He kept *Durūdu'-Salām* (God's blessing) exclusively to the Prophet Muḥammad and his pious progeny without including in it either any wives of the Prophet or his companions.[46] He never gave priority to Caliph 'Othmān over Imām 'Ali.[47]

By admitting the first two Caliphs a harmony between Shi'is and Sunnis could be established. But the situation with the Shi'is was different. They could not budge from their stand nor did they do so. Had they the power of selecting Caliphs, they too would have followed suit. But they believed that the vote of men has no value in the selection or election of Imām or Caliph. This selection is made by no one except God. The matter halted right here. The Żaydīyyas accepted it so the Sunni community embraced them into their fold.

The reverential attitude towards Imām 'Ali and other Imāms from *Ahlu'l-Bayt* was not confined to Imām Abū Ḥanīfa only. It may be called a commonly acceptable attitude of the majority of Sunnis. Barring a few exceptions, the Sunni community regards veneration and love to 'Ali-Ibn-Abū Ṭālib and *Ahlu'l-Bayt* as the base of religious sentiment. A famous couplet of Persian poet Sa'dī, who says:

> "I hold 'Ali close to my heart, for which I am called *Rāfizī* (dissenter). If it is so, then God, his Prophet and Gabriel are *Rāfizī* as well (for they all love 'Ali)."

This is not just a poetic expression of a poet but its thought is based on a famous 'Arabic line asserted by Imām Muḥammad-bin-Idrīs ash-Shāfi'ī. He says:

> "If loving and venerating the *Ahlu'l-Bayt* is to become *Rāfizī* then I make the whole mankind and the whole genii the witness to the fact that I am *Rāfizī*."

There is no doubt that the love and veneration to Imām 'Ali and *Ahlu'l-Bayt* is that fundamental element whose relevance and significance is not only established today, but it is only by adopting it that the dream of Islamic unity can be realized.

Collectively there are two foundations of Sunni faith and thought. One, to follow Ash'arites in the basic principles of theology, and two, to follow one of the four schools of jurisprudence namely Ḥanafi, Mālikī, Shāfi'ī, and Ḥanbalī, in practical code of conduct. The whole Sunni community, barring a few stray differences, is actively based on these two foundations. It would be fitting here to present the contrasting points of the Sunni and Shi'i faiths, so as to make clear the basic difference between the two sects.

Firstly, About the first – four Caliphs

Determining the selection of Imām or Caliph by the vote of common masses, raises a few basic questions. What would be the underlying principle of this selection? What would be the essential qualifications of the man seeking to be selected as Caliph or Imām? Whether a morally deficient man and cruel character can be made a Caliph? What would be the roles and power, rights and duties of judiciary and the executive in the process of the election of the Caliph? What would be the medium of securing balance between them? What would be the rules governing the treasury? Besides these there are other issues and situations also. If the Caliphate of the same Caliph is proved unconstitutional or dubious will his verdicts remain the part of the Islamic laws? If the conduct and behaviour of some caliphs does not come up to mark of Islamic justice, then how far will his teaching and presenting the rules and instruction imparted by the Prophet, will be credible, etc.? These issues have already come up while discussing the Cardinal Beliefs, hence it is not necessary to take them up here again.

Secondly, About the Companions of the holy Prophet

About the companions of the prophet, the Sunni sect believes that:

"All the companions are just"[48]

All the experts of the *Ḥadīth*, theologist and the learned scholars of the Sunni community believe that the companions of the Prophet are the medium and tool of conveying the religion of Islam to Muslims. Even if the slightest doubt is cast on their being just in faith and allegiance, the entire Islam will become dubious. Abu'l 'Olā Maudūdī has the explanation:

> "If the just and true allegiance of the companions to the Prophet is taken in the sense that they were totally committed to the Prophet and all of them were deeply sensitive to the fact that they have the rather heavy and serious obligation to convey the Prophet's traditions and his teachings to the masses of the world, so they would never have imputed any untrue thing to the Prophet, then the statement that 'all the companions are true', will hold good without any exception to all the companions – But if this statement is taken in the sense that without any exception, all the companions, in all the areas of their activities were perfectly dressed with equitable allegiance to the Prophet and no single act of their lives was ever done contrary to justice, then this statement about them would be devoid of truth."[49]

The second point in this clarification is related to the companion's infallibility or being secured from error. But no Sunni individual or any Muslim would never admit that the companions were absolutely secure from errors. Even the first point that none of them would ever attribute any untrue thing to the Prophet is not based on truth. If this assumption were to be believed, then the thousands of spurious *Ḥadīths* will have to be accepted, even though they are contrary to the contents of Qur'an and Sunnat. Moreover, if these *Ḥadīths* were to be accepted, it would amount to overthrowing the achievements of those renowned scholars of Islam, who had involved the special science of testing and sorting the true *Ḥadīths* from the false ones. The science which is known as *'Ilmu'r-Rijāl*, ascertains the narrator's validity and credibility. It is on the basis of this science that the radiant gem and jewel of the genuine *Ḥadīths* were identified and sorted out of the trash heap of fabricated and spurious *Ḥadīths*.

The greatness and distinction of the companions was based on their conduct, character, fidelity and purity, and not on the basis of merits grafted on them. Imām 'Ali while praising the companions says:

> "I have seen the main companions of the holy Prophet Muḥammad. As for me none of you looks like them. They would pass the right till the dawn in a state in which their hair

were dishevelled, their faces filled with dust while they would pass the night in saying prayer, putting down sometimes their foreheads in prostration, sometimes their cheeks, being so restless in minding the day of resurrection, as if they were held on the ambers, prolonged prostration had left corn on their foreheads. Whenever God's remembrance is invoked, tears well up their eyes and gushes forth till the front of their garment is soaked in tears. They would tremble in fear of God's wrath and in joy of God's grace like the trees in fierce wind."[50]

Imām Abū Ḥanīfa's view about those who fought battles against fourth Caliph 'Ali, was clear that they were not on correct path of religion in as much as they were opposed to 'Ali.[51] Clearly this is said about those who were involved in the battles of Camel and Ṣiffīn against Imām 'Ali.[52] The opinion of renowned Sunni scholar, Ibn Ḥajar al-Haytha-mī al-Makkī (d. 1567 AD) was that this was not the view of Imām Abū Ḥanīfa alone, all the Sunni theologists were of the same view.[53] This view assumes special meaning considering the fact that the Sunni faith is based on the Traditions as well as the body of Prophet's companions.

Thirdly, About the Religious Faiths:

With regard to the *Īmān* (religious faiths) there are two basic facts in the Sunni doctrine:

(*a*) *Iqrār-bil-Lisān* (oral declaration) and
(*b*) *Taṣdīq-bil.-Qalb* (affirmation by heart)[54]

Imām Abū Ḥanīfa makes it clear:

> "Action is a thing distinct from *Īmān* and *Īmān* is a thing distinct from action."[55]

The logic of this statement is that at times some actions are left undone but *Īmān* or inner faith never leaves him, such as to say that *Żakāt* is not taxable on the poor but it cannot be said that to have faith in it as a Islamic injunction is not obligatory for him.[56] It is not proper here to put this logic to analysis, however, this would suffice here to say that the reason why the *Żakāt* is not obligatory on the poor is because of his unaffordability to pay it, as God exerts no injunction which a person cannot afford to undertake. On this subject we have discussed in the foregoing pages while discussing the justice of God as the religious obligation of Islamic faith.

About religious faiths, Imām 'Ali ar-Rezā states:

> "*Īmān*'is affirmation by heart, admission by tongue and expression into action by physical organs."[57]

So, in contrast to the Sunni sect, which doesn't believe in the '*Amal-bil-Arkān*, the endorsement of faith into action by physical organs, Shi'is have faith in it in addition to affirmation by heart and expression by tongue. The expression of faith into action as a dimension of *Īmān* is a controversial issue. Shi'is regard all those to be Muslims who admit by tongue the *Kalamahu'sh-Shahadah: Lā Ilāh Ill'allāh Muḥammadu'r Rasūla'llāh* (No gods but God and Muḥammad is messenger of God) but Shi'is do not regard them to be *Mūmin* (true believer) unless their faith manifests into action. To be a *Mūmin* one has to fulfil all the three conditions namely affirmation by heart, admission by tongue and expression by action. But in the belief of the Sunnis, everyone is Muslim who recites oral witness, and every Muslim is *Mūmin* whether or not his actions go against the Islamic essence or his acts may cause Islam to be ridiculed.

Taking advantage of this belief, some cruel and characterless Caliphs of the Umayyite and Abbāsite dynasties, who despite their being an ugly spots on the face of Islam, were believed to be *Mūmin* and used to be addressed as *Amīru'l-Mūminīn* (the leader of the true believers) because of their being in power.

In the Sunni ideology, moral depravity is a sin but it does not turn one out of religion. No Musalmān, howsoever big a sinner he may be, can be said to be a *Kāfir*. As long as he admits that sin is not good, his *Īmān* is not affected and he remains a *Mumin*. It is possible for a Muslim to be utterly as good as detestable in moral conduct, but it is not possible for him to be a *Kāfir*.[58] It is a clear belief of the Sunnis that no one can go out of *Īmān* simply by negating the same thing, affirming which he had entered into *Īmān*.[59] A question arises in this context, if the one who is morally debased is entitled for hell, if so, will he live there on permanent basis or for short period? To tackle this complex question, the scholars don't make a straightforward answer, they make a round about answer, they choose to say:

> "I don't say that such a Muslim will live permanently in Hell, if he is depraved."[60]

or they say:

> "For a person saying prayer with his face toward Ka'ba I say neither that he is entitled for hell nor call him apostate as long as there is traced no evidence of such thing in his conduct, I leave his case with God to decide."[61]

Ironically, how false is this claim that they don't call any Muslim to be a *Kāfir,* whereas the *Fatwās* (edicts) of calling *Kāfir* is frequently practiced in their circle. They keep passing the edicts of being infidel against other Muslims or sects. Apart from calling *Kāfir* the members of other sects, the Sunni sect is in practice calling some of their own sub-sects as *Kāfir*.

In contrast to Shi'is, there was no continuity of Imamate in the Sunnis, so that one Imām after the other would get nominated without a gap. In the Sunnis the Imamate got annexed to the Caliphate. The Caliph would also be the Imam of his time. In following this principle no practical difficulty surfaced in the period of the first four Caliphs (632-61 AD). The deteriorating moral character of the subsequent caliphs strayed away from the *Sharī'a*, so they were not regarded worthy of Imamate.

As a result of gradually out of the bounds of *Sharī'a,* four school of *Sharī'a* came to be established. They are also called the *Muṣalla* (place of worship) of the *Islamic Sharī'a.* Of these, the followers of the school of Imām Abū Ḥanīfa (699-767 AD) are called *Ḥanafī,* those of Imām Mālik-bin-Anas Asḥabī (713-791 AD) are called *Mālikī,* those of Imām Muḥammad-bin-Idrīs ash-Shāfi'ī (767-819 AD) are called *Shāfi'ī,* and those of the Imām Aḥmad-bin-Ḥanbal (780-855 AD) are called *Ḥanbalī.* Majority of Indian Muslims are the followers of the *Ḥanafī school.* In due course, several subsects emerged, such as *Ahlu'l-Ḥadīth, Wahhabī, Muqallid, Ghair-Muqallid* etc.

Ḥanafīs

The founder of the Ḥanafīs was Imām Abū Ḥanīfa No'mān-bin-Thābit-bin-Zotā (d. 767 AD). He had been well known in the Sunni community as Imāmu'l-Āzām. He was trained in the Shi'i theology, was among the pupils of Imām Muḥammad al-Bāqir and Imām Ja'far aṣ-Ṣādiq, and used to give precedence to Ahlu'l-Bayt in support of his own legal judgments. He was involved for a long time in the religions polemics whose centre was Baṣra (Iraq). Having been fed up with it, he turned to Islamic jurisprudence which had two centres of study—one in Baṣra, the other in

Kūfa. Imām Abū Ḥanīfa did not join the *Ḥadīthism* of the people of Baṣra but preferred to be attached to the centre at Kūfa, which had been started by Imām 'Ali. In course of time, however, because of its specific beliefs and ideology, it had become the centre of the *Ahlu'r-Ra'i-w'al-Qiyās*, those who follow their own opinion in the absence of a clear instruction of God in Qur'an or Sunnat. Educated and trained at this centre were many famous scholars like 'Abdu'llāh-bin-Mas'ūd (d. 652 AD), al-Mā'rūf (d. 682 AD), ash-Sharīh (d. 697 AD), Ibrāhīm Nakhafī (d. 714 AD), al-Ḥammād (d. 737 AD), 'Alqamā (d. 814 AD). Out of these scholars, Abū Ḥanīfa remained in service of al-Ḥammād, one of the prominent teachers for thirty years. In course of his teaching he shed light on thousands of religious issues, which were recorded by his disciples.[62] There are unusual similarities in the Ḥanafī and the Shi'i Ja'farī jurisprudence which show that both have sprung from the same source.

An important achievement of Imām Abū Ḥanīfa was the constitution of a kind of unofficial council of Islamic legislation. Because of specific purity, relevance and the moral and religious influence of the individual members of the council, the government was bound to enforce the legal edicts of the council, though, officially it had no patronage. Among the participants of this council were his favourite disciples Abū Yūsuf, (d. 807 AD), Muḥammad Ḥasan ash-Shībanī (d. 805 AD), 'Abdu'llāh-bin-Mubārak, Abū 'Abdu'llāh etc. who were counted one of best scholars of their time.

The methodology of the instruction of Imām Abū Ḥanīfa was to rehear the note taken by his disciples. Abū 'Abdu'llāh says that because Abū Yūsuf, who later emerged as distinguished disciple and called Imām, used to add his own opinion while taking the dictation from Imām Abū Ḥanīfa, he skipped what he had added and read only the text dictated by Imām Abū Ḥanīfa. One day, he missed to skip it and read out his own opinion as well. Upon that the Imām asked him whose opinion was that?[63]

The principle of insertion of the Imām's individual assumption gave variety to the legal matters, it nevertheless, gave rise to sharp disputes, which later helped in bringing various other Sunni sects into existence. This principle of allowing hypothetical presumption is not confined only to the literal interpretation of Qur'an, but attempts to find reasons which may be beyond the text of Qur'an, and *Ḥadīth*, particularly small issues not clearly found in Qur'an and *Ḥadīth*. For example, the wine has been made unlawful on account of intoxication, so all such things which may cause intoxication would become unlawful. Or, since the punishment of theft is to cut hand, and since breaking into house is also theft, so the burglar will also be subjected to the same punishment.

The biggest problem produced by this system of guessing is that it leaves enough room for others to disagree with it and add their own assumptions. The instance of this was Abū Yūsuf, who had mastered artfully twisting the theological laws to suit his various conveniences. Ibn Khalqān ash-Shāfi'ī (d. 1262 AD), by referring to aṭ-Ṭabarī, Ibn Jarīr Abū Ja'far, has said that the *Ḥadīth* narrated by Abū Yūsuf were looked upon with doubts by the enlightened scholars of *Ḥadīth*, because he was in the habit of constantly inventing new proposals of laws.[64] Abū Yūsuf had made the local traditions and customs the part of the Islamic faith, and he termed and styled it as *Istiḥsān* (lenient interpretation) on the basis of which he framed rules according to his own will.[65]

Mālikīs

The founder of the Mālikī School was Imām Mālik-bin-Anas Asḥabī (d. 795 AD). Like Imām Abū Ḥanīfa, he was also the disciple of Imām Ja'far aṣ-Ṣādiq. Though there was no major difference between his theological principles and that of Imām Abū Ḥanīfa, on minor principles and the elaboration thereof, there was sharp difference between them. Imām Mālik had made Medīna, the centre of theological learning. According to him after Qur'an and *Sunnah*, the Medīnian's mode of living and believing were the original ways of Islamic life. If there arose a dispute about a *Ḥadīth*, then according to the Mālikī School, one should rather follow the practice current in the Muslims of Medīna.[66]

Imām Mālik was in favour of following the life-pattern of the people of Medīna, but in case the right direction is not traced either in *Sunnah* or in the life-pattern of the people of Medīna, then he was not in favour of making guesses about doubtful *Ḥadīth* and adding his own assumptions to the theological rules. In fact it was in contradiction of the principle of making hypothetically willful rules, that the Mālikī School had come into existence.[67] The best specimens of the thought-pattern of Imām Mālik is collected in his *al-Muwaṭṭa* in which he has put together the theological evidences under various heads: first the verses of Qur'an, then the *Ḥadīth*, and finally the practice and traditions current among the people of Medīna. His principle was that if the Qur'anic instruction is quite clear then the *Ḥadīth* should be ignored.[68]

Crediting authenticity to the old practices and customs of the people of Medīna, many pre-Islamic habits and traditions of the 'Arabs entered into the legal corpus of Islam. For example, it was a pre-Islamic custom of the 'Arabs to part with the 10th part of the income earned by the water of a new well. This duty tax was enforced even after Islam was adopted as a way of life. Making conditional gift was opposed in many *Ḥadīth*, but as it was practiced by Medīnians before Islam so Imām Mālik allowed it as a proper thing in Islam as well. In the same way it is given in *al-Muwaṭṭa* that a non-'Arab cannot be a heir to an 'Arab, but if the child is born in 'Arabian country, he may be the heir to his mother.[69] But these rulings are not acceptable in other communities of Islam.

Shāfi'īs

The founder of the Shāfi'ī School was Imām Muḥammad-bin-Idrīs ash-Shāfi'ī (d. 819 AD). He had learned Mālikī theology directly from Imām Mālik, and Ḥanafī theology from the disciple and associate of Imam Abe Ḥanīfa, namely Muḥammad-bin-Ḥasan ash-Shabianī. A profound study of both these theologies made him dissatisfied of both, and became the cause of genesis of a new theology. He was dissatisfied with the Mālikī theology because looking at the situations it laid emphasis on following the literal import of *Sunnah*. Moreover, he observed that no distinction between the Prophet's practice and the practices and customs of the Medīnians was maintained. He was against the personal opinions of the theologians. By 8th century, *Ḥadīth* had required the status of the main source of Islamic knowledge. It naturally resulted in the Qur'anic instructions being revoked after expansion of the Muslim imperialism. Many practices and traditions were against the injunctions of the Qur'an, but their roots had gone so deep into social life that it was not easy to uproot them. However, Imām Shāfi'ī became victorious in his battle against the weaker aspects of the Ḥanafī and Mālikī theologies. He attempted to propound such principles which might be free from the defects of the old jurisprudence.[70]

Imām Shāfi'ī, adopted a well thought out method of structuring the rules and determining the sources of theological laws. He agreed to accept old practices and traditions as a regular source but advocated the *Ijmā'*, an essential condition for it. Imām Mālik too believed in consensus but it was applicable to Medīna only. Imām Shāfi'ī expanded it and got included the opinions of the renowned scholars in the body of the Prophet's *Ḥadīths*. These principles gained all the more currency in the course of time because through them were sought the solutions of contemporary problems of the Muslim. Apart from the sacred scholars of Mecca and Medīna, the renowned scholars of all periods and regions were included as a source of laws along with Qur'an, *Sunnah* and *Ijmā'*.

He allowed people to form personal opinions but only when the above three respected sources proved insufficient to derive theological injunctions.

Followers of the Imām Shāfi'ī are found in North Africa, Egypt, South Arabia, Malaya, Sri Lanka and India. Some of the Bohra community of Mumbai follow the principle of Shāfi'ī because of being close to Shi'is.

Ḥanbalīs

The founder of Ḥanbalī School was Imām Aḥmad-bin-Muḥammad Ḥanbal (d. 855 AD). His significance lies in resisting the Mu'tazilīs' ideology dominant during 809-92 AD, the important period of al-Mamūn and al-Mu'taṣim b'Illāh, of the 'Abbāsite caliphates and restoring and asserting the Sunni ideology and beliefs. Had it not been so, the Abbāsite caliphs of the time would have ended the status of the Sunni ideology as part of the state religion and replace it with the Mu'tazilī ideology. The Mu'tazilīs are described elsewhere in this book.

Because Imām Ḥanbal did not propound any new principle, many scholars don't regard him *Faqīh* (theologist) and regard him only a *Muḥaddith* (expert of *Ḥadīth*). But his vision of the Islamic jurisprudence as seen in his interpretation of *Ḥadīth*, cannot be denied. As such, when the Ḥanbalīs attained the political power of the state in the 17th century, they were recognized by consensus to be one of the authentic source of Sunni faith.

Imām Ḥanbal was among the severe opponent of the hypothetical principle of his teacher Imām Shāfi'ī. He was agreeable to the rational interpretation of Qur'an and *Sunnah*. Imām Ḥanbal was only opposed to making any hypothetical assumption based on consensus, which he would call unlawful and unjustified. There is no doubt that in contrast to other sects, the Ḥanbalīs has been more reactionary and extremist, resulting in decrease in the number of its followers. But in the 19th century, the Wahhabī movement restored political strength to Ḥanbalīs, otherwise it would have gone into oblivion.[71] Ḥanbalīs are still in practice in some parts of India.

If a comparative study of all the four sects of Sunni theology is made, it may be said collectively that the followers of the Imām Abū Ḥanīfa were more liberal. In comparison to them the followers of Imām Mālik and Imām Shāfi'ī were orthodox. The most orthodox were the followers of the Ḥanbalīs who refused to accept other Sunni ideologies and beliefs. They made specially the Ḥanafīs the target of their criticism by branding them as *Ahlu'r-Ra'i-w'al-Qiyās*, meaning those who follow hypothetical assumptions and opinion in religion. The Ḥanbalīs bears more affinity to the *Ahu'l-Ḥadīth* than to the three branches of Sunni theology given above.

Even the commoner of Islamic history knows that in course of time as the caliph had become dynastic king and the imperialist order was established, the concern of enforcing the *Sharī'at,* theological laws on the administrative power weakened. Egoism got into the conduct of Muslims leading them to break into fragments of different groups which blocked all the avenues of progress. The door the *Ijtihād*, meaning updating of religious laws by constant re-interpretation in the light of the latest knowledge, was closed. All the same, it resulted into some positive benefits. It stopped the debate and the difference arising out of it. It went on until the Wahhābī campaign in 19th century revived the Traditionist principles and the Sunni beliefs began to be seen in the modern and contemporary contexts.

Ahlu'l-Ḥadīth

Ahlu'l-Ḥadīth, those who followed the Traditions of the Prophet, is the extension of the combination of Mālikī, Shāfi'ī and Ḥanbalī Sunni beliefs. They discard Ḥanafīs for entertaining hypothetical opinions and assumptions. Ahu'l-Ḥadīth emphasize more on *Ḥadīths*. They gave no credit to personal opinion or conjecture. Their important centres were in Medīna, Mecca, Yemen, Baṣra and Syria etc. In course of time Shaykh Ibn Taymiyya, Aḥmad-bin-'Abu'l-Ḥalīm (d. 1328 AD), became leader of Ahlu'l-Ḥadīth. Presently, they are described as a school of theological laws which regards Shaykh Ibn Taymiyya, as its founder and whose belief is:

> "The *Ḥadīth* which was not known to Ibn-Taymiyya, is in fact not a *Ḥadīth*."[72]

Shaykh Ibn Taymiyya raised his voice against the principle of conformity propounded by Imām al-Ghażālī, Abū Ḥāmid Muḥammad (d. 1111 AD) and presented his own logic on many subjects like the earlier experts in Sunni theology. He made an elaborate analysis of the previous four schools of Ḥanafīs, Mālikīs, Shāfi'īs and Ḥanbalīs on the criterion of the Prophets' *Ḥadīths* and the Caliphs life and tried to bring out resolutions to a number of problems.

Shaykh Abdu'l Ḥaq Muḥaddith Dehlawī (d. 1642 AD) has been responsible for establishing this school of Sunni theology in India at Delhi. Having himself trained for three years in the school of Ahlu'l-Ḥadīth by going to Mecca in 1731 AD, Shaykh Abdu'l Ḥaq Muḥaddith was not only the first Indian Ahlu'l-Ḥadīth, also he propagated the principle with such a zeal, that the appellation of *al-Muḥaddith* was tagged to his name.

Historically speaking the first Ahlu'l-Ḥadīth in India was Imām Ḥasan-bin-Muḥammad Ṣan'ānī who lived during the reign of king Quṭubu'd-Dīn Aiybak (1206-10 AD). His book *Mushāriqu'l-Anwār* is famous. But the significance of Shaykh Abdu'l Ḥaqq is that he traced the common points in the Traditions and Jurisprudence, refuted the objection raised against them and established a concord between Jurisprudence and Ṣūfīsm. The best example of this is his book *Taḥṣīlu'l-Ta'rruf-fi-Mu'ārifatu'l-Fiqh-wa't-Taṣawwuf.* In the same period Shaykh Aḥmad Serhindī (d. 1624 AD) started teaching the undesirability of reflecting and thinking and in the name of the purity of speech and action, he opened the front to oppose Ṣūfīsm and Shi'aism.

In India, the Ahlu'l-Ḥadīth school of jurisprudence was founded on firm footing by Shāh Walīu'llāh *Muḥaddith* Dehlawī (d. 1762 AD), whereby a comparative study, all the four Sunni school of theology – Ḥanafīs, Mālikīs, Shāfi'īs and Ḥanbalīs had reached a consensus. He said:

> "By an intuitive support, our hearts agreed and contented to follow the Ahu'l-Ḥadīth school."[73]

Shāh Walīu'llāh's peculiarity lies in his attempt to bring out adjustment among various schools of jurisprudence as per need of the time. He tried to adjust with all the four schools of Sunni theology, and also with the Shi'is on the ground of rationalism, besides he made adjustment with Ṣūfīsm within the framework of *Sharī'a*. His argument was that every school had a strong basis for the rationalization of its own theological laws. Therefore, the proper truth would be found collectively on the basis of evident grounds and the perspectives of time.[74]

Shāh Walīu'llāh did not confine his efforts only to religious thoughts and beliefs but also gave political perspective to his thinking. Declaring the contemporary India to be a *Dāru'l-Ḥarb* (unjust and untrue ruling order) propounded the principal of establishing a justice-predominant state for which he organized a powerful armed political party.[75] The principle of his campaign was *Fakku'l-Niẓām* (the end of each worn out system), for which he called it essential to carry an armed struggle by the name of *Jihād.* And in the name of moral revival, he tried to remove the local customs and habits from the Indian Muslims and bring them in harmony with the other Muslims of the world.[76]

His campaign could not click on political level, but the followers of Ahlu'l-Ḥadīth ideology could achieve strong footing in India. They achieved great success in the expansion of religious education among the Sunni community. The Madarsa of Deoband was founded in 1866 AD. In 1894 AD the Nadwat'ul-'Ulama was established and in 1906 AD the foundation of the Madarsa' ul-Iṣlāḥ was laid in Azamgarh. In this, Shāh Walīu'llāh started the campaign of uniting the Ahlu'l-Ḥadīth with other factions of the Sunni community, which is still going strong.

Wahhābīs

The *Wahhābī* is named after its founder Shaykh Muḥammad-Ibn-'Abdu'l Wahhāb al-Najdī (d. 1792 AD). The *Wahhābīsm* was jointly endeavoured in 1747 AD by Shaykh Muḥammad-Ibn-'Abdu'l Wahhāb and Muḥammad-bin-Sa'ūd, the founder of Saudi kingdom, duly sealed by mutual oaths of loyalty, soon began to prosper in terms of military success and expansion. Even the commoner of Islamic history knows that in course of time the Caliphate based on Sunni ideology had become dynastic imperialist order. The concern of enforcing the *Sharī'at,* theological laws on the administrative system became secondary. Egoism got into the conduct of Muslims breaking them into different groups which blocked all the avenue of progress. The *Ijtihād* the door for updating of religious laws by constant re-interpretation in the light of the latest knowledge, was closed. It stopped debate and dialogue on the differences arising out of it. It went on until the Wahhābī campaign in 18th century revived the Traditionist principles.

The term *Wahhābī* is generally as synonym of *al-Muwaḥḥidūn* (the Unitarians). The term *Wahhābī* is derived from the name of Shaykh Ibn-'Abdu'l Wahhāb, who had risen from the bottom of deeply unequal 'Arab society to the very pinnacles of religious life, because of his hard work, creativity and drive. Wahhābīs' claim that their teachings are puritanical and Traditional, representing the early era of Islam. They condemn anything new as *Bid'ah* (unlawful innovation in Islam), and clearly stand against modernity, which, in their view is evil forbidden fruit. Those who eat it get morally depraved. Wahhābī ideas of religious reformations are actually based on fundamental lines and their teachings are influenced by the Ḥanbalī scholar, Shaykh Ibn-Taymiyya.

Shaykh Ibn-'Abdu'l Wahhāb, began his aggressive propagation against what he considered to be extreme ideas of various exponent of Ṣūfī doctrine in 1736. He wrote a book entitled *Kitābu't-Tawḥīd* (book of unity), which is the main text of Wahhābī doctrine. He was fortunate to find a patron in Muḥammad-bin-Sa'ūd, who used its vitriolic new creed as a powerful weapon to propel tribe forward. Al-Sa'ūd went on to win his descendants the kingdom of Saudi Arabia.

'Abdu'l-'Azīż I (1765-1803 AD), son and successor of Ibn-Sa'ūd, who was largely responsible for his exploits as commander-in-chief of the Wahhābī forces, continued to work in complete harmony with Shaykh Ibn-'Abdu'l Wahhāb, who virtually controlled the civil administration of the country. However, once again the Wahhābī rule was established in 1902 AD under the protection of the British with 'Abdul 'Azīż al-Sa'ūd as its King and assured the Wahhābī religious and political dominance with the creation of the Kingdom of Saudi Arabia in 1932 AD on the 'Arabian peninsula.

Wahhābīs have peculiar doctrine regarding the Divine Unity, Prophethood and the Last Day of Judgment, which did not even match other Sunni sects, let alone of Shi'is. All of Sunni and Shi'a sects strongly believe in Imām Mahdī. His appearance or the arising is awaited decreed by God. Apart from Shi'is, the most eminent Sunni scholars like Ibn Ḥajar al-Makkī and as-Suyūtī, Jalālu'd-Dīn in their respective commentaries, *aṣ-Ṣawa'qu'l-Muḥriqa fi'r-radd 'alā' ahli'l Rafz wa'l Zanadiqā*[77] and *Durru'l-Manthīr fī'l-Tafsīr bi'l Māthūr*[78], and others in their commentaries have specifically mentioned the verses of the holy Qur'an in respect of Imām Mahdī, which have been discussed in the previous pages of this book and the reader is fully aware of them. Apart from Shi'is, there are numerous Sunni Traditions mentioning specific signs of the coming of Imām Mahdī, bearing the name Muḥammad[79], who will be a descendant of Prophet Muḥammad in the lineage of his daughter Fāṭimah aż-Żahrah.[80] He will be accompanied by the appearance of Dajjāl in the East.[81] Imām Mahdī's reign will be prevailed either seven, nine or nineteen years before the end of the world etc.[82] The best known general signs, Traditions in both Shi'is and Sunnis sources, state that Imām Mahdī's reign of righteousness will fill the earth with justice after it has been filled with injustice and tyranny.[83] But everything is denied by the Wahhābīs irrespective of Qur'anic verses and the holy Tradition of the Prophet.

According to the Wahhābīs, reciting *Tasbīḥ* (glorification) of God on the beads of rosary is forbidden. To seek the *Shafā't* (mediation and intercession of a Prophet or a Messenger, including the holy Prophet

Muhammad) or *Walī* (Divine Saint), or *Ṣāleḥ* (perfectly virtuous), and follow them as such or to invoke their help other than God, to visit there grave, or things like that are *Shirku'l-Akbar* (the greatest sin). To recite Qur'an for the dead or make shrine on the grave of the dead etc. are *Bid'ah*. To illuminate the graves, to hold gathering for *Eīdu'l-Mīlādu'l-Nabī* (celebrating the birthday of the Prophet), *Pīrī* (mystic patronage), *Murīdī* (disciplehood of a mystic) and *Mujāwirī* (to be attendant of a shrine) etc. are all sins.[84]

Wahhābīs perceived Divine Unity with its own and specific eyes. Unlike other Sunnis, they do not treat *Risālat* and *Ākhirat* as distinct articles of theological principle. They focus only on *Tawḥīd*, *Ṣalāt* or *Namāż*, *Ṣaum* or *Roża*, *Ḥajj* and *Żakāt*. Whereas the fundamental faith of a common Muslim is oriented to the concept of the Prophethood. He regard a Prophet as an *al-Amīn* and *aṣ-Ṣādiq*. When he accepts the Prophet as an authentic messenger of God, he believes in every word uttered by him, he believes through the Prophet in Divine Unity, in the revelation of the Qur'an, in the voice of revelation brought down by Gabriel, the angel of God, to the audition of the Prophet, recording of the people's words and deeds by the angels, the day of resurrection, accounting for one's deeds, paradise and hell etc. as an outcome of his faith in the Prophet.

Muqallidīn

Muqallid (conformists) is an 'Arabic word, its plural form is *Muqallidūn,* which means the conformitist to particular school of jurisprudence. *Muqalldīn* may not be treated as a separate sect in the sense that a majority of them follows the Ḥanafī School of theological laws. In this there is no religious line separating the *Non-Muqallidīn* and the *Muqallidīn*. But in the practical matters there is all the difference between them. This is evident from their names that they are mutually opposite and rival to each other. The eighty per cent of the Sunni population in the Indian sub-continent is included in the *Muqallidīn*. In them are the various Ṣūfī sects (leaving some sects of the Maqshbandī Ṣūfīs), whose followers prevail in the whole Indian sub-continent. Their various branches and institutions are actively engaged in opposition to the vigorous Wahhābīs, '*Urs* (annual festival) on the shrines, *Qull* and *Fatiḥa* (recitation of Qur'anic verses for the benefit of the dead), spreading *Chādar* (sheet of cloth) on the grave of a saint etc. are regarded by the Wahhābīs as *Shirk* (associating partners to God), *Bid'ah* (unlawful innovation in religion) and *Ḥarām* (sin), while the followers of the Ṣūfīs regard all these as the medium of spiritual upliftment. On these occasions the arrangement of *Qawwālī* (mystic chorus accompanied by music) attract dignitaries also along with the common folk, who share with Muslims in their devotional offering of homage to the saints and sit shoulder to shoulder with them. The mystic principles of the Ṣūfīs are firmly rooted in the Indian soil. It is because of the protection of the Ṣūfīs that it could not be possible for the Wahhābīs to uproot them, though they left no stone unturned.

One sect of *Muqallidīn* is the follower of Aḥmad Razā Khān Barellvī (d. 1921 AD) and calls him '*Ālā-Ḥazrat*. He was connected with the Qādriyya sect of Ṣūfīs, but he also enjoyed the caliphate of other Ṣūfīs. He made the contemporary knowledge and arts the medium for propagating his ideology and thoughts. His followers are called *Razā-Khānī* or *Razāwiyya*. The members of this sect are not different in faith from other *Muqallidīn*, however, they lay emphasis on the practice of standing up for the salutation for the Prophet Muḥammad, which is condemned by the Wahhābīs as *Shirk* and *Bid'ah*. They keep on hurling on each other the *Fatwā* as *Shirk* and *Bid'ah*, so much so that at times they don't hesitate to attribute each other with *Kufr* and *Ilḥād*.

Mahdaviyyas

The name of this sect and declaration of its founder that he was *Mahdī* apparently required to be discussed with other *Mahdī'n* but we have preferred to mention them along with other Sunni sects, because these *Mahdaviyyas* are quite different from the concept of *Mahdī'n* in which Imām Mahdī will emerge in the period preceding the Day of Resurrection. The colour of his flag will be black, which will rise from Khurāsān (Iran) which will indicate the presence of Imām who would be appointed by God as the Divine Ruler.[85] Imām Mahdī will establish peace in the world (*Qur'an: 24: 55*) His rule will last for 7-9 or 19 years.[86] And similar other faiths. These *Mahdaviyyas* follow the jurisprudence of Imām Abū Ḥanīfa and associate with the Sunni in all practical sphere.

The founder of Mahdaviyya sect was Mīr Saiyed Muḥammad Jaunpurī (1443-1505 AD) who, in the beginning tried to eliminate the evils of the Muslim society acting as a social reformer through a reformative movement. He explained to the Muslims that it is this material world which creates distance between God and mankind. So it is obligatory to renounce the world and take to worship, prayer, self-purification and the literal adherence to Qur'an and *Sunnah*. His reformative campaign became very popular with the Muslims. He announced, first at Mecca on the eve of *Ḥajj* (12 Žilḥijjah 901 or 22nd August, 1496) and then at Ahmedabad in December 1497 that he was the Imām Mahdī. After that he at the age of 58 made this announcement for the third time in December 1499. The members of this sect reverently call him *Imāmu'l Mahdīu'l-Maū'd 'Alaihissalām* (Imām Mahdī awaited salute to him).

The teaching of Mahdaviyya sect has two aspects: one, the responsibility, the other, the duty based on Qur'anic injunctions. The first aspect belongs to the area of instructions given in detail by the holy Prophet Muḥammad and everyone has to act upon them. The second aspect belongs to *Vilāyat-i-Muḥammadiyya,* the duties which have been enjoined by the last successor Saiyed Muḥammad Jaunpurī. These duties are as follows:

(i) *Renouncement of the Material World*: This world is your desire, if you curb this desire, the world cannot affect you.

(ii) *Company of the truthful*: Be in Company of those who can teach right conduct, right learning and truthful religions behaviour.

(iii) *Withdrawal from the masses*: Keep aloof from the worldly masses and remain isolated.

(iv) *Maximum recitation of Divine Names*: Recite God's name every moment.

(v) *Contentment*: Make the will and pleasure of God your object, not the contentment based on livelihood.

(vi) *Desire to see God*: God is the originator of human being, if there is a true and sincere devotion to God He shall be seen.

(vii) *Migration from the home-land*: *Hijrat* (migration) is a must for everyone as the attachment to home land resists the sacrifice for faith.

(*viii*) *'U<u>sh</u>ur:* To part with 10th part of your income in the name of God as only after this can the income be purified. So he made *Faqr* (poverty) and *Swait* (The income purified by deducting the *'U<u>sh</u>ur*) obligatory.

His first successor Imām Saiyed Muḥammad Jaunpurī was Imām Saiyed Muḥammad Mahdī (d. 1514 AD), the second successor was Imām Saiyed <u>Kh</u>und Mīr (d. 1524 AD) who was also the son-in-law of Imām Saiyed Muḥammad Mahdī. He was killed along with his 60 associates by the army of Muzaffar <u>Sh</u>āh. His head is buried in Pattan, body in Madrasan and his skin is buried in Chapanir.[87]

Mahdaviyya sect gainded popularity in the regime of the Sūrī-dynasty (1540-55 AD) of the Delhi Sultanate. According to Badā'ūnī, 'Abdu'l Qādir various sects of Mahdaviyyas were established in that period out of them were the two famous scholars Shaykh 'Alāī (d. 1548 AD) and Miyān 'Abdu'llāh Niyāżī (d. 1592 AD). Abu'l Fazl Faizī and his father Shaykh Mubārak were also impressed by the Mahdaviyyas.[88] Emperor Akbar, though indirectly, was, under the influence of the Mahdaviyyas in framing of his religious strategies. The famous Urdu poet of Deccan, Hāshimī Bījāpurī (d. 1667 AD) was also said to be Mahdaviyya. Accepting the migration from home-land as a religious principle, the members of the Mahdaviyya community are well spread in many countries of the world and are still known as an international religious community. Their centre in India is at Hyderabad.

Similar to this religious belief is traceable in the Mahdaviyyas living in Palanpur north of Ahmedabad. They believe that Imām Mahdī has already appeared, so there is left no need for prayers for the dead. They are staunch believers in their faith and they don't establish any relationship outside the circle of their faith.[89]

There are many minor sects of Sunni Muslims, apart from the major sects referred above, if all are described the book becomes too bulky. Only the major sects are discussed here.

Other Communities

There are some Islamic communities, which had their significance in periods of Islamic history on account of their religious beliefs, concepts and certain social and political standing. They influenced Islamic beliefs and thoughts but disappeared in course of time. Most of them merged with one or the other sects of Islam. Eventually only two major sects of Islam namely Shi'is and Sunni remained. But, they cannot properly be placed either under Shi'is or Sunnis because of their specific beliefs and patterns of thought. The best that can be done is to place them closer to one or the other Islamic sects of today.

The peculiarities of all these sects have been described in the foregoing pages. However majority of the orientalists and some of the Indian writers did not differentiate between *Malāḥida, Żanādiqa, Qarāmiṭa* (*Carmathians*), *Bāṭinī'in* or *Ta'līmiyya* and sometimes collectively brand them Shi'is, as if all these sects are of the same belief, which is untrue. Similar is the case of the *Khārijīs, Murji'īs, Mu'tażilīs,* and *Ash'ariīs* for whom they show a peculiar attitude and deny their identity, instead of calling all of them by their specific names, they mingled with the Sunnis.

Khārijīs

Khārijī the singular form of 'Arabic word *Khawārij* means the dissenters or one who exclude or reject. The reason. They are referred to by this name because they supported Imām'Ali in the beginning but rejected him later. They are also known as *Ḥarur'iyya* or *Muḥakamiyya.* Ḥarura' was the place from where originated, so they were called *Ḥarur'iyya.* The basis why they are named *Muḥakamiyya* is the word *Muḥakma,* derived from 'Arabic word *Ḥakam,* which means the judgment. They base their argument on the following verse of Qur'an:

> "The command (*to pass judgment*) rests with none but God." (*Qur'an: 6/57, 40/12*)

The names of other sub-sects of Khārijīs are associated with the names of their founders. For example the followers of Nāfe'-bin-Azariqah are called *al-Azariqahiyyas*; those of Żyād-bin-'Omaru'l-Aṣafar are called *al-Aṣafariyya*; those of 'Abdu'llāh-bin-Abāz are called *al-Abāziyya*; those of Abū Bīhas are called *al-Bīhasiyya*; those of Najda-bin-'Āmir of Hanāfī clan are called *al-Najdiyya;* and the followers of 'Abdu'l Karīm-bin-al-Mujarrad are called *al-Mujārdah.*

As the Khārijīs were earlier supporters of Imām 'Ali against Mu'āwiyah-bin-Abū Sufyyān, third Caliph 'Othmān's governor of Syria, some have wrongly counted Khārijīs as the Shi'is, but at that stage they were Sunnis, who believed in the Caliphate of Abū Bakr, 'Omar and 'Othmān and in turn the Caliphate of Imām 'Ali at fourth place. Shi'is never believed in the Caliphates of Abū Bakr, 'Omar and 'Othmān. They believed Imām 'Ali to be successor of the Prophet Muḥammad without any gap on the basis of his nomination by the Prophet and not through the election by Muslims and so 'Ali-Ibn-Abū Ṭālib as their first Imām. The concept of an elected Caliph is one of the basic principles of Khārijīs who believed in the free election of a Caliph by Muslims to be essential. They also believed that Caliphs must be among the Qurayshites and regarded the earlier Caliphs to be rightful. All these beliefs are the same as that of Sunni faith[90], Shi'i faith does not regard anyone of these beliefs to be acceptable. Therefore, it would be correct to say that the Khārijīs earlier belonged to the faith of the majority of the Muslims established after the Prophet Muḥammad, who believed in the Caliphate constituted through election. They accepted Imām 'Ali as their fourth Caliph but rebelled afterwards being unsatisfied with him. They would equate sin with *Kufr*. According to them accepting anyone to be judged other than God, is a sin. Imām 'Ali had accepted the principle of making arbiter other than God, therefore, he was as good a sinner as Mu'āwiyah-bin-Abū Sufyyān and was entitled to be killed as a religious obligation. So the Khārijīs were repudiated by the Sunni community also.

Khārijīs were killed in large number in the battle of Nahrwān (658 AD) by Imām 'Ali. But they kept on rebelling against the rulers, even in subsequent periods. Their involvement in looting, plundering and committing murders were rampant for a long time until their strength was crushed by the Abbāsites.

Khārijīs have been held as *Fāsidu'l-'Aqīdah* (perverted in belief) but they have not been excluded from Islam as they believe in the fundamental articles of Ialamic faith with exaggerated emphasis on the obedience to God. However, *al-Azariqahiyyas,* the most extreme sub-sect of Khārijīs of Baṣra were separating themselves from the Muslim community and declaring death to all sinners and their families. They regarded other Muslim sects to be *Mushrik*. But other groups of Khārijīs did not call other Muslims as *Mushrik.* The more moderate among the Khārijīs are the *al-Abāziyya,* surviving to the present day in North Africa, 'Oman and Zanzibar.

Murji'īs

Murji'ī is an 'Arabic word derived from *Arija'* which means to hold off. This sect came into existence as a result of its reaction to the belief of the Khārijīs that whosoever commits major sins becomes *Kāfir* and is bound to go to Hell. Murji'īs would say that for any sinner of this world a final, definite and categorical judgment should be held off.

The political and imperial perspective of this belief is clear, in which it was not possible to express any opinion against the rulers (of Umayyite Caliphate), then who would dare to say that the rulers could be held accountable for their acts towards the masses. It was obvious to face adverse consequence of rebelling against the irreligious acts of the rulers. This provided enough room for the rulers and their associates to do what they liked to do. A kind of silent support was secured even if they tried to uproot the very foundation of Islam. What was the worst is the fact that these sinful and un-Islamic acts could in course of time become part of the Islamic traditions. This makes it obvious that this sect did not come into existence only by the reaction against the Khārijīs but also by the support of the imperial policies of the Umayyite dynasty, whose patronage was naturally available to them.

The belief of the Murji'īs in holding off any final verdict of condemnation to Hell for a great sinner as long as he is a Muslim, is in agreement with the basic Sunni faith. It is related to execution of act by the organs of the body which means overall practical agreement with Divine instructions while committing acts of such sinful nature which do not disqualify one to be called a *Mūmin*. This logic is accepted by all Sunnis as a general principle and has been discussed in the foregoing pages. Murji'īs has taken this principle one degree further and said that every sinful act is pardonable except *Shirk*.[91] Some of them have taken the same principle still further and said that any one living in Islamic state will have no fear of life, even if he utters *Kufr*, worships idols, adopts Jewish or Christian faith. He will continue to be a true Muslim. He is still a heir to God and entitled for Paradise.[92]

These notions encouraged a lot the acts of sin and voluptuous indulgence and with such beliefs in mind no act of the rulers howsoever sinful, could be opposed and no voice could be raised against them. With the result, corruption and injustice found an open passage. They declared any armed struggle to re-establish religious doctrine as seditions. If any evil act is found inside the ruling system, it may be pointed out but the contemporary ruling-system could in no way be opposed.

Murji'īs, securing existence under the political strategy of the Umayyite dynasty, gave considerable strength through its principle to the acts of injustice, sinfulness and corruption and damaged the vital principles of Islam. This was why Gilan al-Damishqi was put to death by 'Abbāsi Caliph Hishām (d. 743 AD). Despite being of the Murji'īs, he emphasized on the principle of self-determination and said that every man was free in his will, because this principle might give one the right to destablish the unjust and corrupt ruler from the ruling authority. In contrast to this emphasis on freewill, another group of Murji'īs called *al-Jahmiyya,* whose founder was Jahim-bin-Ṣafwān (d. 746 AD) would refute the principle of freewill and said that human will is pre-determined by God, so no act committed by a human being leaves any responsibility on him. His thought has been a part of the Sunni faith for about a century.[93]

The Murji'īs were the group which took some of the important early steps which formed the basic doctrine of *Ahl'us-Sunnat-w'al-Jama't* in matters of theology as well as polity.[94]

It is also interesting to note that some Shi'i *Ghulāts* were associated with the Murji'īs, such as *Āftābiyyas* or *Fatḥiyyas* and *Muḥaddithiyyas*.[95]

Mu'tażilīs

Mu'tażilī is an 'Arabic word derived from *I'tizal,* which means to remain isolated. The founder of this sect was Wāṣil-bin-'Aṭā (d. 748 AD), disciple of the famous Islamic mystic Khwāja Ḥasan Baṣrī. It is said that on the issue of the occurrence of an act of sin, he differed with his mentor Khwāja Ḥasan Baṣrī on which he said to his disciple *I'tizal-'Annā* (get separated from me). Wāṣil separated himself along with his brother-in-law 'Amarū-bin-'Obayd (d. 763 AD), which became the reason why this sect is called *Mu'tażila* (Mu'tazilite). But others say it may be just a co-incidence, the word *Mu'tażila* was already prevalent for those who had separated from Imām 'Ali and maintained to be neutral at the events of Camel and Ṣiffīn Wars (656-7 AD).[96]

The real significance of the Mu'tażilīs lies in its developing a branch of knowledge known as *'Ilmu'l-Kalām* (the science of religious polemics). Among the Sunni scholars and other men of authority the *'Ilmu'l-Kalām* had always been treated out of bounds. Any argument on the basis of intellect, logic and philosophy had been *Bid'ah* and *Ḥarām*. Mālikī and Ḥanbalī theologists have been in forefronts in this regard. But these oppositions did not cause any decline in the importance of the Mu'tażilīs, instead it became the cause of its popularity.

The Mu'tażilīs maintains peculiar viewpoints, which cannot be reached without analyzing them in right perspective. Their reaction against some of the commonly accepted Sunni beliefs and thinking is rather uncommon. For example, the Mu'tażilīs did not credit *Ḥadīth* and *Ijmā'* as the reliable principles.[97] They refuse to accept an unjust and corrupt man as Imām or Caliph.[98] They refuse to say prayers led by such a man. They were against the election of a Caliph in a state of controversy and revolt.[99] They did not accept the condition of the Caliph being a Qurayshite, rather they preferred the Caliph to be a non-'Arab so much so that would rather like to elect a freed slave to be a Caliph in preference to a Qurayshite or an 'Arab, because it was easier to dethrone him in case he was found corrupt or unjust.[100] They also asserted that if the election of a Caliph was held in a state of controversy and revolt, it was meaningless, and Muslims should themselves adhere to justice.[101]

This is how the Mu'tażilīs, having created a controversy, made rather complex the basic principle of Sunnis, with respect to election of a Caliph. Their judgments on the early Caliphates were rather aggressive. They would call one of the two fighting parties in the battles of Camel and Ṣiffīn to be *Fāsiq* (sinful). Though they were clearly favourable to Imām 'Ali, but for political reasons, which side was fair, they would not take sides. They would severely criticize the third Caliph 'Othmān.[102] They did not refrain even from blaming second Caliph 'Omar.[103]

Mu'tażilīs shared in many Shi'i beliefs and thoughts. Like the Shi'is they adhere the theology that emphasized the doctrine of the Unity and Justice of God, the Createdness of Qur'an, the Freewill of human beings and upheld rationality. They explained the subjects related to the essence and attributes of God as the Shi'is. They accepted *Jabr* and *Qadr* as basic principles, which are the as did the Shi'is. Their belief with regard to *Kufr* and *Īmān* were also similar to that of the Shi'is.[104] Their belief was that a sinner is neither a *Muslim* nor a *Mūmin* nor a *Kāfir* but he is somewhere in between them. Similarly, they emphasized revolution against a corrupt and unjust ruler in order to restore and establish religious laws.

Mu'tażilīs established various logical, rational, and elemental thought-systems. They interpreted the Greek philosophy afresh and discovered common grounds between it and Islamic ideology. They struggled against their opponents and defended the logic and rationale of Islamic faith and beliefs. In this connection they had to face theological debates with their opponents, whose records are available in writing.

As a matter of fact, the Mu'tażilī sect was born out of the political context of the last phase of the Umayyite dynasty. The founder of the Mu'tażilīs sect Wāṣil was the teacher of Żaydīyya sect's founder Imām Żayd. The discontentment with the Umayyite regime prevailed in the then Muslim society. The political revolt was on the rise. On the religious front the popularity of the Murji'ī ideology was on the decrease to the extent that some of the Murji'īs were openly in opposition. The political constraint demanded that all the common points in the opposition of the Umayyite regime be put together. Naturally, the Shi'a community was supposed to be in the forefront and it did so. Others who eagerly came in support of the Mu'tażilīs, were the *Ṣūfīs* and some *Ulama* who had sharp ideological differences with the Murji'īs of course there were people of different ideologies but the majority was of Shi'is ideology with specific faiths and thoughts.

In the development of the Mu'tażilīs religious thought Abū Hażīl al-'Allāf (d. 849 AD) of Baṣra, who was an enthusiastic Shi'i[105], played a critical role. A little older than him was his contemporary Bashar-bin-Mu'tamir of Baghdad, and a little younger than him was Ibrāhīm Nāẓim (d. 844 AD). Mu'tażilīs have two different schools, which were known as the Baṣra and Baghdad schools. The philosophical approach of these two schools were altogether different. The chief figure of the Baṣra school was Abū 'Ali al-Jubbāī (d. 915 AD) whose two disciples became prominent: one was his son Abū Hāshim (d. 935 AD), and the other was Abu'l Ḥasan *al-Ash'arī* (d. 941 AD), who founded a separate school known as the Ash'arīs. Other prominent Mu'tażilīs have been al-Jāḥiẓ (d. 869 AD), Abu'l Qāsim Balkhī Ka'bī (d. 929 AD) 'Abdu'l-Jabbār (d. 1024 AD) and al-Żamakhasharī, Jāru'llāh (d. 1143 AD).

The Mu'tażilīs did not survive the 'Abbāsite rule. They got lost into their own individualized beliefs. And thus the Ash'arīs emerged as a school of thought and replaced the Mu'tażilīs. Yet the way Mu'tażilīs had set the tradition of logical analysis, objective study, intellectual and rational approach to religion, and the way they had introduced Islam in new perspectives, remained engrained in Islam forever.

Ash'arīs

Abu'l Ḥasan *al-Ash'arī* (d. 941 AD), beloved disciples of Abū 'Ali al-Jubbāī and the foremost figure of the Baṣra school of Mu'tażilīs was the founder of this sect. He cut himself off from the Mu'tażilīs and established a separate school based on conventional lines. Abu'l Ḥasan al-Ash'arī started his school of thought by opposing Imām Ahmad-bin-Muḥammad Ḥanbal and other Ahlu'l-Ḥadīths. He allowed use of argument and logic in matters of religious principles and made references to Qur'an and *Ḥadīths*. It resulted in the division of Ahlu'l-Ḥadīths into two separate groups: Ash'arīs and Ḥanbalīs. Ash'arīs, who believed in the religious polemics and reasoning, while the Ḥanbalīs treated it as a sin. Ḥanbalīs scholar Shaykh Ibn Taymiyya had issued the judicial degree to the effect that those who believe in religious polemics and reasoning are *Kāfir*.

Ash'arīs became popular among the masses, because of their mass-appeal. Public in general liked conventions and avoided reasoning and discussion in religious matters. They surrendered to Qur'an and the *Ḥadīths* of the Prophet or both. Moreover, the common man was frustrated with the oppression and exploitation of the Mu'tażilīs under the patronage of the imperial power of the 'Abbāsites caliphs in which thousands had been humiliated and killed for not toeing their faith. A gulf was growing wider between the Mu'tażilīs and the ordinary believer. People were in search of a religious system, which could ensure equality and restore again the dignity of their faith. All their woes found a remedy in the Ash'arī principle of convention, which later became the basic principle of Sunni theology.

Some scholars among the Ash'arīs were renowned, such as Abū Bakr Bāqlānī (d. 1012 AD), Abū Isḥāq Aṣfarā'nī, al-al-Ghażālī, Abū

Ḥāmid Muḥammad (d. 1111 AD) and ar-Rāzī, Fakhu'r-Dīn Abū 'Abdu'llāh Muḥammad (d. 1209 AD). In course of time certain changes occurred in the theology of the Ash'arīs. al-Ghażālī, Abū Ḥāmid Muḥammad's pioneer book *Aḥyāu'l-'Ulūmu'd-Dīn* diverted them towards Islamic mysticism. ar-Rāzī, Fakhru'd-Dīn Abū 'Abdu'llāh introduced some aspects of the religious polemics and reasoning. Finally, when Khwāja Naṣīru'd-Dīn aṭ-Ṭūsī (d. 1274 AD) authored the book *Tajrīdu'l-E'tqād*, the perspective was ninety percentage changed to philosophy. It is amazing that the influence and impact of Shi'i elite Khwāja aṭ-Ṭūsī became so elegant that both Mu'tażilīs and the Ash'arīs have been following the path shown by him. Even the books have been written to interpret the *Tajrīdu'l-E'tqād*. With the passage of time it has resulted in deviation from the ideology of the founder Abu'l Ḥasan al-Ash'arī and getting closer to Mu'tażilīs, which is the current tendency of Sunni theology.[106]

Żanādīqah

Żanādīqah, an 'Arabic word derived from *Żandaq,* means believing in duality of God. Formerly, by definition this word was attributed to the group following the principles of the Irani nationalist movement called *Taḥrīk-i-Shu'ūbīyyat.* Though literally means, the movement of the families, but actually, it was the Irani campaign which arose in reaction to the 'Arab nationalism of the Umayyite Caliphs and announced that 'Arabs can have no superiority over non-'Arabs. Later, this movement took the colour of anti-'Arab feelings. Many books were written in opposition to 'Arabs. We find many books written in condemnation of the Qurayshites and other clans of 'Arabs, in the list of al-Nadim.

The opponents generally denounced the Iranians, saying that their ancient beliefs are still alive in their hearts. As a result of this, they believe in the duality, instead of the Divine Unity. They say that the Iranians have brought the germs of their ancient faith of Manicheans and Magianism, which have injected them into the body of Islam.[107] These accusations were never accepted by the *Shu'ūbī.* But, the fact that they are a separate group, cannot be denied, irrespective of the name they are given. They had gathered so much dominance on the Islamic state by the time of 'Abbāsite Caliph al-Manṣūr (d. 775 AD), that even the Caliph was afraid of them. When they embarrassed the Caliph al-Mahdī (d. 785 AD), he tried to curb them by force. He appointed religious scholars to engage in debate with them and write books in refutation of their faith. He opened a separate department whose objective was to suppress them and subject them to torture. In this way the group organized under the Irani influence, was given the abusive name of *Żanādīqah.* Even now the 'Arabs call their adversaries, specially the Iranians by the same name.

The political perspective of naming the *Taḥrīk-i-Shu'ūbīyyat* as the party believing in duality of God, cannot be negated. Abu'l 'Olā al-Mu'arra, in that period would count all the renowned Iranians among the *Żanādiqah,* such as, Dā'bal, Bashshār-bin-Burd, Abū Nuwās, Abū Muslim Khurāsāni etc. The discussion on the faith of these renowned Iranians was punctuated by abusive words. According to Ibn 'Abdarya the wine, debauchery and corruption were the essential part and identity of the *Żanādiqah.* Since then some people have been referring to their adversaries by this abusive word. Muḥammad Iqbāl writes:

> "In the *Żanādiqah,* according to me, was more stability and consistency compared to their opponents. Their belief was that the earliest souls are mutually separate and have permanent existence. In contrast to this, the Parsis believed in the oneness of all souls. The supporters of monotheism tried to vie the *Żanādiqah* in many forms. But the fact is that in order to explain the monotheism of the earliest twin souls, they use different expressions and illustrations. This proves how powerful were their opponents and that they were not themselves contented with their own philosophic explanation."[108]

Qarāmiṭa (Carmathians)

The name of this sect has come from *Qarāmiṭa* (Carmathian) the title of its founder, Ḥamdān who was famous for his exalted character and saintliness. It is said that he used to ride bull so he began to be called *Qarmṭiyya* (bull-rider) by the common folk and 'Arabs as *Qarāmiṭa* (followers of bull-rider). Ḥamdān, who had extraordinary administrative and managerial abilities, was taken by a missionary of Ismā'īlīs to their faith in 877 AD. In the beginning he started propagating the Ismā'īlī faith, which gathered strength and assumed the form of a movement. Abādān, a close relative of Ḥamdān, started secret campaign in the adjoining areas of Kūfa (Iraq). He revolted in 890 AD and captured Yemen. From there the missionaries of the Ismā'īlī faith reached North Africa where Fāṭimite movement had raised its head. Egypt got victory and the Fāṭimite rule was established as a rival to the 'Abbāsite rule. The capital of the Fāṭimite kingdom was Egypt. They ruled for about 262 years (909-1171 AD) with 12 rulers in all-over the period. The Qarāmiṭa, who in the beginning, were a branch of the Ismā'īlī sect, in course of time, became famous as a sect in its own right. Qarāmiṭa established their kingdom in the North East 'Arabia in Alhasa. They made several attacks on Syria and Iraq. Their leader Abū Sa'īdu'l-Ḥasan al-Jannābī made Bahrain his headquarters. His son and successor Abū Ṭahir Sulaymān Qarāmiṭī captured Baṣra in 923 AD. He attacked with huge mob the holy city of Mecca and massacred numberless pilgrims there, looted the scabbard of the holy Ka'ba, pulled down its door and took away to Yemen the *Ḥajaru'l-Aswad* (black stone of the holy Ka'ba), believed by Muslims to have come from Heaven. They kept this holy place under their control for twenty two years, until they gave it back on the intervention of the Fāṭimite Caliphs.

The Qarāmiṭa regarded the open killing of their adversaries, looting and plundering their property and shedding their blood as excusiveable acts. They considered these acts were in their defence and reaction to the ceaseless killing and looting and savage cruelties perpetrated on Ismā'īlīs by Umayyites Caliphs and then by the 'Abbāsites. But why did they kill the pilgrims and the innocents? Is ravaging the Ka'ba not an open heresy? The fact is that the Qarāmiṭa had started their religious journey from the Ismā'īlī beliefs but afterwards transcended its bounds and went far away and adopted the path of sin and apostasy so much so that they framed such beliefs as the basis of their religious thought which are directly opposed to Islam – e.g. condemning prayer, fasting, and *Ḥajj* and upholding debauchery, sensuous pleasure, drinking wine etc. But like the Mahdaviyya sect they believed in the *'Us̲h̲ur*, the 1/10th as the poor-rate, and like the Sunnis they believed in *S̲h̲ūra,* the election of Caliph or settlement of matters by an advisory body. They had organized the *Majlisu'l-S̲h̲ūra* (council of consultation) in Bahrain, which looked after all the issues of administration of Qarāmiṭa and served also as a guiding light. In all there were five rulers in the Qarāmiṭa period which lasted for 72 years (903-77 AD).

Bāṭinī'in or Ta'līmiyya

Bāṭin (internal or hidden) and *Ta'līm* (the teaching or education) both are 'Arabic words. They are called the Bāṭinī'in, because of their belief that there is the *Baṭn,* the internal or hidden meaning behind every *Ẓāhir*, the external or literal meaning of the all revealed Scripture, which is concealed and out of sight from the common eyes. Similarly, they are called *Ta'līmiyyas*, because of their belief that the Imām is the dispenser of the Divinely-ordained *Ta'līm,* the teaching or education.

This is well known to the learned men how this division of the external and internal forms of the Divine injunctions, hurts the body of laws contained in Islamic jurisprudence. The external or literal meaning is obvious and can be learnt from the books, but internal or hidden meaning can be given only by the Imām, who is the dispenser of the Divinely-ordained *Ta'līm,* the teaching or education. Using such arguments, the basic religious laws and its other obligations were disobeyed, and defied.

As has been pointed out, the Bāṭinī'in had started as a sub-sect of the Ismā'īlī sect, but in course of time, they formed a separate sect of their own like the Qarāmiṭa based on their specific beliefs and ideology, and gradually assumed the form of a community. Bāṭinī'in regarded God to be devoid of attributes and believed that God was put off. Contrary to the common Islamic belief about God, they regarded each attribute and quality of God to be His absolute component. They believed that there was no attribute of God. If there were attributes they would take a form and shape. The qualities which are attributed to God imply that He has imparted those qualities to his created beings. God is not Almighty in the sense that he has all might, but that he imparts might to others. This is how the Bāṭinī'in would negate the attributes of God. They would call him *Lā-Nūr* (No-Light) instead of the *Nūr* (Light), *Lā-Ḥa'ī* (No Ever-Living) instead of *Ḥa'ī* (Ever-Living) and so on. They would call such terms as the Divine injunctions to be external and believed that there was an internal form of text.

The author of this philosophy was Ḥasan-bin-Ṣabbāh (d. 1124 AD), the leader of Nizārī Ismā'īlīs and the class-fellow of Niẓāmu'l-Mulk aṭ-Ṭūsī (d. 1067 AD), who was richly equipped with a bold and courageous personality. He was able to lead an ascetic existence and imposed a puritanical way of life on his followers: when one of his son was accused of murder and other of drunkenness, he had them both executed. Ḥasan-bin-Ṣabbāh had written a number of cogent theological treatises and his expression of the doctrine became widely accepted by the contemporary Nizārī Ismā'īlīs.

Ḥasan-bin-Ṣabbāh proclaimed to be the seventh Imām of the Ismā'īlīs as Imām Ismā'īl had incarnated himself into his person. He also claimed that all kinds of Imamate had come together into his person. He made all the Muslims to break the fast on the 27th of the holy month of Ramazān and made it a day of celebration. The whole day was spent in sensuous pleasures and luxurious acts.

Ḥasan-bin-Ṣabbāh is commonly believed to be the founder of Assassins. *Assassin*, the 'Arabic version of *Ḥashshash*, plural *Ḥashshāshīn*, meaning the Ḥashīsh smoker, referred to the *Assassins* alleged practice of taking Ḥashīsh to induce ecstatic vision of paradise before setting out to face martyrdom. Its historical existence is not proved but is widely circulated in the form of stories told by Marco Polo and other travellers. On account of such stories Ḥasan-bin-Ṣabbāh became very controversial person. Numerous false and exaggerated wrong allegations were ascribed to his name.

It cannot, however, be denied that Shi'is in general and Ismā'īlīs in particular were subjected to ceaseless torture, collective murder and savage behaviour of the Umayyite and 'Abbāsites Caliphs and their dynasties, so an intense feeling of vengeance and retaliation was enflamed in the hearts of the Ismā'īlīs. How to pay them in the same coin became a major issue for them. Ḥasan-bin-Ṣabbāh, who made numerous converts, enhanced his power and with the help of converts made within its garrison, was able to seize the great fortress of Alamut fort of Rodbar, north Kazvin, in Daylām (Iran), a province of the Seljuq empire on 4th November, 1090. He made the fort imprisoning every evil spirit by its invulnerable reconstructions. He carried out organized schemes in areas around Rodbar-Alamut by multiplying the strength of his army. He was grand master, who commanded a network of the corps of devoted terrorists and numerous agents in the enemy camps and cities, claimed many victims.

The corps of devoted terrorists were designated as *Fidāī'* (devotee, who willingly hazards his life), plural *Fidā'īn.* There were three ranks of the Bāṭinī'in order of administration – *Dā'ī Rafīq* (comrade) and *Fidāī'*. The *Dā'ī* would excite the responsibility of propagating the faith, *Rafīq* would co-operate and assist the *Dā'ī* and *Fidāī'* was the extremist militant order which remained steadfast (ready to kill or die) like inevitable death. On this ground, the *Dā'ī* would instruct his followers against *Sharī'a* without any hesitation, and the followers would strictly adhere to this instruction. Within a period of about 150 years not only numberless generals, commanders, rulers, ministers of the 'Abbāsite Caliphate as well as some Caliphs but also other elites, statesmen, scholars, theologists of the Sunni faith were murdered by the *Fidā'īn.* That is why the Sunni community is the greatest opponent of the Bāṭinī'in.[109]

In an attempt to resist his growing power, the Seljuq ruler Malik Shāh (d. 1092 AD) was killed by sword of a *Fidāī'*. Seljuqs once laid seige to Alamut but failed. Ḥasan-bin-Ṣabbāh after the major siege of

Alamut in 1118 AD, kept the Alamut fort under his control for thirty five years with stronghold of all-over Persia and Iraq. He appointed Kīya Buzurg Umīd his successor. After him his son Muḥammad, and then his son Ḥasan occupied the throne. After him many rulers came one after the other until in October 1256, it was captured by the Tartars who effaced the Bāṭinī'in sect leaving no vestige of it.[110]

The Mahdī'n Communities

Mahdī'n is the plural form of the 'Arabic word *Mahdī* which means guide or spiritual guide. The last twelver Imām Abu'l Qāsim Muḥammad Mahdī Āḵhiru'ż-Żamān son of Imām Ḥasan 'Askarī is also called *Mahdī,* who will appear before the advent of *Qiyāmah.* Broadly speaking Mahdī'n do not differ from the Sunnis or Shi'is, except on a few stray points. The main difference lies in the definition of Mahdī. Different sects have evolved among themselves. Some of these Mahdīs claimed to be Imams, some also claimed to be a Prophet, while the common and undisputed Islamic belief is that Muḥammad is the last Prophet, after whom the chain of Prophethood ceased. So, the claims of the Mahdī to be a Prophet in addition to his claim as an Imām, has been objected and declared as non-Islamic. These Mahdīs have, however, their own arguments to justify their claims. We include them in the Islamic community on the ground of their own claims that they belong to Islam or have started from Islam.

We have already discussed in the previous pages regarding the Occultation and Return of Imām Mahdī. The best known general signs, Traditions in both Shi'is and Sunnis sources, state that Imām Mahdī's reign of righteousness will fill the earth with justice after it has been filled with injustice and tyranny. It may be said safely that the incumbents are altogether different from the ideology agreed upon the Traditions of both Shi'is and Sunnis. They may be categorized in three groups as under:

(*i*) Those who abide by Islamic jurisprudence and have faith in Divine Unity and Muḥammad as the last Prophet and also claim themselves to be Muslim.

(*ii*) Those who abide by Islamic jurisprudence with certain modifications and have faith in Divine Unity and Muḥammad as the Prophet but not the last and claim themselves to be the last Prophet. Their splitting group has faith in Divine Unity and

Muḥammad as the last Prophet but some serious *ghuluww* tendencies. Both of them claim themselves to be Muslims.

(*iii*) Those who have their own jurisprudence and have faith in Divine Unity and Muḥammad as the Prophet but not the last and claim himself to be the last Prophet. They never claim themselves to be Muslims. They have separated themselves and assumed a distinct name and faith. They, nevertheless, had started their journey from Islam.

Mahdī'n of Islamic faith

They are of the first category of the Mahdī'n cited above. Actually speaking, there has been some sects among the Shi'is, who rose with a dazzle at some point of time only to fade out. Some of these sects, who claimed to be real Shi'is, disputed the successorship of some Imāms[111], were by comparison in greater number. They are mentioned as under:

Wāqifiyyas

They hesitate over the death of a particular Imām, contrary to *Qat'iyyas* who believed that Imams also died. *Wāqifiyyas* maintain that a particular Imām did not die and awaited his return to fill the earth with justice. They have different branches named after a particular Imām or some time after their founders. They have their separate identity also, such as *Bāqiriyyas, Ja'fariyyas* and *Mūsāwiyyas,* who have their further branches. Their enemies call them *Mumtūrā*, the rained upon.

Bāqiriyyas

They were so named because they believed that the Imamate ceased with Imām Muḥammad al-Bāqir, who had not died. He has gone in concealment and would return.

Ja'fariyyas or Nāwusiyyas

Ja'fariyyas believed that the Imamate has ceased with Imām Ja'far aṣ-Ṣādiq, who had not died but had gone in concealment and would return. They are called *Nāwusiyyas,* because the Nāwus of Baṣra was prominent in this faith.

Afṭaḥiyya or Faṭaḥiyya

They maintain that after Imām Ḥuasin the succession had always gone to the eldest son. Accordingly, after Imānı Ja'far aṣ-Ṣādiq his eldest son 'Abdu'llāh al-Afṭaḥ ought to be Imam. *Afṭaḥ* means the flat-footed or flat-headed. It is said that he disagreed with certain doctrines of his father Imām Ja'far aṣ-Ṣādiq and followed the Murji'īs in some way or other. Some believed that the Imamate has ceased with him but others joined other sects but continued al-Afṭaḥ as the rightful Imām before Imām Mūsā al-Kāẓim.

Shumaytiyyas or Sumaytiyyas

The followers of Yaḥyā-bin-Abī Shumayt (or Sumayt) maintained that after Imām Ja'far aṣ-Ṣādiq his son Muhammad, who was popularly known as *ad-Dībāj* (the handsome) succeeded him. Ad-Dībāj believed in Żaydīyya type Imamate. He fought against Abbāsite Caliph al-Mamūn in 814 and defeated them. But al-Mamūn treated him respectfully and made him part of his court in Khurāsān.[112] Ad-Dībāj's followers believed that Imamate would remain in his family and Imām Mahdī shall be from his family.

Mūsāwiyyas or Mamṭūras

They were named *Mūsāwiyyas* because they believed that Imām Mūsā al-Kāẓim had not died but escaped from the prison and remained in concealment. Likewise, *Mamṭūras* (the rained-upon) believed that Imām Mūsā al-Kāẓim died but raised to heaven like Jesus Christ and will return later. Both the groups, who are called by the general name *Wāqifiyya*, believe in Imām Mūsā al-Kāẓim as Imām Mahdī who will fill the earth with justice.

Mu'allifas

They maintained the doctrine of *Wāqifiyyas* i.e. after his death Imām Mūsā al-Kāẓim would return. Similarly, the other group of *Mu'allifas* believed for Imām Ḥasan 'Askarī and await his return.

Bajaliyyas

This sect was named after its founder Ibn Warsand al-Bajalī who was one of the leading *Mūsāwiyyas.* He took his doctrine to Morocco and

Spain in the beginning of 9th century. He and his descendants succeeded in converting some of the Amīrs of Idrīs regime into his faith. This sect died after the advent of Alamut movement in 12th century.

Bashīriyyas

It was named after the founder Muḥammad-bin-Bashīr of Kūfa. They maintained that Imām Mūsā al-Kāẓim was not imprisoned and did not die. He was in concealment and appointed Muḥammad-bin-Bashīr his representative, and the Imamate later on. He asserted that only the five daily prayers and fasting were obligatory, rest were optional. They believed in the *Tanāsukh*, the transmigration of soul and the *Tafwīz*, the delegation of God's power to any other person.

Aḥmadiyyas

They maintained that Imām Mūsā al-Kāẓim had nominated his next son Aḥmad to be Imām after Imām 'Ali ar-Rezā. Ahmad is said to be buried in the shrine of Shāh Chirag in Shīrāz.

Muḥammadiyyas

They asserted that tenth Imām 'Ali al-Naqī *al-Hādī* during his lifetime had nominated one of his sons, Muḥammad who died but another group believed that he had not died but had been a ruse to put off his enemies. He was concealed and would return as Imām Mahdī. Some of them maintain that the nomination of Muḥammad was necessary because Imām 'Ali al-Naqī's son Imām Ḥasan 'Askarī was childless and other son Ja'far was immoral, both did not fulfil the conditions required for the Imamate.

Ja'fariyyas

They believe in the Imamate of Ja'far son of tenth Imām 'Ali al-Naqī *al-Hādī.* According to them he succeeded to Imām Ḥasan 'Askarī, who was childless. It appears that confusion and fragmentation prevailed at the death of Imām Ḥasan 'Askarī. According to al-Mas'ūdī, 'Ali-bin-Ḥusain twenty sects[113], as per al-Qommī, Sa'd-bin-'Abdu'llāh fifteen sects[114] and to an-Naubakhtī, Abī Muḥammad al-Ḥasan-bin-Mūsā fourteen sects[115] broke out at the time. As earlier stated Ja'far after due verification had withdrew his claim and accepted the Imamate of twelfth

Imām Mahdī Ākhiru'ż-Żamān but a group of his followers continued to accept him as their Imām. When Ja'far had claimed to be Imām, he was nicknamed the *Każżāb* (the liar) and when he repented, he got the title of *Tawwāb* (the repented).

Qaṭ'iyyas

They maintained that each and every Imām from Imām 'Ali up to Imām Ḥasan 'Askarī has died and has nominated his successor in his lifetime. Accordingly, Imām Ḥasan 'Askarī has also died and nominated his only son Muḥammad to succeed him. Some of *Qaṭ'iyyas* believe that Muḥammad was a matured person at the death of his father but others say that he was born eight months after the death of his father. Every group of them believe that Imām Ḥasan 'Askarī had a son, Muḥammad, who is the twelfth Imām Mahdī Ākhiru'ż-Żamān and who has gone into occultation until the last days and will return to fill the earth with justice.

Mahdī'n of *ghuluww* tendencies

They are of the second category of the Mahdī'n cited above. They were repudiated and anathematized for their *ghuluww* tendencies with extremism, and deviated elements of religion in the name of spiritual guidance and sanctity, holding doctrines that are so heretical as to put those holding them outside the pale of Islam. To mention some of them as under:

Mansuriyyas or Kisfiyyas

The chain of this sect is traceable from the time of Imām Muḥammad al-Bāqir (677-733 AD). The founder of the sect Abū Manṣūr al-'Ijlī, was initially the follower of *Ahlu'l-Bayt* but was repudiated by Imām Muḥammad al-Bāqir on account of his *ghuluww* tendencies. He quoted the verse in his favour:

> "And if they were to see a *Kisf* (fragment) of the heaven falling would say: A heap of clouds." (*Qur'an: 50/44*)

Abū Manṣūr al-'Ijlī claimed to be himself the *Kisf* (fragment) of heaven falling down, as mentioned in Qur'an. He maintained that first creation of God was Jesus Christ and the next after him was 'Ali-Ibn-Abū Ṭālib. He had given such interpretation of the terms like, *Ghayāba* (occultation), *Tafwīz* (hand-over of power), *Bada* (change in intention),

Rij'ā (returning from past), *Ḥulūl* (incarnation) and *Tanāsukh* (transmigration of soul). He asserted that the things forbidden in the Qur'an were nothing but the allegory for the names of certain evil men. This created all types of immorality and sin among his followers.

Mughīriyya

They are named after the founder of the sect Mughīra-bin-Sa'īd al-'Ijlī (d. 737 AD), who changed his allegiance over the years several times. Sometimes he was among the *Ghulāts* and sometimes in the Żaydīyyas. Mughīra believed in anthropomorphism of God. He also made claim for himself to be Imām after Imām Muḥammad al-Bāqir and then claimed to be prophet. After his death his followers merged with the *Muḥammadiyya* of Muḥammad-bin-'Abdu'llālh *Nafs-aż-Żakiyya.*

Khaṭṭābiyyas

They are named after the founder Abu'l Khaṭṭāb Muḥammad-bin-Abū Żaynab al-Asadī al-Ajza', who was accused of having denied all religious observances and declaring everything as lawful. He was executed in Kūfa in 755 AD. His close associate Mufazzal-bin-'Omar al-Jū'fī, who was said to be teacher of Imām Ismā'īl of Ismā'īlīs and also accused of having led him astray from several Traditions of Imām Ja'far aṣ-Ṣādiq.[116] Khaṭṭābiyyas are said to be condemned as heretics but in someone of the Ismā'īlīs has been maintained as its founder. No doubt, after the death of Abu'l Khaṭṭāb most of his followers have shifted their allegiance to Imām Ismā'īl.[117] Fatimid Caliph al-Mui'żż li-dīn-Illāh was successful in bringing Khaṭṭābiyyas to his sect. Khaṭṭābiyyas has the following branches –

Bāżighiyyas: Its founder Bāżigh-bin-Mūsā was a weaver, who claimed the man reached perfection never dies and his followers are superior to the angels.

Mufażżaliyyas: Its founder Mufażżal aṣ-Ṣayrafī believed in the lordship of Imām Ja'far aṣ-Ṣādiq but repudiated the apostleship of Abu'l Khaṭṭāb.

Ghurābiyyas: They believed that God had sent the angel Gabriel with divine revelation for 'Ali-Ibn-Abū Ṭālib but he by mistake given to Muḥammad who was matured person of forty and Imām 'Ali was only of eleven years.[118]

'Omayriyyas or *'Ijliyyas*: Its founder 'Omayr-bin-Bayān al-'Ijlī was straw dealer of Kūfa.

Mu'ammariyyas: Its founder Mu'ammar-bin-Khaytham was corn dealer who claimed to be prophet in succession to Abu'l Khaṭṭāb.

Muslimiyyas

A Persian proverb reads: *pīrān namī parānd, murīdan mī prānand*: the saint never (miraculously) fly, the devotees fly him! The nomenclature of *Muslimiyyas* is because of being believers in the divinity of Abū Muslim Khurāsānī. Surely, he was an energetic and capable leader, who was instrumental in the downfall of the Umayyite Caliphate and in placing the 'Abbāsites in throne. Owing to his military victories and political prowess, 'Abbāsites Caliph al-Manṣūr became leery of a vassal with so much power and popularity. He was treacherously put to death by the Caliph in February 755. Abū Muslim had richly equipped bold and courageous personality. He led puritanical and ascetic Shi'i way of life. He was faithful follower of the holy progeny of the Prophet Muḥammad.

Many wrong assumptions are current which cannot be believed. They are just tales. As for Abū Muslim, it may be said about him that the official machinery of both the Umayyites and 'Abbāsites dynastics might have engaged in defaming and slandering him. What is truth is known only to God. Abū Muslim, who never claimed to be divine in his life-time, after the death his followers started to make him to be divine. A number of groups emerged with their respective assertions. To name of them as under:

Riżāmiyya: It was named after their founder Riżām-bin-Riżm considered that Abu Muslim had inherited the Imamate from 'Abdu'llāh as-Saffāḥ, the first 'Abbāsite Caliph. They believe in the divinity of Abū Muslim and assert that he was greater in rank than Gabriel. He had not died but rather he was in concealment. Abū Muslim would return to fill the earth with justice.

Barkūkiyyas or *Khurramiyya* or *Khurramdīniyya*: This group is known by different names but their faiths regarding Abū Muslim are the same. They were active in Herat and Marv. According to them Abū Muslim was not killed but a devil who took his shape.

Isḥāqiyya: They believed that Abū Muslim was in fact a Prophet sent by Zoroaster to revive his religion. They had been active in Khurāsān and Trasoxania and link their sources with Zoroastrianism and Mazdakism.

Mubayyazis or Nakhshabīs

Mubayyaz is an 'Arabic word meaning the one who adopts white clothing. As the members of this sect always wear white clothes, so they were identified with this name. Their founder was Hāshim-bin-Ḥakīm, famous by the name Ḥakīm Maqna' (d. 779 AD). *Maqna'* (veil) was the part of his mysterious personality, as he would put on golden veil on his face. The other name of this sect by which it became famous is *Nakhshabī*, because Ḥakīm Maqna' did skilful magic and black arts at famous city Nakhshab (Central Asia).

Ḥakīm Maqna' proclaimed to be Imām Mahdī, then to be a prophet. For his miracle he announced the rise of a moon. He made a vessel and told the people that it would rise from a well of Nakhshab city, go up to a height, stay for a time and then return to the same well. When he was exposed, the people dug out and extracted a big vessel from the well, the vessel was filled to the brim.

Later, Ḥakīm Maqna', proclaimed to be a God, he would justify his claims by explaining that God created Adam who transformed into his person, then He created Noah who also transformed into him and likewise getting transformed into many figures, he came to be transformed into Abū Muslim Khurāsānī to be finally transformed now into the form of Ḥakīm Maqna'. He had special adherence to Abū Muslim and would regard him above the prophet. Some people would say that he regarded Abū Muslim as God. He believed in the transmigration of soul and claimed that the soul of Abū Muslim has transmigrated into him.

There are many stories about the death of Ḥakīm Maqna'. In the history, however, only this much is given that on the order of al-Mahdī, the Abbāsite caliph, a huge army was sent in 777 AD to fight a battle against Ḥakīm Maqna' and he was killed. Majority of the historians maintain that before the domination of 'Arabs on his stronghold at the Sanām Castle, he had ended his life himself. Even after the death of Ḥakīm Maqna', the people of the Mubayyazis or Nakhshabīs of the central Asia, were present for a long time who, in later times, got submerged into other sects.

Roshaniyya Sect

The founder of this sect was Miyān Bāyażīd Anṣārī, who was born in 1525 in Jullundhar. In the earlier life, he was a soldier in the Moghal army. Afterward, he organized the Afghanis and set a movement against the Mog<u>h</u>als, which later took a form of sect, called Roshaniyya sect. Miyān Bāyażīd called himself the *Mahdīu'l-Maū'd*, Imām Mahdī whose return is promised. Miyān Bāyażīd was also famous by the appellation *Pīr Roshan* (lighted guide). This sect regarded loot and plunder to be a proper act, which found special favour with the *Qabā'līs*, the folk tribal clans. They whole-hearted came into the fold of the Roshaniyya sect and became active with full force. Their opponent was A<u>kh</u>und Duwiżah. He fought a war with Pīr Roshan. He called him as *Pīr Tārīk* (obscure guide). They conflicted many times with Mog<u>h</u>als.

Badā'ūnī, 'Abdu'l Qādir has written about the Roshaniyya sect that there was a clear impact of Hinduism on their faith and thinking.[119] Their ideology of *Waḥdatu'l-Wujūd,* the philosophy of the Muslim mystics regarding Unity of Essence was nothing short of the *Advaitwād* of the Hindu philosophy. In the Roshaniyya sect, the belief in the transmigration of soul was in vogue. They regarded heavens not only as a prophet but like a God. They did pray but facing the Ka'ba was not obligatory for them. They would not regard water to be indispensable for bath. Eventually, Pīr Roshan was killed, but his followers remained settled in the tribal areas, who, in course of time got merged into the Sunnis.

Mahdī'n who left Islam

They are of the third category of the Mahdī'n cited above. They have been repudiated and anathematized by Muslim community. By now they are well established with their separate identity, religious faiths and obligations.

The Bahāī's

The *Bahāī's* have originated from I<u>th</u>nā-'Asharī or Imāmiyya sect's <u>Sh</u>ay<u>kh</u>ī school of thought. We have already discussed the <u>Sh</u>ay<u>kh</u>i school of thought elsewhere. I<u>th</u>nā-'A<u>sh</u>arīs have a religious rank of *Nā'ib* (Deputy), *Wakīl* (Advocate), *Safīr* (Ambassador), *Bāb* (Gate) etc. There had been four representatives, who claimed to make direct contact with the hidden Imām Mahdī Ā<u>kh</u>iru'ż-Żamān, receive instruction from him and convey it to the believers. The appointment of the *Bābs* has ended under the orders of Imām Mahdī after the fourth incumbent 'Ali-bin-Muḥammad Sāmarrī (937-40 AD).[120]

The founder of *Bahāī'* religion, Mirża 'Ali Muḥammad (d. 1055 AD) of <u>Sh</u>īraż, was a follower of I<u>th</u>nā-'A<u>sh</u>arī sect's <u>Sh</u>ay<u>kh</u>ī school of thought and later became its leader. He was also most revered Persian poet of his time. He borrowed heavily from the teaching of other religions in formulating his own doctrine. It was 23rd May, 1844 when Mirża 'Ali Muḥammad in an inspired fervour wrote and simultaneously intoned a commentary, the *Qayyumu'l-Asmā'* on the chapter of Joseph from the Qur'an and proclaimed to be *Bāb,* the spokesman of the hidden Imām Mahdī. In the same year, he was successful in making 18 disciples, who along with him added up to the sacred *Bābī* number 19, called *Huruf u'l-Ḥayy'* (living letters). Later he abandoned the title *Bāb,* but to be Imām himself, the *Qā'im* (constant), the *Nuqtah* (point) and finally the divine manifestation, claimed to be the prophet. Bābīs, later Ażalīs, call him *Nuqta-i-Ūlā* (primal point), *Hazrat-i-Ālā* (supreme presence), *Jamāl-i-Mubārak* (blessed perfection) and finally *Ḥaqq-i-Ta'lā* (Truth Almighty). Among his followers was the famous Persian poetess Qurr'atul 'Ain Ṭāhira. Mirża 'Ali Muḥammad was declared *Murtad* (apostate) and executed in 1850, poetess Qurr'atul 'Ain Ṭāhira and his other followers too were put to death. In the year 1848 AD, two years prior to the execution of Mirża 'Ali Muḥammad, the Bābīs had assembled at the convention and declared a final break with Islam.

In the Bahāī' religious hierarchy the next name is Mirża Ḥuseyn 'Ali Nūrī known as *Bahāu'llāh* (Glory of God), the follower of the Bāb, who after some years of his execution, took the leadership of the community and in the year 1867 AD (or 1863 AD), publically proclaimed himself *Him Whom God Shall Manifest*, a Divine spirit foretold by the Bāb. The Bahāī's believe Bahāu'llāh to be the latest of the series of the past and the future divine manifestations that include Jesus Christ, Muḥammad, Zoroast and the Buddha. Bahāī's believe that Mirża Ḥuseyn 'Ali Nūrī known, the Bāb and Mirża Ḥuseyn 'Ali Nūrī Bahāu'llāh both are the ministrations of God, who in his essence is unknowable. The writings of Bahāu'llāh are inspired and constitute the revelation of God. His literary legacy of more than hundred works includes *al-Kitāb al-Aqdas* (The Most Holy Book), *Kitāb-i-Īqān* (The Book of Certitude) etc.

The third important figure in the Bahāī's religious hierarchy is *'Abdu'l-Bahā* (Servant of Glory) (d. 1921 AD), the eldest son of Bahāu'llāh, who is said to be infallible interpreter of his teachings. The writings and spoken words form the basis of the Bahāī's religion and literature.

The Bahāī's religious obligation include to pray daily, to fast 19 days a year, to abstain from narcotics, alcohol or any substance that affect the mind etc. Their principal teachings are the unity of religions and unity of mankind. There also exist Bahāī' faith appointive institutions, such as the Hands of the Cause of God and the continental counsellors. They work under an elected supreme governing body known as the Universal House of Justice and its judicial is the commonwealth of all Bahāī's. Its institutions are spread all-over the world which are engaged with heart and soul in spreading their specific faith and ideology. The seat of their Universal Houses of Justice is at Haifa, which is located in Israel.

The Aḥmadīyahs or *Qādiānīs*

They called *Aḥmadīyah* for being named after its founder Mirża Ghulām Aḥmad (d. 1908 AD) and *Qādiānīs* for being the name of the birthplace of the founder and the foundation place as *Qādiān*, a town in the province of Indian Punjab, which is now a place of pilgrimage for the Aḥmadīyahs. After the partition of India in 1947, a group evolved a separate organization and moved their headquarters from Qādiān to Rabwah in Pakistan.

Mirża Ghulām Aḥmad Qādiānī (d. 26th May, 1908) claimed to hear voices and declared in 1889 that he had a revelation from God to receive the *Bai'at* (oath of religious allegiance). He was successful in attracting a small group of devoted disciples, which steadily increased, despite strong opposition from the Muslim community, he proclaimed not only to be Imām Mahdī but also to be the *Burūz* (reappearance) of the Islamic Prophet Muḥammad, the Jesus Christ of the Christians and the incarnation of Krishṇa of Hindus. He did not announce, however, any new revelation or a new law. After his death, his followers disputed whether he really claimed to be a prophet and if so what he meant by his prophethood. Nonetheless, his followers formed a community of believers and after the death of the founder, elected the Maulvī Nūru'd-Dīn (d. 1914 AD) as *Khalīfah* (Caliph) to lead them.

In 1914 AD, a schism over succession occurred among the Aḥmadīyahs after the death of Maulvī Nūru'd-Dīn. A group of old Aḥmadīyahs accepted Mirża Ghulām Aḥmad Qādiānī as their *Nabī* (prophet) and his son Mirża Bashīru'd-Dīn Maḥmūd Aḥmad as the second Caliph. But the new society of Aḥmadīyahs living in Lahore (Pakistan) refused to accept Mirża Ghulām Aḥmad as a prophet and regarded him only a *Mujaddid* (revivalist). The concept of the *Mujaddid* has been well known in Sunni sect.[121] These claimants too have been making claims of special rights like those who would lay claims to be Imām Mahdī, out of whom Shaykh Aḥmad *Mujaddid-i-Alfsanī* (d. 1624 AD) of Sarhind (India) has a special significance, who had propounded the principle of *Qayūmiyyat,* like that of the Mahdī'n. The Aḥmadīyahs in India and Lahore in Pakistan have their religious centres separate from the Muslims. They are rather better organized community in comparison to Muslims, in general, on economic and social levels.

Aḥmadīyahs claim to be the representative of the original Islam, but their beliefs and concepts are quite different from other Islamic sects. At the level of the basic Islamic principle, there is wider difference in their faith and concept of prophethood. All the sects of Islam are unanimous in the belief that the holy Prophet Muḥammad was *Khātimu'n-Nabīyyīn* (the last in the chain of prophets) after whom no other prophet would come. But the Aḥmadīyahs argue that in this verse the word *Khātim* (last) is correctly pronounced as *Khātam*, which means ring or golden seal. So the holy Prophet Muḥammad is like a ring or a golden seal among the prophets and not the last prophet. On the basis of this logic they regard Mirża Ghulām Aḥmad as their prophet. Likewise they also believe in the embodiment of God, who adopted the form sometimes of Jesus Christ, sometimes of Krishṇa and sometimes of Muḥammad. This is radically different a faith or principle from Islam. This is why the Aḥmadīyahs are regarded to be the sect beyond the pale of Islam, otherwise, treating Mirża Ghulām Aḥmad as a revivalist finds no objection with some Islamic sects. Aḥmadīyahs of Lahore are a bit nearer to Sunni sects, their relations are found among them.

There are some other beliefs of the Aḥmadīyahs which are contrary to the common beliefs of other Muslims. Having the patronage of the then colonial British rulers, who were extending full support to Aḥmadīyahs because they had become the dividing force among the Sunni Muslims, whose *Ulama* had waged *Jihād* against Britishers and Christians. Mirża Ghulām Aḥmad adopted the doctrines of modernist Muslims, like Sir Saiyed Aḥmad Khān (d. 1887 AD), who has been a great luminary in the sphere of the history of Indian Muslims and leader of the most progressive section of the Indian society. With a view to counter the endeavour of Sunni Muslims *Ulama*, Mirża Ghulām Aḥmad abrogated the *Jihad by the sword* and replaced it with the *Jihād* by pen. He also declared that Jesus Christ had unnatural death and was not assumed into Heaven, contrary to the belief of all the sects of Islam. They further added that Jesus Christ made an excuse of death, rose from his grave and escaped to India where, having attained the age of 120 years, died.

On the basis of the above-mentioned doctrines of Aḥmadīyahs, the restrictions were imposed on them in 1974 AD and again in 1984 AD by the Government of Pakistan, which declared that Aḥmadīyahs were not Muslims and prohibited them from engaging in various Islamic activities.

In the secular India the Aḥmadīyahs are as free and enjoy equity as any other religious community of the country.

Out of the sects enumerated above, there is hardly any confusion about the first category of the Mahdī'n cited above to be in Islamic pale, considering their religious beliefs in general, whose theological principles are based either on Shi'is or the Sunni community. Though the second category of the Mahdi'n cited above claims to be Muslim, their extremism, and astray elements of religion in the name of spiritual guidance and sanctity, has resulted to be repudiated and anathematized and put them outside the pale of Islam. The third category of the Mahdī'n cited above did not claim to be in Islamic pale, except a group of Qādiānīs, who regards Mirża Ghulām Aḥmad only as revivalist, but their other faith did not match with Islam. The followers of the third category of the Mahdī'n themselves have already declared a final break with Islam and are known with their identity and faith. I have included their descriptions within the Islamic sects simply because they started as Islamic sects but ended as non-Islamic. Moreover, the student of Islamic sects should be aware of realities about them in the historic perspective.

Mahdīyah of Sudan

The Mahdīyahs of Sudan are different from the Mahdī'n communities discussed so far. They were seen as restorers of the political power and religious purity of Islam. The title of al-Mahdī has tended to be claimed by the social revolution in the Islamic society. They tended to receive new emphasis in every time of crisis. Thus after the battle of Navas de Tolosa in 1212 AD, when most of Spain was lost for Muslims, the Spanish Muslims circulated the foretelling traditions of Prophet Muḥammad that Spain will be again conquered by al-Mahdī. During the Napoleonic invasion of Egypt, a person had appeared claiming to be al-Mahdī and astounded the people briefly in Lower Egypt. Muḥammad-bin-Tumart on the basis of similar claims founded Almohad movement in Morocco in the 12th century. Mahdīyah of Sudan may also be placed in the same category, of course, with certain peculiarities.

The Mahdīyah of Sudan, Muḥammad Aḥmad son of as-Sayyid 'Abdu'llah (d. 1885 AD) was the creator of a vast Islamic state extending from the Red Sea to Central Africa and founder of a movement that remained influential in Sudan a century later. As a youth he moved from orthodox religious study to a mystical interpretation of Islam. He joined the Sammaniyah order and grew to manhood in a wholly Sudanese religious setting, purposely separating himself from the official ruling class. He proclaimed his divine mission as al-Mahdī with the object to purify Islam and the official ruling class and the governments that defiled it. He captured Khartoum and established a theocratic state in the Sudan, with its capital at Omdurman. All the efforts of the ruling classes and the learned men of Khartoum, who mocked al-Mahdi's divine claim, failed miserably.

The Mahdīyah of Sudan referred to himself as the *successor to the apostle of God*, but only in the sense of continuing his work. He confined himself to the enunciation of the principles of Sunni Islam and on the pattern of its *Khilāfatu'r-Rāshidah*, which is believed to be the legitimate body to rule the Islamic nation. He appointed four Caliphs to be the living successors of the four earliest Caliphs mentioned above. Three of these appointees were Sudanese, including his most trusted counsellor and chief of staff, 'Abd Allad son of Muhammad; The fourth appointee was Muḥammad al-Mahdī son of as-Sanusi, head of Sausiyah order in the western desert, who ignored the appointment. The Mahdīyah of Sudan was, no doubt, great visionary and innovative. He has been the principal motivating force behind the revival of Sudanese Muslims.

Some Indian Converts

While studying Indian Muslim communities, it should be borne in mind that there are three forms of the Muslim existence in Indian sub-continent – by foreign invasions, by exile and by conversion. All the three of these forms have got so mixed up that their separate recognition is not easy. The Indian communities which adopted Islam, had a large number among them who were not converted of their own will, but having been defeated in the battle, they had joined the Muslim army and because of this they were turned out from their religious fraternity. So they being disgusted with the social disregard, adopted Islam. Once Muslim rule was established in India, many Muslims from elsewhere migrated to India. Among them were artists, poets, intellectuals, mystics, priests and the common folk etc.

The foreign invasion of Muslims was not on a huge scale, it was rather gradual and slow in pace. But the entire clans of the Muslim community living across the north-eastern region entered Indian territory. That is why the Pathān community is at present in clear majority compared to the Saiyed and Shaykh communities in India. Even after having come to India they kept on moving from place to place. About the influx of the Saiyeds, it is said that first they settled in Sindh and Punjab. Then they settled at Delhi, Muzaffarnagar, Bijnore, Meerut, Lucknow,

Faizabad, Jaunpur, Allahabad, Patna and in the south at Hyderabad, Aurangabad, Ahmedabad, and Chennai etc., and thus were widely spread. In some places the S͟hayk͟hs settled along with them. Muḥammad Tughlaq shifted his capital from Delhi to Daulatabad so many of them shifted over there.

There are various reasons behind moving from one place to another; religious conversion is also an important reason. The Turkian gypsies of Rampur claim that originally they belong to Multan (Pakistan). After conversion, they were disgusted with social torture which forced them to leave their native land. Similarly, the Aryno of Montgamari (Pakistan) claim that they were *Suryavanshi* Rajput, who were formerly settled in the adjoining areas of Delhi.

At time whole area and the communities living there had become Muslims, under the influence of the Muslim saints and mystics. In this context, the Kashmirī Pandits are specially mentioned, who almost all, had taken to Islam. It is said that there was a time when only eleven families of Hindus had been left there, whose descendants are the present Kashmirī Hindus. Kashmirī Muslims are the staunch followers of Islam but they write the name of their *Gotr* (clan) with their names even today. The same is true also with the Bengalis that despite being staunch Muslims, they write their names with their original *Gotr*. So are the Maimans who write their *Gotr* with their name. Conversion has different and various forms. Some have adopted Islam completely while a few have not given up some practices of their old religion even after their conversion, instead they made those practices the part of their Islamic faith, so they are usually satirized by the bigoted Muslims.

Indian Muslim community mainly consists of two Islamic sects, Sunnis and Shi'is, others are negligible. In the Shi'is, *Ithnā-'As͟harī* (the believers in 12 Imāms) and Ismā'īlīs are the main. In the Sunni sect, all the subsets which have been described in this book, are present in one or other form. The theological principles of the Shi'a and Sunni sects in India are the same as they are throughout the world. However, some sects of the Indian Muslims owing to their conversion, still retain some specific traits which have set them apart from the mainstream Shi' as and Sunni Muslims of the world and they have made these traits their own identity.

A comprehensive knowledge about the various Muslim sects in such a huge country like India, is not available. Only a few reference books are there, some of which had been published over a hundred years earlier. In the meantime revolutionary changes have taken place. The Indian nation got divided into five sovereign countries – Bharat, Pakistan,

Bangladesh, Sri Lanka and Myanmar. Religious conversion has also been made in large scale. In the phase of religious passion, material temptation and religious propagation, it would be difficult to say how many people would have saved their family religious values, rites and sacraments. In the meantime, no official or individual survey has been properly conducted to help us get a knowledge of the present situation seen on the basis of the past information. So whatever information is available in the surveys made in the past, would make the basis of the following findings about the Muslim sects in India.

In order to understand the composition of Islamic converts of the Indian sub-continent, we should bear in mind that the bi-religious-rites group of the coverts, despite holding fast to his old religion, has made the beliefs and faiths of other religions the part of his own religion, and makes it his identity among their religious fraternity. This group is found in both the Hindu and Muslim communities, the following are prominent among themselves:

Ḥusainī Brahman

Many views are current about Ḥusainī Brahmans, which are even mutually contradictory. Some scholars have enlisted them as Muslims who still maintain a few Hindu rituals, as they wear *Janev* (sacred thread), apply *Tilak* (dot on forehead), but accept charity only from the Muslims not from the Hindus. They recite the episode of the sacrifices of Imām Ḥusain made at Karbala, whence they are called Ḥusainī Brahman. But other scholars maintain that basically they are Bhat Brahman, belong to their respective *Gotr* (clans) such as Gappe, Bhakar, Lande, Gare, Dargopal, Rati, Chhatchhust, Rabat, Bharadwaji, Dangmar and many more.[122] Because of being called Bhatt, they narrate Ḥusainī heroism and martyrdom.[123]

Ḥusainī Brahman do marry in their religious fraternity but don't do so in the four *Gotras* of their own. They don't marry in *Bhat Gotr*, but accept water from their hands. They wear *Janev* by the hands of a Brahman and follow them in the matters of deciding auspicious hours and omen. In religious beliefs and conduct they are different in many ways from other Brahmans. They are indifferent to Hindu rites, neither they study Hindu religion in prescribed schools, nor they go to temples for idol-worship. Mohyaloli caste of Hindus is also called Ḥusainī Brahman. On the tenth day of Muḥarram, they mourn his martyrdom. famous Urdu poet Jamnadass *Akhtar* told the author that he belongs to Ḥusainī Brahman family and at least in his family food is not taken on the tenth day of Muḥarram. In the *Imambara* (Sanctuary) of Zeydibal, Srinagar (Kashmir) the holy hair of Imām Ḥusain is present, which was brought over from Kabul (Afghanistan) by a Ḥusainī Brahman some 100 years ago.

Regarding the attachment of the Ḥusainī Brahmans with Imām Ḥusain, it is generally said that their ancestors were martyred for the cause of truth and justice, along with Imām Ḥusain, his family, companions, kith and kin at Karbala on 10th Muharram 61 AH or 10th October, 681. After the cruel butchery of Karbala the family of the Ḥusainī Brahman was driven out of 'Arab to Iran. I could not trace any historical reference to it but the possibility of this claim cannot be rejected, because Hindus lived in 'Arab before the advent of Islam. Once their delegation met the Prophet of Islam, the holy Prophet showing affection to them had used Sanskrit word *Kushal* (safety) in wishing for their well-being.[124]

To lay one's life in defence of truth and justice has been the nature and sacrament of Indians, therefore, if some Hindus living in 'Arab had sacrificed their life in defence of truth and justice, there is nothing improbable about that. But Ḥusainī Brahman's own Tradition is that the troop of Umayyite king Yazid I (d. 683 AD), while on their return, after cutting off Imām Ḥusain's head, stopped in Rahab, their ancestor's home at Bathowal in the Sialkot district (now Pakistan) and placed the head in his house. In the morning, finding the head to be that of the Prophet's grandson, he kept it, and gave the soldiers his own son's head instead, but they discovered that it was not the same as the one they had brought. So Rahab cutt-off all his seven sons' heads in succession and gave them to the soldiers. Since then Ḥusainī Brahmans beg from Muslims.[125]

The word *Rahab* has been used in the above event which may be the 'Arabic word *Rahib*. It is commonly used for the Christian monastic. The mention of obtaining the head of Imām Ḥusain from the Yazidi army by Rahib against the temptation of money, is found in the episodes of Karbala. But there is no mention of the place Bathowal in the Sialkot district. It is just possible that the story orally narrated for over thousand years, might have changed in long course of time.

In the Saraiki language, we find poetical compositions based on the event of Karbala, which is said to be of Hindu-Shāhī period (950-1000 AD). In this poetical compositions the sacrifice of the Ḥusainī Brahman is described as follows –

> "Raj Siddhojha Dutt lived in 'Arabia. From among his progeny, Raiputra Birsar and Mirad too lived in 'Arabia. The

> Umayyites persecuted the justice-loving Imām. The Dutts supported the Imām and killed his enemies and terrorized them. Imām became triumphant and the world felt blessed and applauded the Imām."[126]

The Priests of the goddess

There are many pilgrimage places where many temples of special significance are found in which are placed the idols of Hindu gods and goddesses. Thousands of devotees visit these idols on special occasions and throughout the year. Among these, Badrinath is the chief temple of the four main centres of pilgrimage. This is situated in the North at a higher point of Himalaya. In this chief temple Nar-Narayan (Human-Divine) duality is worshipped. A lamp remains alit without break which symbolizes the light of knowledge. There are idols of Bhaironath and Kuber. Some of the rites of the Badrinath temple are performed by a Muslim priest, who is known by his Muslim name. May the ancestors of the priest were Brahmans to begin with. They became Muslim, as a result of conversion but did not give up their family tradition of performing the rites, and in due course of time they were given recognition by the inter-faith communities.

Likewise, the priest of a Hindu temple near Suratgarh (Rajasthan) is a Muslim. He accepts gifts from the devotees. This has been going on for many generations onward. This had raised controversy also but the state legislative gave its judgment in favour of the Muslim priest.[127] There are many other examples of this nature but are not being described to avoid unnecessary extension of time and space.

Worshipper of god and goddess

There are several tribes in India who got converted to Islam yet kept on worshipping their beloved gods and goddesses as well. In the following lines some of such tribes are being mentioned:

Many families of the Deshmuk and Deshpandey tribes of Muldana, were converted Muslims, yet they kept on worshipping their beloved gods. They secretly invite Hindu priest and get the rites of worship performed.[128]

The butchers of Ahmadnagar and Bijapur invite *Qāzī* at the marriage ceremony for *Nikāh* rituals and also worship idols of gods and goddesses and keep the idols in their home.[129]

In the neighbourhood of Indore some Muslims Patels and Mirdha, even after their conversion, keep Hindu names and dress also like Hindus. They also believe in goddess Bhavani and other gods.[130]

In Karnal there is a population of the cultivator Muslims, who recite the *Kalamahu'sh-Shahadah* to profess the Muslim creed and also get their children circumcised, yet worship the gods and goddesses as their forefathers used to worship before conversion.[131]

There are little differences between the Hindus and Muslims of the backward groups of Purnea. In every house there is a place for the goddess Kali, where she is worshipped. Likewise in Muslim houses, there is place for prayer called *Khudai Ghar* (Divine House). In their prayers they call both God and Kali together. Even in the house of the Muslims, the marriage is solemnized in the *Deval* (shrine) of the goddess Bhagvati. Goats, hens, pigeons, fruits and vegetables are offered to Hindu gods and goddesses. Their favourite god is Maharaj, whose gateman's name was Hādī, on whose worshipping place a bamboo would be pinched, on which is hung old sop, arrow, bow, the old net of fishing and the fishing hook. Likewise, in Kishanganj, there is subtribe of Bengali Muslims, whose custom it is to build a temple for the Nagdebi Bishhori. They say that their ancestors had both the house of god and the house of Nagdebi Bishhori.[132]

The people of Khadra community wear female dresses, call themselves Muslim *faqīrs* but worship Bhakrasar or Davel goddesses. The place where they keep idols is called Mastareai by them. They offer the preparation of flour, mashed into clarified butter and sugar, to their goddesses.[133]

About Kamalias Muslim tribe living at 40 miles north of Ahmedabad within the city of Chandanwal-Pattam, in a village Sankhanpur there is a temple without any idol in it, however, there is *black-stall*, which is famous by name of *Bahuchara,* one of the many names of goddess Bhavani. Its worshipper Muslims are classed into two groups – Pawayya (eunuch), and Kamaliyya. Kamaliyyas use to be soldiers and keep the mark of Bahuchara *trishul* (tri-point spear) with them. Both of these Muslim tribes offer sacrifice of buffalo to the Bahuchara temple and stamp their foreheads with its blood. Despite being Muslims, they would not get their children circumcised. They bury their corpses like Muslims, but burn their chests.[134]

The names of the Merh and Manihar Muslims are like those of Hindus but they add *Khan* at the end of their names. In this community only a few of them know the *Kalamahu'sh-Shahadah.* They have their own places of worship in which there is a stone called – Panchpira (five spiritual guides) which is offered to five saints. Bhayya is a kind of platform on which a stone is placed to prevent the lamp from going off. They believe that this is a protector of the holy spirits. The platform is also called *Hiradev*. On this platform sacrifice is offered to *Mahadevi*. In the religious thought of the Merh, warriors and heroes have a special significance. Out of whom the commander Masu'd Ghāżī Miyan of Bahraich has an important place. In every village of the Merh community the flag of the Ghāżī Miyān is worshipped on the eve of *Shabbara't*. They do not marry in their *Gotr* (clan). In the marriage of their daughters, they take money from the bridegroom's family. Their population is mostly found in Alwar and Bharatpur in Rajasthan.[135]

The people of the Mina community worship specially Bhairov in the form of Shiva, and Hanuman. A kind of spear (wide turned up knife) which they call *Kover* is used to administer oath. Except the pork and beef to be unlawful, they take all kinds of meats. In the marriage of their daughters they take money in return. Among them there is a custom known as *Gharicha* in which a widow is married to man lower in caste than her. This community is also found in Alwar and Bharatpur in Rajasthan.[136]

Torat is not the name of any tribe but the name of their custom. They believe in the goddess *Shitla* (small pox). At the time of marriage they dress up the bridge in a round shape called the *Torat*, in its centre they place a parrot made of wood and hang a plough on the door-step of the house. They are found 50 miles north of Rallaur (M.P., India).[137]

Baluchis are populated apart from India, in Pakistan and Afghanistan. There are many opinions about their genesis. They have several clans. All of them are Muslims. They maintain religions values. But in the Baluchis of the Dera Ghāżī Khan (Pakistan), it is not obligatory to follow the Islamic laws in the marriage of a widow. They call it *Tan Bakhshī* (bestowed body). In this custom the widow has just to announce that she had accepted a man as her husband. In the inheritance of property all children share equally but the daughters and the grand-daughters are deprived of inheritance. Their Mazārī and Darishak clans, allow the eldest son to get more than other sons.[138]

The Sindhi community has much faith in the living or dead mystics and Saiyeds. There are two bases of Sindhi beliefs – firstly, the River, which symbolizes the male-power and chivalry and secondly, the Nature, which symbolizes female power and creativity. The Sindhis have great faith in Shaykh Ṭabrī or Shāh Ṭahir. According to them, God used to reveal to these mystics in the form of a camel. They visit the shrines of these mystics on special occasions. Women who have been betrothed or the married may also visit their shrines. Hindus call them *Adir-o-Lal*, who are the incarnations of the River God, and in time of distress they come to protect their devotees in the form of soldiers. For having a special attachment to the Sindhu River, they are also called *Nadi Panthi* (river sect). Sindhis of Lohana, pray to the River God: 'O master of the waves, listen to our prayer!' In Sakhkhar, the worship of the River has assumed the form of the *Khizr* worship. According to the Qur'anic story a youth had accompanied the Prophet Moses (*Qur'an: 18 /60-82*), who is believed to be *Khizr* by the Muslims and he lives near the river and guides the people. Similarly, in Thatha the Shah Jhandu is worshipped as the *life-protector sailor*. Some also worship the crocodiles. In one way they appear to be a corrupt form of Sufis in which mystics are worshipped. Nature worship is closely related with female-worship. The Thatha and Mirpur's Sindhis worship the goddess Shrub, which is taken to mean that the successor of the clan of the *tree-mystic* used to be always a woman. A similar faith is found in the neighbouring areas, where near the Rixal river is found the shrine of *Mai Pīr*. This shrine is made of low mud wall of a 100 yard circular shape in the middle surrounding the goddess Shrub. No male person is allowed to enter into it. They believe that Mai Pir was maiden. At present it is in the form of a small cottage, from whose roof hangs the neck-belts of the animals.

Along the banks of the Sindhu and Jhellum rivers are the '*Advans* populated. '*Advans* is an 'Arabic word, meaning the helpers. They claim to be descendants of 'Ali-Ibn-Abū Ṭālib. They came to India as soldiers and settled here. Their religious values are all Islamic but they don't marry in their own clan. From their ancestor Qutub Shah's three wives, were born Khokhar and Char Muhin. Many sub-clans were produced by Char Muhin in which Gujjar Khanjar are also included. Among the Gujjars those belonging to Hazara families are Shi'is. They are hated by Afghani Sunnis. Gujjar ladies mourn the death of their domestic animals just as they mourn the death of their family-members. There are many views about the genesis of the Jat clan. Muslim Jats also don't marry in their clans. Same tradition is found in Muslim Aroras.[139]

Saddis are the clan of the African slaves, who had been brought from Somalia. They were singers and dancers. They regard their musical instruments holy, if touched by an unholy person, they fear that gods would punish them. Likewise the Mol-Salam were the Rajputs, before their conversion. They maintain Islamic rituals but also worship gods and goddesses.[140]

The Panch-Mahal-Wasi of Godhra (Guajrat) have faith in Ghanchi Manur, though they know not much about him. They hate Muslims and like Hindus. Dhuniyas, who call themselves Mansūrī, are found in Barar, Thana, Ahmadnagar etc. The way they slaughter a cock is very ridiculous. Placing the knife on the throat of the cock, they say:

> "Father and son, Shaykh Farīdu'llāh! slaughter the cock. The order of God is that cock be slaughtered by my hand."

They also slaughter the egg, while breaking its shell, they say:

> "While dome under which there is nothing but moisture, I know not if there is male or female in it, I slaughter you in the name of God".[141]

Numerous customs and practices based on superstitions are not being described for it would take many pages.

Devotees of Swami Naraiṇ

Rathors call themselves Sunni Muslims but they don't say *Namāż* nor recite Qur'an. They don't follow other principles of Islam. They establish relation with Hindus without entering into marriage. They keep the portrait of Swami Naraiṇ in their houses and worship it.[142]

Near Ahmedabad there is a place called Pīrānā. The inhabitants of this place are called Shaykh Das. There is a shrine of Pīr Bālā Muḥammad Shāh, whose devotees they are. They call themselves Muslims but don't get their sons circumcised. They stamp Tilak on their foreheads like Hindus. They don't take food together with Muslims. In marriage, they observe the customs of both Hindus and Muslims – for this they invite both a Brahman and a *faqir*. They bury the dead like the Muslims. They keep the image of Swami Naraiṇ in their houses and worship it.[143]

Devotees of tenth incarnation of Shiva

There are some Muslim communities which regard their religious' *Maha Guru* (high priest) to the tenth incarnation of Shiva. Some of them are described below:

There is a Pīrżada sect in Sunni community, whose centre is Burhanpur, which was founded some 200 years ago by some Pīr Muḥammad Shāh Dullah, whom the people of this sect regard as the 10th incarnation of Vishṇu. They believe that he was free from all sins and blemishes. They believe in all the incarnations of Vishṇu. But they don't believe in other gods and goddesses of Hindus. Among his devotees are also the Hindu Kunbi and Gujjar, who are at liberty to observe the practices of their own castes and creed. Every year a huge fair is held around the shrine of S͟hāh Dullah. They have a religious book of their faith in which the religious matters of both Hindus and Muslims have been put together. These people call themselves to be bigoted Muslims.

Among the believers of the 10th incarnation of Shivas are a group of Niżārī Ismā'īlīs sect, who mainly live in Punjab (Pakistan). They regard Imām 'Ali as the 10th incarnation of Vishṇu. They assert that God had told Gabriel to give the Qur'an to 'Ali-Ibn-Abū Ṭālib and by mistake he gave it to Muḥammad. They put in its place the *Kalāmī Pīr.* Their religious books are known as the *Ginans*; and of these *Das Avtar*, written by Pīr Sadrud-Dīn is by far the most important, which consist of ten chapters, each describing one of the incarnation of Vishṇu, of which 'Ali is last. The whole book but particularly the last chapter is accepted as scripture, and is read in the homes, at festivals, at meetings in *jama't-khana* and at death-bed.[144]

All the various Muslim communities described above, all sects, tribes, *gotras* etc, call themselves Muslims except the Husaini Brahmans who call themselves Hindus and other too regard them as Hindus. Most of their customs are like Muslims. They can reasonably be called as ones who manage to be respected by both Hindus and Muslims. Most of the Muslim sects accept the fundamentals of Islam.

If the conduct and behaviour are put to test on the touch stone of the perfect conformity and expression of Islamic principles, then the so, called religious leaders and clergies are found to be the most affected. This is a different matter if they have one standard for themselves and another standard for others. It is not my duty to obtain any edict from them nor it is my rank to pass judgment on any issue. I have described them simply on the ground that they claim themselves to be Muslim, and the society too accepts them as Muslims. To go beyond that is not within the purview of my work.

The Chinese Muslims

Islam is the belief of 10 of China's 56 nationalities, they are Uighur, Kaza͟kh, Kirgiz, Tajik, Uzbek and Tatar (in Xinjiang, the eastern Turkemanistan), besides the Hui, the Manchu, the Salar and the Dongxiang. Salars reside in Qinghai Gansud and the Dongxiang in the Xinjiang and Gansu. Manchu and Hui speak Mandarin and use Chinese characters. The Hui are the descendants of the Chinese who adopted Islam, when it penetrated China in the 7th century. They are intermingled with the Han, the non-Muslim majority group, throughout much of the country and are distinguished as Hui only in the area of their heaviest concentration, the Hui Autonomous Region of Ningsia. Other Hui communities are organized as *tzu-chih-chou* (autonomous prefectures) in Sinkiang and as *tzu-chih-hsien* (autonomous countries) in Tsinghai, Hopeh, Kweichow and Yunnan. Uighur and Hui constitute 40 and 50 per cent of Muslim population respectively. The Uighur are Turkics, speaking their own language mixed with Mongol dialect. Hui are the ethnic Chinese primarily north-western mandarin, practicing Muslims with many mosques. The Manchu call themselves to be the descendants of the Manchu warriors who invaded China in the 17th century and founded the Ch'ing dynasty (1644-1912 AD). During the last years of their rule Islam suffered great setback. As they had assimilated into Han Chinese culture, Manchus were influenced by the *Taiping* (Great Peace) rebellion, which was crushed by Gordon in 1864 AD. It was a religio-political movement started by Hung Hsiu-Ch'un, an ecstatic epileptic noble. It opposed magic, idols and belief in spirits.

There has been growing tendency for the practicing Muslims to move from their scattered settlements into the areas of major concentrations, possibly, as firm adherents of Islam, in order to facilitate intermarriage with other Muslims. Because there had been attempts to weaken the attachments to Islam by assimilating the Muslims, along with other minorities, under Ming Law which prescribed that all Mongols or Semus must marry Chinese, prohibiting marriage between themselves. The offender must receive 80 stokes, and both men and women be conscripted as slaves.

Ancient Chinese' religious and philosophical traditions which originated in 5th or 6th century BC, have survived in the form of the Taoism and the Confucianism. The two schools differ in the orientation: Taoism stressing mystical experience and individual's harmony with nature and Confucianism emphasizing the importance of rational process over inspiration and divination. The later has several common factors with Islam, such as the duty of the individual in society. During the Ming rule (1368-1644 AD) Muslims made remarkable contribution to Chinese culture. They were excellent astronomers, architects, physicians and writers. The astronomer *Tcha Ma-Lu-Ting* (Jamālu'd-Dīn Muḥammad) brought 'Arabic-Persian astronomy to China and invented ten-thousand-years *Wan-Nien-Li* calendar, which was officially adopted in 1281 AD. The city walls of Dadu and Yuan capital, which is now known as the city of Beijing, was planned and its foundations laid by Ikhtiyanu'd-Dīn. Muslim physicians introduced Unanī system, which became part of Traditional Chinese medicine.

Islam has influenced Chinese life in many ways. It has grown in importance and its principles are referred in their general behaviour such as rewards and punishments depended on man's virtue, for the *Heaven is always kind to the virtuous*. Religious sacrifices continued to play a great role in the lives of the people and the spirituality being pure expressions of reverence. That means to make a firm promise with the purity of heart to refrain from disobedience committed in the past and compensate for those sins. The religion has always been pious.

After the Communist Revolution in 1949 AD, Muslim came under tight control and various restrictions were imposed on them. Human rights were voilated and they were told that 'the right of national self-determination is not absolute, but must be subject to the basic interest of the proletarian revolution and to the struggle against the enemy.' Various tactics are adopted to undermine Muslim identity. It has resulted in continued struggle and protest marches demanding human rights. They were suppressed only after brutal reprisals by the Chinese army.

Central Asian Muslims

The Central Asia consists of five largest ethnic groups of the Uzbek, Kazakhs, Tajik, Turkmam, and Kyrgyz, in descending order of size. Together they constitute a majority in Central Asia, which was known to the ancient Greeks as Trasoxania and to the 'Arabs as *ma-wara-an-nahr* (that which lies beyond the river). It consists of the area between the rivers Amu Darya (the Oxus of the Greeks and the Jayhun of 'Arabs and Syr Darya (the Jaxartes of the Greek and Sayhun of the 'Arabs). Central Asia is Turkic in ethnicity and language, except the Persian Tajiks. They lend their names to the five republics, after separating from Soviet Union. The sixth largest ethnic group, the Turkic Kara-Kalpaks, who occupy territory in the Amu Darya delta plain, was created under the subordination of the republic of Uzbekistan, and has Russians, Ukrainians, German, Koreans and Jews, to form a multi-ethnic group. The major central Asian nationalities identify strongly with the Sunni Islam.

With the dissolution of Soviet Union in 1991 AD, Islamic religious affiliation has been growing for new regional connections with the neighbouring Islamic countries like Turkey, Iran and Saudi Arabia. Their renewed interest in Islam after decades of suppression of religion under the Soviet Governments has become a feature of the cultural life and the fervent young followers of the Imams and *Ishan* (Muslim religious leaders) has promised a change in the direction toward a much closer attachment to the Islamic heritage as well as life-style.

The Central Asia has been famous for the leading seats, the *Madrasas* (seminaries), at Bukhārā, Khiva, Samarkand and the Farghānā Valley. After a long period in decline they could see a revival only in the late 18th and early 19th centuries, that prepared entirely a new generation in the Central Asia. Owing to the models offered by sudden activism among modernizers called *Uṣūl-i-Jadīd* (new methods) instituted its own educational reform movement, which flocked thousands of *Madrasas* throughout the Central Asia. The leaders of *Jadīd* (modern), as they called themselves, included Munawwar Qari in Tashkent, Mahmud Khwāja Bahāu'd-Dīn in Samarkand, Sā'du'd-Dīn 'Aynī in Bukhārā and 'Āshūr 'Ali Ẓahirī in Kokand (Qoqan). It was strongly affected by the *Glasnost* (openness) and *Perestroika* (restructuring) introduced in 1986.

The Black Muslims

The Black Muslim is the popular name of the Islamic movement, which arose among blacks in United States, after World War II, whose members called themselves the Nation of Islam. It started as a movement of various qausi-religious black nationalist organizations. Prominent among these precursor groups was the Moorish Science Temple of Newark (New Jersey), founded in 1913 AD by Timothy Drew, who posited the Moorish, and thus Muslim, origins of all blacks and advocated a return to Islam as the only way of redemption from racial oppression. He acclaimed to be the Prophet, later known as Prophet Drew 'Ali. Universal Negro Improvement Association was founded in 1914 AD by Marcus Garvey, also espoused the principles adopted by the Black Muslims.

Wallace Fard Muhammad, also known as W.D. Fard or Wali Fard, was born in an orthodox Sunni family in Mecca, around 1877 AD, who migrated to the United States in 1930 AD. He clustered together in the black ghettos of the great northern industrial cities. He claimed to be an inspired Prophet, interpreted the doctrine of Resurrection in an unorthodox sense as the revival of oppressed (dead) people. His followers believed Fard to be an incarnation of God, who had come to liberate, the *Lost-Found Nation of Islam in the West*. His successor Elijah Muhammad developed the movement, which was called the Nation of Islam, which professed the moral and cultural superiority of black men and women, who were seen as destined by God to assume religious, cultural and political leadership of the Earth. The black men and women were enjoined to give up Christianity, which was regarded as the chief stratagem for their enslavement. During the 1960s, Malcolm X, also called al-Hajj Malik al-Shabazz, Elijah Muhammad's spokesman forcefully articulated the racial pride and Muslim principles made the black people religious-cultural hero. The publication of the book *The Black Muslims in America* by C. Eric Lincon in 1961 AD, standardized, though never official, the name in the public mind. Disagreements among the sects hierarchy led to formation of a rival group by Malcolm, which resulted into his assassination in 1965 AD.

Elijah Muhammad was succeeded by his son Warith Deen (or Wallace D.) Muhammad in the late 1970s AD. Under his leadership all the precepts of colour-consciousness and the racism, were repudiated and the organization was renamed as the American Muslim Mission. In May 1985 W.D. Muhammad announced dissolution of the American Muslim Mission, so that its members might become a part of the worldwide orthodox Muslim community. However, a splinter group, under leadership of Louis Farrakhan, existed in New York retaining both the name and founding principles.

The Black Muslims at the early stage of their movement had adopted some Islamic social practices, the group was in large part a black separatist and social protest movement. But currently characterized with their network of mosques and their attendant religious, educational and economic programmers continued to function.

Muslims of Europe

Muslims have been an integral part of the European continent and especially of the Britain and its way of life, at home and abroad, for centuries. The British Museum in London contains an 8th century gold coin minted by King Offal of Marcia with 'Arabic text both sides. It does demonstrate the earliest known connections between the European continent and the Islamic world. These connections and contacts continued between an advanced and civilized Islamic civilization and a backward impoverished West throughout the Middle Ages, with Europe and Britain being the main beneficiaries, who inherited a rich scientific and philosophical traditions, universities, advances in medicine, mathematics and countless other benefits. These benefits of Islamic civilization had triggered the Renaissance and allowed the European continent to slowly emerge from the Dark Ages.

Muslims have established and flourished in the European continent some of the most outstanding communities like Spain, Portugal, Sicily and Crete. The Spain was conquered by Muslims from North Africa, defeating the Visigothic ruler King Roderick in 711 AD and slashed their reign on almost entire peninsula until 1492. The domination of Muslims almost for 800 years, is still visible on their culture and language. The contributions of Spanish Muslims cover almost every sphere of knowledge and learning, in the field of Qur'anic science, *Ḥadīths*, history, humanities and science. Islamic influence and impact on Portuguese language and culture became more evident when Sidi Barakat, who legitimated the Sa'di family of *sharifs,* had expelled the Portuguese and established an independent state (1511-1603 AD) strong enough to expand far to the south. The Muslims of Sicily had the history of several years. Sicily was the part of Tunisian state and then became an independent Muslim state in 827 AD. After lasting for a total of 418 years, the Muslim community of Sicily has been completely extinguished due to new rebellions in 1245 AD, but their influence and impact on language and culture is still alive. Islam came to the island of Crete between 1645 and 1669 AD. The Muslim community, which was Greek-speaking, suffered continuous persecution in 1889 and final expulsion to Turkey in 1923 AD.

Balkons, liberated by 'Ottomans defeating the Serbian armies in 1389 AD. Bogomilist territories of Bosinia, Hercegovina and Albania were not molested but when the Bogomilist cried for help, Muhammad al-Fatih liberated them and accorded freedom of worship to all. Many of these Muslims lost their language in favour of Turkish, but the majority kept their distinctive heritage, as the Bosnians, Albanians and Bulgarians.

In Bosnia the Bogomils embraced Islam *en masse* in the year 1463 AD, in the open field 36,000 families voluntarily accepted Islam. It highly delighted 'Ottoman authorities. The new converts were given a dispensation by declaring them free from the painful rite of circumcision, which encouraged the chain of mass conversion. After a few years thousands of others converted at a public gathering in Hercegovina, a dukedom. Within the present borders of Bosnia-Hercegovina the Muslim population is above the half. Unfortunately, as soon as Bosnia declared independence in 1992 AD, an unjust war was imposed upon it by the Serbs and an ethnic cleansing similar to that of Andalusia and Palestine was set in.

Islam reached Albania, the most remote and mountainous country in Europe, via Macedonia in 1381. Albanians are the deeply divided society, into the followers of three religions – Muslims, Bahā'īs and Aḥmadīyas or Qādiānīs. Muslims are divided among the Sunnis and Shi'is. Apart from the Sunnis, who form the majority group, there are Bektashiyyas, who are one of the *Shi'is* mystics orders. They consist of 20 per cent of Muslim population of Albanians. Unlike their practice in Turkey, the Bektashiyyas of Albania are precious Shi'is and openly espouse their religious practices. Bektashiyyas had been prominent in late 19th century reformatism, particularly in the field of education. They have separate identity as one of the four religions of Albania. Their tribal leader Ahmet Bey Zoqoli, better known as King Zog, who reigned until ousted by Mussolini in April 1939. Bulgarians state continued to encourage atheism, since the reforms of 1989-90 AD, but the religious activity was increasingly tolerated, barring the Islam. Muslims are among the minority religious groups of Bulgaria and face continued expulsion toward Turkey. No mosque is allowed to be built or rebuilt. During two centuries of Muslim presence in the Balkan area, Bosnia and Hercegovina (in former Yugoslavia) and Albania and Thrace became Muslim majority areas. Similarly, Bulgaria and Greece have the migrations not only from Turkey but also from Spain. Besides these countries most of former Yugoslavia, Romania and Hungary were by the end of the 15th century in the Muslim hands.

The growth of the Muslim inhabitants of western Europe in the current perspectives had different types and patterns. They are mostly emigrant workers from almost all-over the Muslim world. With the growth of colonialism in the 19th and 20th AD centuries most of the *Dar es-Salam* came in the hands of the western European powers. The days of Muslim hegemony was gone and they became modern slaves. Most of Muslim immigrants, were denied their human rights, their jobs were taken away; they were subjected to the terrible pressure of assimilation. Morever, today's Europeans are not prepared to tolerate the presence of non-Europeans, especially non-white people.

Muslims at Cross-Roads

The 18th century was a period of degeneration for Muslims and a prelude to European domination, symbolized by the Napoleon's conquest of Egypt in 1798 AD. Muslims were largely unaware of the causes of their decline and the rise of Europe. In 19th century selective westernization of 'Ottoman empire coexisted with a reconsideration of Islam. In some areas Muslim leader's attempt was limited to revive the existing political system. In Iran, for example, the restoration of combined military and religious reforms were initiated. Nādir Shāh extended the borders of the

Ṣafavīd state further than ever and also defeated the 'Ottomans and may have been aspiring to be called leader of all Muslims, for which he made overtures to the neighbouring rulers. After he was killed in 1747 AD, his attempts did not revive. In the 'Ottoman empire, the restoration involved various phases. The military and political reforms referred as *Niẓām-i-Jadīd* (New Order) was nothing short of making use of things European. In other areas, leaders envisioned new political orders of self-consciousness.

In the 1860s AD, a group of Young Turks tried to identify the fundamental principles of European liberalism and even love of nation itself. In Iran, the Qajars brought in a special *Cossack Brigade* trained and led by Russians. At the same time Shi'i *Mujtahids* of Iran viewed that the decision of their spiritual leaders, the *Marjau't-Taqlīd*, as binding on all brothers-in-faith and declared themselves to be independent of the Shah. Like the Young Turks, Shi'is leadership came to be identified with constitutionalism in opposition to the ruler and took part in the positional revolutions of 1905-11 AD.

Sunni activist movement and its protests often took the form of *Jihād,* had been directed less at non-Muslims than at Muslims, who, according to them, have gone astray by decreasing reliance on Islam as a source of public value, it was counter-balanced with reforms ranging from educational reform to *Jihād,* as its various examples demonstrate. In northern Nigeria when discontent erupted, 'Ottomans Fodio declared a *Jihād* against the Hausa rulers. Among others Muḥammad al-Jaylnai in Aiir, Shehuh Ahmadu Lobbo in Macina, 'Omar Tal in Fouta Djallon and Samory in the Malinke (Mandingo) states and the Salihi mystics in Somalia, led by Saiyed Muḥammad, who was abusively nicknamed by the Europeans as *Mad Mullā.* Similarly, there had been *Jihād* by Southeast Asians against Dutch, Sanusi mystics over Italian control in Libya. Muḥammad Aḥmad *al-Mahdī* of Sudan declared *Jihād* against European occupation. Shāh Walīu'llāh (d. 1762 AD) has been best exemplar for the *Jihād* against British rule. In the recent years *Jihād* against America and his allies has taken a new turn. It has orchestrated a bloody campaign of violent attacks and beheading of hostage, had remained elusive in Afghanistan, Iraq, Sudan, Somalia, Chechnya, Bosnia and number of other countries.

Sometimes the need to throw out the European occupation has promoted the fortunes of secular nationalism and other forms of loyalty. It would not be out of place to printout that the nationist fervour has actually increased since 1905 AD, after Japan's defeat of Russia. Despite being deeply committed to resisting and removing European occupation or control, many nationalist enthusiastically admired European way of life and often accepted their assessment that the Traditional religion was a barrier to modernization. They sought identity in their pre-Islamic past. Kemal Ataturk sought the identity in the Turkic past in Central Asia and Anatolia with the aim of transforming the traditions set by 'Ottoman Caliphate into a Turkish identity not fully dependent on Islam.

Kemal Ataturk's attempt to establish new Turkish identity was not merely change of dress-pattern of every Turkish men and women, it was an assault on Islamic principles and practices. In 1929 Islamic *Sharī'a* was abolished and the Western laws substituted, the *Ḥijāb* (veil) was banned, monogamy was made compulsory; *Nikāh* was replaced by the civil marriage system, so much and so far these liturgical reform went that the pillar of Islamic faith, the *Namāż* was discouraged. Muslim males, who prayed covered heads, were now asked to replace the fez, which could be kept on during the prayer, with the brimmed hat, which could not. *Ażān* and the *Namāż,* prescribed and practiced since the life of the holy Prophet were changed and translated in Turkish language. An amended and modified Qur'an in Turkish language, by Mehmet Akif, the author of the Turkish national anthem, was published. Such desperate actions were highly resented by the people-in-faith and the author fled the country to save his life.

In 1920s-30s AD, Ataturk served as a role-model for Muslim dictators everywhere such as Amānu'llāh Khān of Afghanistan, Reza Shāh Pahlavī of Iran and King Zog of Albania. 'Arabic script, too closely associated with Islam was replaced with Roman. Reza Shāh Pahlavī argued that Iran had the continuous history, since Achaemenid times and the Islamic period was but accidental interlude in that continuity. The Egyptian connected their identity with the period of Pharaons and the Mediterranean times. 'Arabs emphasized the unity of all sons of soil, regardless of their confession. On the other hand, in Egypt, Sayyid Qutb and Ḥasan al-Banna were the mentors of the Muslim Brotherhood, who fought for the educational, moral and social reforms.

Muslims associated the nationalist fervour with the related ideologies, such as pan-'Arabism, pan-Turkism, or 'Arab-Socialism. Actually, much of the activity was pan-Islamic sentiment that had drawn on the old conception of the *Ummah,* the ultimate solitary group for Muslims. Among others, three most prominent Islamic reconstructionist were Jamālu'd-Dīn al-Afghānī, his Egyptian disciple Muḥammad 'Abdh'ū and Indian poet-philosopher Sir Muḥammad Iqbāl. They argue that Muslims themselves are responsible for their weaknesses, because they had lost the progressive spirit of social, moral, and intellectual reconstruction that had made early Islamic civilization, one of the greatest in human history. They warned against blind pursuit of Westernization, arguing that the Western technology could advance Muslims only if they retained and cultivated their own spiritual and cultural heritage, and may lead the world, as in its Golden Age during the 8th-9th centuries. Like al-Afghānī, Iqbāl asserted that Muslims should regain the strength they had possessed when they were the vital force in the world, united in a single international community, irrespective of caste, creed, colour, or ethos of nation and language. Thus, aggressive recovery of the past had became vital theme of the Islamic reconstruction.

The Islamic activities and the ideological orientations appeared more important between the end of World War II and the declaration of the Islamic Republic of Iran on 11th February, 1979. It was against what many people expected that religion would recede as modernization progressed. In the early 1960s, new circumstances began to foster increased Islamic activities and the people of Iran started to rally around the exiled Imām K'homenī; the writing of 'Ali Sharī'atī influenced Muslim inside and outside Iran. After a landslide victory in the national referendum of 1st April, 1979, Imām Khumaynī declared an Islamic republic, subsequently invested with a new constitution reflecting the Shi'a ideology of Islamic Government. There are sharp paradoxes, the twists and turns of political developments in Islamic countries, but this much may be said without any hesitation the awareness of a new system of Islamic democracy is on the rise, the future would decide how far successful the Islamic democracy proves. Presently, only a few Muslim states are there, which are still under imperial rule, and the campaign for liberation is on in full swing. The scene of the imperial power coming to an end. Muslim Imperialism has totally lost the creditability and shall die within a few years.

Modern Islam's unifying forces suffer by labels such as Sunni, Shi'is etc. and their sub-sects, which always carried an oppositional quality, may be non-essential attributes that have become salient in the wake of a new valence. Modern Islam may appear diverse and defying the description, yet it is held together by stronger centripetal forces than any other pan-national solidarity religious group. The *Ḥajj* is a living example, in which millions of Muslims meet annually; and, despite significant religious cleavages, Islam remains an undivided house. Although, the *Hajj* has unique glory and grandeur of the congregation which acquaints the people with the reality of the great Islamic identity which transcends the nation, races, colour and languages. The great congregation of Muslims during the *Ḥajj* may become the starting point and launching pad to march towards the comprehensive movement. Islamic awakening is spreading and the youth, elite and masses of many Islamic countries have brought to the scene, exposing the bullying politicians. Islam continues to compete, spurred on the freshness of its own demands, by the outstanding ability of many mundane and spiritual that has been proved to be the hallmark of all religious life.

The above introductory summary of the global Muslim community is a token recognition of their important existence. Some of the countries have been omitted, not because they are unimportant but because the space for discussion is limited. Our object has been to present global Islamic spectrum in brief. There are a large number of countries where Muslims have their identity as one of the religious minorities and they are contributing immensely to its socio-cultural life. As well as Islam dominates as the state religion of most Southwest Asian countries and has by far the largest number of adherents in Asia. From the Arabian Peninsula, where it was founded in the 7th century, Islam has spread throughout the Middle East, into Central Asia and across the southern part of the continent to Indonesia, which remains predominately Muslims. The majority of Asian Muslims belong to the orthodox Sunni community, except Iran, Iraq and Bahrain, where members of more esoteric Shi'a community are in majority. However, the number of Shi'is in India is next to Iran and if the entire Indian sub-continent is kept in mind, the number of Shi'is may exceed that of Iran. Muslim constitute important minority in India, China, Philippines, Japan, Myanmar, Sri Lanka, and numerous Islands etc.

The classical Islamic civilization presents a model for the people from varied races and creeds. How to live together and learn from each other to create a cultural whole much greater than the sum of its parts. Nevertheless, the relationship between various communities had been by no means always harmonious or straightforward, this has provided an early example of the multicultural society different from, but never alien to, the one we aspire today. Its diversity has resulted in a creative mix of ideas to give rise to literary masterpieces and scientific achievements far ahead of their times. If a historian would argue about the exact reasons for the flourishing of Islamic civilization, it is clear that the inspiration of Islam teaches tolerance and peaceful coexistence, equality and justice, which has a major role in creating the progressive model for at global society.

References

1. *al-Milal wa'l Niḥal*, Vol. 1, p. 16.
2. *Maqālātu'l-Islāmiyyīn*, Vol. 1, p. 1.
3. *al-Milal wa'l Niḥal*, Vol. 1, pp. 11-43.
4. *al-Milal wa'l Niḥal*, Vol. 1, pp. 11-43.
5. *Anwāru'l-Qur'an*, p. 931.
6. *al-Muqaddima*, p. 102.
7. *Shi'a dar Islam*, pp. 4-5.
8. *A Socio-Intellectual History of Isnā 'Asharī Shi'īs in India*, Vol. 1, p. 72.
9. *Khutūtu'sh-Sham*, Vol. 5, p. 25.
10. *Dīn-i-Islām aur Auwallīn Musalmānon kī do Mutazād Taṣwīren,* pp. 6-7.
11. *The Book of Certainty,* p. 30.
12. *al-Firaqu'sh-Shi'a*, p. 1.
13. *Kitābu'l-Mabsūt*, Vol. 10, p. 125.
14. *Tārīkh-i-Alfī,* Introduction.
15. *al-Fitnau'l-Kubrā,* Vol. 1, pp. 132-34.
16. *al-Fitnau'l-Kubrā,* Vol. 2, pp. 89-100.
17. *al-Milal wa'l Niḥal*, Vol. 1, p. 115.
18. *as-Sunan*: Abū Dāwūd, Vol. 2, p. 20, *al-Musnad:* Aḥmad, Vol. 2, p. 92, *Yanābia'u'l-Muwaddah,* p. 308.
19. *al-Uṣūl-min'al-Kāfī*, Vol. 1, p. 178, *Bihāru'l-Anwār*, Vol. 23, p. 22.
20. *An Introduction to Shi'i Islam*, p. 82.
21. *Karbala se Karbala tak*, pp. 64-5.
22. al-Ḥurr al-'Āmulī's *Wasa'l ash-Shi 'as* quoted in Kumaynī's: *Vilāyat-i-Faqīh dar khṣūṣ-i-Ḥukūmat-i-Islāmī i*, pp. 100-101.
23. *Tārīkhu'r-Rusūl wa'l-Mulūk,* Vol. 4, p. 188, *al-Kāmil fī't-Tārīkh,* Vol. 3, p. 234 & Vol. 4, p. 154 *Khilafar-o-Mulūkiyat*, p. 162.
24. *Kitābu'l-Mabsūt*, Vol. 10, p. 125.
25. *Nahju'l-Balāghah* Sermon 204, p. 571.
26. *Yanābia'u'l-Muwaddah,* p. 266.
27. *al-Kāmil fī't-Tārīkh,* Vol 2, p. 55.
28. *Tārīkhu'r-Rusūl wa'l-Mulūk,* Vol. 2, p. 1179.
29. *Tārīkh-i-Fātimīn-i-Miṣr,* p. 9.
30. *A Short History of Saracens,* p. 592.
31. *Polemics on the Origin of the Fatimid Caliph*, p. 25.
32. *Kalami Pir: A Treatise of Isma'ili Doctrine*, p. 44.
33. *Khilāfat-o-Mulūkiyat,* p. 246.
34. *al-Milal wa'l Niḥal*, p. 67.
35. *Muwaddatu'l-Qurba,* pp. 71, 77.
36. *Kitābu'r-Rijāl,* p. 70.
37. *al-Faṣl-fī'l-Milal wa'l-Aḥwa wa'l-Niḥal,* Vol. 1, p. 45.
38. *al-Fitnau'l-Kubrā,* Vol. 1, pp. 132-34, Vol. 2, pp. 89-100.
39. *The Spirit of Islam*, p. 343.
40. *al-Kāmil fī't-Tārīkh*, Vol. 2, p. 28.

41. *A Short History of the Saracens*, p. 46.
42. *The Spirit of Islam*, p. 134.
43. *Munāqību'l-Imāmu'l-Āẓam Abū Ḥanīfa*, Vol. 1, pp. 65-66.
44. *Khilāfat-o-Mulūkiyat,* p. 213.
45. *Munāqību'l-Imāmu'l-Āẓam Abū Ḥanīfa*, Vol. 2, p. 72.
46. *Khutabāt*, p. 155.
47. *al-Ittaqan fī 'Ulūmu'l-Qur'an*, p. 163.
48. *Khilāfat-o-Mulūkiyat,* p. 264.
49. *Khilāfat-o-Mulūkiyat,* p. 279.
50. *Nahju'l-Balāghah*, Sermon no. 95, pp. 287-88.
51. *Sharḥu'l-Ṭaḥāwiyā,* p. 397.
52. *Khilāfat-o-Mulūkiyat,* p. 216.
53. *al-Iṣābah fī Tamayyażu's-Ṣaḥābah,* Vol. 2, p. 502.
54. *Sharhu'l-Fiqhu'l-Akbar,* p. 103.
55. *al-Jauhar fī Sharh Waṣīyatu'l-Imām Abū Ḥanīfa*, pp. 6-7.
56. *al-Jauhar fī Sharh Waṣīyatu'l-Imām Abū Ḥanīfa*, pp. 6-7.
57. Qouted in *Nahju'l-Balāghah* (Urdu tr. Ja'far Ḥusain) p. 224.
58. *Sharhu'l-Fiqhu'l-Akbar;* p. 86-89.
59. *Sharḥu'l-Ṭaḥāwiyā,* p. 265.
60. *Munāqību'l-Imāmu'l-Āẓam Abū Ḥanīfa*, Vol. 1, pp. 124-125.
61. *Munāqību'l-Imāmu'l-Āẓam Abū Ḥanīfa*, Vol. 1, pp. 124-125.
62. *Munāqību'l-Imāmu'l-Āẓam Abū Ḥanīfa*, Vol. 1, p. 96, Vol. 2, pp. 136-38.
63. *Munāqību'l-Imāmu'l-Āẓam Abū Ḥanīfa*, Vol. 1, p. 109.
64. *Wafiyyātu'l-'Ayān wa anbā'aż-Żamān,* Vol. 2, p. 302.
65. *Kitābu'l-Khirāj*, pp. 108, 116.
66. *al-Muwaṭṭa:* Mālik, Vol. 2, pp. 302-60.
67. *Tārīkhu'r-Rusūl wa'l-Mulūk*, Vol. 3, p. 250.
68. *al-Muwaṭṭa:* Mālik, Vol. 2, p. 359.
69. *al-Muwaṭṭa:* Mālik, Vol. 2, pp. 315, 365, 376.
70. *Kitābu'l-Muārif*, pp. 346-51.
71. *The Heart of 'Arabia*, Vol 1, p. 18.
72. *Tajdīdu'-Aḥyāi'-Dīn*, p. 71.
73. *Anfāsu'l-'Ārifīn*, p. 193.
74. *Uṣūl-i-Fiqh aur Shah Waliu'llah*, pp. 191-97.
75. *at-Tafhīmātu'l-Ilāhiyyā*, Vol 3, p. 120.
76. *The Muslim Community of the Indo-Pakistan Sub-Continent,* p. 229.
77. *aṣ-Ṣawa'qu'l-Muḥriqa,* vide verses 11/86, 43/61, 9/32, 24/55.
78. *Durru'l-Manthūr fī'l-Tafsīr bi'l Māthūr* vide verses 9/32, 11/86, 43/61, 24/55.
79. *Jām'au's-Ṣaḥīḥu't-Tirmiżī,* Vol. 2, p. 36, *as-Sunan*: Abū Dāwūd, Vol. 2, p. 420.
80. *as-Sunan*: Ibn Māja, p. 1367, Tradition no. 4085, *Jām'au's-Ṣaḥīḥu't-Tirmiżī,* Vol. 2, p. 36, *as-Sunan*: Abū Dāwūd, Vol. 2, p. 422.
81. *Jām'au's-Ṣaḥīḥu't-Tirmiżī,* Vol. 2, pp. 36-7, *Kitābu'l-Kāmilu'd-Dīn*, pp. 525-32.

82. *Jām'au's-Ṣaḥīḥu't-Tirmiżī,* Vol. 2, p. 36, *as-Sunan*: Abū Dāwūd, Vol. 2, pp. 422-3,*Kashf al-Ghumma fī Ma'rifat al-Ai'ma*, Vol. 3, pp. 257, 269.
83. *as-Sunan*: Ibn Māja, p. 1367 Tradition nos. 4085, 4084 & p. 1366 Tradition nos. 4085, 4082, *as-Sunan*: Abū Dāwūd, Vol. 2, p. 422.
84. *Kitābu't-Tawḥīd*, pp. 28-155.
85. *Sabih Sunnan* Ibn Maja, pp. 1366-67 (tr. 4082, 4087) *Kashf-al-Ghummah*, Vol. 3, pp. 62-63, *Bihar-al-Anwar*, Vol. 13, p. 159.
86. *Jām'au's-Ṣaḥīḥu't-Tirmiżī,* Vol. 2, p. 36, *as-Sunan*: Abū Dāwūd, Vol. 3, pp. 257-69.
87. *Bustān-i-Wilāyat*, p. 222.
88. *Muntakhabu't-Tawārīkh*, pp. 262-76.
89. *Indian Muslims*, p. 12.
90. *Khilāfat-o-Mulūkiyat,* p. 199.
91. *al-Milal wa'l Niḥal*, Vol. 1, p. 104.
92. *al-Faṣl-fī'l-Milal wa'l-Aḥwa wa'l-Niḥal,* Vol. 4, p. 203.
93. *Khilāfat-o-Mulūkiyat,* p. 203.
94. *Islāmic Philosophy and Theology*, pp. 32-5.
95. *An Introduction to Shi'i Islam*, pp. 54, 58.
96. *Islāmī 'Ulūm kā Ta'rruf,* p. 203.
97. *al-Farq bayn al-Firāq*, pp. 138-39.
98. *Maqālātu'l-Islāmiyyīn*, Vol. 2, p. 124.
99. *Kitab al-Milal wa'n-Nihal*, Vol. 1, p. 51.
100. *Murūju'ż – Żahab-wa'l-M'adinu'l-Jauhar,* Vol. 2, p. 191.
101. *al-Milal wa'l Niḥal*, Vol. 1, p. 63.
102. *Khilāfat-o-Mulūkiyat,* p. 204.
103. *al-Farq bayn al-Firāq,* pp. 133-4, *al-Milal wa'l Niḥal*, Vol. 1, p. 401.
104. *al-Farq bayn al-Firāq*, pp. 94-95.
105. *The Development of Metaphysics in Persia*, p. 57.
106. *Islāmī 'Ulūm kā Ta'rruf,* p. 208.
107. *Khilāfat-o-Mulūkiyat,* p. 185.
108. *The Development of Metaphysics in Persia*, p. 18.
109. *Jām'au't-Tawarīkh,* pp. 99-100.
110. *Tārīkh-i-Gużīda,* pp. 517-27.
111. *al-Irshād fī Ma'rifat Ḥujāj Allāh 'Alā 'Ibād*, pp. 227, 308, 314, *al-Milal wa'l Niḥal*, Vol. 1, pp. 56, 76-120, *Murūju'ż – Żahab-wa'l-M'adinu'l-Jauhar,* Vol. 5, pp. 68, 467, Vol. 6, p. 186, Vol. 8, p. 40, *Bihāru'l-Anwār*, Vol. 45, p. 116.
112. *al-Irshād fī Ma'rifat Ḥujāj Allāh 'Alā 'Ibād*, p. 268.
113. *Murūju'ż – Żahab-wa'l-M'adinu'l-Jauhar*, Vol. 8, p. 40.
114. *al-Maqālāt wa'l Firaq*, pp. 102-16.
115. *al-Firaqu'sh-Shi'a*, p. 79.
116. *Kitābu'r-Rijāl*, p. 48.
117. *Umm'ul-Kitāb*, p. 11.
118. *al-Faṣl-fī'l-Milal wa'l-Aḥwa wa'l-Niḥal,* Vol. I, p. 56.
119. *Muntakhab al-Tawarikh*, pp. 262-76.
120. *al-Kafi*, Vol. 1, p. 178, *Bihar-al-Anwar*, Vol. 23, p. 22.

121. *Tajdid-o-Ahya-e-Din*, pp. 42-9.
122. *A Glossary of the Tribes and Castes of Punjab and North-West Frontier Povinces,* Vol. 2, pp. 141-2.
123. *Billochon kī Tārīkh, Qabāyal ke Ā'ine mein*, Vol. 1, p. 150.
124. *Malfūzāt,* p. 160.
125. *A Glossary of the Tribes and Castes of Punjab and North-West Frontier Povinces,* Vol. 2, p. 142.
126. *Durr-i-Gauhar,* p. 9.
127. *Indian Muslims*, p. 22.
128. *Central Provinces District Gazetteer* (Seoni Dist. Allahabad), Vol. 17, p. 221.
129. *Central Provinces District Gazetteer* (Seoni Dist. Allahabad), Vol. 23, p. 296.
130. *Indore State Gazetteer,* p. 59.
131. *Indian Muslims*, p. 11.
132. *Purnea District Gazetteer* 25/58, *Bengals District Gazetteer* 3/47-76.
133. *Sindh Gazetteer*, Vol. A9 (1907) p. 160.
134. *Gazetteer of the Bombay Presidency*, Vol. 9 (3), p. 12.
135. *Gazetteer of Alwar*, pp. 37, 70.
136. *Bundi State Gazetteer*, p. 223.
137. *Indian Muslims*, p. 12.
138. *A Glossary of the Tribes and Castes of Punjab and North-West Frontier Povinces,* Vol. 2, p. 49.
139. *A Glossary of the Tribes and Castes of Punjab and North-West Frontier Povinces,* Vol. 2, pp. 27-8, 317.
140. *Gazetteer of Bombay Presidency,* Vol. 9(3), pp. 72, 226 & Vol. 9(2), pp. 64, 69.
141. *Central Provinces District Gazetteers* (Seoni Dist. Allahabad) Vol. 17, p. 221.
142. *Gazetteer of the Bombay Presidency*, Vol. 9(2), pp. 64, 69.
143. *Indian Muslims*, p. 18.
144. *The Shi'a of India*, pp. 382-3.

Conclusion

If I am asked to summarize the nature and principles of Islam in one word, I would say *justice*. Islam is synonymous with justice. Justice to Creator by having faith in Him and by obeying His injunctions and mandate, as He is justice. Justice to the Prophet of God by following him as he represents the authority of God. Justice to one's own self by keeping it secure from sinfulness and egoism. Justice to body by keeping it healthy and free from undue exertion and illness. Justice to his soul by keeping it pure with piety. Justice in the matrimonial sphere. Justice to parents as they have been instrumental in gifting our existence. Justice to the spouse who shares the burden of leading a family life. Justice to the offsprings as they are the extensions of our own life by motivating them to take right direction in life. Justice to neighbours by sharing with them in their moments of trial. Justice to the sick by helping to restore health. Justice to the downtrodden and poor by supplementing their basic needs. Justice to the motherland by enjoying the fragrance of its soil, by loving and promoting its prosperity and being ready to sacrifice for it. Justice to the entire humanity by contributing to its development. Justice to knowledge by making it reach far and wide, by enabling mankind to enjoy its fruits without discrimination. Justice, therefore, is the foundation of Islamic principles and occupies a place next to oneness of God.

Has the author of this book done justice to his subject, shall be the judgment of the learned readers. In his defence the author would like to clarify that Islam is multidimensional global religion and Islamic creed has spread across the world and obtained a permanent and powerful hold over billions of people. In this book the author has confined himself to the study of the origin and development of the Islamic faith and people in uplifting humanity and its true place in the history of religions. Spirituality has a great place in Islam. It teaches realization of God while leading a normal but pious social life. Among the many sects of Islam the one that made a pious living devoid of unholy worldly temptations as its goal is called *Taṣawwuf*– 'Our pride is hermitage', declared they. It is a subject of the full length book, so I have not touched the topic in this book. If it could be possible, I would like to write a separate book on it. Similarly, the contributions of Muslims to human knowledge, culture, art, literature etc., besides socio-political history are various subjects of independent books. How could everything be accomplished in this humble book.

In the pages following an attempt has been made to underline the vital planes of Islamic thought and principles which came as a legacy of Islam for cultural enlistment of human society in the subsequent ages in general and in the current cultural development in particular. To avoid details only those vital points have been touched which are central and highly important, and also regarded as the basic principles of the current cultural life. In the analysis of these principles, Islamic personalities who have left their influence, have been considered as an integral components of these principles. All these have been discussed in the foregoing pages of this book to underline the commonly acceptable principles of Islam to have an idea of how the Indo-'Arab: Iranian civilizations have combined into one civilization, specially in the sub-continent of India and serves as a light-house to the global people. Indians have shown love and respect to the holy Prophet Muhammad and his holy *Ahlu'l-Bayt*. They also colour them with their own beliefs.

All the four sources of the Islamic laws namely Qur'an, *Sunnah*, *Ijmā'* and *'Aql* have been described earlier in this book. This is further sub-divided into four parts:

(*i*) *'Ibādat* (Obedience): the laws governing the worship of God.
(*ii*) *'Uqūd* (Obligations): the laws which obtain between two parties entering into a deal such as marriage, purchasing, selling etc.
(*iii*) *'Eqā't* (Red-Shelling): the laws where involvement of two parties is not essential. One party itself can effect the act like Talaq, Khula etc.
(*iv*) *Aḥkām* (Orders): the laws for all those acts which are not covered by the above three categories namely *'Ibādat, 'Uqūd* and *'Eq'āt*.

There are further sub-division of all these four categories. Apparent by these division and sub-division of these laws and sub-laws they don't seem to have any relationship but each seems to have a separate ground of its own. Nevertheless, there is a consistent and in-depth relationship running through them, all widely based on a single source, to regulate and promote human life on earth.

With *'Ibādat* man purifies his soul. *'Ibādat* is like a mirror in which man realizes his self and God is revealed to his self. In *Uqūd* man finds the principles of practical conduct to look after his family, his spouse, children, relatives, neighbnour, his teacher, his disciple, and all those whom he has to confront in his practical life. For his individual concerns, he has *'Eq'āt*. The sphere of *Aḥkām* is fairly wide in which all affairs of life are observed and checked.

According to Islam, every Muslim has four responsibilities:

1. *Responsibility, he bears to God*: Belief in the absolute oneness of God, submission to Him and to His Messenger, and worship of God, saying Prayer, paying the Poor-Due, Fasting, Pilgrimage and Holy struggle.
2. *Responsibility, he bears to his own self*: Making use of those things made lawful by God and keeping away from those made unlawful and forbidden by God. Using things good for health and spiritual enhancement. Bearing good conduct in society. Earning livelihood from clean sources and spending it on lawfully desirable objects.
3. *Responsibility, he bears to others*: Commitment to his family, society and nations. Bearing no grudge, no fraud, no evil design against anyone. Performing no act which might do wrong to anyone. Forgiving those who fail to pay what is duly payable to you, because even God cannot forgive the dues unless pardoned by the man to whom the dues were payable. A man not forgiven by the man, will deserve punishment in Hell, howsoever virtuous he might be otherwise.
4. *Responsibility, he bears to the Cosmos and other creatures:* God has created numberless creatures. Man gets them under his control by using his power, and derives benefits from them. Man is the noblest and highest of all creatures. God has given him right to make use of them, but this does not entitle him to abuse them. If they are put to use it must be done within a dignified limit and their use must be made good – if a tree has been cut-off, another tree must be planted, and so forth.

Islamic equality and brotherhood is universal, there is no discrimination of colour, sex, language, region or country. Islam binds all human beings with the thread of fraternity and brotherhood. Islamic equality has special significance in the global context. If we look at the present plight of the great religious country like India, we will notice that corruption is rampant on every level. Moral degradation is growing wider like cancer. Masses are suffering from exploitation and injustice. Casteism has prevented many from availing themselves of human opportunities. Communalism is bent on breaking the nation. Consumerism has overpowered social justice. An atmosphere of fear is spreading because of violence, robbery, murder and rape. Human dignity and human right are being violated. A large number of masses are still below the poverty line – longing anxiously for bread, clothes and shelter. Unemployment has gripped the youth with growing disappointment. Women are feeling insecure, etc. I am a proud Indian, so I referred here to my country, otherwise, truly speaking, it is the global phenomenon, which is challenging the human existence.

In this horrible and explosive situation, it is highly imperative for a peaceful, just and harmonious change that the followers of different faiths find a common plane among themselves, build a friendly attitude and explore the common religious, spiritual and human values in each religion and struggle to form a healthy society serving the common human interest and social welfare. This is, in fact, the discovery of truth. This is the very object of human interest. The need of a constructive inter-faith dialogue among the followers of diverse religions of the world, was never greater than today. The inter-faith dialogue is possible only by understanding the principles and identifying the nature of each other's faith. This book places the Islamic aspect before the readers. If this book helps to acquaint with and identify Islam in the right direction, it would register its achievement.

Annexures

List of Qur'anic Verses

Chapter I: *al-Fateḥa* (The Opening): 1, 2, 3, 4, 5, 6, 7.

Chapter II: *al-Baqarah* (The Cow): 29, 30, 43, 44, 45, 60, 62, 83, 107, 117, 124, 128, 129, 148, 154, 156, 164, 165, 168, 169, 170, 171, 183, 188, 189, 190, 191, 193, 200, 207, 220, 229, 230, 255, 256, 269, 274, 275, 280.

Chapter III: *Āl 'Imrān* (The Family of Imran): 6, 7, 17, 18, 19, 32, 56, 60, 63, 66, 82, 85, 102, 103, 104, 133, 150, 159, 172, 186, 192, 194.

Chapter IV: *an-Nisā'* (The Women): 1, 3, 7, 10, 16, 21, 24, 34, 36, 59, 80, 86, 136, 148, 157, 158, 159, 174.

Chapter V: *al-Māi'dah* (The Table Spread): 3, 4, 5, 32, 33, 48, 55, 64, 67, 76, 169.

Chapter VI: *al-In'ām* (The Cattle): 12, 29, 42, 57, 60, 65, 73, 76, 83, 88, 98, 109, 115, 122, 124, 126, 126, 153, 159, 162, 214.

Chapter VII: *al-'Arāf* (The Height) 9, 29, 54, 69, 74, 85, 129, 156, 157, 181, 189.

Chapter VIII: *al-Anfāl* (The Spoils of War): 41, 61.

Chapter IX: *at-Tawba* (The Repentance): 6, 12, 19, 32, 34, 38, 39, 41, 71, 119,

Chapter X: *Yūnus* (Jonah): 7, 14, 23, 25, 44, 47, 100.

Chapter XI: *Hūd* (Hūd): 86, 104.

Chapter XII: *Yūsuf* (Joseph): 41, 55, 101, 109.

Chapter XIII: *ar-Ra'd* (The Thunder): 19, 41, 43.

Chapter XIV: *Ibrahīm* (Abraham): 4, 10, 11.

Chapter XV: *al-Ḥijr* (The Rock): 10, 21, 31, 46, 94, 95, 99.

Chapter XVI: *an-Naḥl* (The Bee): 32, 76, 87, 90, 125.

Chapter XVII: *Banī Isrāel* (Children of Israel): 23, 24, 32, 33, 34, 36, 44, 85.

Transliteration

The internationally accepted principle of having the words as pronounced in its original form has been followed. With a view to further simplification, a few deviations have been allowed in some cases of 'Arabic phonetics. Similarly, the complications of special diacritical marks of vowels and diphthongs have also been avoided in case of Urdu, Persian, Sanskrit and other phonetics. While transliterating it into English, same system has also been followed in the words of identical sounds, especially in 'Arabic for non-'Arabic readers. It is at providing authentic material to the readers. However, some words and names commonly occurring in the book carry no transliteration marks, because the readers are better familiar with their present form, such as Islam, Sunni, Shi'a etc. instead of Islām, Sunnī, <u>Sh</u>ī'a etc.

The following table is intended to assist them:

ا अ	=	a	آ आ	=	ā
اَ ए	=	ē	ا इ	=	I
اِ ई	=	ī	ء	=	'
ا उ	=	u	و ऊ	=	ū
ب ब	=	b	بھ भ	=	bh
پ प	=	p	پھ फ	=	ph
ت त	=	t	تھ थ	=	th
ٹ ट	=	ṫ	ٹھ ठ	=	ṫh
ث	=	<u>th</u>	ج ज	=	j
جھ झ	=	jh	چ च	=	<u>ch</u>
چھ छ	=	ch	ح	=	ḥ
خ	=	<u>kh</u>	د द	=	d
دھ ध	=	dh	ڈ ड़	=	ḍ
ڈھ ढ़	=	ḍh	ذ	=	ž

ر र	=	r	ڈ ड	=	ṛ
ڑھ ढ़	=	ṛh	ز	=	ż
ژ	=	żh	س स	=	s
ش श	=	sh	ص	=	ṣ
ض	=	z	ط	=	ṭ
ظ	=	ẓ	ع	=	‘
غ	=	gh	ف	=	f
ق	=	q	ک क	=	k
کھ ख	=	kh	گ ग	=	g
گھ घ	=	gh	ل ल	=	l
م म	=	m	ن न	=	n
ہ/ة ह	=	h	و व	=	w
ي य	=	T	ے ऐ	=	y

The following alphabets, set of symbols or characters used to represent some specific sounds of ‘Arabic language, which have also been adopted in Persian, Urdu and some other languages:

ء(***ḥamżah***): penultimate letter of ا (alif).
ث (***thē***): pronounced with a lisp like ***th*** in ***thin***.
ح(***ḥē***): strong aspirate, stressed guttural ***h***.
خ(***khē***): guttural sound, as in German ***machen.***
ذ (***žāl***): close to soft ***th*** in ***father***.
ز (***żē***): close to ***z*** in ***zebra.***
ژ (***żhē***): close to ***sion, television.***
ص (***ṣād***): strong articulated ***s***.
ض (***zād***): stressed, explosive ***z***.
ط (***toē***): strong palatal sound, strong articulated ***t***.
ظ (*ẓoē*): strong palatal sound, articulated *z*.
ع(***‘ēn***): guttural sound close to ***a***.
غ(***ghēn***): gargling sound similar to French ***r.***
ف (***fā***): close to soft ***f*** in ***first***.
ق (***qāf***): ***k*** sound at back of throat, close to ***qua.***

Glossary

With a view to convey the import of the technical terminology to the reader, it has been explained right at the place where it is used for the first time and given its English equivalents. However, with a view to avoid repetition in explaining the same technical terminology again and again at various places, a brief glossary is given here for the readers' convenience:

'Abbāsites (*'Abbāsī*): Descendants of 'Abbās-bin-'Abdu'l-Muṭṭalib, uncle of the Prophet Muḥammad. This family seized the Caliphate for 507 years (750-1257).

'Adl: Divine Justice, one of the Principles of Islām.

Ahlu'l-Bayt or *'Itrat:* Household or Progeny of the Prophet Muḥammad.

Ahlu'l-Kitāb: The people of the revealed Books. Some have restricted it to Jews and Christians, but others include Zoroastrians, Hindus and all the claimants of the Divine Book.

Ahlu'r-Ra'i: Those who follow their own opinion in the absence of a clear instruction of God in Qur'an or Sunnat.

Ahlu'r-Ra'i-w'al-Qiyās: Those who follow hypothetical assumptions and opinion in religion.

Ākhirat: Last Judgment, one of the three most important Pivots of Islāmic faith, mainly four components; *Ma'd* (Resurrection), *Barżakh* (Purgatory), *'Adālat* (Judgment) and *Nijāt* (Salvation).

Amr-bil-Ma'rūf: Enjoining of God, things permitted in Islam.

Amīn: The truthful person, trustee to God.

Amīr: Commander, chief, leader.

Amīru'l-Mominīn: The leader of the faithful, the term used for the Caliph.

Angra Mainyu or *Ahriman:* Destructive Spirit, as believed by Zoroastrians.

Anṣār: Helpers, the residents of Yathrib who were ready to sacrifice anything to their brothers-in-faith.

'Aql: wisdom,

'Aqlī: Intellectual.

Asās (or *Asāsu'l-Imāmah*): Founder of the Imamate. Ismā'īlīs regard 'Ali-Ibn-Abū Ṭālib to be the bedrock of the Muslim Ummah, with Universal Soul, more than just an Imām.

Asurās: Demons.

'Ażādārī or *Tā'żiādārī*: Commemoration ceremony, which in course of time became guiding force to institutionalise the message of the martyrdom of Karbala and became the inseparable part of Islāmic religious life, especially for Shi'is.

Bada: Change in intention.

B'adu'l-Ijtihād: Closing of the door of the *Ijtihād*, completely and permamently by *al-Ghażāli*.

Barżakh: Isthmus or purgatory. Interval period between Death and Resurrection, as per Islāmic theology.

Bātini'īn: Secretistics, sub-sect of Ismā'īlīs.

Baytu'l-Māl: State Exchequer.

Bid'ah: Unlawful innovation in Islam.

Bin (or *Ibn*): Son of.

Bint: Daughter of.

Burhān: Demonstration, evidence of fact as universally observed and confirmed.

Dā'ī: Claimant, missionary, emissary; Nāyab-Imām in the Ismā'īlīs.

Dā'īsm has three steps – In the first step is *Makāsir*, the second is *Māżūn* and the third is *Dā'ī*.

Dā'īu'l-Muṭlaq: In absolute charge in Ismā'īlīs.

Dāru'l-Ḥarb: An unjust and untrue ruling order, propounded the principle of establishing a justice-predominant state, Shāh Wali'ullāh declared the contemporary India to be a *Dāru'l-Ḥarb* for which he campaigned the principle of *Fakku'l-Nizām* (the end of each wornout system), organised a powerfully armed struggle by the name of *Jihād*.

Dauru's-Sitar: veiled or covered period of Ismā'īlīs. Imamate in which the Shi'is were exposed to calamities perpetrated on them by the Abbāsite Caliphs.

Dā'wat: Feast; propagation, extension programme.

Dā'wat-al-żul-'Ashīra: Feast of the Family.

Devas: Gods.

Diyat: Wehrgeld, the price which any homicide pays to the family of the victim, if they so consented.

Durūd-wa'l-Salām: God's blessing.

'Eīdu'l-Mīlādu'l-Nabī: Celebrating the birth anniversary of the Prophet Muḥammad.

Faqīh (pl. *Fuqaha*): Expert in the *Fiqh*, theologist of Islām. Shi'is prefer to say him *Mujtahid*.

Faraiz ad-Dīn: Religious Obligations. Shi'is call it *Furū' ad-Dīn* (Branches of

Religion) and Sunni term as *Arkān ad-Dīn* (Pillars of Religion). These are, actually, compulsory duties for each and every Muslim, such as *Ṣalāt* or *Namāż* (the prayer), *Ṣaum* or *Rożah* (the Fasting), *Ḥajj* (the Pilgrimage) and *Żakāt* (poor-rate) *Khumus* (fifth part of wealth sacrifice and *Jihād* (struggle)

Fāsid-al-'Aqīdah: Perverted in belief.

Fāsiq: Sinful.

Fatwā: Edict.

Fidaī' (pl. *Fidaī'n*): Devotee, who willingly hazards his life. A rank of the extremist militant of al-Bāṭiniyya or Ta'līmiyya order of the Ismā'īlīs which remained steadfast ready to kill or die like inevitable death.

Fiqh: Islamic jurisprudence, elucidation and application of the *Shari'a.*

Firqah (pl. *Firaq*): Sects, differences.

Ghadīru'l-Khumm: It is known for general announcement of the Prophet regarding 'Ali to be his successor. Shi'is' celebrate in the commemoration of this event every year on 18th Żilḥajjah AH.

Ghulāt (sing. *Ghālīn*): One who exaggerates in religious matters, follower of the *Ghuluww* or *Ghalīyya,* holding such heretical doctrines, which put them outside the pale of Islām.

Ḥādī: Spiritual Guide.

Ḥadīth: Tradition, the words of the holy Prophet, Muḥammad. *Hadīths* are classified into four categories – *Ṣaḥīḥ* (correct), *Ḥasan* (fine), *Muwaththaq* (proved authentic), and *Za'īf* (weak).

Ḥadīthu'l-Qudsī: Heaven Traditions, the holy Traditions in the words of Gabriel.

Ḥadīthu'th-thaqalayn: Because it has deal with 'two things of immense gravity' *viz. Qur'an* and *Ahlu'l-Bayt,* it is popularly known as *Hadīthu'th-thaqlayn.*

Ḥajaru'l-Aswad: Black Stone, believed by Muslims to have come from Heaven.

Ḥajj: Pilgrimmage to Ka'ba (Mecca) in the Islamic modes of worship, is an obligation which has to be fulfilled once in the lifetime.

Ḥaqqu'l-Allāh: Religious Obligations regarding God Himself.

Ḥaqqu'l-'Ibād: Religious Obligations regarding the servants of God, i.e the Society.

Ḥaram: Mosque and sacred well Zemzem, located inside and in the central courtyard is Ka'ba, the holiest shrine of Islām.

Hijrā: Prophet Muḥammad's flight from Mecca to Medina in 622 AD, the base year of Muslim calendar called AH.

Ḥikma: Wisdom, considered to be the aim of philopophy.

Ḥikmat-i-Ilāhī: Divine Wisdom or Philosophy, Theosophy.

Ḥujjat: Proof of God, high position in hierarchy.

Ḥukama (sing. *Ḥakīm*): Philosophers, who are divided into two categories – *Masha'īyūn* (peripatic philosophers) who believe that the wisdom may be achieved through intellectual efforts and rational process. *Ishrāqīyūn* (illuminationist philosophers) who consider that the true wisdom could only be achieved under the spiritual discipline, the cleanig the soul from all defilements and acquisition of the virtues.

Ḥulūl: Incarnation.

Hurqālya or *Huvarqālya:* Intermediary world, between the physical world and the spiritual world. Every human being in the physical world has two bodies, one in physical shape and the other in the *Hurqālya.*

Ijmā': To agree or to resolve – in Shi'is it is possible only by the consensus of all the clergies. According to Shi'is principles like *Qiyās* (analogical reasoning), *Istiḥsān* (lenient interpretation) and *Masāelu'l-Mursala* (expedient issues) do not help reach an authentic judgment, so it is not wise to act upon them. But according to Sunnis these three principlees are the constituent elements of *Ijmā.* Similar is the case with *Taqlīd* (emulation) and *Ijtihād.*

Ijtihād: Exertion; the process of innovative exegesis to arrive at judgment on points of religious law using reason and principles of jurisprudence.

Ikhtiyār: Free-will, the human being is responsible for his actions.

Ilḥād: Heresy.

'Ilmu'l-Ghayb: Knowledge of Unseen.

'Ilmu'l-Ḥadīth: Science of Tradition in Islāmic academics.

'Ilmu'l-Kalām: Science of religious polemics.

'Ilmu'r-Rijāl: The science of testing and sorting the true *Ḥadīths* from the false ones and ascertaining the narrator's validity and credibility through the study of their biographies and other sources.

Imām: Head, leader or guide, other pivot of Islām, after *Rasūl.*

Imāmu'l-Ākhiru'ż-Żamān: The Divine Guide of the last period, whose Imamate will persist now for every age to come until the Last Day, who will appear in the time preceding the Dooms Day.

Imāmu'l-Maktūm: Undisclosed Imām, a chain of Ismā'īlī Imamate.

Imāmu'l-Muntaẓar: Awaited Imām, Imām Mahdī.

Imāmat: Imamate.

Imāmu'ż-Żamāna: Contemporary Imām of the period.

Irādah: Will.

'Irfān: Spiritual wisdom.

'Iṣmat: Sinlessness and infallibility.

Istiḥsān: Lenient interpretation of Sharī'a.

Ithna-Ash'arī: Twelver Shi'is.

Jabr: Predeterminism, the human being is bound to do as he is predestined, he has no choice.

al-Jafr: the Divination.

Jāhilīyah: Age of Ignorance.

al-Jāmi'a: the Compilation.

Jidāl: Dialectics, in which the fact is reached through the scientific debate.

Jihād: Struggle, to strive hard in the path of God.

Jizia: Tax for newly converted Muslims.

Kāfir: Infidel, apostat.

Kalām: Dogmatics, speculative theology.

Kalamatu'sh-Shahadah or *Kalamah:* Profession of Faith. It is read or recited in two different forms among the Shi'is and Sunnis. For Sunnis it is quite simple – *Lā Ilāh Ill'allāh Muḥammadu'r Rasūla'llāh.* (There is no good but God, Muḥammad His Prophet.) But Shi'is add their faith in the Imamate and read or recite as – *Lā Ilāh Ill'allāh Muḥammadu'r Rasūla'llāh 'Aliyan Ḥujjatu'llāh.* (There is no good but God, Muḥammad His Prophet, 'Ali is Argument of God.)

Khayr: Good.

Khārijī (pl. *Khawārij*): A sect driven out of Islam.

Khālwah: Spiritual retreat.

Khilāfat: Vicegerency, succession of the Prophet after his death.

Khilāfatu'r-Rāshida: Rightly Guided Caliphate. First-four Caliphates of Abu Bakr, 'Omar, 'Othmān and 'Ali.

Khula': Dismissal, the rights of wife to get separated from her husband, lent within the limits set by God.

Khumus: 1/5 of the annual tax on net profit.

Kisf: Fragment of heaven falling down.

Kufr: Blasphemy.

al-Mahdī: Rightly Guided One. The last saviour of the Divine and Justice on earth. He has a large number of other titles, all indicative of specific qualifications – *Ṣāḥib-aż-Żamān* (the Lord of the Age), *Ṣāḥib-al-Amr* (the Lord of Command), *Al-Qā'im* (He who will arise) and the *Baqīyyātu'llāh* (the Remnant of God) etc. The doctrine of the *Ghayāba* (Occultation) and *Rij'ā* (Return) maintains that Twelfth Imām Abu'l Qāsim Muḥammad, al-Mahdī has not died but has been concealed by God, that is what he is called *Imāmu'l-Ghayāb* (Hidden Imām).

Manṣūṣ-mina'llāh: Divinely ordained and appointed exclusively by God.

Marjau't-Taqlīd: Reference point for emulation; source of authority; great religious scholar who through his learning and probity is qualified to be followed in all points of religious practice and law and whose teachings should be observed by all Shi'is.

Marthiya: Elegy, in commemoration on the martyrdom of Imām Ḥusain and his companions.

Meḥrāb: Central place, specifically provided in to lead the congregation-prayers.

Mūmin (pl. *Mūminīn*): Believer, the person perfect in Islām.

Muḥaddith (pl. *Muḥaddithīn*): Expert of *Ḥadīth*.

Muhājirīn (sing. *Muhājir*): Emigrants, who had foresaken their birth-place the ties of kith and kin and every tie of home for the sake of Islām.

Mujtahid (pl. *Mujtahidīn*): Competent religious scholar having permission to practice.

Muṣḥafu'l Fāṭimah: Book of Fāṭimah aż-Żahrah.

Mushrik (pl. *Mushrikīn*): Polytheist.

Mulāḥedah (sing. *Mulḥid*): Heretics in religious matters.

Mulūkiyat: Imperialism.

Munāfiqūn (sing. *Munāfiq*): Hypocrites, who actually did not believe in Islam but mingled with Muslims, outwardly Muslim, inwardly dangerous enemies of Islām, while remaining within Islām, had started playing foul with it.

Nabī (pl. *Anbiya*) or *Rasūl* (pl. *Rusūl*): Prophet, Messenger or Apostle of God. (Christians use the word *Apostle* for one of the disciples of Jesus.)

Nahī-'anil-Munkir: Prevention and obliteration from Bad.

Naqlī: Transmitted.

Naṣṣ: Authority of God, specific designation used in relation to designation of 'Ali by the Prophet or any Imām by his predecessor. The process is sometimes may be in the *Mithāq* or *'Ahd* (convenant).

Nātiq: Vocal. Ismā'īlīs emphasize the circle of seven Grand-Prophets, who brings the revelation of truth. They are – Adam, Noah, Abraham, Moses, Jesus Christ, Muḥammad and Ismā'īl.

Qadr: Fate, self-determination.

Qiyāmah: Catastrophe.

Qazā: Divine Decree.

Qāzī: Judge in Islamic legal court.

Qur'an: Word of God.

Rāfizī (pl. *Rawāfiz*): Dissenter and swindler, a pure abusive term often used by some Sunnis for Shi'is.

Rāsikhūn-fil-'Ilm: Firmly established in knowledge.

Rāwī: Narrator, the one who had directly heard the words of the holy Prophet, Muḥammad.

Risālat: Prophethood, the second unanimous pivot of Islām, embassy, messenger which stands for that Embassy which God employs to communicate with mankind and sends some infallible human being to act as the representative of the Divine Kingdom in human world.

Rūḥ: Spirit.

Sabath Day: Saturday, special day for Jews.

Ṣabr: To deconstruct self-confidence and strength of willpower.

Ṣādiq: Absolutely truthful person.

Ṣaḥāba: Prophet's Companions.

Ṣaḥifa: the Book.

Saiyed (pl. *Sādāt*): Venerable, descendant of the progeny of the holy Prophet Muḥammad, in the family-tree of his daughter Fāṭimah aż-Żahrah, but due to political reasons the 'Arab world in general now use the word *Saiyed* as an equivalent of *Mr.*

Ṣalāt or *Namāż*: the prayer, the foremost pivot of the Religious Obligations of Islām, which occupies the central place in the elements of Islāmic practices to draw closer to the Almighty. It has seven components – *Azān* (formal call), *Aqāmat* (staying), *Qayām* (standing), *Rukū'* (the bowing position), *Sajdā* (placing forehead on the ground in prostration), *Tashahhud* (bearing witness) and *Salām* (Salutation).

Ṣāmit: Silent, Isma'ilias emphasize the circle of seven Grand-Imāms. They are: Shith, Sam, Ishmail, Aroan, Shamun, 'Ali and Muḥammad-bin-Ismā'īl.

Ṣaum or *Roża:* Fasting is observed daily during the holy month of Ramazān for special blessing of the Almighty.

Shafā't: To seek the mediation and intercession of the Prophet.

Shahādah: Profession of Faith.

Shar: Evil.

Shari'a: Sacred Law of Islām, the Divine Jurisprudence.

Shi'a or *Shi'i:* Friend and follower, from the earliest time to the present, the theologian have used, this word for the followers of Imām'Ali.

Shi'atu'l-'Ali: Followers of Imām 'Ali.

Shirku'l-Akbar: The greatest sin.

Silsilahu'ż-Żahab: Golden Chain. The spiritual chain of *Ṣūfīs* starting from Imām 'Ali to Imām ar-Reza. One of its main branches gave rise to the branch of Khwāja Ma'rūf Karkhī which in turn gave rise to many other branches like Saqṭiyya, Junaidīyya, Qādarīyya and Chishtīyya etc.

Spenta Mainyu or *Yażdān:* Beneficent Spirit, as believed by Zoroastrians.

Ṣūfī: Muslim Mystic. Other terms associated with *Ṣūfīs* are: *Walī* (Divine Saint), *Ṣaleḥ* (Perfectly virtuous person), *Pīrī* (mystic patronage), *Murīdī* (disciplehood of a mystic), *Mujāwirī* (to be attendant of a shrine), *'Urs* (annual festival on the shrines), *Qull* and *Fātiḥa* (recitation of Qur'anic verses for the benefit of the dead), *Chādar* (sheet of cloth spreading on the grave of a saint) etc.

Sultān: Monarch, addressed as *Zille-Ilāhī* (Shadow of God) and *Zille-Subḥanī* (Shadow of Glory).

Sunnī or *Ahlu'l-Sunnat-wa'l-Jamā't:* The people of tradition and group. This naming makes it clear that in this sect, it is essential to have faith in the life-pattern of the holy Prophet, and the collective model of the companion of the Prophet in general and *Khilāfatu'r-Rāshidūn* in particular. The majority of Muslims belong to *Sunni* community.

Sūra: Chapter of Qur'an.

Tabarrah: To be detatched emotionally from the enemies of the Prophet and his pious Progeny. A few enthusiastic Shi'is feel no wrong in openly condemning and using abusives terms for the enemies of the Prophet and his pious family, but the large majority of Shi'is is against this.

Tafsīr: Commentary or exegesis of whole or part of Qur'an.

Tafwīz: Hand-over of power.

Talāq: Divorce, the rights of husband to get separated from his wife, lent within the limits set by God.

Tanāsukh: Transmigration of soul.

Taqiyyah: Self-protection, concealment of faith when it causes life to be threatened.

Tasbīḥ: Reciting glorification of God on the beads of rosary.

Tawalla: To be in love with the Prophet and his pious progeny. The difficulty arises with extremes, holding doctrines that the persons loved are so heretical as to put those holding them outside Islām.

Tawḥīd: Divine Unity, the first and foremost unanimous pivot of Islām.

Thaqīfa Banīu's-Sa'da: Portico of Sa'da clan, where Abū Bakr was chosen as first Caliph.

'Ulama (sing. *'Ālim*): learned persons, scholars, erudites – the religious class.

Ulul-Amr-Minkum: Best in knowledge and character to merit a commanding position in the Muslim nation.

'Ulūmu'l-'Aqliyah: Intellectual Sciences.

Umayyites: Descendants of Umayya-bin-'Abdu'sh-Shams. 'Abdu'sh-Shams was brother of Prophet Muḥammad's grandfather 'Abdu'l Manāf. This family seized the Caliphate for 89 years (661-750).

Ummah: Islāmic Commonwealth.

Ummu'l-Mūminīn: Mother of Believer, the title used for the wife of the Prophet.

Uṣūlu'd-Dīn: Principles of Islām.

Uṣūlu'l-Fiqh: Principles of Islāmic jurisprudence.

Walī: Religious guardian, helper or defender, a title used for Imām or Sūfī saint.

Waḥy: Revelation from God.

Wikāla: Agency.

Wilāyatu'l-Faqīh: Guardianship of Expert theologist of Islām, a concept that government belongs by right to those who are most learned in Islāmic jurisprudence.

Żakāth: poor-rate, which is 2.5 per cent annual tax on the capital or total assets for the poor.

Ẓan: Strong presumption.

Żanādiqa: Followers of the ancient religion of Persia.

Ẓawāhiru'd-Dīn: the literal and textual explanations of Islām.

Bibliography

A Glossary of the Tribes and Castes of Punjab and North-West Frontier Province: Denzil Ibbetson, Edward Maclagan & H.A. Rose, Patiala 1970.

A History of Western Philosophy: Bertrand Russel, London 1948.

A Short History of the Saracens: Saiyed Amīr 'Ali, New Delhi 1998.

A Socio-Intellectual History of the Isnā 'Asharī Shī'īs in India: Saiyid Aṭhar 'Abbās Rizvi, Canberra (Australia) 1986.

A'yānu'sh-Shi'a: al-'Āmulī, Muḥsin Amīn, Damascus 1944.

Aḥqāqu'l-Ḥaqq: ash-Shūshtarī, Mar'ashī, Qāzī Nūru'llāh (Urdu tr.), Lahore n.d.

Aḥyā'u'l-'Ulūmu'd-Dīn: al-Ghażālī, Abū Ḥāmid Muḥammad, Cairo 1939.

al-Bābu'l-Hādī 'Ashar: al-Ḥillī, Ḥasan-bin-Yūsuf, (tr. Miller, W.W.) London 1928.

al-Bayān fī Tafsīru'l-Qur'an: al-Khū'ī, Saiyed Abu'l Qāsim, Beirut 1974.

al-Bidāyah w'an-Nihāyah: Ibn Kathīr, Abu'l Fidā, Ismā'īl-bin-'Omar, Cairo 1929.

al-Durru'l-Manthūr fī'l-Tafsīr bi'l Māthūr: *as*-Suyūtī, Jalālu'd-Dīn, Cairo 1896.

al-Farq Bayn'ul-Firāq: al-Baghdādī, 'Abdu'l Qāhir-bin-Tāhir, (tr. Halkin, Abraham S.: *Moslem Schisms and Sects*), Tel Aviv 1935.

al-Fārūq: Shiblī No'manī, Azamgarh 1956.

al-Faṣl-fī'l-Milal wa'l-Aḥwa wa'l-Niḥal: Ibn Ḥażm, Abū Muḥammad 'Ali-bin-Aḥmad, Cairo 1929

al-Firaqu'sh-Shi'a: al-Naubakhtī, Abī Muḥammad al-Ḥasan-bin-Mūsā (tr. Hellmut Ritter, Bibiliotheca Islamica), Instanbul 1931.

al-Fitnatu'l-Kubrā: Ṭāha Ḥusain, (Urdu tr. 'Abdu'l Ḥamīd No'mānī), Karachi 1978.

al-Irshād fī Ma'rifat Ḥujjāj Allāh 'Alā 'Ibād: al-Mufīd, Ibnu'l-Ma'allim, Shaykh Abū 'Abdu'llāh Muḥammad, (tr. Howard, IKA), London 1981.

al-Irshādu'l-Bārī fī Sharḥu'l-Ṣaḥīḥul-Bukhārī: al-Khaṭību'l-Qasṭalānī Aḥmad-bin-Muḥammad, Kanpur n.d.

al-Isti'āb fī Mā'rifatu'l-Aṣḥāb: 'Abdu'l-Barr 'Omar Abū Yūsuf-bin-'Abdu'llāh, Hyderabad 1900-1.

al-Istibsār fī Mukhtalifa fihi mina'l-Akhbār: Shaykhu't-Ṭā'fa, Abū Ja'far Muḥammad-bin-Ḥasan aṭ-Ṭūsī, Lucknow 1889-90.

al-Iṣābah fī Tamayyażu's-Ṣaḥābah: Ibn Ḥajar al-'Asqalānī, Abu'l Fazl Aḥmad, Cairo 1939.

al-Ittaqan fī 'Ulūmu'l-Qur'an: as-Suyūtī, Jalālu'd-Dīn, Cairo 1888.

al-Jauhar fī Sharh Waṣīyatu'l-Imām Abū Ḥanīfa: Ḥusain, Hyderabad 1903.

al-Kāmil fī't-Tārīkh: Ibn Athīr, 'Iżżu'd-Din, Abu'l Ḥasan 'Ali-bin-Muḥammad (ed. C.J. Torberg & E.J. Brill) Leiden, 1868.

al-Kashshāf 'an Ḥaqāyiqu'l-Tanżīl: al-Żamakhasharī, Abu'l Qāsim Jāru'llāh Maḥmūd-bin-'Omar, Calcutta 1859.

al-Khaṣayṣ Murtazwi: Nasā'ī, 'Abdu'r-Rahmān, (Urdu tr. Abu'l Ḥasan Aḥmad), Varanasi 1985.

al-Milal wa'l Niḥal: ash-Shahristānī, Abu'l-Fatḥ Muḥammad, Cairo 1948-9.

al-Mīżān fī Tafsīr al-Qur'an: aṭ-Ṭabāṭabāī, Saiyed Muḥammad Ḥusain, Tehran 1976.

al-Mu'jam al-Mufhras li-Alfaẓu'l-Qur'ani'l-Karīm baḥashiya al-Muṣḥafi'l-Sharīf: Muḥammad Fawād 'Adu'l Bāqī Miṣrī, Tehran 1962.

al-Mukhtaṣar fī Akhbāru'l-Bashar: Abu'l Fidā, 'Imādu'd-Dīn, Ismā'īl-bin-'Ali, ash-Shāfi'ī, Cairo 1907

al-Muqaddima: Ibn Khaldūn, Abū Żayd 'Abdu'r-Raḥmān (tr. R. Rosethal), New York 1958.

al-Murtaza: an-Nadawī, Abu'l Ḥasan 'Ali Ḥasanī, Lucknow 1988.

al-Musnad: Aḥmad-bin-Ḥanbal, Cairo 1895.

al-Mustadrak: al-Hākim an-Naysābūrī, Riyādh n.d.

al-Mustadrak'ala's-Saḥiḥayn: an-Naysābūrī, Abū 'Abdu'llāh

al-Muwaṭṭa: Mālik-bin-Anas, Cairo 1862.

al-Nubūwwat wa'l Khilāfat: Saiyed Najmu'l Ḥasan (tr. L.A. Ḥaidarī) Lucknow 1934.

al-Uṣūl-min'al-Kāfī: al-Kulaynī, Abū Ja'far Muḥammad-bin-Y'āqūb, Tehran 1972.

al-Yaqīn fī Imāra Amīr al-Mu'minīn: Ibn Ṭāwūs Raziyu'd-Din 'Ali, Qomm 1950.

An Approach to the Understanding of Islām: 'Ali Sharī'atī (tr. Venus Kaivantash), Tehran 1979

An Introduction to Shi'i Islām: Moojan Momen, Oxford 1985.

Anfāsu'l-'Ārifīn: Shāh Walī'ullāh Muḥaddith Dehlawī, Delhi 1897.

Ansābu'l-Ashrāf: al-Balāżurī, Aḥmad-bin-Yaḥyā-bin-Jābir, Cairo 1935

Anwāru'l-Qur'an: (Urdu tr. & exegesis by Žīshān Ḥaider Jawādī), Lucknow 1992.

Anwāru't-Tanżīl: al-Bayzāwī, Abdu'llāh-bin-'Omar ash-Shāfi'ī, Cairo 1912.

'Aqā'idu'l-Imāmiyyau'l-Ithna 'Ashariyya: aż-Żanjānī, Ibrāhīm al-Mūsāwī, Beirut 1973.

'Aqā'idu'sh-Shi'au'l-Ithna 'Ashariyya: al-'Āmulī, Bahāu'-Dīn, Tehran n.d.

'Aqā'idu'sh-Shaykh Ṣadūq: Urdu tr. *Hadya-i-Ja'fariya:*Shaykh Muḥammad A'ejaz Ḥasan: Dehli 1928.
Arjaḥu'l-Maṭālib: 'Obaydu'llāh Amritsarī, Lahore n.d.
ar-Risālah: ash-Shāfi'ī, Muhammad-bin-Idrīs, Cairo n.d.
ash-Shamsu'l-Bāżighā: Mullā Maḥmūd Jaunpurī, Lucknow 1871.
Aspects of Islam: MacDonald, D.B., New York 1911.
as-Sunan: Abū Dāwūd Sulaymān, as-Sijistānī, Lucknow 1900.
as-Sunan: Ibn Māja, Abū 'Ali Muḥammad-bin-Yazīd, Cairo 1895-96.
as-Sunan: Nasā'ī, Abū 'Abdu'r-Raḥmān-bin-Shu'ib-bin-Baḥr, Kanpur 1881-2.
Aṣlu'sh-Shi'a wa Uṣūliha: al-Kāshifu'l-Ghīta, Muḥammad Ḥusain, Najaf 1962.
aṣ-Ṣawa'qu'l-Muḥriqa fi'r-radd 'alā' ahli'l Rafz wa'l Zanadiqā: Ibn Ḥajar, al-Haythamī, al-Makkī, Cairo 1955.
ath-Thaqāfatu'l-Islāmia: Rāghib at-Tabākh: (Urdu tr. Iftekhār Aḥmad Balkhī:*Tārīkh-i-Afkār-o'Ulūm-i-Islāmī*), Delhi 1998.
'Umdat'ul-Qārī Sharaḥu'l-Bukhārī:'Aiynī, Badru'd-Dīn, Cairo n.d.
at-Tafhīmātu'l-Ilāhiyyā: Shāh Wali'ullāh, Bijnor 1936.
at-Tārīkh: al-Yā'qūbī, Ahmad-bin-'Ali Yā'qūb al-Wāziḥ (ed. Houtsma), Leydon 1883.
aṭ-Ṭabaqātu'l-Kabīr: Ibn S'ad, Abū 'Abdu'llāh Muḥammad, Leiden 1914-15.
Bayānu'l-Qur'an: Ashraf 'Ali Thānwī, Thanabhwan 1933.
Bhartiya Islāmī Sanskriti: Saiyed Jafar Reza, Allahabad 2011.
Bihāru'l-Anwār: al-Majlisī, Muḥammad Bāqir, Tehran 1887-8. (Urdu tr. Saiyed Ṭayyab Āghā al-Mūsāwī), Lucknow 1999-2001.
Billochon kī Tārīkh, Qabāyal ke Ā'ine mein: al-Hyderī, Mīr Aḥsan, Multan n.d.
Bustān-i-Wilāyat:Rushdī, Saiyed Khudā Bakhsh, Hyderabad 1956.
Cambridge History of Islam: (ed. P.M. Holt, *et al.*), Cambridge 1970.
Conflict and Tensions in Islamic Jurisprudence: Coulson, Noel J., Chicago 1969.
Dabistān-i-Mażāhib: Mīrżā Żulfaqār Āżar Sāsānī Mobad (author's name wrongly mentioned as Muḥsin Fānī; tr. David Shea & Anthony Troyer), London 1901, (Urdu trs. Ḥāfiẓ Ghulām Murtazā & Rashīd Aḥmad Jalandharī), Lahore 2002.
Dīn-i-Islām aur Auwallīn Musalmānon kī do Mutazād Taṣwīren: al-Nadawī, Abu'l Ḥasan 'Ali, Lucknow 1984.
Durr-i-Gauhar: Akhtar Waḥīd, Multan n.d.
Faizān-i-Abū Ṭālib: Saiyed Badr'ul Ḥasan 'Ābidī, Varanasi 1987.
Fatḥu'l-Bārī: Ibn Ḥajar al-'Asqalānī, Abu'l Fazl Aḥmad, Cairo 1901.
Fatḥu'l-Bayān fi Maqāṣidu'l-Qur'an: Ṣiddīq Ḥasan Khān, Bhopal 1883.
Fatḥu'l-Qadīr: Muḥammad-bin-'Ali, Beirut n.d.
Fuṣūlu'l-Muhimmah: Ibn al-Sabbāgh Mālikī, Najaf n.d.

Futūhul-Buldān: al-Balāżurī, Aḥmad-bin-Yaḥyā-bin-Jābir (tr. Philip K. Hitti & F.C. Murgotten – *The Origins of Islamic State*), New York 1916-24.

Gazetteers: Gazetteer of Alwar, Gazetteer of Bombay Presidency, Bengals District Gazetteer, Bundi State Gazetteer, Central Provinces District Gazetteers, (Seoni/Dist Allahabad). *Indore State Gazetteer, Purnea District Gazetteer, Sindh Gazetteer.*

Gharā'ibu'l-Qur'an wa'l-Raghā'bu'l-Furq'an: al-Nīshāpurī, Nizāmu'd-Dīn Ḥasan, Tehran 1864.

Hayātu'l-Muḥammad: Haykal, Muḥammad Ḥusain (Urdu tr. Abū Yaḥyā Imām Khān), New Delhi 1988.

Hayātu'l-Qulūb: al-Majlisī, Muḥammad Bāqir (tr. Merrick, J.L.), Boston 1850.

History of the Fātimid Khaliphate: O' Lear, de Lacy, New York 1923.

Ḥusain Sabżwarī – *Żādu'l-'Uqba*) Lahore n.d.

Ḥusnu'l-Muḥāzara fī Akhbār Miṣr wa'l-Qāhira: as-Suyūtī, Jalālu'd-Dīn, Cairo 1981-2.

'Iqdu'l-Farīd: 'Omar-bin-Aḥmad-bin Muḥammad, Cairo 1884.

Ḥayātu'l-Ḥaywānu'l-Kubrā: ad-Damīrī, Kamālu'd-Dīn Muḥammad, Cairo 1950.

Inkeshāfāt-i-Qur'an: (ed. 'Abul Majīd Miṣbāḥī & Saiyed Bashārat Shikoh), Bombay 1992.

Islām – Nāmā: Saiyed Khairāt Ḥasan, Lucknow 2011.

Islām, Sidhānt aur Swarūp: Saiyed Jafar Reza, Allahabad 2004.

Islām, the Straight Path: Morgan, Kenneth W. (ed.), New York 1958.

Islāmī 'Ulūm kā Ta'rruf: Murtazā Muṭaharī, (Urdu tr. S.M. 'Askarī), Tehran 1996.

Islāmī Rājya banām Muslim Rājya: Saiyed Jafar Reza, Allahabad 2004.

Islāmic Philosophy and Theology: Watt, W.M., Edinburgh 1962.

Ithnā 'Asharīya: Sell, Canon Edward (Urdu tr.), Lahore 1925.

Iżālatu'l-Khulafā: Shāh Walīu'llāh, (Urdu tr. M. 'Abdu'r Shakūr), Karachi n.d.

Jām'au'l-Bayān fi Tafsīru'l-Qur'an: aṭ-Ṭabarī, Ibn Jarīr Abū Ja'far, Cairo 1902-3.

Jam'au'l-Baynu' r-Rijālu's-Ṣaḥīḥayn: Ibnu'l-Qaysarānī, Abu'l Fazl Muḥammad-bin-Ṭāhir, Hyderabad n.d.

Jām'au'sh-Shawāhid fī'l Dakhūl Ghayr-Muslim fī'l-Masjid: Abu'l Kalām Āżād, Delhi 1923.

Jām'au'ṣ-Ṣaḥīḥ al-Muslim: al-Muslim, Abu'l Ḥusain Ibnu'l-Ḥajjāj, Cairo 1930, (Urdu tr. 'Abdu'l-Dai'mu'l-Jalālī), Delhi 1998.

Jām'au'ṣ-Ṣaḥīḥu'l-Mishkātu'l-Maṣābīḥ: al-Khaṭīb, Walīu'd-Dīn Muḥammad-bin-'Abdu'llāh, Amritsar 1895-6, (Urdu tr.'Abdu'l Ḥakīm Akhtar), Delhi 1987.

Jām'au'ṣ-Ṣaḥīḥu't-Tirmiżī: at-Tirmiżī, Abū Īsā Muḥammad, (Urdu Tr. Fazl Ahmad) Lucknow 1894.

Jām'au'ṣ-Ṣaḥīḥul-Bukhārī: al-Bukhārī, Abū 'Abdu'llāh Muḥammad-bin-Ismā'īl, (ed. L.K. Krehl), Leiden 1862, (Urdu tr. Mirzā Ḥairat Dehlawī), Deoband n.d.

Jām'au't-Tawarīkh: Rashīdu'Dīn, Lahore n.d.

Jilā'u'l-'Uyūn: al-Majlisī, Muḥammad Bāqir, Tehran

Kalāmī Pīr, A Treatise of Ismā'īlī Doctrine: Ivanow W., Bombay 1935.

Kanżu'l-'Ummāl-fī-Sunnau'l-Aqwāl-w'al-Afā'l: 'Alā'ud-Dīn 'Ali Muttaqī-bin-Ḥisām'ud-Dīn al-Hindī, Beirut 1981.

Kanżu'l-Ansāb: Shāh Malik Shujāu'l-Malik, Lahore 1919

Karbala se Karbala tak: Reyaz Husain Jafri, Lahore n.d.

Kashf al-Ghiṭā: Shaykh Ja'far-bin-Khizr an-Najafī.

Kashf al-Ghumma fī Ma'rifat al-Ai'ma: Irbīlī, Ibn al-Fakhr, Bahāu'd-Dīn 'Ali-bin-'Īsā, Tehran 1877.

Kashfu'l-Mahjūb: Dātāganj Bakhsh, 'Ali-bin-'Othmān al-Jalābī, (Urdu tr. Muḥammad Alṭāf), Dehli 1992.

Kashfu'z-Zunūn: Hājī Khalīfā (tr. G. Flugel), London 1835-58.

Kashifu'l Bayān fī Tafsīru'l-Qur'an: ath-Thā'bī, Abū Isḥāq Nīshāpūrī, Raza State Library, Rampur (Mss.)

Kāshu'n-Niqāb: Saiyed 'Ali Naqī Naqavī, (Urdu tr. *Raddu'l Wahhābīyya*), Bombay 1986.

Khilāfat-o-Mulūkiyat: Abu'l 'Olā Maudūdī, Dehli 1981.

Khutabāt: Abu'l 'Olā Maudūdī, Dehli 1993.

Khutūtu'sh-Sham: Muḥammad 'Ali Kurd, Lahore 1986.

Kitābu'l-'Ibar: Ibn Khaldūn, Abū Żayd 'Abdu'r-Raḥmān (Urdu tr. Aḥmad Ḥusain 'Othmānī), Allahabad 1899-1930.

Kitābu'l-Ansāb: al-Sam'ānī, Abū Sa'd Abdu'l-Karīm, London 1912.

Kitābu'l-Fihrist: Ibnu'l-Nadīm, 'Abdu'l-Faraj Muḥammad (tr.& ed. D. Dodge), Columbia 1970.

Kitābu'l-Ishārāt: Ibn Sīnā, Leiden 1892 (commentary by Naṣīru'-Dīn Ṭusī – *al Shifā'*), Cairo 1950.

Kitābu'l-Kāmilu'd-Dīn: Ibn Bābūya, Abū Ja'far Muḥammad-bin-'Abdu'llāh al-Qommī, Tehran 1959.

Kitābu'l-Khirāj: Abū Yūsuf (Urdu tr.) Hyderabad n.d.

Kitābu'l-M'ārif: Ibn Qutayba, Cairo 1850.

Kitābu'l-Mabsūt: as-Sarkhasī, Abū Bakr-bin-Aḥmad, Cairo 1906.

Kitābu'l-Maqālāt wa'l Firaq: al-Qummī, Sa'd-bin-'Abdu'llāh, Tehran 1963.

Kitābu'r-Rijāl: al-Najāshī, Abū 'Abbās Aḥmad, Tehran n.d.

Kitābu't-Tawḥīd: Muḥammad-bin-'Abdu'l-Wahhāb, al-Najdī (Urdu tr. 'Abdu'l-Mālik Mujāhid), Delhi n.d.

Lababu't-Tāwīl fī Mā'nī-at-Tanzīl: al-Khāżin, Shaykh 'Alāu'd-Dīn 'Ali-bin-Muḥammad 'Alāu'd-Dīn, 1899.

Laṭā'fu'l-Ishārāt, Tafsīr Ṣūfī Kāmilu'l-Qur'anu'l-Karīm: (ed. Bisyūnī), Cairo 1981.

Lawām'au'l'Tanżīl wa's-Sawāṭ'au't-Tāwīl: al-Ḥā'rī, Saiyed 'Ali, Lahore n.d.
Madārijul-Nabūwat: Shaykh 'Abdu'l Ḥaqq, (Urdu tr. Abdu'l Majīd), Kanpur n.d.
Majālisu'l-Mominīn: al-Majlisī, Muhammad Bāqir, Tehran
Majm'au'l-Baḥrain: Aḥmad Ḥusain 'Aẓīmābādī
Majm'au'l-Bayān fī 'Ulūmu'l-Qur'an: aṭ-Ṭabarsī, Fazl Ibn Ḥasan, Tehran 1959.
Malfūzāt: Shāh 'Abdu'l Ażīż (Urdu tr.), Karachi 1960.
Man Lā Yahzurūhu'l-Faqīh: Ibn Bābūyā, Abu Jā'far Muḥammad-bin-'Abdu'llah al-Qommī, Tehran 1972.
Maqālātu'l-Islāmiyyīn: al-Ash'arī, Abu'l Ḥasan-bin-Ismā'īl, (ed. H. Ritter), Istanbul 1929-30.
Minhāju's-Sunnau'n-Nabawiyyā: Shaykh Ibn Taymiyya, Bulāq, 1903-5.
Modern Islam in India: Smith, Wilfred Cantwell, Lahore 1943.
Mufātīḥu'l-Ghayb, al-mushtahir bi'l Tafsīru'l-Kabīr: ar-Rāzī, Fakhu'ru'd-Dīn Abū 'Abdu'llah Muḥammad-bin-'Omar, Cairo 1890
Muḥarram Nāma: Khwāja Ḥasan Niẓāmī, Delhi 1953.
Muḥammad-bin-Ḥākim, Hyderabad 1921.
Munāqīb Ahlu'l-Bayt: Ażīżu'l Ḥaqq Nadawī, Varanasi n.d.
Munāqīb Āl Abī Ṭālib: Ibn Sharāshūb, Abu 'Abdu'llāh Muḥammad, Najaf 1956.
Munāqību'l-Imāmu'l-Āẓam Abū Ḥanīfa: al-Kurdarī, Hyderabad 1903.
Muntakhabu't-Tawārīkh: Badā'ūnī, 'Abdu'l Qādir, (tr. G.S.A. Ranking, W.H. Lowe & T.W. Haig) Calcutta 1864-1925.
Muqaddima-i-Tafsīr-i-Qur'an: Saiyed 'Ali Naqī Naqavī, Lucknow 1976.
Murūju'ž – Žahab-wa'l-M'adinu'l-Jauhar: al-Mas'ūdī, 'Ali-bin-Ḥusain, Beirut 1966, (ed. & tr. C. Babier de Meynard) Paris 1861-77.
Musalmānon ka 'Urūj wa Żawāl: Sa'īd Aḥmad Akbarābādī, Delhi 1947.
Mushkilu'l-Āthār: aṭ-Ṭaḥāwī, Abū Ja'far Aḥmad, Hyderabad 1968
Mussulman Culture: Bartold, Vassily Vladimirovitch (tr. from Russian – Shāhid Suhrawardy), Calcutta 1934.
Mutālia-i-Qur'an: Žīshān Haider Jawādī, Lucknow 1994.
Muwaddatu'l-Qurba: 'Ali Ḥamedānī, Mīr Saiyed, (Urdu tr. Sharīf
Nahju'l-Balāghah: Imām 'Ali-Ibn-Abī Ṭālib (compiled by Saiyed Razī Sharīf), Urdu tr. Ja'far Ḥusain, Lucknow 1996, Eng. tr. Saiyed Moḥammed Askarī Jafery, Karachi 1971.
Nūru'l-Abṣār fi Akhaž al-Thār: Saiyed Muḥammad Ibrāhīm, Lucknow, n.d.
On the Sociology of Islam: 'Ali Sharī'atī, Berkeley 1979.
Origin and Early Development of Shi'a Islam: Jafrī, S. Ḥusain M., Beirut 1979.
Polemics on the Origin of the Fātimid Caliph: Mamour, Princep. H., London 1934.
Rawā'hu'l-Qur'an: Muḥammad 'Abbās, Lucknow 1888.

Rise and Fall of the Roman Empire: Gibbon, Edward: London 1948

Riyāzu'l-Munẓarah fī Fazāyilu'l-'Ashrah: Ṭabarī, Muḥibu'd-Dīn Aḥmad, Lahore n.d.

Rūḥu'l-Ma'ānī fī Tafsīru'l-Qr'anu'l-'Aẓīm wa'l Sab'āu'l Mathanī: Ālālūsī, Abu'l-Fazl Shihābu'd-Dīn Saiyed Maḥmūd, Cairo 1883.

Selected Works: Karl Marx & Frederick Encels, Moscow 1962.

Sharhu'l-Fiqhu'l-Akbar: 'Ali Qārī, Delhi 1929.

Sharḥu'l-Ṭaḥāwiyā: Ibn Abī 'Izzā al-Ḥanafī, Cairo 1953.

Shi'a dar Islam: aṭ-Ṭabāṭabāī, Saiyed Muḥammad Ḥusain, (tr. & ed. S. Ḥossein Naṣr), London 1975.

Sifātu's-Shi'a wa'l Fazāilu's-Shi'a: Ibn Bābūya, Abū Jā'far Muḥammad-bin-'Abdu'llāh, al-Qommī (tr. A.A. Fyzee – *A Shi'ite Creed*), Oxford 1942.

Sīrat Rasūlu'llāh: Ibn Hishām 'Abdu'l Malik (tr. Guillaume, Alfred: *The Life of Muḥammad*) London, 1955

Sīratu'n-Nabī: Ibn Isḥāq, Muḥammad-bin-Isḥāq-bin-Yasār (Urdu tr. Nūr Ilāhī), New Delhi 2000.

Some Aspects of Religious Politics in India: Niẓāmī, K. A., Delhi 1974.

Sūratū'l-Ikhlaṣ wa'l-'Alaq: Ibn Sīnā (Avicenna), Abū 'Ali al-Ḥusain-bin-'Abdu'llāh, Delhi n.d.

Ṣaḥīfahu'l-Kāmilah: 'Ali-Ibnu'l-Ḥusain, Imām Żainu'l-Ābidīn (Urdu tr. & exegesis by Ja'far Ḥusain), Bombay n.d.

Ṣawaṭ'au'l-Ilhām: Abū Faiz Faizī, Lucknow 1888.

Ta'wīlu'l-Mukhtalifu'l-Ḥadīth: Ibn Qutayba, Cairo, 1908

Ta'wzīḥu'l-Majīd fī Tanqīḥ Kalāmu'llahu'l Majīd: Saiyed 'Ali, Lucknow 1841.

Tafsīr-i-Qur'an: Saiyed 'Ali Naqī Naqavī, Srinagar 1983-9.

Tafsīr-i-Sāfī: Ḥasan Fayzī, Lucknow 1924.

Tafsīron mein Isrāēlī Rawāyāt: Nizāmu'd-Dīn, Deoband 1985

Tafsīru'l-Ḥusainī: al-Wāiẓ al-Kāshifī, Ḥusain-bin-'Ali, Lucknow 1895.

Tafsīru'l-Jalālayn: as-Suyūtī, Jalālu'd-Dīn & al-Maḥallī, Jalālu'd-Dīn, Delhi 1864.

Tafsīru'l-Maẓharī: Thināu'llāh 'Othmanī Pānīpatī, (Urdu tr. 'Abu'l Dāyam) Delhi 1961-2

Tafsīru'l-Qommī: al-Qummī, Abu'l-Ḥasan 'Ali-bin-Ibrāhim, Najaf 1966-7.

Tafsīru'l-Qur'anu'l 'Aẓīm: Ibn Kathīr, 'Imādu'd-Dīn, Abu'l Fidā Ismā'il, Cairo 1937.

Tafsīru'l-Qur'anu'l-Karīm: Sufyān Thūrī, Abū 'Abdu'llāh (ed. Imtiāż 'Ali 'Arshī), Rampur 1965.

Tahzību'l-Aḥkām: Shaykhu'ṭ-Ṭā'fa, Abū Ja'far Muḥammad-bin-Ḥasan aṭ-Ṭusī, Najaf 1959.

Tajdīdu'-Aḥyāi'-Dīn: Abu'l 'Olā Mū'dīdī, Delhi 1986.

Tārīkh-i-A'imma: Saiyed 'Ali Ḥaider, Lucknow 1998.

Tārīkh-i-Alfī (Vol. 1): Aḥmad-bin-Naṣru'llāh Thattawī, University Library, Bombay (Mss.)

Tārīkh-i-Dā'wat-o-'Azīmat: an-Nadawī, Abul Ḥasan 'Ali Ḥasanī, Lucknow 1959.

Tārīkh-i-Dā'wat-o-'Azīmat: an-Nadawī, Abul Ḥasan 'Ali Ḥasanī, Lucknow 1984.

Tārīkh-i-Fātimīn-i-Misr: Žāhid 'Ali, Hyderabad n.d.

Tārīkh-i-Gużīda: Qażwīnī, Ḥamdu'llāh-bin-Abī Bakr, (ed. Edward G. Browne), London 1910.

Tārīkh-i-Islam: Saiyed 'Ali Naqī Naqavi, Lucknow n.d.

Tārīkh-i-Karbala wa Ḥāi'r al-Ḥusain: al-Kilidār, 'Abdu'l-Jawād, Najaf 1967.

Tārīkh-i-Wahhābiyat: 'Ali Aṣghar Faqīhī (Urdu tr. Iqbāl Ḥyder Ḥydery) Qomm 2006

Tārīkhu'l-Baghdād: al-Khaṭību'l-Baghdādī, Cairo 1931.

Tārīkhu'l-Khmīs fī Aḥwāl'u-Nafīs: Dayār Bakrī Ḥusain Muḥammad Mālikī, Cairo 1866.

Tārīkhu'l-Khulafa: *as*-Suyūtī, Jalālu'd-Dīn (tr. Jarrett, H.S.), Calcutta 1881.

Tārīkhu'r-Rusūl wa'l-Mulūk: aṭ-Ṭabarī, Ibn Jarīr Abū Jā'far, Lucknow 1874.

Tarjima-i-Kalām-i-Ilāhī: Saiyed Farmān 'Ali, Lucknow n.d.

Tarjimānu'l-Qur'an: Āżad, Abul Kalām, New Delhi 1996.

The Book of Certainty: Abū Bakr Sirāju'd-Dīn, London 1952.

The Caliphate, its Rise, Decline and Fall: Muir, Sir William, London 1891.

The Caliphate: Arnold, Sir Thomas, Oxford 1913.

The Deoband School and the Demand for Pakistan: Fārūqī Z.H., Bombay 1963.

The Development of Metaphysics in Persia: Muḥammad Iqbāl, Sir, (Urdu tr. *Falsafa-i-'Ajam*: Mīr Ḥasanu'd-Dīn), Ḥyderabad 1956.

The Glory of the Shi'a World: Sykes, Sir Percy & others, London 1910.

The Heart of 'Arabia: Philby H.S.J., London 1922.

The History of Moḥammedanism and its Sects: Taylor, W. Cooke, London 1851.

The Indian Muslamāns: W.W. Hunter, London 1871.

The Indian Muslims: Muḥammad Mujīb, London 1969.

The Islāmic Dynasties: Bosworth, Clifford E., Edinburgh 1967.

The Miracle Play of Ḥasan and Ḥusain: Pelly, Sir L., London 1879.

The Muslim Community of the Indo-Pakistan Sub-continent (610-1974): Qurashī, Ishteyaq Ḥusain, (Urdu tr. *Barr-i-Āẓam-i-Hind-o-Pak kī Millat-i-Islāmia*), Karachi 1967.

The Muslim Creed: Wensinck, A.J., Cambridge 1932.

The Reconstruction of Religious Thought in Islam: Muḥammad Iqbal, Sir, Oxford 1934.

The Shi'a of India: John Norman Hollister, New Delhi 1979.
The Shi'ite Religion: Donaldson, Dwright M., London 1933.
The Spirit of Islam: Saiyed Amīr 'Ali, New Delhi 1997.
The Story of Philosophy: Will Durant, New York 1955.
Umm'ul-Kitāb: Ivanow, Valdimir (ed. & tr.), Der' Islam 1936.
Uṣūl-i-Fiqh aur Shah Walīu'llah: Maẓhar Baqā, Islamabad 1973.
Vilāyat-i-Faqīh dar Khṣūṣ-i-Ḥukūmat-i-Islāmī: Khomeinī, Rūhu'llāh, Tehrān 1980.
Wafiyyātu'l-'Ayān wa anbā' aż-Żamān: Ibn Khallikān, Aḥmad (tr. Baron MacGuckin de Slane) Paris 1842-71
War and Non-violence: Gandhi, M.K., Delhi, n.d.
Whither Islam: Gibb, H.A.R., London 1932.
Yake Aż Shākh-i-Thamarbār: Saiyed Khairāt Ḥasan, Allahabad 2011.
Yanābiya'u'l-Muwaddah: Shaykh Sulaymān Ḥusainī Balkhī (Urdu tr. Malik Muḥammad Sharīf), Lucknow 2002.
Zakhayiru'l-'Uqbā: Ṭabarī Muḥību'd-Dīn Aḥmad, Lahore n.d.

Index